NEW
MEDIA

NEW MEDIA

AN INTRODUCTION

CANADIAN EDITION

TERRY FLEW & RICHARD SMITH

OXFORD

UNIVERSITY PRESS

OXFORD
UNIVERSITY PRESS

8 Sampson Mews, Suite 204, Don Mills, Ontario M3C 0H5
www.oupcanada.com

Oxford University Press is a department of the University of Oxford.
It furthers the University's objective of excellence in research, scholarship,
and education by publishing worldwide in

Oxford   New York

Auckland Cape Town Dar es Salaam Hong Kong Karachi
Kuala Lumpur Madrid Melbourne Mexico City Nairobi
New Delhi Shanghai Taipei Toronto

With offices in

Argentina Austria Brazil Chile Czech Republic France Greece
Guatemala Hungary Italy Japan Poland Portugal Singapore
South Korea Switzerland Thailand Turkey Ukraine Vietnam

Oxford is a trade mark of Oxford University Press
in the UK and in certain other countries

Published in Canada by Oxford University Press

Library and Archives Canada Cataloguing in Publication

Flew, Terry

New media : an introduction / Terry Flew & Richard Smith. — 1st Canadian ed.

Includes bibliographical references and index.

ISBN 978-0-19-543181-0

1. Mass media—Technological innovations—Textbooks. 2. Mass media—Influence—Textbooks. 3. Mass media—Social
aspects—Textbooks. 4. Mass media—Political aspects—Textbooks. I. Smith, Richard Keith II. Title.

P96.T42F64 2011   302.23   C2011-900196-9

Cover image: Kheng Ho Toh / Veer

Contents

8   The Global Knowledge Economy   166

9   Internet Law, Policy, and Governance   192

Tables and Figures

Tables

Figures

Preface

My mission in this adaptation was to preserve as much as possible of Terry's fine book, while adding material to make it more relevant to Canadian students of new media. I also wanted to include more historical material and a larger section on mobile devices and life, which have been given their own chapter in this edition. I am hopeful that students will appreciate the mobile devices chapter, but they might wonder about the history, especially delving back as far as I have. I respectfully submit that we can learn a lot about new media and the Internet from looking back at where we have been. Not just the trivial (today's 'L33T'-speak was anticipated by telegraph abbreviations by almost a century) but also fundamental features of our present system, such as network topologies, business practices, and regulatory regimes were all pioneered by previous generations.

Any text on new media faces the challenge of dealing with a topic that is subject to constant change. I have endeavoured to provide a combination of well-established as well as current information, but I encourage readers—when you encounter a fact or reference that you suspect might be out of date—to use the descriptive material in the text to do a quick search on the Internet to identify more recent information. Not only will you have the new facts but you'll also have an appreciation for how quickly things change and, most importantly, a visceral sense of the way in which the Internet and new media are self-revealing to the diligent and inquisitive scholar.

Constant change isn't the only challenge a new media text faces these days. The biggest question has to be, 'why?' Why do we need another new media textbook? The simple answer is in part the same response given to the challenge mentioned above—constant change in the field invites new perspectives that are current, that are abreast of the latest developments, and that situate the historical and theoretical issues in the context of the present age. If staying up to date were our only rationale, however, it might have been better to direct students to a website or blog about new media. There are some clever ones, to be sure. In my view, the larger issue is what does this book add that other books don't cover? Here the answer seems to lie in the specific mix of elements, the factors that are included and emphasized, sometimes at the expense of others. Some texts focus on new media as an art form (Manovich would fall into this camp), some seek to identify the social psychology of new media, seeking insight into the impact. Other texts include reprints of 'classic' treatises or important milestones in our thinking about new media. All of these have their place but their topics aren't the focus here.

In this book I've tried to draw together the views of a number of the most important writers on new media, presented through our own lens. I've included a significant section on history, going back to media forms that certainly wouldn't be called 'new' these days, although I am sure they seemed so at the time. And, in fact, that point—that new media is in part a time-and-place dependent description—is an important take away from the chapter on history (Chapter 2). I've also positioned the book as an explicitly pedagogical project, with chapter objectives, questions to ask yourself, discussion questions, and further reading included in all of the chapters. This isn't to pre-empt the work of instructors, rather I hope these elements contribute to their repertoire of material as they seek to animate the text for their students.

The book was originally created for an Australian audience and while it provided a solid introduction to new media, many of the examples would have been unfamiliar to Canadian students. This adaptation brings the book home to Canada while preserving much of the original text. This version is explicitly and unashamedly Canadian in its approach, examples, and almost all of the case studies. Without making it parochial, I have tried to position this book as a Canadian exploration of new media. Some things, such as our specific regulatory and legal history in relation to new media, are distinct and require a specifically Canadian treatment, keeping in mind of course the international context in which all new media operate. Other facets of new media (and the history of new media) are, in fact, Canadian contributions to the global environment. The BlackBerry from Research in Motion, for example, has not just popularized smartphones in North America but it has changed the way business, government, and social life are conducted in this country, as well as around the world. The 'constantly in touch' executive or socialite or student is both a caricature and a reality because of RIM, a Canadian company. Reading about that doesn't just bring the world of new media alive to Canadian students but—potentially—it can also inspire interest in the larger topic and demonstrate how Canadian new media inventions fit into global media empires.

I hope readers of this book will come away with an appreciation of both the origins and context for new media, as well as the operations, implications, benefits, and constraints of this new form of communication.

Adapting Terry Flew's *New Media: An Introduction* for the Canadian market has been an honour and a privilege and it wouldn't have been possible without Ryan, Jodi, Mark, Luke, Johanne, the anonymous reviewers, and (especially) Deborah. Ryan Chynces and Jodi Lewchuk got the project off the ground at Oxford University Press, until Mark Thompson took over and shepherded it the rest of the way through the OUP system to completion. Mark was gracious and understanding when I missed my first deadline and firm and helpful in making the second. Here at SFU, Luke Freeman (a visiting Australian, as it happened) was an invaluable assistant in the early stages. Johanne Provençal then stepped in and has been a colleague, and a conscience with a copywriter's attention to detail, an editor's sense of the whole and parts, and—most importantly—an educator's eye to the pedagogical features of the book. Finally, and most importantly, I need to thank Deborah, my wife of twenty-five years and partner in all things, who has been unfailingly positive and encouraging throughout this project.

Richard Smith
December 2010

Introduction

This book aims to provide a text that can be used in undergraduate courses on new media in a range of disciplines in the arts and social sciences, including (mass) communication, journalism, sociology, and anthropology. It could also be used in a business or marketing course given our attention to innovation and the business setting for new media. We don't assume a great deal of prior knowledge about theories, approaches, or technology and we attempt to cover new media from a variety of perspectives.

Throughout the text, we pay special attention to the role of the new 'read-write-web' or 'Web 2.0' as it is commonly called, which has both captured the popular imagination via sites like Facebook (http://facebook.com) and demonstrated the political and economic power of new media as we saw in the use of YouTube (http://youtube.com) videos following the G20 protest in Toronto, or the incredibly successful 'Old Spice' campaign in July 2010. We do not sugar coat the new media, however, and show the negative as well as the positive cultural, social, environmental, and civil rights implications of the widespread adoption of new media tools. Our objective is that readers are critical and analytical users and students of new media.

The first chapter asks the question, 'what is new for society in new media?' and then looks at the role of new media in social change. New media is already deeply embedded in the debates, processes, and practicalities of our society. We explore new media as an outcome 'convergence'—the process by which media technologies, industries, and services are merging—through changes in computing and communications networks and content. Although convergence is important, we attempt to put these changes in perspective and recognize that long-standing social, cultural, political, and economic forces remain significant factors affecting technological change. The chapter then examines the characteristics of digital information and how those characteristics result in interactive communication and communication practices. Since the Internet is one of the most important new media forms of the late twentieth and early twenty-first century, we review the history of the Internet, its social implications, the recent growth of Web 2.0, and the importance of search engines. We also look at the importance of online encyclopedias, status updates, friend lists, and online video, in the context of a growing and globalizing technology. The chapter concludes with a review of the implications of convergence and Web 2.0 for the creation and consumption of media content.

Chapter 2 provides the historical context for new media. Connections are drawn between current network technologies and prior inventions such as the telegraph, radio, and television. Although the path has been twisty sometimes, ever since we have been able to send messages without moving physical objects (the first telegraph), that immediacy has forever changed our expectations about communication media. With new capabilities came new institutions and social arrangements and these have proven to be foundational and influential for subsequent generations of media. Journalism, politics, and business were all transformed by their use of the telegraph and the telephone, as this chapter demonstrates. The radio and, later, television provided a testing ground for key elements of new media and in particular the business model in which the content could be accessed for free, if one was willing to accept a little bit of advertising. The chapter concludes with a brief discussion of the educational potential of earlier new media.

Chapter 3 is premised on the notion that a well-rounded view of the role and effects of new media in society can only be gleaned by taking a number of perspectives. For this reason, the chapter presents several theoretical approaches to new media while providing insight into their strengths and weaknesses. For example, we critically examine technological determinism, and point out its weaknesses while acknowledging that existing technological configurations inevitably influence society once they are widely adopted. Particular emphasis is placed on a 'social shaping' perspective in which groups and individuals are understood as able to influence how media is used and how it evolves. We explore some of the hype that surrounds new media and try to understand why science-driven messages are so compelling, while critically examining both the overly positive and the unnecessarily negative (frequently deterministic) portrayals of the effects of new media. Both cultural context and media forms are explored as ways of understanding new media, along with social, psychological, and economic explanations.

Chapter 4 is about mobile technologies and examines how they are a vital and important part of new media today. This chapter explores the mobile phone and related technologies, such as the tablet computer and netbook, from historical, technological, and economic perspectives. Some of the key features of mobile phones are explained and examined with an eye to making this sometimes mysterious technology more comprehensible. We also look at how social software such as Facebook or Twitter is deployed on mobile devices, and the implications of location on these services. We examine, as well, some of the cultural impacts of mobile new media technologies as well as social, health, and environmental implications.

Chapter 5 is about social networks and the use of these networks for the production of culture and cultural goods. In the first half of the chapter we consider the concept of social networks and how these enable a culture of mass participation—a 'participatory culture'. We also examine how these networks enable and enhance many other social processes. Although networks are not new phenomena, they are enhanced and extended by new media and we explore this process in more detail in this chapter. Networks are economic and political as well as social phenomena and, given their importance, it is not surprising that new research methods have arisen to study them. One of these, social network analysis, is considered in detail from both a practical and an historical point of view. Social network theories are also critically examined in this chapter. The second part of the chapter looks at social production and participatory culture as it has emerged in information- and communication-technology-enhanced social networks.

Chapter 6 presents a rounded and broad examination of computer games. Game play and the game industry are a prime example of new media in the twenty-first century. We examine games as a significant part of popular culture, extending beyond their economic impact. We also look at how the immersive nature and rapid pace of change places online and computer games at the centre of debates about gender roles, culture, childhood experiences, and intellectual property. We take a look at the economics of the game industry, including its dependence on subcontractors. This is followed by a consideration of the tension between the creative side of the business and the investment side, as well as the complex value chain between production and distribution. The last part of the chapter looks at some of the most significant gaming developments in the first decade of the twenty-first century, such as the role of producer-consumers 'modding' games, and the issues arising from that. The chapter concludes with a discussion of the political economy of the game industry, as well as a section on the game industry in Canada.

Chapter 7 is about creative industries and considers how creativity has been industrialized, a process that has accelerated, broadened, and deepened with digital media. We begin with an examination of the concept of creativity and, especially, under what circumstances it can flourish. We next consider the notion of a 'creative industry' and how and why this has become a policy objective of cities, provinces and states, and countries around the world. The rise of a creative economy, creative cities, and the creative class both as reality and as vision or ideal, is considered and debated.

Chapter 8 looks at the global knowledge economy and new media as a powerful force for globalization. The chapter explains the complexity of globalization and reviews some of the main criticisms of these developments as part of an overall knowledge economy. We examine both technological change and its role in the economy as well as more practical matters such as e-commerce strategies and the role that new media play in 'disintermediation' in order to better understand the forces that drive the global knowledge economy. We look at the nature of digital goods and how they have disrupted many industries that relied on the expense of reproducing and transporting ideas (news, music, movies, for example) for a competitive advantage and now find themselves without their former basis for extracting value. In this context, we return to some of the themes on creativity from Chapter 7 and examine the creative economy more closely from a business perspective. Here we examine topics such as technological innovation and innovators' dilemmas.

Chapter 9 examines law, policy, and governance for new media. We consider the interesting and sometimes difficult issues that have arisen in a world in which two of the foundational principles of law—property and the state—are significantly altered by digital and global information flows. In the absence of a strong legal foundation for new media, nations have attempted to use policy initiatives to establish priorities and create programs that will boost the power and role of their own citizens and corporations in the use of information and communication technologies. Governments have also intervened by subsidy or procurement strategies. We examine these issues along with implications for copyright and property rights, and the open source software movement.

Chapter 10, the concluding chapter, considers how new media are evolving at the start of the first decade of the twenty-first century. We look at several additional topics that are particularly relevant in considering the continued evolution of new media, including the future of mobility, the growing presence of an 'Internet of things', and our reliance on the Internet as something that is always on and always there. We also return to look further at social media and their implications for social interaction, whether for personal, business, political, or other purposes. Finally, we look in some detail at the surveillance implications of our networked, digital new media.

Abbreviations

3G	Third generation (in the context of mobile telephony)
4G	Fourth generation (mobile phones, internet protocol based)
ACTA	Anti-Counterfeiting Trade Agreement
AIMIA	Australian Interactive Multimedia Industry Association
APEC	Asia Pacific Economic Co-operation grouping
API	Applications Programming Interface
ARPA	Advanced Research Projects Agency
ASEAN	Association of South East Asian Nations
ASCII	American Standard Code for Information Interchange
B2B	business-to-business
B2C	business-to-consumer
BBC	British Broadcasting Corporation
CAR	computer-assisted reporting
CBC	Canadian Broadcasting Corporation
CC	Creative Commons
CCI	Creative Industries and Innovation
CCTV	closed-circuit television
CDS	Center for Digital Storytelling
CED	Committee for Economic Development
CERN	Conseil Européen pour la Recherche Nucléaire (European Organisation for Nuclear Research)
CMC	computer-mediated communication
CRTC	Canadian Radio-television and Telecommunications Commission
CWTA	Canadian Wireless Telecommunications Association
DARPA	Defense Advanced Research Projects Agency
DIY	Do-it-yourself
DRM	Digital Rights Management
EA	Electronic Arts
ECI	Entertainment-Communication-Information
EFF	Electronic Frontier Foundation
ESA	Entertainment Software Alliance
EULA	End-User Licensing Agreement
FPS	first-party shooter
GATS	General Agreement on Trade in Services
GII	Global Information Infrastructure
GPL	General Purpose Licence
GPS	Global Positioning System
GUI	Graphical User Interface
HCI	human–computer interaction
HSPA	High speed packet access
HTML	Hypertext Markup Language
HTTP	Hypertext Transfer Protocol
ICANN	Internet Corporation for Assigned Names and Numbers
ICTs	information and communication technologies
IGO	international governmental organisation

IHAC	Information Highway Advisory Council
INGO	international non-governmental organisation
IP	Internet Protocol
IPR	intellectual property rights
ISOC	Internet Society
IT	information technology
ITCP	IT-related creative practice
ITU	International Telecommunications Union
LAN	local area network
LTE	Long term evolution (mobile phone technology)
MIT	Massachusetts Institute of Technology
MMOG	massive multiplayer online game
MNC	multinational corporation
MOO	Multi-User Object-Oriented Domain
MPPW	massively populated persistent world
MMORPG	massively multiplayer online role playing game
MUD	Multi-User Dungeon
NAFTA	North American Free Trade Agreement
NCSA	National Center for Supercomputer Application
NES	Nintendo Entertainment System
NGO	non-government organisation
NII	National Information Infrastructure
NLS	On-Line-System

NTIA	National Telecommunication and Information Administration
P2P	peer-to-peer
PBS	Public Broadcasting Service
PDA	personal digital assistant
RFID	Radio frequency identification
RPG	role-playing game
RSS	Really Simple Syndication; Rich Site Summary
RTS	real-time strategy
SME	small and medium enterprise
SMS	short message services
TCP/IP	Transmission Control Protocol/Internet Protocol
TPM	Technological Protection Measure
TRIPS	Trade-Related Aspects of Intellectual Property Rights
UNCTAD	United Nations Committee on Trade, Aid and Development
WAIS	Wide Area Information Service
WAN	wide area network
WiFi	a trade name for wireless networking devices (often thought to stand for 'Wireless Fidelity', although this is not the case)
WIPO	World Intellectual Property Organization
WSIS	World Summit on the Information Society
WTO	World Trade Organization
WWW	world wide web

1 Introduction to New Media

Questions to Consider

- In what ways is communication mediated by technology? Why is this significant?

- Why is it important to think about nuanced understandings of what 'new media' means?

- How can 'digital divide' be variously understood and what are the causes and consequences of such divides?

- In what ways is globalization significant when thinking about new media?

- Why do you think the Internet and Web 2.0 have become so popular? What are some benefits and drawbacks of this popularity?

Chapter Outline

In this chapter we consider what society finds novel in new media and what role new media plays in wider social change, as it is already deeply embedded in the debates, processes, and practicalities of our society. We explore how new media is an outcome of the digitization of content, which has enabled '**convergence**'—the process by which media technologies, industries, and services are merging—through changes in computing, communication networks, and content. Although convergence is important, we attempt to put these changes in perspective and recognize that long-standing social, cultural, political, and economic factors remain important and mitigate and filter the impact of technological change. This chapter explains the characteristics of digital information and how those characteristics result in a particular type of communication that can be summed up as **interactive**. We examine the Internet as one of the most important new media forms of the late twentieth and early twenty-first centuries, and review Internet history, social implications, and recent growth into **Web 2.0**, focusing on the importance of search engines. We also look at the importance of online encyclopedias, status updates, friend lists, and online video, in the context of a growing and globalizing technology. The chapter concludes with a deeper examination of the implications of convergence on how we create and consume media content and the role of Web 2.0 in this process.

Why 'New' Media?

In any discussion of new media, a question that needs to be addressed is why some media are considered 'new'. There is a temptation to simply list the latest developments in media technologies and call these *new*. Yet this approach is inadequate, partly because the rate of change in media technologies, services, and uses is so rapid that any list of this sort will quickly become dated. It also conflates what is new with what is novel. At one extreme, 'newness' can simply refer to updates of long-established commodities, as when car manufacturers reveal their 'new' line of vehicles for the coming year, television networks present the 'newest' sitcom or game show, or mobile phone companies announce a new model that is jewel-encrusted or locates the camera in a new place on the device.

Such an approach is also problematic because media technologies now considered to be 'old', such as film, radio, and television, were themselves once new (Gitelman and Pingree 2003; Marvin 1988). To many of those born after the 1980s, whom Marc Prensky (2001) terms 'digital natives', even the idea of a world without the Internet, email, mobile phones, computer games, digital cameras, and instant text messaging is simply preposterous: only the folks on reality TV shows such as *Big Brother* and *Survivor* don't have access to such devices, and that was their choice. Indeed, in developed countries, networked personal computers and other digital media technologies are now so common in our work, our home lives, and the myriad everyday interactions we have with each other, that they are ceasing to be 'new' in any meaningful sense of the term. As a result, any approach to new media that simply catalogues the technologies themselves, and fails to ask broader questions about the contexts of their use and their social and cultural impacts, ignores the central question of why there is a need to look at new media in the first place.

There is a need, as Sonia Livingstone notes, to ask 'what's new for society about the new media?' rather than simply 'what are the new media?' (1999: 60). This takes us to the larger question of whether, and how, technologies can act as factors in wider social change while being already embedded in a social context (Cowan 1997; Flichy 2005a). In *Novum Organum*, first published in 1620, the English philosopher Francis Bacon proposed that three discoveries had been central to marking out the period in which he lived as one that was dramatically different from those preceding it:

> It is well to observe the force and effect and consequences of discoveries. These are to be seen nowhere more conspicuously than in those three which were unknown to the ancients, and of which the origin, though recent, is obscure: namely, printing, gunpowder, and the magnet. For these three have changed the whole face and state of things throughout the world; the first in literature, the second in warfare, the third in navigation; whence have followed innumerable changes. (Quoted in Graham 1999: 26–7)

One way that *new media* has been defined—in previous editions of this book (Flew 2002, 2005a) and elsewhere—has involved the combination of the three *C*s:

1. computing and information technology (IT);
2. communications networks; and
3. content and digitized media, arising out of another process, (a fourth *C*), convergence (cf. Barr 2000; Miles 1997; Rice 1999).

Convergent media can be seen as combining computing, communications, and media content in the way shown in Figure 1.1.

Convergence

Convergence refers in the first instance to the interlinking of computing and IT, communications networks, and media content that occurred with the development and popularization of the Internet, and the convergent products, services, and activities that have emerged in the digital media space. So, for example, we not only have media companies that own Internet companies, but television shows with complementary websites, all available on devices such as mobile phones and computers that were formerly dedicated to conversations and calculations. Many see this as simply the tip of the iceberg, since all aspects of institutional activity and social life—from art to business, government to journalism, health and education, and beyond—are increasingly conducted in an interactive digital media environment, across a plethora of networked information and communication technology (ICT) devices. This ubiquity, the possibility that one might speak of convergence from three quite different perspectives (technology, services, and industries) makes the term not only 'slippery' but prone to confusion among writers and students of new media and the Internet.

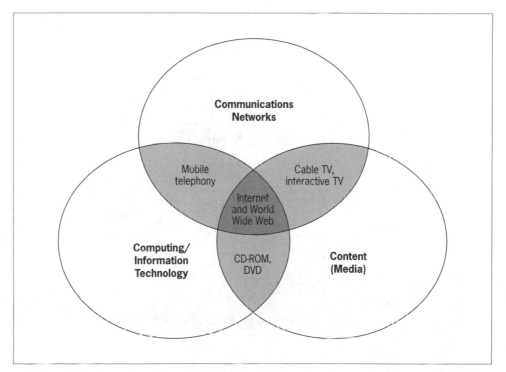

FIGURE 1.1 The Three Cs of Convergent Media
Source: Barr (2000).

The careful reader is wise to pay attention to which of the three (or which combinations of these aspects) is being referred to when reading about convergence.

A recent report by the Canadian Radio-television and Telecommunications Commission (CRTC) shows that, 'In 2008, over 80% of communications revenues were generated by converged companies offering both broadcasting and telecommunications services' (2009: i). Figure 1.2 illustrates how convergence is situated within a larger dynamic of telecommunications operating platforms. It should be noted, however, that interactivity and the complexity of convergence are not fully captured here; both of these are discussed later in the chapter.

For writers such as Thomas Friedman (2005), convergence is in turn generating a global 'flat earth', where activities conducted through digital media can occur in any part of the world. We note in Chapters 8 and 9 that there are reasons to question this claim, and that culture, policy, and other variables remain critical to the geographical location of new media activities, particularly with the shift towards a global knowledge economy.

The second element of convergence is the morphing of devices (computers, mobile phones, televisions, etc.) as they become multi-purpose conduits for a range of activities involving digital media (Zetie 2004). For example, computers become telephones via Skype, mobile phones like the iPhone are now major platforms for playing games, and even televisions are acquiring multimedia capabilities through widgets that display web content.

New media can also be thought of as digital media. **Digital** media are forms of media content that combine and integrate data, text, sound, and images of all kinds; are stored in digital formats; and are increasingly distributed through networks such as those based on

FIGURE 1.2 Broadcasting and Telecommunications Operating Platforms
Source: Communications Monitoring Report 2009, p. 100. Reproduced with the permission of the Minister of Public Works and Government Services Canada, 2011.

broadband fibre-optic cables, satellites, and microwave transmission systems. Such media, or forms of digital information, have the characteristics of being:

- manipulable: digital information is easily changeable and adaptable, at all stages of creation, storage, delivery, and use;
- networkable: digital information can be shared and exchanged between large numbers of users simultaneously, and across enormous distances;
- dense: very large amounts of digital information can be stored in small physical spaces (e.g. USB flash drives) or on network servers;
- compressible: the amount of capacity that digital information takes up on any network can be reduced dramatically through compression, and decompressed when needed; and,
- impartial: digital information carried across networks is indifferent to how it is represented, who owns or created it, or how it is used.[1]

This still leaves open, however, the question of what is new for society from the new media. In this text, we take a broad social focus towards new media and stress the need to be aware of the importance of how communication is mediated by technology. We follow Lievrouw and Livingstone (2005: 2) in their observation that any approach to thinking about new media needs to take account of three elements: (i) the artifacts or devices that enable and extend our ability to communicate; (ii) the communication activities and practices we engage in to develop and use these devices; and (iii) the social arrangements and organizations that form around these devices and practices.

Lievrouw and Livingstone also make the point that these three elements should not be thought of as linear or layered—technologies influencing communications practices, in turn shaping social arrangements and institutions—but rather as constituting an ensemble characterized by 'dynamic links and interdependencies among artifacts, practices, and social arrangements that . . . guide our analytic focus' (2005: 3). In this way, critical analysis of new media also has wider implications for how the media are studied more generally, since media studies as it emerged in the twentieth century understood media production, texts, and audiences as discrete forms, following a linear model of different moments in the media production-consumption cycle.

In practical terms what differentiates old media from new media, when you take into account the five characteristics of digital media listed above and Lievrouw and Livingstone's 'three elements', (artifacts, activities, and arrangements) is that new media are interactive in a way that previous media were not usually thought to be. Old and traditional media, however, are still the basis for much of the conceptual apparatus that we bring to the media both as audience and media producers. We regularly see new media undertakings that reconceive, or '**remediate**' in Bolter and Grusin's language (Bolter and Grusin 2000), existing media forms.

Online and console-based games, websites, and instant messaging services, for example, all extend our abilities, change our practices, and transform social arrangements through significant levels of interactivity. Media technologies that were previously dominated by a one-way flow of content (newspapers, film, radio, television) are giving way to media forms that are inherently and profoundly interactive and two-way.

While interactivity has been around a long time (telegraph, telephone, and point-to-point radio), these were limited to individual, one-to-one conversations. New media takes the power of the mass media to aggregate large groups and takes the ability of interactive media to involve participants and blends these as never before. It is this blend that makes new media distinctive from previous media forms; it is also why the power of new media is not simply a matter of newness or specific technologies.

Internet History

The concept of new media is integrally bound up with the history of the Internet and the web. While convergence has now spread across a range of platforms and devices, it was the emergence and mass popularization of the Internet that heralded the rise of new media, bringing together computing and information technologies, communications networks, and media content. It should be noted, here, that the Internet refers both to:

1. a technical infrastructure of computers and other digital devices (e.g. servers, routers) permanently connected through high-speed telecommunications networks; and
2. the forms of content, communication, and information sharing that occur through these networks.

In their analysis of the social implications of the Internet, sociologists DiMaggio, Hargittai, Neuman, and Robinson define the Internet as 'the electronic network of networks that links people and information through computers and other digital devices allowing person-to-person communication and information retrieval' (DiMaggio et al. 2001: 307). A more technical definition has been developed by the Internet Society (ISOC), which, in 1995, resolved that the Internet:

> refers to the global information system that: (i) is logically linked together by a globally unique address space based on the Internet Protocol (IP) or its subsequent extensions/follow-ons; (ii) is able to support communications using the Transmission Control Protocol/Internet Protocol (TCP/IP) suite or its subsequent extensions/follow-ons, and/or other IP-compatible protocols; and (iii) provides, uses or makes accessible, either publicly or privately, high level services layered on the communications and related infrastructure described herein. (Leiner et al. 2003)

It is vitally important to observe that the history of the Internet, while developing in parallel with the general development of personal computers and other devices for digital information processing and retrieval, is both a history of the common networking protocols for the transfer of digital information and a history of systems for the publication, organization, and distribution of this information.[2]

The technical history of the Internet has been well documented and will not be presented in great detail here; however, it is worth reviewing several elements of this history. First, while the commitment to developing an integrated communications network arose in the US as a consequence of the Cold War with the Soviet Union, the priorities of the Advanced Research Projects Agency (ARPA)—established in 1957 after the Soviets launched the Sputnik satellite—were arguably driven as much by the desire of the American scientific community to perfect mechanisms of communicating with one another as by the demands of the military.[3] The most significant development to come from ARPA in the 1960s was packet switching. **Packet switching** meant that long messages could be broken down into smaller 'packets'; messages could be rerouted if there was a blockage at one message route or point of connection between two computers; and messages would be sent in an asynchronous mode, meaning that the receiver would not receive the message until some time after the message was originally sent. Not only did packet switching overcome limitations of the telephone system, such as the potential for access to be blocked by heavy use by others, it also established the principle of a decentralized network with no single point from which control can be exercised, which has been so central to the Internet's development (Gillies and Cailliau 2000: 18–25). With the establishment of ARPANET as a national long-distance computer network in the US in 1969, packet switching became central to this network, with the transfer of electronic mail being perhaps the major communications innovation arising from this development. In 1972, ARPANET demonstrated to the public its capacity to send and receive data at the International Conference on Computer Communication in Washington, DC, where perhaps the world's first email was sent (although not called this at the time!) (Hassan 2004: 13).

Another landmark in Internet technical history was the development of a common set of networking protocols, which enabled researchers in the various local area networks (LANs) to communicate with one another, through the interconnection of these LANs within a wide area network (WAN). The major breakthrough came in 1974, when Robert Kahn and Vinton Cerf proposed a common switching protocol that could meet the needs of an open-architecture network; this came to be known as TCP/IP (Transmission Control Protocol/Internet Protocol). The quasi-privatization of ARPANET in 1983, which allowed universities and commercial interests to play a larger role on the network and which marked the birth of the Internet we know today, was premised on the adoption of TCP/IP as a common interconnection protocol. In sharp contrast to other media, the Internet would become both a public and a global communications medium, as all computers and computer networks could communicate with one another in a common language, whether they were Apples, PCs, or mainframes, regardless of the local or national computing network they were operating within. As Internet use spread in the 1980s from outside its core constituency of the US government and military, scientists, and defence contractors, the importance of TCP/IP being established as a common Internet protocol would be of increasing significance to more and more people worldwide.

The development of the web in the 1990s, however, was a major advancement that made the Internet what it is today. While developments such as TCP/IP and packet switching provided the means by which networks could connect with networks, and computers could connect with computers, the question of how people could connect with other people through such electronic networks had not received as much attention. The conception of the web by Tim Berners-Lee in 1989, and its development by Berners-Lee and colleagues at CERN (Conseil Européen pour la Recherche Nucléaire, or European Organization for Nuclear Research) from 1991 onwards would dramatically change the communications capabilities of the Internet. The significance of developing the web became even more apparent in 1992 when Marc Andreesen of the National Center for Supercomputer Applications (NCSA) developed Mosaic as the first popular web browser. Andreesen went on to become one of the founders of Netscape Communication, which developed Netscape, the first major commercial web browser, in 1994. Microsoft quickly followed suit in 1995 with its Internet Explorer browser, released as part of its Windows 95 software suite, to much fanfare and to the sounds of the Rolling Stones' 'Start Me Up'.

The ability to use web browsers such as Netscape and Internet Explorer to access online content through the web saw the mass popularization of the Internet, with the number of Internet users worldwide growing by over 1,300 per cent between 1994 and 1998 (see Table 1.1 on page 14). Several features of the web were particularly important in this popularization. First, it allowed for the display of colourful pictures, music, and audio as well as data and text, and introduced multimedia capability to the Internet. Second, it was based on **hypertext** principles. Hypertext allows for the linking of information, where links from one information source provide simple point-and-click access to related information available from other sources. The concept of hypertext had circulated in various domains since the publication of Vannevar Bush's article 'As We May Think' in 1945, which proposed the development of a computational machine (the 'Memex') that not only could store vast amounts of information, but could allow users to create ancillary 'thought trails' (Bush 1996). Ted Nelson's experimentations with hypertext through 'Project Xanadu' in the 1960s and early 1970s pointed to the possibilities of interconnected electronic writing, and both the French Minitel system (developed as a national teletext system in 1983) and the Hypercard storage system (available on all Apple computers from 1987 and well into the 1990s) drew on hypertext principles in different ways. The value of hypertext became even more apparent with the development not only of web browsers such as Netscape Navigator and Microsoft Explorer, but directories and search engines such as Yahoo!, Alta Vista, and Google, which provided vast and easy-to-use databases that gave users easy access to information stored on the Internet. Third, the web was associated with the development of both the common Hypertext Transfer Protocol (HTTP), which provided a platform-independent means of interconnection between websites, and Hypertext Markup Language (HTML) as a relatively straightforward means of writing source code for the web. As a result, a much wider range of people could become producers, as well as consumers, of content on the web. This trend would gain momentum as commercial software for developing web pages became increasingly available—such as Macromedia Dreamweaver and Microsoft Front Page—and this has been further accelerated by the development of programs associated with what is known as Web 2.0 (see below for more on the nature and impact of Web 2.0).

The people behind the Internet and the applications side of Internet history

It is tempting to think of the Internet in terms of its signature technologies (switches, fibre optic cables) and software (TCP/IP, SMTP, DNS) and certainly these played a key role in the making of the Internet, but there is more to the story. Internet technologies enabled information to move from place to place and enabled email and computer sharing but these capabilities, alone, were not sufficiently attractive to great masses of people to account for the mass popularization of the Internet.

The Internet graduated from being a computer network akin to a highway, to a 'place' with attractions along the way, in part because key entrepreneurs and their companies helped create valuable online destinations for everyday folks. Many of these destinations allowed people to consume and share new media. Some of these sites provided services—like search engine Google (or, before it, Alta Vista and Yahoo!)—or hosted users' content, like Wikipedia and YouTube. In appreciating the history of the Internet, it is important to consider some of the remarkable people involved and their significant contributions.

Cataloguing and searching

At first, the problem of finding things on the Internet was a non-issue because the only things on the Internet were things that one user put there for another user. Typically, one user would send another user an Internet address—perhaps in the form of login information to a File Transfer Protocol (FTP) server—and then, whatever had been placed at that Internet address could be retrieved, using the expertise of both users. There was little content available or even of interest to anonymous and non-expert users.

This all changed with the arrival of the web.[4] Very quickly, online content proliferated and finding something online became an enormous challenge. People tried to keep up, at first, by saving and sharing links to interesting Internet websites, but this was both overwhelming and inadequate. Some organizations—perhaps recalling the challenges that a profusion of new products meant for retailers at the beginning of the last century—decided to set up catalogues of all these new websites. They would turn this into a business by selling advertising alongside the listings. One of the most successful of these and still in business more than a decade later—a remarkable achievement in the dot.com era—is Yahoo! (with its signature exclamation mark).

Yahoo! was built by a couple of Internet entrepreneurs—the classic story of college students with a great idea (founders Jerry Yang and David Filo were engineering students at Stanford University when they started their web project)—as a site that would bring together all kinds of useful website links, categorize them, and let the user either flip through them by heading or search within the entire set. This latter feature quickly became the most popular feature and the company focused on it, while adding additional properties (email, picture sharing, and so on), either by building them themselves or buying promising young companies. The famous picture sharing site, Flickr, a small start-up in Vancouver, Canada, was purchased by Yahoo! in 2005, for example.[5]

Searching for things, as anyone who has lost their keys knows all too well, can be a tedious business at best. Until recently humans coped with disorder by devising, implementing, and (often failing to) stick to a plan of organization (Weinberger 2008). If you have not yet filed your latest bank statements or income tax forms, you are not alone. Once we leave the realm of physical objects, however, searching is proving to be remarkably efficient, even if things are not filed properly. Computers don't complain about the humdrum tasks assigned to them. Still, searching, as it turns out, is not a simple task and doing it well proved to be the making of another key Internet entrepreneurial duo: the founders of Google. Sergey Brin and Larry Page, also college students, sought to help computers arrive at better answers to people's search questions. Brin and Page did such a good job of it that Google became one of the most well known companies in the world and it performs more Internet searches than any other search engine on the entire planet.

Search engines are doubtlessly important from a technical and ease of use perspective, but they have profound social, political, and cultural implications as well. Alex Halavais' 2008 book, *Search Engine Society*, tackles these important questions and in particular examines how search engines affect politics and privacy. The search engine, as Halavais concludes, is an important tool in the exercise of power in an information society. For example, it has become common practice that the first step to finding something online is to 'Google' it. For many people, online searching is now second nature and rather than book-marking or remembering where they have been, users search again and again ('re-finding' in Halavais' words). In this way users are allowing search engines to determine the best path to navigate, with profound implications for sites that do not rank highly in a search engine.

Encyclopedias

For more than a hundred years average folks have looked to an encyclopedia for answers to everyday topics. The family encyclopedia set was a resource for homework assignments for young people and helped settle many a kitchen table argument. Not many people, however, would have imagined that they would participate in the creation of one. Early on in the history of the Internet it became evident that computers and networks would be a good way to distribute the type of knowledge that encyclopedias contained. In fact, even before the Internet was in widespread use, Microsoft founded a company based on selling encyclopedias on CD-ROM.

For Jimmy Wales, founder of Wikipedia, putting an encyclopedia online seemed like an obvious thing to do, but how to get started? His first attempt seemed promising from a technical point of view but it took too long to get the encyclopedia entries through the editorial process. In frustration, he decided to open up the submission and review system, using a new set of tools known as 'Wiki' technology. The rest, as they say, is history. People loved creating, editing, and most of all, having access to the encyclopedia entries.

While there have been (and continue to be) controversies over the validity or reliability of Wikipedia, it has survived both serious scientific scrutiny and public acceptance and has become one of the most widely used sources of information on the Internet. Thousands of Wikipedia entries are created each day and tens of thousands undergo constant revision.

Although Wikipedia's very popularity has also made it a target for pranks and attacks, the 'many editors' approach that the Wiki software makes possible mitigates such problems. When necessary, the managers of the site lock down a Wikipedia entry, but for the most part, the site is maintained by the goodwill of many hundreds of thousands of amateur experts who strive for a neutral point of view.

(Amateur) film-making

While the amateur bird watcher or automobile enthusiast might be inclined to write an online article about their favourite raptor or roadster, the Internet also drew the attention of those working with audio-visual content. Although the Internet was launched and initially functioned as a largely text-based medium, images and videos increasingly began to appear online in the twenty-first century. Much of that content came from home users who created so-called 'user-generated' content.

Getting video online was difficult for amateurs until the arrival of video clip sharing on YouTube. Now owned by Google, YouTube was also started by a small team of enthusiasts who famously uploaded a video of a trip to the zoo to start their web-based service.[6] The team of three former PayPal employees (Steve Chen, Chad Hurley, and Jawed Karim) launched the service in February 2005 and sold it, less than two years later, for USD $1.65 billion. The videos on YouTube (as with the textual contributions on Wikipedia, although mainly less serious, and frequently silly or inane) can be enormously popular, becoming in some instances among the most viewed images in history. Justin Bieber's 'Baby', for example, had over 424 million views at the beginning of 2011.[7]

The circulation of amateur video is made much easier by sites such as YouTube, but the creation of such video in the first place is the outcome of a downward spiral in the cost of recording, editing, and compressing audiovisual material. As recently as the mid-1990s creating video content was expensive and cumbersome, and once created it was confined to tape or film archives, difficult and expensive to duplicate and distribute. The rise of low-cost digital video recorders, coupled with staggering leaps in the processing power of personal computers, particularly in the area of graphic processing capabilities, has made the raw material of sites like YouTube something that can be accomplished by just about every Internet citizen. In recent years the addition of video recording capabilities to mobile telephones has resulted in a second explosion of videos uploaded and circulated on the net, often with explosive (literally) content. In fact, the distribution of videos from the July 2005 bombing in the London Underground is considered a turning point in both the awareness and acceptance of amateur video as a record of serious events, and not just the results of frat parties and stupid pet tricks.[8]

Status/friends

There was a time when the word 'friend' was not used as a verb and 'following' someone had a very different connotation from what it does today. Social media sites such as Facebook and Twitter have not just redefined language used in socializing online, but they have become hubs for socializing, political organizing, and commercial promotions. With over 500 million members in the middle of 2010, Facebook is by far the largest community online and continues to grow rapidly. Although controversies have flared up from time to time over photographs or comments inadvertently shared, or inadequate or ill-understood privacy policies, the site that founder Mark Zuckerberg envisioned as a place to help people 'understand the world around them' continues to grow.[9]

Facebook's assertion that its mission is to serve its customers first is not uncommon on the Internet. A claim of working for the public good is typical of Internet companies, including Google's famous claim that they will 'not be evil'. Along the way to 'aiding understanding' or doing an Internet search, however, companies such as Facebook have spawned an entire industry of add-ons, applications, and linkages to other online software that generates considerable revenue. On Facebook, people can play Scrabble, farm, send each other (virtual) gifts, and indeed, spend a great deal of money doing so. The tractor sales in the Facebook application FarmVille, according to *Fortune* magazine, exceed annual tractor sales—in numbers, if not revenue—in the US by a large margin (purportedly 500,000 a day versus 5,000 a year for John Deere, one of the largest manufacturers).[10] That selling virtual tractors for $20 each is a good business to be in is lost on nobody, and Zynga, the creators of FarmVille and other similar games, reportedly made over $500 million in 2010.

Twitter was founded by Jack Dorsey, Biz Stone, and Evan Williams in March 2006 as a side project or spin-off from a company called Odeo. As with the YouTube pioneers, some of the Twitter founders had experience in previous social media sites, including Blogger (sold to Google). They used their expertise to create Twitter, one of the first popular sites in North America to have an explicitly mobile focus (the limitation to 140 characters was designed for messages to be sent and received as text messages—or SMS—on mobile phones), although it has since morphed into much more of an online service.

Both Facebook and Twitter emphasize the sharing of brief updates, also known as 'microblogging'. Facebook currently gives you a small box with, 'What's on your mind?' (the question changes from time to time), while Twitter's web interface has retained its simple look, but dropped the question and instead has a simple blank box with a countdown of how many characters are left as users enter text. Both services emphasize creating, maintaining, and building a social network. While these services could be used to leave messages for the general public, those actively using them soon acquire friends (Facebook) or followers (Twitter), to share pithy remarks about life, the universe, and lunch ideas.

Each of these examples (Yahoo!, Wikipedia, YouTube, Facebook, Twitter) has a different kind of sharing at work. People share their words to create knowledge (Wikipedia), their videos to entertain (YouTube), and their status to create/maintain social networks (Facebook and Twitter). And while it may not be immediately obvious, people using Yahoo!'s or Google's search engines also contribute. Every Google search (and the choices users make as a result of the search) provides a list of options, which are fed back into the Google search engine to enhance and refine the search performance. This 'implicit work' is as much a form of user-generated content as that found with the other sites, if somewhat less obvious to the untrained eye.

The fact that we are working to create the very things we consume is not lost on critics of online services such as Google, Facebook, and Twitter. As with earlier criticism of how television viewers were 'working' by watching advertisements and thereby learning to consume, Internet critics charge that not only are we working by viewing online ads, we are actually providing all of the content, as though we had to produce our own television programs in the heyday of TV. In particular, critics such as José van Dijck note that this activity is 'immaterial labour'—unpaid work that is captured and capitalized by the owners of the websites (van Dijck 2009: 50).

Others, such as danah boyd and Oscar Gandy, have remarked on the considerable potential for privacy invasion by tools that encourage users to over-share through the use of default settings that are too wide open and the creation of a false sense of community and privacy through the requirement that users log in with a user name and password (boyd 2008). Despite this criticism these sites continue to be enormously popular, in large part because they serve what seems to be a real need. Or, at least, people find them useful and entertaining.

The growth of the Internet

The Internet has become the world's second-fastest growing medium, after mobile phones. It is estimated that, as of November 2010, there were 1.967 billion Internet users worldwide, having grown from 360 million users in 2000 (30.6 million users in 1995), or by almost 400 per cent over a nine-year period (Internet World Stats 2010). Table 1.1 on page 14 indicates the number of Internet hosts worldwide, or the number of sites from which the Internet is accessed, as well as the rate of growth of Internet use over time.[11]

The incredible penetration rates and growth for mobile telephones and the Internet are blending in many countries, as more and more mobile phones are Internet enabled. Depending on how you define access (since many Internet services such as Twitter and Facebook are accessible in some fashion through SMS), one could use the mobile subscriber numbers in place of the Internet numbers. In this case, the number of people with some access to the Internet is approaching two thirds of the world's population (ITU 2010).

The Global Internet

In the 2000 US presidential election campaign, the Democratic Party candidate Al Gore (now a leader in raising awareness about global warming) made the claim that as Vice-President during the Clinton administration, he had 'invented the Internet'. Gore was roundly criticized for his hubris, particularly as the collaborative nature of the Internet meant that no single person could claim to have invented it, let alone a senior politician. Yet there is a subtext to Gore's claim that cannot be ignored. At the time of its mass popularization in the mid-1990s, the bulk of the major initiatives that led to the Internet's emergence came from the US, its user base was predominantly North American, and the policies of the Clinton Administration—such as the promotion of a National Information Infrastructure (NII) and a Global Information Infrastructure (GII) modeled on the US NII—played a key formative role in the way in which the Internet evolved globally.

Year	Estimated number of Internet hosts worldwide	Annual rate of growth (%)
TABLE 1.1 Estimated Internet Hosts Worldwide		
1991	376,000	
1992	727,000	96.4
1993	1,313,000	80.6
1994	2,217,000	68.8
1995	4,852,000	188.5
1996	9,472,000	95.2
1997	16,416,000	73.3
1998	29,670,000	80.7
1999	43,230,000	45.7
2000	72,398,092	67.5
2001	109,574,429	51.3
2002	147,344,723	34.4
2003	171,638,297	16.5
2004	233,101,481	35.8
2005	317,646,084	36.2
2006	394,991,609	24.3
2007	433,193,199	9.7
2008	541,677,360	25.0
2009	625,226,456	15.4

Yearly figures are for January.
Source: Internet Software Consortium, www.isc.org/solutions/survey/history.

By contrast, the Internet today has a far more globally diverse user base. Of the estimated 1.967 billion Internet users in November 2010, the majority are now from Asia and Europe, and the fastest growing regions for Internet take-up are the Middle East, Africa, and Latin America.

North America, with just 13.5 per cent of Internet users, is no longer the dominant player that it once was. This diversification has been growing for more than a decade, as the regional Internet populations have come to more closely resemble their absolute numbers in the world population figures. Although current statistics haven't taken the impact of mobile phones into account, the rise of the mobile Internet, accompanied by high and growing penetration rates for mobile phones in the developing world, suggests that mobile phones will be a factor in the growing access to the Internet around the world. As the use of the Internet spreads beyond its origins in the US and Europe, two key issues have been

TABLE 1.2 World Internet Usage and Population Statistics

World Regions	Population (2010 est.) (million)	Population % of world	Internet Use Dec. 2010 (million)	% of Population as Internet Users	% of World Internet Users	User Growth 2000–10 (%)
Africa	1,013.80	14.81	111.00	10.90	5.60	2,357.30
Asia	3,834.80	56.02	825.00	21.50	42.00	621.80
Europe	813.30	11.88	475.00	58.40	24.20	352.00
Middle East	212.30	3.10	63.00	29.80	3.20	1,825.30
North America	344.10	5.03	266.00	77.40	13.50	146.30
Latin America and Caribbean	592.60	8.66	205.00	34.50	10.40	1,032.80
Australia/Oceania	34.70	0.51	21.00	61.30	1.10	179.00
WORLD TOTAL	6,845.60	100.00	1,967.00	28.70	100.00	444.80

Source: Internet World Stats, www.internetworldstats.com/stats.htm.

highlighted: (i) the 'digital divide' separating rich and poor; and (ii) the importance of globalization as an economic and political force.

Digital divide

The National Telecommunication and Information Administration (NTIA) used the term **'digital divide'** in the late 1990s in its 'Falling Through the Net' reports on the differential access to networked personal computers. The term digital divide has been defined as 'the differential access to and use of the Internet according to gender, income, race, and location' (Rice 2002: 106). The term has also been important in the context of globalization, in clarifying the extent to which, as the United Nations observed in 1995, 'more than half of the world's population lived more than two hours away from a telephone' (quoted in Couldry 2002: 186). Recent figures (2008) from the International Telecommunications Union (ITU) suggest that access to a phone is much more widespread in the twenty-first century then in the twentieth century. In fact, almost two thirds of the world population (4.1 billion of the 6.7 billion people) subscribe to mobile cellular services (see www.itu.int/ITU-D/ict/statistics).

In an overview of digital divide research, Norris (2001) proposes that it is important to distinguish between: (i) the 'global divide' or differential Internet access between nations based on access to networked ICT infrastructures, computers, information transmission capacity, local website hosts etc.; and (ii) the 'social divide', or the gaps within nations in terms of access to the Internet as a means of social engagement. Critics of the digital divide concept argue that inequalities related to new media involve far more than access, but also include opportunities to participate effectively in online environments (Gandy 2002). Murdock and Golding (2004) argue that because the computing hardware, software, and skills required change so quickly, and opportunities to learn these new skills are unequally distributed, inequalities in the digital environment continue to reflect other sources of social inequality, such as those arising from income, occupation, or geographical location.

While these data certainly provide considerable evidence of a global digital divide they nonetheless also highlight how the world's Internet-using population is becoming more globally diverse. A good indicator of this is the change in the top ten languages used on the web. While English remains the dominant language, accounting for 29.7 per cent of languages used globally in 2009, quickly proliferating online are Chinese and Spanish (the written and spoken languages of about 30 per cent of the world's population), as well as Korean, Portuguese, and Russian (not as widely used worldwide, but these are the languages of some of the world's fastest growing Internet-using populations). There is also a **'long tail'** of languages used, with over 30 languages used by at least one million people on the Internet (see Figure 1.3).

Globalization and new media

New media is also implicated in one of the most widely used concepts in social theory today: **globalization.** Globalization is a term used to both describe and make sense of a series of interrelated processes such as the rise of multinational corporations (MNCs); international production, trade, and financial systems; international communications flows; global

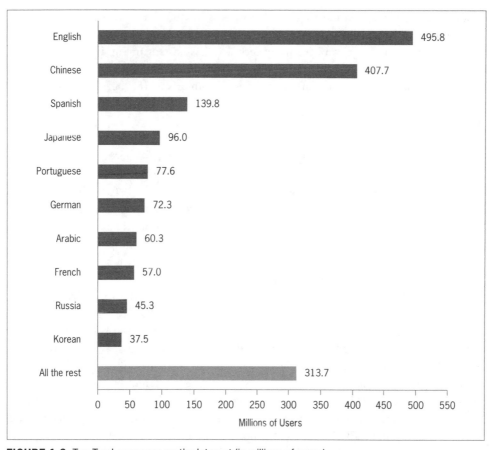

FIGURE 1.3 Top Ten Languages on the Internet (in millions of users)
Source: Internet World Stats 2009, www.internetworldstats.com/stats7.htm.

movements of people and the increasingly multicultural nature of societies; developments in international law; global social movements such as the environmental movement; the development of international governmental organizations (IGOs), regional trading blocs, and international non-governmental organizations (INGOs); and global conflicts such as the war on terror after the attacks on the World Trade Center and the Pentagon on 11 September 2001. While many of these developments are not new—trade and empire have been features of the world for millennia and evident in North America since Columbus crossed the Atlantic in 1492—the speed, intensity, and interconnectedness of these developments are seen by many as marking a new stage in human social development. As technologies that enable borderless communication, new media are central to debates about globalization and its impacts.

Globalization has turned out to be a key issue for social justice activists and scholars, in particular since the famous 'Battle In Seattle', which was a watershed moment for both new media and activism in the sense that new media tools were widely used to both organize and document those resistance movements. From that day in 1999—a protest outside the

World Trade Organization meetings in Seattle, Washington—right through to the recent G20 protests in Toronto, Ontario, the role of new media has been front and centre for social justice activists. In fact, a whole cadre of tech activists has sprung up in the years since, creating sites such as Indymedia to share alternative news and tools like Crabgrass to enable anonymous and easy facilitation of group discussions in private (Milberry 2009).[12]

The Conduit and the Content

The development and popularization of the Internet was a high-water mark in the process of convergence. Through the web, a rapidly growing number of Internet users were able to access a dramatically increased range of forms of digitized content (text, images, sound, video), delivered across telecommunications networks, via their personal computers, which increasingly became a single media platform able to deal with multiple media forms. This process of technological convergence, or the bringing together of computing, communications networks, and media content, was matched by the development of convergent products and services, and processes of industry convergence, or the range of takeovers, mergers, and strategic alliances that strengthened links between the computing and IT industries, the large telecommunications companies, and media corporations (Barr 2000; Flew 2005: 11–2).

At the same time, early Internet content was frequently quite impoverished in terms of the capabilities of the new media form. Indeed, the imperative to provide content was often the problem, as it frequently led to the dumping of already existing text online with little consideration of how such material was viewed and used differently from its print-based variants. The much-publicized early initiatives to digitize the entire contents of the US Library of Congress envisaged not only a veritable army of minimum wage information workers undertaking endless document scanning, but also an Internet where content was largely synonymous with that of the world of print media. One problem was, of course, download speeds: with most domestic users reliant on 28.8 Kilobyte per second modems for much of the 1990s, access to audio and video was bound to be slow for many.

The development of the web gave a renewed focus to the nature of the **interface**, or the 'front page' from which users accessed websites, typically through a web browser and search engine. The quality of interface design draws attention to the nature of human-computer interaction, which is fundamentally a consequence of technical design and the computer programming aspects of the interface, but which can only operate effectively when, as Anne Cranny-Francis observes, it recognizes 'the cultural practices that enable users to engage with the technology', since it constitutes the 'hidden engine of the user's interaction with the text' (2005: 120). The importance of interfaces to the usability and, hence, the popularity of computers was apparent well before the web. The success of Apple Computers in the 1980s was strongly related to its development of a Graphical User Interface (GUI) that, in simulating the environment of a desktop (with files, folders, in-trays, trash cans, etc.), was intuitively more usable when compared with the PC-DOS system that was the leading personal computer interface at the time. Indeed, Apple fought a long, bitter, and ultimately unsuccessful legal case against Microsoft between 1994 and 1998 over its claim that Microsoft had infringed Apple's copyright when it incorporated the desktop metaphor into its Windows software, raising the question of whether or not the look and feel of a GUI—and software generally—is protected by copyright.

The question of the technical conduit or the means by which online content is distributed, delivered, and accessed by the user, has become considerably more complex in the age of new media. With broadcast media, access to a suitable reception device (a television set or radio) gave its audiences content that looked and/or sounded more or less the same, regardless of the device being used to access it (except in instances such as the transition from black-and-white to colour televisions). With the Internet, by contrast, a variety of factors come into play in terms of both the accessibility and the quality of the user experience in accessing online content, including:

- the age of the computer being used and the software installed on that computer;
- whether the user is accessing the content from a dial-up or broadband connection and the speed of downloads available from that connection;
- the overall quality of service and the available modes of delivery (dial-up, broadband, wireless broadband, etc.) in the physical location from which the content is being accessed;
- the type of computer being used (e.g. some material is not available for PCs or Mac computers);
- the software being used to access the content (e.g. the web browser); and,
- the nature of the users themselves; for example, they may have a physical or mental condition that makes certain types of web design inappropriate.

Sites such as Vincent Flanders' Web Pages That Suck (www.webpagesthatsuck.com) delight in demonstrating the principles of good web design by drawing attention to examples of bad web design in a highly amusing manner. In response to the often baroque features of many early websites, where the designers seemed to forget about both their users and the means by which they would access such sites, there was a turn towards usability in web design, led by writers such as Donald Norman (1998) and Jakob Nielsen (2000).

The paradox of convergence and the reason why the concept becomes more problematic over time is this: as the computing, communications, and media industries are brought closer together by technological and industry changes, the disparities between and across content forms become more significant. For example, if we simply consider computer-based media, interactive online games require content that is sufficiently rich and compelling to provide an immersive experience for the gamer. What gamers seek from online media is, therefore, considerably more complex than the functionality and usability sought in most web-based user interfaces.

While the discussion of new media has thus far tended to focus on the Internet and computer-based digital media, a range of wireless technologies and applications have been developed that are increasingly shifting the locus of ICTs from the desktop to a range of portable, handheld devices. At the forefront of this has of course been the mobile phone. As noted above, almost two thirds of the world population subscribe to mobile cellular services. There have also been important transformations in how the mobile phone is used, with devices being increasingly used for short message services (SMS) or text messages, taking and sending pictures, viewing video, playing games, listening to music, and accessing email and the Internet. With these developments, the increased content that users seek to access from mobile devices has added to the complexity of issues of convergence: with the proliferation of interconnected digital media technologies and devices, the question of developing content that works across multiple media—in both a technical and a consumer demand sense—becomes more and more complex.

Given the importance of mobile devices for our understanding of new media in the years to come, we will return to this topic in a later chapter for a more thorough examination of what is different—and what is the same—about the mobile Internet and mobile new media in general. While mobile technologies are clearly the emerging face of new media, the current face is what is known as Web 2.0. This development has transformed the Internet and the way it is used (leading one site to call itself 'ReadWriteWeb'), from a passive consumption and selection process (surfing), to active production of new media content on sites such as YouTube and Flickr. The remainder of this chapter considers the Web 2.0 phenomenon in more detail.

Web 2.0

The concept of **Web 2.0** is central to understanding new media in the twenty-first century. The term was first circulated in 2003 and the first conferences were held on Web 2.0 through O'Reilly Media (formerly O'Reilly & Associates) in 2004. Tim O'Reilly (2006), who has been a key thinker and promoter of Web 2.0, defines it as 'the business revolution in the computer industry caused by the move to the Internet as platform, and an attempt to understand the rules for success on that new platform. Chief among those rules is this: *'Build applications that harness network effects to get better the more people use them . . . [or] harnessing collective intelligence'* (emphasis added).

There are both Web 2.0 evangelists and skeptics—as seems to be the case with most new media concepts. *Time* magazine drew particular attention to the Web 2.0 phenomenon when it declared that its 'Person of the Year' for 2006 was 'YOU', for each person's collective contribution to Web 2.0 (Grossman 2006). Not surprisingly, such prognoses generate equal doses of skepticism about both the sustainability of the phenomenon and the extent to which it is really marketing hype or what Steve Woolgar (2002) calls 'cyberbole'.

Nonetheless, the concept of Web 2.0 has caught on for two main reasons. First, it has embedded within it a range of features that have long been seen as central to the web as a communications infrastructure, such as the scope for participation, interactivity, collaborative learning, and **social networking** ('social networking media' or just 'social software' are commonly used, alternative terms), as well as positive networking effects from harnessing collective intelligence. In other words, the quality of participation increases as the number of participating users increases, and this in turn attracts more new users to the sites. Second, some of the fastest growing websites of the 2000s have been based on Web 2.0 principles. These include sites such as the photography site Flickr, the online encyclopedia Wikipedia, the online **user-generated** video site YouTube, aggregated web log (blog) sites such as Blogger, Livejournal, and Technorati, and the various personalized web space sites such as MySpace, Facebook, and Bebo.

Software programs and Internet sites that conform to Web 2.0 principles have core principles, in that they are:

- many-to-many in their connectivity;
- decentralized in terms of control;
- user-focused and easy for new users to use;
- open in terms of their technology standards and their Applications Programming Interface (API);
- relatively simple and lightweight in their design, their administrative requirements, and their start-up and ongoing development costs; and,
- expected to evolve and change over time, as users make new modifications to the sites.

In their overview of design and application principles that underpin and drive Web 2.0, Musser and O'Reilly (2007) identify the following principles (Table 1.3 on page 22).

The concept of Web 2.0 clearly implies a relationship to an earlier form of the Internet (Web 1.0). O'Reilly (2005) identifies some of the differences as related to a move from personal websites to blogs and blog site aggregation; from publishing to participation; from web content as the outcome of a large up-front investment to an ongoing and interactive process; and from content management systems to links based on **tagging** or what is known as '**folksonomy**'. A significant factor in the promotion of Web 2.0 has been the dot.com crash of 2000 and lessons learned from it, where very large numbers of small investors lost wealth due to the unrealistic business models of a plethora of Internet start-ups which, in contrast to the Web 2.0 model, had high initial costs in developing infrastructure, personnel, and marketing strategies.

Bloggers such as Carr (2005) and Shaw (2005) have expressed skepticism about Web 2.0, arguing that such a term is simply marketing bait that will promote over-capitalization in a new Internet capital-raising bubble (Bubble 2.0), on the basis of poor understanding of the Internet as a social technology. Moreover, the decision by News Corporation to buy MySpace in July 2005 raises a series of questions, yet to be resolved, about the relationship between established, incumbent media and the emergent start-up enterprises that arise in the Web 2.0 space.

Nevertheless, second generation web content continues to dominate Internet usage. One of the interesting outcomes of this is the way that traditional media and new media have formed hybrid forms. The CBC, Canada's national public broadcaster, has pioneered in this area (see Case Study, below) as well as continuing to support new media elements in their existing offerings.

TABLE 1.3 Principles of Web 2.0

Principle	Examples
Harnessing collective intelligence—deriving the benefits of large-scale ongoing participation and user co-creations and peer review of content to continuously improve the quality of the service	Google Wikipedia Flickr Amazon Del.icio.us
Data as the next 'Intel inside'—new wealth from online enterprises to be derived from database management	Amazon eBay Craigslist
Innovation in assembly—open APIs that allow for online remixing of content (mash-ups) and the use of RSS (Really Simple Syndication)	Google Maps Yahoo! Flickr
Rich User Experiences, that promote user interaction and immersive engagement with the available online content	Google Maps GMail Netflix
Software above the level of a single device—services that can span across media devices, particularly mobile media such as mobile phones and PDAs	iTunes TiVo
Perpetual Beta testing—software is incrementally released, and understood as a service rather than as a final product	Google Flickr Open source software more generally
Leveraging the 'long tail'—recognizing that there is a move from mass markets to niche markets, but that niche markets can be sustainable over a long period of time (cf. Anderson 2006)	Amazon eBay Google
Lightweight models and cost-effective flexibility—Web 2.0 marketing works off word of mouth rather than high up-front costs in business set-up and marketing	Digg.com (allegedly established with an up-front investment of USD $2,800) Flickr

Source: Musser and O'Reilly (2007).

One of the key benefits of new media is that it is endlessly adaptable. This is changing from something to be feared by old media to something to embrace. Old media—newspapers, radio, television—may not be as threatened by new media as was originally thought, once they begin to adopt and adapt to the new possibilities that digital distribution presents. Some recent Canadian examples include the expansion of CBC into digital multimedia broadcasting, the adoption of user forums by *The Globe and Mail* newspaper, and the extensive use of streaming video by Global Television.

CBC Radio was one of the early adopters of new media, with extensive use of rich media websites from an early stage. There are several ways in which new media provides an interesting and compelling companion to the old medium of radio. New music is one of these, as is radio drama. In the case of new music, the core of the experience is the music itself. That is what draws people in, and music has to be listened to. But if you are not familiar with a piece of music, how can you find it again? What if you forgot the band's name, after the announcer moved on to the next song? What if you want to know what other songs the band has made, or buy their CD? Here is where new media excels. The music can be accompanied by links to other songs by the band, photos of the band members, links to the online sales of their album, and histories and stories about the band. It can provide information about upcoming live shows as well. Importantly, you can branch out to other music similar to the song you've just listened to, make comments and tag the music, and follow the recommendations of others.

All of these things are available on the excellent website for CBC Radio. In addition to live streams of national and regional content of the broadcast network there are multiple Internet streams including live—with a host, and in real time—as well as pre-recorded (podcast) concerts, and themed stations that run without a host. Listeners can tune in via their web browser or mobile Internet device such as an iPhone. New media markedly increases the CBC's ability to present new material as well as the quality and richness of that material, as with 'Concerts on Demand', which is particularly in need of background and linking since it is, by definition, new or unknown to its audience.

The other aspect of radio that benefits from a new media complementary website is radio drama. At first this wouldn't seem obvious, but there are some types of radio drama that are very difficult to carry off successfully without some sort of supplement, at least in the present style of listening. These days, people rarely schedule their lives around a broadcast times. Gone are the days when a family might set aside Saturday afternoons to listen to an ongoing radio program. As a result, modern listeners may find it difficult to keep track of the complex plot or diverse array of characters required for some dramatic forms. These might perish except for the interesting solution of an accompanying website. Such a website was built for an ongoing CBC drama about farm life in Saskatchewan that aired several years ago. The plot was complex and the number of characters was very large. It was broadcast every day, but if you missed an episode you might lose the thread of the drama and decide to stop listening. With the website, not only were you able to catch up by listening to archived recordings but you could also click through to biographies of the main characters, read plot summaries of past episodes, and even get additional background information and images that are not possible in an audio-only medium. The result was a winning combination of sound and story.

As we have seen, new media is a rapidly evolving and complex assemblage of technology, social uses, and business models. While much remains up in the air, and the future is far from certain even for popular services such as Facebook, the pathways that new media is following have, in many ways, been laid down by pervious generations of 'new media' such as the telegraph and television. The next chapter will examine the roots of new media in previous media forms and the influence that these developments continue to exert.

Case Study: Radio3

Before reading this case study, perhaps take a minute to visit the Waterlife website (http://waterlife.nfb.ca). It is a wonderful example of new media at its best. The production is slick, the visual elements are artfully combined with facts and data, and there is lovely music. The producer of that piece, Rob McLaughlin, is based at the National Film Board, but he started at CBC Radio3,[13] which began its life in Vancouver in January of 2000. Radio3 still exists (http://radio3.cbc.ca), but the earlier version was quite different, more like Waterlife than the present version.

When Radio3 was conceived, the CBC already had some experience with the Internet, via a program on CBC radio called 'Real Time'. That program incorporated the Internet to some extent, making early experiments with streaming and trying out live chat lines (IRC) during the show.

In 1998, Robert Ouimet, one of the members of the Real Time team, worked on a proposal for a third radio network in Canada, one targeted at younger people and adding elements of what was, then, still a rather new Internet. CBC decided not to proceed with the broadcast network but decided to launch instead on the Internet. Ouimet started putting a team together in late 1999 and they were live on the Internet—as well as producing about 40 hours of traditional radio material a week for use on the existing Radio 1 and Radio 2 networks—by June of 2000.

Some of their early challenges were technical. In 2000, streaming was just beginning. Most people connected to the Internet by modem, and the idea of a live stream—where there is no intervening stage in which the files

are prepared for streaming, but rather, are pumped directly to the net—was a very new thing. They had to work closely with one of the pioneering firms in the field, Real Networks, Inc., of Seattle, to get beta versions of software to run on their servers. They had much the same story with Macromedia, the creators of Flash, the software used to create their web pages. They were pushing the envelope in those days and many people looked at what they were doing as state of the art, or indeed as cause for inspiration.

Much of the content on the three websites came from the public. But it wasn't user-generated content as we know it today. The notion of user-generated content, the driving force behind sites like Flickr and YouTube, scarcely existed when the CBC Radio3 team started. The idea that you could build a successful website with material from the public was initially greeted with some skepticism. The Radio3 team worked hard to support their contributors, which they called pro-consumers, and created a model in which their story ideas were nurtured and shaped, sometimes by helping them form partnerships with other people that had complementary skills.

Musicians were well along in creating digital versions of their work, at this point. A site called MP3.com already had 15,000 Canadian artists by 1999, at a time when Canadian radio stations in aggregate were playing perhaps 400 musicians. Graphic artists, animators, and photographers also had begun to work in digital formats but translating that to an online experience did not always come easily. Unlike sites such as Flickr or YouTube, which do not get involved in the things users upload, the Radio3 team worked hard to support their contributors in order to keep the quality of the web content high. They also made sure that the material featured on the site (the front page, etc.) was the best of what was received, even though they accepted almost everything.

These efforts were widely recognized, in the form of continuing financial support from the company and various awards, both in regular media and the emerging new media categories. CBC Radio3 won awards in California and New York—at a time when Vancouver was far from the epicentre of new media—bringing attention and recognition to the new media

scene in Canada. They also had local admirers who drew inspiration from their work and even tried to outdo them.

This sort of friendly competition led to a very high level of web capability (including Flash programming and audio streaming) in the Vancouver area. Although Radio3 has moved on to a more generic site now, integrated with the rest of CBC's web presence, the people responsible for the initial efforts continue to have an impact. Some of the team moved into local advertising and graphic production houses, gaming companies and, of course, Rob McLaughlin has moved to the National Film Board.

Useful Websites

Internet Society—Histories of the Internet
←www.isoc.org/internet/history→

This is an excellent collection of papers on the early development of the Internet and the Web. It includes Vinton Cerf's 'Brief History of the Internet', Tim Berners-Lee on the past, present, and future of the Web, and the website for the series Nerds 2.0.1, produced by the US Public Broadcasting Service (PBS) in 1998.

Internet World Stats—Usage and Population History
←www.internetworldstats.com/→

This site has the most up-to-date information on how many Internet users there are worldwide and where they are geographically located.

Alexa—Web's top ten
←www.alexa.com/topsites→

Alexa, a service that monitors the most popular websites, publishes a live list of the most popular sites in the world. It is available in a number of formats and provides in-depth information about each site that it has ranked. As of early 2010, the list starts with these in the top ten:

The top 500 sites on the Web.

1. google.com
2. facebook.com
3. yahoo.com
4. youtube.com
5. live.com
6. wikipedia.org
7. blogger.com
8. baidu.com (a music search engine – China focus)
9. msn.com
10. qq.com (an instant messaging service, like MSN – China focus)

Further Reading

Handbook of New Media, Leah A. Lievrouw and Sonia Livingstone (eds) (2006)

This handbook provides an excellent and broad perspective on new media. First published in 2001, it was updated in 2006, and while it misses some of the latest developments this is more than compensated for by its rich treatment of new media from a theoretical point of view and its firm grounding in 'social shaping' method. This focus on method gives students a perspective and a toolkit on new media that can be adapted and extended to more recent developments. Lievrouw and Livingstone also provide useful introductions to the way in which networks form an essential metaphor for understanding new media. Finally, the book also helps the student with historical, economic, social, and political background and context for new media.

New Media Reader, Noah Wardrip-Fruin and Nick Montfort (2003)

This reader provides an excellent collection of original texts, articles, and book excerpts that sets the new media revolution in context for the student reader. If a reader would like to find a comprehensive collection of scholarship, from a wide array of sources, this is a helpful companion.

Remediation: Understanding New Media, Jay David Bolter and Richard Grusin (2000)

A welcome reassessment of what it means to be new media, and in particular the borrowing that goes on when web pages, streaming video, and podcasts emulate, modulate, and simulate previous media forms by re-mediating them. As Bolter and Grusin remind us, it isn't just the media who are altered in this process but ourselves (especially when we are participating in the social web/Web 2.0, a term that was not in circulation at the time they wrote the book).

Discussion Questions

1. What are some key differences between what we would today refer to as 'new media' and the media that preceded it?

2. How is 'convergence' a term that is prone to confusion? In what ways are the current trends in convergence perhaps only the tip of the iceberg?

3. In what ways do new media devices affect our communication activities and practices, as well as larger social arrangements and organizations?

4. Comment on the following: 'The quality of participation increases as the number of participating users increases, and this in turn attracts more new users to the sites.'

5. What does it mean to describe the Internet as having graduated from being a computer network akin to a highway to a 'place' that can allow people to 'understand the world around them'?

6. What are some of 'the cultural practices that enable users to engage with the technology' and what best describes the 'hidden engine of the user's interaction with the text'?

7. Give a close reading to the following: 'Media studies as it emerged in the twentieth century understood media production, texts, and audiences as discrete forms, following a linear model of different "moments" in the media production-consumption cycle.' What does this mean and what are the implications?

8. In what ways do trends in new media reflect trends in globalization?

Class Activities

1. In groups of five with your classmates, discuss which websites you spend the most time at per day and the activities you engage in with those sites. Consider if those activities were the same a year ago, what changes have occurred, and why. Discuss with your group what you think about the growing use of social media.

2. Visit a website, such as Alexa, that provides a list of the 'top ten' sites in the world. Take a look at the sites you might not be familiar with and classify these sites into different types.

3. Given the global nature of much new media, compile a list of local, or regional, websites that you are aware of or use for news, information, entertainment, and so on. Compare these with some national or multinational sites. What are the key differentiators?

2 The History of New Media

Questions to Consider

- What are some challenges of human communication in terms of sending and receiving messages across distances? How have these changed over time?

- In what ways have advances in communications and connectivity been historically linked to key enabling technologies, institutional configurations, business models, and products and services? How are these links still evident today?

- In what ways was privacy a concern in media technology of the past? How does it remain a concern today?

- What ideological or political implications are there to consider in regard to policies, practices, and changes/advances in communications and new media?

Chapter Outline

This chapter sets new media in its historical context, drawing connections between current network technologies, convergence trends, and prior inventions such as the telegraph, radio, and television. Although the path has been circuitous, ever since we have been able to send messages without moving physical objects (the first telegraph), the immediacy factor has forever changed our expectations about communication media. With new capabilities came new institutions and social arrangements and these have proven to be foundational and influential for subsequent generations of media.

Journalism, politics, and business were all transformed by the use of the telegraph and the telephone. Radio, and later television, provided a testing ground for key elements of new media and in particular the business model in which content could be accessed for free, if one was willing to accept a little bit of advertising with that content. The chapter concludes with a brief discussion of the educational potential of earlier new media.

Early Traces of New Media

Although some online accounts suggest otherwise, new media did not spring, wholly formed, from the minds of computer and network engineers. Just as Newton famously claimed that he was able to see further and do more than his contemporaries because he was able to 'stand on the shoulders of giants', advances in new media have their roots in technologies that predate the Internet by at least fifty, if not one hundred years. The pioneers of new media also built on foundations laid long before and sometimes in unexpected places. As discussed in the introductory chapter, although new media are profoundly different from old media in many ways, there are some aspects of old media and old telecommunications technologies that set the pattern for things to come. In this chapter we look at some of these antecedent technologies to better understand how they have shaped present-day understanding of media.[1]

Institutionalized, Instantaneous, Worldwide Communication: The Telegraph

One of the challenges of human communication has always been that to send a message any further than you can see, you had to send some sort of physical object to carry the message. Various attempts to overcome this limitation—with towers, balloons, or smoke signals—ultimately proved unwieldy, and most people settled down to writing letters and sending them by post. In the 1700s, there was some experimentation in sending messages by relay stations, using towers with semaphores or other signaling apparatus. Although this worked reasonably well it could still take hours for a message to go a long distance. These early attempts to overcome the problem of sending messages across distances did get people thinking about the possibilities of these kinds of technologies, however, especially for military applications.

In the 1800s, with a better understanding of the properties of electricity, attention turned to the potential of wires to send messages. Samuel Morse, an American, is widely credited with bringing the **telegraph** into popular use, even if he did not invent it. His name is still attached to the coding system—which is digital and formed of dots and dashes—that was used on the telegraph, that is, Morse Code (see Figure 2.1, on page 30).[2]

Morse Code, the system of dots and dashes used to represent the alphabet, has had remarkable impact, conceptually at least. While no one (or almost no one) uses this system to encode messages anymore, the idea of using a digital coding scheme to break a message down into smaller components was both revolutionary and incredibly prescient. The system of dots and dashes at one end of the telegraph line corresponding to long and short pulses

Postal twittering?

A recent article by Sarah Milstein asks the question, 'What Would Jane Austen Have Twittered?' It turns out that during Jane Austen's day (1775–1815), the post was delivered up to six times a day in London. After watching a show about Austen's life and letters, Milstein reflects that, 'The speed of mail at the time and the content of the Austen sisters' letters suggest that the desires to communicate instantly and to let other people know what you ate for breakfast aren't [just a] modern phenomenon. [. . .] The Jane Austen show [. . .] suggests just the opposite: our human patterns are surprisingly consistent, and technology evolves to meet us.'

Source: Milstein (2009).

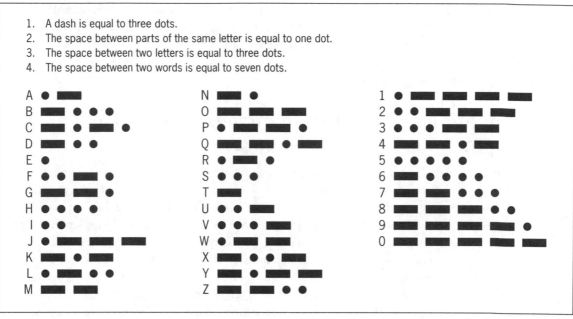

1. A dash is equal to three dots.
2. The space between parts of the same letter is equal to one dot.
3. The space between two letters is equal to three dots.
4. The space between two words is equal to seven dots.

FIGURE 2.1 International Morse Code
Source: http://en.wikipedia.org/wiki/File:International_Morse_Code.svg.

of electricity that triggered a buzzer at the other end of the telegraph line can be seen as an antecedent to the contemporary binary system used by computers, with dots as zeros and dashes as ones. Telegraph encoding was done by hand, at first, by telegraph operators who converted words into letters and each letter into code. Much of this later became automated by the teletype machine, speeding up the process.

Morse code was a practical method of sending information, since it was simple, reliable, and easy to implement. More importantly, it established an approach to the digitization of information that has persisted into the present day.

When the telegraph was launched in the 1840s it soon became enormously popular. Telegraph offices were built in cities and towns and within a few decades the world was overlaid by a network of wires and cables on land and under sea. You could visit any telegraph office in the world and send a message instantly to a receiving office. As antiquated and limited as the telegraph may seem now, at the time it provided a new and relatively immediate level of connectivity, as people were able to send messages to each other across the globe. It should be noted that global communication did not come easily, especially across oceans. The first trans-Atlantic telegraph took many attempts, finally reaching land at Heart's Content in Newfoundland. Canada again served as the nearest land to Great Britain several decades later, when Guglielmo Marconi first sent a radio signal across the Atlantic, to Signal Hill in Saint John's. In early telecommunications revolutions the proximity of eastern Canada to the centres of commerce in New York, Boston, and London provided economic and strategic importance to these small Canadian communities.

If the telegraph had the effect of making instantaneous communication worldwide seem normal, it also set the tone for the kinds of businesses that would later be built to run communication networks and for the regulations that governments would impose on them (we discuss this in more detail below). The use of the telegraph also prompted cooperation and collaboration among global institutions for technical standards and payment transfers that were necessary to ensure that a message could pass seamlessly from one network to another, and that all parties would be reimbursed for carrying it.[3] The telegraph brought attitudes, awareness, and an appreciation of immediacy to the general population but, behind the scenes, it also fostered key enabling technologies, institutional configurations, regulatory schemes, and business models that would also be foundational for future new media products and services. For example, telegraphs pioneered input devices, storage devices, and underlying technologies such as 'multiplexing' (sending more than one message at a time to make the most of the limited amount of capacity available on wires). Telegraph companies grew into large monopolies that attracted regulation and configured themselves as cooperative networks, sharing revenues and carrying each other's traffic. These product, service, and business innovations had repercussions that are evident today.

The telegraph, however, is not just a technological and business achievement and antecedent for the web. It also served as a pivotal technology in terms of its ability to break the seemingly obdurate link between moving information and moving things. As noted above, the telegraph broke this link and allowed instantaneous communication over long distances for the first time (Carey 1989). As Canadian theorist Harold Innes notes, however, bridging this gap inevitably had its costs in terms of how people used the media. Specifically, the content of new 'space binding' media forms such as the telegraph were biased toward more ephemeral topics, like news from afar (Innis 1951).[4]

The telegraph as scanner

While an appreciation for worldwide, instantaneous communication was surely one of the most important contributions of the telegraph, some other—more technical—aspects were important, as well. One of these is the concept of 'scanning'.

Morse Code, as we noted above, was a breakthrough in transmitting content. The process of encoding information—in effect digitizing it—allowed for the movement of complex ideas using simple 'on and off' electrical impulses. Yet, this was still limited to text, not pictures. Sending pictures through the telegraph required an additional leap forward. Telegraphs were eventually adapted to send photographs (wire photos) by having a light-sensitive sensor scan for light and dark parts of a picture. A white area would be a dot and a dark area would be a dash. The picture was wrapped on a drum that was slowly rotated while the sensor moved back and forth in front of it. In this way, the whole picture was eventually scanned and represented as a string of dots and dashes. The telegraph operator would send this content down the line to a remote printer, which was equipped with light-sensitive paper wrapped around another drum. The paper would be exposed to a bit of light for each dash and the result would be a dark spot. The process eventually produced a facsimile of the original.

Scanning like this was crude, but seemed miraculous at first. Today, computer scanners, digital cameras, camcorders, and just about anything else that works with images uses a similar system of breaking a picture into 'bits' (binary digits) of black and white (and now shades of grey and millions of colours) to encode media for transmission on networks and for further processing by software.

Telegraphs as storage and pricing pioneers

The torrent of telegraph messages being sent from large cities all over the world meant that the system could become overwhelmed and messages lost. Telegraph operators worked out a system of 'punching'—using a small device to create holes in a paper tape to represent the code—and then running those tapes through another machine that read those holes and generated Morse Code. This allowed the company to send the telegram later, when the system was less busy. The same could be done at the other end, where messages would be received en masse and then printed out later, to distribute to homes and businesses. This helped to balance the load on the system and increase overall capacity.

These and many other innovations helped to solve the technical problem of capacity in the system, and telegraph companies used these to identify new business opportunities. Given the ability to store and forward messages, they were able to offer pricing options based on how quickly a message needed to be delivered (similar to the 'evening and weekends' pricing that is familiar to today's users of cell phones). Modern computer networks carry on this same storage and forwarding model with email, making copies and letting messages pile up wherever necessary, resending if required.

Telegraphs as network pioneers

Telegraph systems extended all over the world and there were literally hundreds of telegraph companies in the United States by the 1850s. Bringing them all under one umbrella company, as Western Union did in the 1860s and 1870s, was a shrewd business move that provided an illustration of the value of networks, now known as **Metcalfe's Law.** First described by Robert Metcalfe in the 1980s and popularized by George Gilder in a *Forbes* article in 1993, Metcalfe's 'law' is more of an observation, describing the increasing value of a network according to the number of connections it has.[5] According to Metcalfe's Law, 'the value of the network increases at the square of the number of connections', which can be mathematically represented as $O(n^2)$, where O is the value and n is the number of connections (see Figure 2.2).

Metcalfe's law has driven the business side of communications networks for over 100 years and famously incited serious economic hysteria during the dot.com boom. As such it is worth exploring further and is perhaps best explained with an example.

> The foundation of his eponymous law is the observation that in a communications network with n members, each can make $(n-1)$ connections with other participants. If all those connections are equally valuable—and this is the big

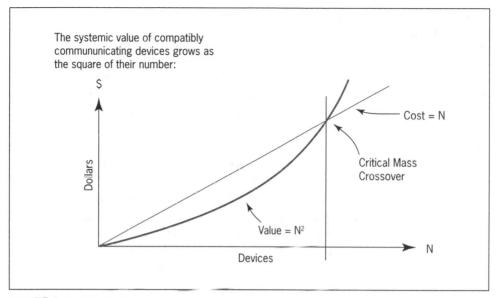

The systemic value of compatibly commununicating devices grows as the square of their number:

FIGURE 2.2 Metcalfe's Law
Source: Adapted from Metcalfe's original slide, reproduced by Simeonov (2006), http://blog.simeonov.com/2006/07/26/metcalfes-law-more-misunderstood-than-wrong.

if as far as we are concerned—the total value of the network is proportional to $n(n-1)$, that is, roughly, n^2. So if, for example, a network has 10 members, there are 90 different possible connections that one member can make to another. If the network doubles in size, to 20, the number of connections doesn't merely double, to 180, it grows to 380—it roughly quadruples, in other words. (Briscoe, Odlyzko, and Tilly 2006)

To illustrate this in a different way, consider this: If there are two networks, both with 50 nodes and thus 50(50–1) or 2,450 connections each, if they were joined, then suddenly, there would be 9,900 possible connections (100(100–1)), simply by putting a link between the two networks. Western Union quickly understood the value of linking networks and began to acquire hundreds of small telegraph companies over a very short time.

Metcalfe's Law also explains why at some point, most people do end up getting a telephone, or buying a fax machine, or signing up for email, because: (1) the value of the network grows enormously as more and more people join; and (2) *not* being part of the network means not having access to something that is increasingly valuable. At the same time, however, there is also some skepticism that the math of Metcalfe's Law continues to work in the same way throughout the life of the network (at some point you run out of people to call or do not care to call everyone), but nevertheless, it is a powerful economic force for network owners and subscribers.

The telegraph and early signs of communications media monopolies

The telegraph proved to be the impetus for many successful enterprises, but it also carried with it the risk that these newly consolidated companies would start to behave as monopolies and raise prices beyond what the market would bear. At first, telegraph messages were considered luxury items, and could be priced accordingly (early prices for telegrams sent across the Atlantic were several dollars per word and this was in an era of 25 cent meals!). As the telegram became integrated into business and social life, however, pressure was put on governments to regulate the operations of telegraph companies (as we will see, this would be the case with subsequent new media innovations).

The telegraph spread rapidly and became dominated by large monopolies, often by combining with the railways, using their rights of way as a convenient place to string wires and poles. Their importance for other businesses and their monopoly practices eventually led to calls for regulation.[6] In the 1870s, control of the telegraph system in the United States was almost entirely in the hands of Western Union, which had an exclusive contract with The Associated Press, ensuring that that organization used only Western Union telegraph services (rather than rival telegraph companies). As newspapers were the principal users of the telegraph at the time and paid for much of the telegraph traffic, it is not surprising that this business arrangement was lucrative for Western Union. Using their dominant position with the major users of the telegraph system, Western Union continued to buy up rival companies, eventually becoming synonymous with telegraphy in the US and carrying over 90 per cent of telegraph traffic in the country (Nonenmacher 2001).

Despited repeated calls for regulation of the telegraph business in the United States—and bills to that effect being introduced in Congress in practically every sitting of the House from 1850 to 1900—the Western Union lobbyists were able to fend off almost any serious control of their industry (Nonenmacher 2001). Those following the debates on 'net neutrality' in the US today will remark that the role of lobbying by the telecommunication industry is a continuing story.

Telegraphy arrived in Canada in 1846 with a demonstration at Toronto's City Hall and followed soon after with the creation of the Toronto, Hamilton, Niagara and St. Catherines Electromagnetic Telegraph Company. Railways, both Canadian National Railway and Canadian Pacific Railway, were the primary operators of telegraph systems in Canada (Burnet 1996) and, because railways were already regulated in Canada, their operations were at first governed by the system in place for the regulation of transportation systems.

The telegraph and newspapers—dire end or happy marriage?

As the Internet has spread to more and more corners of the world, and home and mobile access to the web has made online readers of so many people, newspapers are suffering from a decline in print readership and advertising dollars. Many from the newspaper industry—most notably, outspoken publisher Rupert Murdoch—have accused Google and other Internet search

Early 'text speak' on telegraphs

The costliness of telegrams led to individual responses, as well as broader social calls for regulation. To combat the cost, those sending telegrams began using abbreviations. The practice of abbreviating telegram messages—where every letter, every space between words, was precious—created a convention that continues to this day: the text speak of today and the codes and abbreviations in the telegraph age, in this sense, are rather surprisingly alike.

Abbreviations only work, of course, if they are understood. Code books for telegraph abbreviations were therefore published and circulated widely. One of the most popular codes was called the 'Phillips Code' and the code book was first published by Walter P. Phillips in 1879 in New York.[7] It contained thousands of abbreviations (even for relatively short words). In addition to economy of space, abbreviations permitted an economy of time: using these abbreviations, Walter Phillips was able to copy 2,731 words in a single hour. This was not typing as we know it, but tapping out letters using dots and dashes in Morse code. For this he won a gold pen from Samuel Morse himself![8] The speed of entering messages was particularly important to court reporting and so too for news agencies, which competed with each other to get the scoop on breaking news. The practice of doing telegraphy with abbreviations even had a word: stenotelegraphy, meaning, a kind of shorthand with dots and dashes.

engines of being the cause of their woes. While this may seem to be a thoroughly Internet-age problem, the telegraph was implicated in a similar 'death of newspapers' scare more than 150 years ago, when James G. Bennett, founder and publisher of the *New York Herald*, predicted in 1845 that some newspapers must 'submit to destiny, and go out of business'.[9]

The telegraph was able to shake up the newspaper industry because, prior to the early 1800s, newspapers operated on a casual sharing of old news, with relatively little attention to timeliness. Towards the mid-nineteenth century, particularly in the rising commercial centres on the east coast of the US, some newspapers sought to distinguish themselves by being 'first with the news'. By the 1830s, newspapers were employing a wide range of techniques to beat their competitors to publish the latest international news, including semaphores, carrier pigeons, even rowing out to meet ships arriving from Europe and elsewhere, then racing back to port faster than the cumbersome ocean-going vessels. To the press barons of the day, the arrival of the telegraph seemed to make competing on the basis of being first with the facts a losing proposition, as newspaper operators, business people, and just about anyone else, would all have access to the news at the same time. In hindsight, this concern may seem ridiculous and in fact, it quickly proved to be so. While the telegraph could effectively move the news from one city to another, it had a terrible 'last mile' problem: the news would arrive by telegraph to offices across the globe, but how to get it from those offices to thousands of people at once? People were not going to stand in line to wait for the news and they were not likely to pay for it, unless it could be delivered to them, in one way or another.

As it happened, newspapers provided their own solution: As the biggest customers of telegraph services, they quickly became outlets for a steady stream of wire clippings. Indeed, journalist W.J. Stillman, writing in *The Atlantic Monthly* in 1891, complained that, 'America has in fact transformed journalism from what it once was, the periodical expression of the thought of the time, the opportune record of the questions and answers of contemporary life, into an agency for collecting, condensing and assimilating the trivialities of the entire human existence.'[10] Others wondered if the telegraph (and thus newspapers) would convey nothing but inanities. Henry David Thoreau, upon hearing of the plans to build a telegraph line across the United States, wrote in his journal: 'We are in great haste to construct a magnetic telegraph from Maine to Texas; but Maine and Texas, it may be, have nothing important to communicate.'[11] Both of these comments recall Innes' observation of the bias of communication toward the ephemeral in 'space-binding' media such as the telegraph.

Yet, the changes in journalistic writing style brought on by the telegraph were not entirely without benefit. The market and the technology led to the kind of newspaper content that is now expected: a dependence on facts and (the appearance, at least) of a neutral point of view. The ability of the telegraph to transmit news instantly also meant that politicians could be held more accountable; for example, they could not take a particular position on an issue in one city and then take a different position in another city. They had to be more consistent in their messages.

Newspapers thrived under the telegraph and eventually adapted the newspaper business to take advantage of the features that it offered, including ready access to foreign news, easy sharing of stories via telegraph-connected news agencies, and the wire photo.

> What lessons does the telegraph hold for newspapers now grappling with the internet? The telegraph was first seen as a threat to papers, but was then co-opted and turned to their advantage. "The telegraph helped contribute to the emergence of the modern newspaper," says Ford Risley, head of the journalism department at Penn State University. "People began to expect the latest news, and a newspaper could not succeed if it was not timely."[12]

Some people see the proliferation of handheld reading devices (the Apple iPad, or the Kindle from Amazon, for example) as possibly leading to an increase in newspaper and magazine subscriptions. At this point, however, it is too early to know and the dynamics of the industry continue to evolve.

One of the defining features of new media in the twenty-first century is how it has been turned to commercial ends and in particular, to advertising. Everything from animated television commercials to advertisements that pop into the background of an iPhone 'app' are evidence of the ways in which new media are integrated with the advertising industry. The telegraph, however, was similarly entangled with advertising. The telegraph, in fact, is implicated in the development of the advertising industry (and specifically, the advertising agency). Just as the telegraph made it possible for trains to better coordinate their activities on single tracks, the insertion of advertising copy in multiple newspapers—and all the billing and coordination that entailed—made it possible for advertising agencies to use the telegraph to move into this 'coordination business' by becoming adept at buying and then re-selling blocks of space (and later time on radio and television) in newspapers. Canadian writers and advertising men, Terry O'Reilly and Mike Tennant, who are the forces behind the popular radio program, *O'Reilly on Advertising*, draw attention the role of the telegraph in their history of advertising, *The Age of Persuasion*:

> [The telegraph] revolutionized marketing. The telegraph followed on the heels of the European industrial revolution, and in North America, manufacturing had mechanized and expanded. Rural families had gravitated to cities to work in the fast-growing factories, which in turn churned out products for burgeoning urban populations. With the rise of railways through the nineteenth century, goods could be transported over land, en masse, to distant markets, resulting in more product choices in stores. And how did the telegraph fit into the picture? It allowed manufacturers to communicate instantly with newspapers in distant cities and towns, buying advertisements to attract thousands of potential new customers. (xvi)

While this helps explain the importance of the telegraph to the development of advertising, O'Reilly and Tennant go on to discuss the meeting point between manufacturers and newspapers—the advertising agency as technology-enabled middleman—in this way:

> Barely a year after Morse dotted, dashed, and dotted his way into history, Philadelphia businessman Volney Palmer opined, quite rightly, that many manufacturers had neither the time nor the inclination to place ads in dozens—even hundreds—of newspapers on a regular basis. Palmer offered his services as a sort of middleman, buying large amounts of advertising space in several newspapers and parceling and selling it to businesses, who would have to create their own messages. And so . . . the advertising agency was born. (2009: xvi)

In all, the telegraph contributed significantly to a multitude of innovations in long distance, instantaneous communication as well as in technology, business, and regulatory changes.[13] Presented throughout this chapter are further examples of both the rather clear and the less obvious links between the telegraph and other new media technologies.

From Telegraph to Telephone: A Revolution in Sound

Visiting a telegraph office and speaking to someone who would write down a message and then send it through the wire was simply the way things were done in the early days of the telegraph—there was no system for home telegraph terminals. Morse Code, while relatively simple, still had to be learned and remained out of reach for most people. It was clear that taking the encoding out of the equation would make the ability to transmit messages more useful for people.[14]

Several inventors set to work on the problem of sending voice across wires and Alexander Graham Bell's telephone emerged as the winner (after some trouble in the patent office).[15] Bell, a Canadian, was working in his lab in Boston, as well as his lab at home in Brantford, Ontario, throughout the years and months leading up to his successful first call. The obvious benefit of the telephone was the ability for people to speak directly to others, with their own voices, without reducing everything to code. Understandably, the telephone very quickly became popular, for both workplace and household. In fact, once people started installing telephones in their homes, it was so difficult for the telephone companies to keep up with demand that they started running promotions urging people to reserve phones for emergency or important use. It is testimony to a shared human interest in communication that over-use of new communication media is a recurring problem. Most recently, it has affected the telephone company, AT&T. In 2009, AT&T struggled to keep up with the data usage of all the new iPhone users, who loved their apps so much that they drove mobile data use up by as much as 4,000 per cent. The AT&T response has been to urge customers not to use the service so much.[16]

Telephone use became a widely adopted form of communication in the early twentieth century because as soon as a telephone connection was set up, it was ready for use. That said, the telephone was also a new tool and people had to learn how to use it properly. Knowing to pick up the ear-piece (the microphone was typically built into the device itself) and saying 'hello' had to be learned, as is the case with other communication tools. In fact, in the early days of the telephone, companies mounted advertising campaigns, in print and at the opening of movie reels, introducing people to the telephone and urging them to, 'pick it up, and say hello'.

It may seem comical now to think that instructions were needed on how to use a telephone. Most new communication technologies, however, not only have an adoption curve (in which people acquire the devices), but also a learning curve (in which people learn how to use the devices properly and work out appropriate etiquette). The mobile telephone experienced a similar curve: at first, people did not know how to put them on silent mode or they spoke loudly in classrooms and restaurants. Again, both private and public campaigns were launched to encourage people to use their communication devices responsibly.

Although it was relatively easy to use the telephone and a standard way of greeting was adopted, another problem arose: with so many people using the telephone, the process of connecting everyone—a manual process in the early days—began to put a strain on the system's resources. There were not enough telephone operators to handle the volume and an automated means had to be found. The answer was the mechanical telephone switch, which replaced local operators first and later, long-distance operators.

Changing telephone connections—the telephone switch and 'network neutrality'

The telephone switch or telephone exchange was a wonderful invention in terms of saving labour but it also gave users the freedom to make calls without involving other people.[17] The secret call, the late night call, calls between teenagers without their parents knowledge; all these were enabled by putting a machine instead of another human being in the middle of the call. Although telephone operators were trained to uphold professional standards and were not supposed listen in on calls or judge who was calling whom (and when), callers could not be sure of the privacy of their conversations. In fact, the inventor of the mechanical telephone switch was supposedly motivated by his suspicions that an industry rival's girlfriend was diverting business to her sweetheart.

Human beings have generally preferred making contact directly rather than through an intermediary. At the time of the invention of the automated telephone switch, people were well acquainted with the postal system's approach: they put addresses on letters and did not concern themselves with how the letters got to their destinations. Similarly, the telephone switch allowed people to dial a phone number directly and make their own calls.[18] In a way, the mechanical telephone switch made **network neutrality** a reality. Although network neutrality is a term used today for Internet technologies, in the early days of the telephone a similar principle applied: 'common carriage' law, which is a reference to the regulation of railroads. These regulations were originally put in place to keep railroads from charging different rates to different companies (for example, subsidiaries) and giving unfair advantage to some at the expense of others. In telephone terms, the common carriage laws meant that everyone paid according to a common fee/charge structure and—more importantly— telephone companies could not discriminate on the basis of what callers were saying. This separated 'carriage' from 'content' and this remains a cornerstone of telecommunications law to this day. Common carriage law protected the telephone companies, too, since they could (and did) argue that they could not be held responsible if someone used the telephone to plan a crime, for example.

Network neutrality has emerged as a key issue in the debates about control of and payment for Internet services. In principle it means that the network is unbiased in relation to the content that is transmitted, but this has been under stress in recent years by both user behaviour and competition between telecommunication carriers. User behaviour became an issue as data-heavy new media forms such as music and movies began to move onto the Internet. These activities (mainly downloading of content) threatened to swamp services that were deemed both more important for business and lighter in terms of data load (e.g., email). In response, some Internet service providers sought to charge differential rates or to limit the amount of bandwidth available for these activities. Users, as might be expected, protested. The issue became more complicated as telecommunications and media companies merged and it became possible to imagine a world in which a broadband network owned by a media giant (as is the case for several Internet service providers in

Canada) might provide preferential access to their network to services that come form their corporate family. More about network neutrality and common carriage agreements is presented later in the text, in the discussion of Internet service providers and data services (see Chapter 9).

The cost of communicating—early regulatory frameworks on products and services

Early telephones were expensive. People leased their telephone service and did not own any part of the system, not even the phone itself, which was the property of the telephone company. This arrangement lasted until well into the 1960s and only slowly eroded as customers gradually won the right to purchase 'terminal equipment' of their own choosing. For a long time telephone companies argued that the system was so finely tuned and complicated that they could not keep it operating unless they had complete control of all parts. This argument gradually became untenable in both practical terms and from a legal point of view.

In practical terms, telephone companies wanted to take advantage of the reliability and cost advantages of using standardized products and had long set rigorous standards for all aspects of their system. In fact, at first, telephone companies owned their own manufacturing arms. Northern Electric, later Northern Telecom, was once a wholly owned subsidiary of Bell Canada (itself a subsidiary of Bell Telephone, the US parent company). As other manufacturers began to prove that they could also make telephone equipment, the telephone network gradually evolved into one with competitive provision of components from a multitude of suppliers and eventually consumers were able to purchase and install their own telephones and businesses were able to buy (or lease) small office switches (a PBX or 'private branch exchange'). This evolution in the industry was brought about for business reasons, spurred on by legal challenges and regulatory changes. As a result, telephone companies were closely regulated, almost from the outset.

As with the telegraph companies, the economics of operating a network meant that consolidation happened early and quickly in the industry. The bigger the network (and getting bigger by buying others was a fast way to grow), the more money the network could make. Consolidation of networks also made sense in the way that consolidated electricity distribution makes sense: having one company provide the service prevented wires from blocking the pathways and ensured that the system was reliable and well maintained. In exchange for permission to operate as a monopoly, telephone companies were either nationalized (owned by the local or national government) or regulated, or both. This kept companies that had no competitors from charging excessive rates, limiting them to a regulated rate of return, and it ensured that they met certain performance standards, including coverage of all the homes in a service area. Telephone service, in North America especially, gradually came to be seen as a basic service for everyday life. In fact, in many rural areas, telephones were more common than electricity, and arrived decades before. Treating telephones as a universal service was a foundation of government intervention into telecommunications in Canada, either through state monopolies (in the prairie provinces) or regulation of private companies (Mussio 2001: 3–4).

In Canada, with the vast distances and extreme climate, telephone service was regarded as a lifeline. Doctors (and veterinarians) were called out over the telephone service, as were fire trucks and ambulances. As a result, telephone service has been deemed an essential service.[19] For example, in Canada, monthly telephone costs are included alongside housing costs and utilities in calculating income social assistance levels. Other countries have recently taken the essential service argument much further into the arena of new media, making access to high speed Internet a human right (as is discussed in more detail in Chapter 9).

By the Flickering Light We Will Conjure Movement: Film

While the telegraph managed to transmit a still image from one part of the world to another (almost) instantly, such transmission was not possible with moving images, as this required another innovation. Photography was developing at the same time as the telegraph and people were enchanted by the realistic images that photography produced. Although photographs are not altogether different from paintings, photographic images are considered a nineteenth century new media form because many images, presented in rapid order and with slight variations between them, give the illusion of movement. This illusion is derived from what is known as 'persistence' in human vision: What the human eye sees will remain in the mind's eye for a brief period of time and so, if one image is quickly replaced with another image that differs only slightly from the preceding one, the human brain interprets the change as movement. This effect can be exploited in a number of ways (such as flip books), but to make the illusion of movement realistic very accurate images—such as photographs—are needed.

It took enormous initiative and invention by a wide range of people, including Thomas Edison in the US and the Lumière brothers in France, but eventually the 'moving picture' was perfected. In moving picture systems, which only recently are being replaced by digital projection systems, small frames of film with a still image are projected with a strong light behind them onto a screen at the front of a room. Then, a small shutter very briefly—and imperceptibly to the human eye—blacks out the image while the next frame is moved into position. This process of projection, blackout, movement, and then a stop and projection again, is responsible for the characteristic clatter of a movie projector as the film moves, stops, moves, and stops again, at 24 frames per second.

The effect, to the audience, is the 'magic of movies' and much of what digital technologies have been seeking to perfect over the past half century is to recreate what was achieved, mechanically, at the turn of the twentieth century. This is another example of what Lev Manovich might have been referring to when he said, 'We will see that many of the principles [of new media] are not unique to new media, but can be found in older media as well'.[20] The 'many frames' approach, however, remains the way of achieving the illusion of movement in the present age. Today, the frames are no longer whole images but, rather, are painted pixel-by-pixel by computers. In fact, the images built on computer screens are assembled much in the same way that the telegraph assembled photographic images: line-by-line. Computers perform essentially the same function, just in more detail and very, very quickly! These same early traces of new media can also be found with the television, but to connect the new media dots, so to speak, some attention must first be given to further innovations in sound.

Speaking Without Wires: Radio

As magical as the telephone was, it was nothing compared to the mystery and magnitude of radio. How could sounds, created in one place, be heard at once in so many other places, so far away? Radio technology brought forth a number of developments that proved extremely important for the Internet and new media. Key among these are: (i) the importance of hobbyists (radio amateurs or 'hams'); (ii) the identification of new business models, including advertising and sponsorship; and (iii) the regulation of content.

Unlike the telephone and the telegraph, which required knowing other subscribers in a network in order for it to be useful, the radio was useful to listeners immediately, simply by turning it on, once there was something to listen to, that is. Moreover, the basic elements of a radio transmitter-receiver, once the technology was reasonably well understood, were relatively inexpensive and the parts needed to build a radio were available in kit form. Indeed, before the First World War radio was primarily a hobby activity, particularly popular with young men and boys. Prior to the 1920s, radio was not a **broadcasting** undertaking.

Radio pioneer Marconi and a few companies operated radio telegraph stations as a point-to-point communication technology for ships at sea or as an alternative to wired telegraphs in difficult terrain. Since only Morse code was being used at the time, radio telegraphy did not have much widespread appeal, beyond use among trained operators for commercial messages. Nevertheless, there was a dedicated group of amateurs who liked experimenting with radio and in fact, it was among these hobbyists that many of the early technical advances were made. Plans circulated in special hobby magazines and an important industry of radio parts/kits suppliers grew, providing the parts for both the entry-level and more advanced radios that could be built at home. Marconi himself owned and operated radio stations in Canada through a subsidiary, Marconi Canada. One of these—CFCF—went on to become a pioneer in the soon to emerge world of radio broadcasting (Godfrey 1982: 56–71).

A Canadian living in the US, Reginald Fessenden, is credited with sending the first spoken words over the radio.[21] In one of his early experiments, Fessenden played his violin and some Christmas carols from a record player and, much to the surprise of radio operators who had been encouraged to listen in on their headphones, it turned out that the airwaves were entirely suitable for voice, once Fessenden figured out how to get the signal from a microphone onto the channel. One thing that spurred hobbyist creativity was the growing commercial importance of radio after the First World War (all non-military use of the radio waves was curtailed during the war). With business taking over the airwaves, amateur radio operators found themselves banished to higher and higher frequencies (up where AM radio is now) and they had to be creative about how they could make use of the radio spectrum there.

In many ways, these developments paralleled and anticipated how early computer users would meet in user groups to discover how to program and build their own computers and connect them to bulletin boards and later, to the Internet. These early, informal social connections were both enabled by the medium and by the topic that members of a group were interested in, so it was a felicitous match. Where telegraph operators had developed some camaraderie, it was constrained by the need to get work done and by the limited number of people connected through the telegraph. Radio amateurs could connect with a seemingly limitless group of people and without restrictions on the time they spent on the air. They used that time to socialize, to compare notes on equipment, and to learn more about their hobby. The early radio universe was not without conflict, of course. There were people who hogged the airwaves and people who voiced extreme opinions and annoyed others, much like chat rooms and discussion forums have trolls and flamers today. But the fact remains that hobbyists helped advance radio technology in significant ways. Early web page design also had similar hobby roots, with HTML code being shared and many people *using* the technology *to learn about* the technology.

Hobbyists can also be credited with finding the business model that would take radio from being more than a military or point-to-point communication medium (as it was used by telegraph companies that wanted to reach beyond their wires, for example). It was Frank Conrad, a radio amateur from Pennsylvania, who is widely credited with transmitting the first commercial radio broadcast in 1919, playing records provided by a local record store.[22] When Conrad saw a store that was advertising receivers capable of bringing in these radio signals and broadcasts, he convinced the executives where he worked (Westinghouse) that there might be a market in selling radio receivers. Up until that time, radio technology had been considered only a business tool or the domain of the hobbyist. Canadians living in Montreal in 1919 would have been surprised to hear that a Pittsburgh station claimed to have the first commercial broadcasts, however, as they had been listening to CFCF—a privately owned station—since late 1918 (Godfrey 1982).

More important than a claim to the first radio broadcast or the oldest broadcasting station is how the commercial content of radio broadcasts changed the way governments regulated radio, which up until that time—and well into the 1920s in Canada—was very light-handed.[23] As commercially sponsored radio grew quickly through the 1920s and 1930s to become big business, the content changed: in particular, soap operas—named because of the many soap commercials they carried—and comedies began to displace high culture content such as symphonies or news reports.

In the UK, radio broadcasting was assigned to a public agency, the British Broadcasting Commission. In the US, private interests were behind almost all of the broadcast activity. In Canada, a model emerged in which there was a role for both private and public broadcasters (Dewar 1982). In all cases, however, much of the impetus for the regulation was the content of the broadcasts and—in the case of Canada—the need for a national voice distinct from the American voices pouring across the border via the radio waves. Canadians were particularly concerned about having a national system. To respond to the situation, Canada set up a Royal Commission to look into the situation of broadcasting in Canada. Led by John Aird, a prominent banker from Toronto, the Commission on Radio Broadcasting resulted in a report in 1929, which recommended the establishment of publicly funded radio broadcasting in Canada. This resulted in the creation of a national broadcaster, the Canadian Radio Broadcasting Commission (CRBC) in 1932. The CRBC had the task of being both a national radio broadcaster and a regulating force for the emerging industry. Parliament subsequently split these roles and created the Canadian Broadcasting Corporation (CBC) to focus on broadcasting while the CRBC continued with the regulatory aspect, eventually becoming the Canadian Radio-television and Telecommunications Commission, or the CRTC. As with radio, modern new media have also stirred calls for regulation and raised concerns related to material unsuitable to national audiences (in some countries), influence on children (in most countries), impact on politics, on business, and on the family.

From early radio broadcasts to commercial radio

Both Westinghouse (Conrad's KDKA station in Pittsburgh, Pennsylvania) and Marconi (the CFCF station in Montreal) were originally interested in broadcasting because they thought it would be a great way to sell radio receivers. They would soon discover, however, that the profit and power was elsewhere. The large corporations that came after Westinghouse and Marconi—including companies that remain important today, such as NBC, CBS, and ABC—brought a new approach to the radio business, and ever since advertising has been a mainstay of commercial radio.

If the telegraph helped set in motion the *mechanics* of advertising (moving advertising *copy* from headquarters to the market, creating a demand for advertising *agencies*), radio (re)created these conditions and went even further. Newspapers had for a long time charged a nominal price for the paper itself, making most of their money selling print space to advertisers. But radio didn't have that option. How could you broadcast and charge a subscription fee?[24]

The answer, it seemed, was to embed ads, either before and after radio programs as we are familiar with these days, or right in the middle of the program, with actors taking time out of their story to shill, or even working the product itself into the story (what we would call product placement today). This form of embedded advertising persists to this day: in the advertising that lines Google search pages and in many commercial blogs and news sites; in the advertisements that appear within video games; and in the pop-ups that appear at the foot of email. Thanks to the precedent set by radio, it has been incredibly difficult to get people to shift back to a subscription model, which would, in theory, work with the new Internet technologies because online content can be encrypted to a single machine or user and can be delivered without broadcasting it to the entire world. But, media consumers had come to expect free content (though not content free of advertising), something the new media pioneers had to inherit.

Radio also achieved something unprecedented by a mass medium: It took hold of people's attention in the privacy of their homes and during their daily routines. Shortly thereafter, with transistor and automobile radios, the medium also accompanied people on their travels. Terry O'Reilly and Mike Tennant capture this well in their book, *The Age of Persuasion*: 'Print ads could be skipped, set aside, or noticed at the reader's pleasure. In contrast, radio ads reverberated through people's homes on the broadcaster's own schedule, adding the evocative nuances of voice and personality, and the subconscious power of music, to the language of persuasion' (2009: xvi). The power of radio, however, would soon be eclipsed by something even more powerful: television.

Pictures and Sound, Educational Potential: Television

We have discussed the telegraph's capability to send a single-frame image from over long distances (by scanning and reprinting the scan) and film's creation of the illusion of movement by showing a series of images, but how to combine these two innovations? The idea was obvious to many people and was widely predicted, even in the 1920s, but it was a devilishly difficult problem to solve. Both telegraphic scanning and film-making were difficult. Combining them made for a long series of frustrating experiments and the challenges involved were not overcome until just before the Second World War. The eventual solution—after ill-fated attempts at mechanical scanning systems—involved television receivers that contained an electron beam yoked between powerful magnets at the end of a vacuum tube. The other end was painted with material that would glow when struck by the beam. By moving the beam from side to side and top to bottom very quickly (much faster than the human eye can perceive), an image is 'painted' onto the screen.

Although the war put the advent of television (and much else) on hold, by the 1940s, television burst onto the airwaves and was in widespread use by the 1950s, coming to Canada on a commercial basis with the CBFT station in Montreal in 1952 (the first experimental broadcasts were in 1932, also in Montreal).[25] Not long afterwards, the CBC cemented popular interest in television by arranging to have footage of the coronation of Queen Elizabeth II flown across the Atlantic on a jet bomber and thereby made available to Canadians on the same day it took place.[26]

Many of the hopes and dreams that people had for television mirrored the early aspirations held for radio: that it would be a civilizing force for society. Although commercial radio had largely degenerated into an endless stream of advertisements, proponents of television thought that the educational aspects of the medium would prove extremely powerful. Some of the CBC's first broadcasts were of political events (the opening of parliament) and educational programs. In the twenty-first century, however, the allure of television appears to be fading. Television audiences are shrinking (especially in key demographics) and the power of the TV schedule (once the stronghold of television networks) is slipping away. Television networks with set schedules based on target demographics, requiring viewers to watch the programs they provide and the advertisements that fill those programs, now face the challenge of audience time-shifting: with a personal video recorder or the ability to download shows from the Internet, people can now watch when and where they want and are able to strip the annoying ads from the shows. This shift seems almost inevitable today, but in the 1950s and 1960s television was all-powerful, dominating the media landscape in ways that are now scarcely remembered.

Television—and the satellite transmission of broadcast signals that arrived in the 1960s—brought together the key features of all preceding new media up to that point: it had the global reach of the telegraph and telephone (and even extra-terrestrial reach, with the coverage of the moon landings), the movement of film, and the sound and private consumption aspects of radio. In 1972, Canada led the world in the use of broadcast satellites for national television when its Anik 1 came into service, responding to the need to deliver service to the far north and other remote areas of the country.

With the advent of television, there were concerns that both film and radio would disappear in the face of this new medium and, certainly, both film and radio had to evolve, and have found new niches. Radio has since become more of a companion technology in cars, at work, and around the house, providing a kind of background. Film has adapted and advanced with wide screens, elaborate sound, special effects, and 3D effects. From a new media perspective, early television represented the arrival of the small screen in the living rooms of the nation. Television was the multimedia of its day— with the arrival of the TV remote control a form of interactivity existed, albeit one restricted to flipping channels and pressing pause on the VCR/DVD player. Still, television was a remarkable achievement technically and culturally. No longer were people required to go out for their entertainment, as they had done with the movies. With television, personal and private interaction with multimedia began to establish itself. The early television networks initiated a willingness among people to sit in front of a small screen, which is carried forward today as people spend so many hours a day in front of a computer, at home or at work.

The educational, children's, and documentary features of television were among the first areas of focus for early multimedia developers. Similarly, when the CD-ROM format emerged in the 1980s, much of that early, non-networked, content was educational, including dictionaries, encyclopedias, and nature and science material. As with the media that had come before it, however, television quickly succumbed to commercial pressures. Television was simply too powerful a tool (for advertising, in particular) to be left in the hands of educators and news organizations. In order to attract as wide an audience as possible, television gradually became the 'vast wasteland' that prompted writers such as Neil Postman (*Amusing Ourselves to Death*) and Noam Chomsky (*Manufacturing Consent: The Political Economy of the Mass Media*) to decry its very existence. Although the television as an electronic device can hardly be blamed for the ills of society, 'television' has become a short hand for a larger 'media ecology' that includes the pieces and all of the players of today's media landscape.[27]

One of the lessons that can be learned from the advent of television is that new media entering society do not entirely displace old media forms but rather, they rearrange relationships (in some ways, significantly so). Although movie studios and radio station owners were disrupted by television, both found new niches and mutually compatible roles or reconfigured their offerings to fit the new reality. In exploring the newer new media forms, it is important to keep in mind that there will always be a balancing act between old and new forms, without a complete displacement (or not for awhile, at least). Further, although media forms and media uses have precursors or antecedents, new media (such as Twitter or Facebook, today) do bring with new them behaviours and effects that shape society in new ways.

Case Study: Canadian Radio Pioneer Edward Rogers: Making Radio Easier and Better

Today, the latest in new media arrives smoothly on your computer screen courtesy of high speed Internet technologies. The new media of an earlier era—the radio programs of the 1920s—were also enjoyed around the world, but people struggled with the heavy, dangerous, and expensive batteries required to power a radio set in those days (IEEE n.d.). Although household electricity was widely available in cities, there was no way to connect a radio to the alternating current that reached households. The solution to this—a vacuum tube design that took alternating current (AC) and converted it to the direct current (DC) that radios required—was provided by Edward Samuel Rogers, of Toronto.

Rogers did not invent the AC tube itself, but he purchased the Canadian patent rights for the design and improved it dramatically. The new tubes not only allowed radios powered by household electricity, eliminating trips to the battery store with large, heavy batteries, but also the stains and damage to floors and carpets from the inevitable acid spills of those early wet cell batteries. Radios powered by these tubes—ingeniously—also made use of the wires in the house as an antenna for the radio set, eliminating the need for an external antenna. Rogers not only designed radios with internal tubes, he also created an external power supply that could be hooked into a household socket and then subsequently to a radio from another manufacturer (Anthony 2000).

Rogers was born in 1900 and began his radio career as a precocious child, operating radio sets from his home and winning international contests from the age of thirteen. He appeared in both Toronto newspapers (for hearing about a shipwreck off the coast of Ireland, via a radio alert sent from Massachusetts) and American magazines (*QST*, the American Radio Relay League's monthly magazine, noting his achievement of contacting Scotland in 1922) (Anthony 2000).

Rogers was a radio operator on Great Lakes ships through his teen years and helped build a radio station (called 9HA) for the *Toronto Star* newspaper in the early 1920s. He also built a 'Radio Car' to help publicize the newspaper and its radio station. His AC tube was perfected in 1924 and Rogers founded the Rogers Radio Company to manufacture and build the 'batteryless radio' (Foundation Radiomuseum Luzern). Rogers first thought he could sell the tubes for the power supply to other radio manufacturers, but he found little interest and ended up building the whole radio himself (Murray 2003: 196). He went on to build a whole line of radios and later merged with an American company to produce radios for that country under the name Rogers-Majestic (Foundation Radiomuseum Luzern).

In 1927 Rogers founded the radio station CFRB ('Canada's First Rogers Batteryless'), which continues to this day at 1010 AM in the city of Toronto. Although Rogers died quite young (at age 39), his son went on to turn this one radio station into a media empire: Rogers Communications. Rogers Communications is now one of the largest media companies in Canada, owning cell phone, cable, Internet, and sports franchises. Interestingly, it all started with getting the batteries out of radios.

Useful Websites

YouTube
←http://youtube.com→

The idea of turning to YouTube for historical information might seem a little odd at first, but once you have searched for 'semaphor telegraph' or 'telegraph' or 'how does radio work', you will be convinced. This video-sharing site is full of interesting and explanatory videos that help the lay person understand information and communication technologies. Many of these videos are professionally produced and added to the site from the BBC and other sources.

About
←http://about.com→

This site has explanations for and history behind most media and communications technologies. A search on 'history of radio', for example, will turn up many entries including 'The Invention of Radio', 'Radio History', and so on.

Canadian Broadcasting Corporation Archives
←http://archives.cbc.ca/→

The CBC Archives are a treasure trove of media history from the earliest days of the CBC to recent days. For media history, look in the 'Arts and Entertainment/Media' category (http://archives.cbc.ca/arts_entertainment/media) and for technology history, look in the 'Science and Technology/Technology' or 'Science and Technology/Computers' categories. A special radio broadcast, commemorating the centenary of Alexander Graham Bell's first phone calls, is a good example: http://archives.cbc.ca/science_technology/technology/clips/6256.

The Secret Life of Machines
←http://www.secretlifeofmachines.com→

This series of British television programs, available online, had its early inspiration from a series of newspaper comic strips depicting the workings of machinery from the sewing machine and internal combustion engines to the elevator and video camera. The series captures the early days of radio and television, including easy-to-understand explanations of how the technology works.

On The Air, CBS (1937)
←www.youtube.com/watch?v=6VHtZr_xsT8→

This recreation of Lodge's 1887 demonstration of Hertz's radio waves is particularly fascinating. This short documentary, spelling out in simple but understandable terms how radio works, is in the public domain and available on YouTube.

Further Reading

Spirit of the web, Wade Rowland (1999 and 2006)
This text offers a historical approach to the Internet, generally, with chapters on major inventors and technologies from the semaphore telegraph to search engines. The book was recently revised and Rowland's attention to the people and the players at each stage, including fascinating accounts of those who laid the first undersea telegraph cable, for example, makes for a marvelous read.

The Victorian Internet, Tom Standage (1998)
This book provides a detailed look at the telegraph and how it predicts the modern Internet in many ways. Standage offers many examples of modern media use and communication that have their roots in behaviours and techniques first worked out at the end of the nineteenth century. It is a fascinating chronicle.

'History of the U.S. Telegraph Industry', Thomas Nonnenmacher (2001)
http://eh.net/encyclopedia/article/nonnenmacher. industry.telegraphic.us.
A concise history of the history of the telegraph told from an economic perspective. This article contains a timeline and key technological features of the telegraph

as well as useful explanations of the business drivers and uses of the telegraph, including interesting facts about the benefit of the telegraph for the railroad industry and how it allowed them to better coordinate trains and thereby avoid double-tracking their system, saving enormous capital costs.

Introduction to *New Media Reader*, Lev Manovich (2003)
In addition to his *Language of New Media,* Lev Manovich has provided a useful historical perspective to new media in his introduction to Noah Wardrip-Fruin and Nick Montfort's *New Media Reader,* (2003) called, 'New Media from Borges to HTML'. The original text for that introduction is available on the web at www.intelligentagent.com/CNM200/manovich_new_media.doc

Canadian Railway Telegraph History, Robert Burnet (1996)
Burnet's history of the telegraph in Canada is packed with historical anecdotes and interesting features, with a focus on the people and technology that helped make telegraph communication—especially that which was carried out by the railways—possible in Canada.

'Sandford Fleming and the Pacific Cable: The Institutional Politics of Nineteenth-Century Imperial Communications', Graham Thompson (1990)
In this article Graham Thompson makes the case for seeing Canadian investment in telegraphy as part of a larger project of integration into the (British) imperial project and becoming a key link in a global network. Thompson's view is that we are too quick to see the national aspects of our early telecommunications (and transportation) systems and fail to realize how they were viewed at the time of construction as part of Canada's contribution to the successful running of a global empire.

Discussion Questions

1. In what ways has connectivity changed over time? What are some examples of communication technologies that were soon taken for granted? Why might that be the case?

2. In your view, is there a problem with overuse of communications technology and new media and, if so, with which technologies and what are the consequences?

3. To what extent is privacy a concern for you as a user of communications technology and new media? How has privacy as a concern changed over time?

4. What are some changes in how news has historically been moved from one location to another and what effects have these changes had on how news is captured, presented, and shared? What are the corollary effects on society?

5. In what ways does the value of a network increase as more people make use of it (or could the argument be made that the opposite is true in some cases)? What are some other consequences of increased network activity, in terms of points of contact as well as content?

6. How has telecommunications technology historically been used for connectivity between and among people with shared interests (whether personal, professional, political, etc.)?

7. What are some of the implications of user expectations of free content, whether for creators of content, copyright owners, vetting of content, quality of content, access to content, searching content, etc.? Do such considerations change depending on genre and medium?

Class Activities

1. Locate a 'how does it work' video or web-site for a technology from the history of new media—using a search strategy such as 'how does the telegraph work'—and then retell this in your own words or make a storyboard for a video of your own.

2. Choose an historical antecedent technology, such as the telegraph or the telephone, and trace the linkages between that technology and present day new media. Consider economic linkages, technological linkages, and sociocultural linkages (usage).

3. Several examples of 'prior art' for everyday new media activities (abbreviations and text speak found in telegrams, 'twittering' via the postal system) have been described in this chapter. Can you find examples of these from your own family, either memories of grand-parents or historical artifacts (old postcards, for example)?

4. Locate a piece of very early 'new media' (the CBC Archives on the web are good for this) and review it in class. What is similar and what is different to new media today?

3 Approaches to New Media

Questions to Consider

- In what ways do different approaches to new media bring with them different perspectives?
- What hype and counter-hype has accompanied the evolution and discussion of new media?
- What is meant by McLuhan's phrase, 'the medium is the message'? Why do you think it has become so widely known?
- In what ways can the term 'technoculture' invite you to consider both technology and culture as multifaceted and complex?

Chapter Outline

In this chapter we examine the notion that a well-rounded view of the role and effects of new media in society can only be gleaned by taking a number of perspectives. The different views presented in this chapter are useful in different ways. For this reason, we look at several theoretical approaches to new media while providing insight into their strengths and weaknesses. Particular emphasis is placed on a 'social shaping' perspective in which groups and individuals are understood as able to influence how media is used and how it evolves. We explore some of the hype that surrounds new media and we try to understand why science-driven messages are so compelling, while critically examining both the overly positive and the unnecessarily negative portrayals of the effects of new media. Both cultural context and media forms are explored as ways of understanding new media, along with social, psychological, and economic explanations.

Getting Perspective

This chapter examines different approaches to new media and asks you to consider what it means to have an approach to new media and what different perspectives contribute to how new media are understood. In some ways, learning about a new topic is like going to a new city. If you were new to a city, how would you approach it? Would you stand on a hill nearby and look down, or walk the streets? Would you buy a map, look at it using Google Earth, or read a travel book? Whether from above or from the ground, with a book, a map, or Google Earth, each of these different approaches offers a different view. Once you have chosen an approach, you might then consider an appropriate tool to inform your perspective. A telescope would help with the view from a hill. A computer would be required for Google Earth. You can use your own eyes for reading a book or you could listen to an audio book. Different tools or methods of looking at a topic and different perspectives on that topic are part of your approach to it and together shape your understanding. In the case of new media, there is a wide range of approaches ranging from the technical, artistic, social, political, economic, and historical.

This multi-disciplinary interest reflects both the importance of new media for society and the special place that communications media occupy as both a technological form and a cultural form. A wide variety of theorists have developed many approaches to account for both the form and the content of media. These are further complicated by the way in which the content of media is affected by the form. Media technologies, especially *new media* technologies, are part of the social world and as such their influences are felt through the people who develop them and are heavily affected by how people interpret the messages they contain. This is especially true in how people modify the intended use of new media through their own adaptations and creativity. The mashup, scratch music, the 'response' video on YouTube; these are all examples of people making something new out of the content of others' messages.

For a student of new media, familiarity with multiple theories not only helps with your own investigations but also proves invaluable when you encounter commentary from others: you will know what the strengths and weaknesses of an approach might be and when one perspective might be more appropriate or useful than another. Such an understanding can also give you an appreciation of how multiple perspectives are helpful—as with the many ways of exploring a new city, each offers a different vantage point.

As you read the remainder of this book and in your own encounters with new media, we encourage you to try to deploy multiple views, to think about how the perspective you take influences what you find and your understanding. And we particularly encourage you to see human beings as creative actors in the media world they live in, not simply reacting to or being affected by the new media world around them, but independent thinkers with agency, with free will.

What to Believe: The Hype or the Counter-Hype?

Writing in 1998, Kitchin (1998: ix) described **cyberspace** as 'probably one of the most universally over-hyped terms of the latter part of the twentieth century'. A decade later, this has not changed. Indeed, a recurring feature of the development of the Internet and the popularization of digital media technologies has been their capacity to generate hype about how they are expected to change everything, typically for the better.

Lister and colleagues (2003: 11) suggest that this tendency is linked to the modernist belief in technology as socially progressive: 'new' is the 'cutting edge' or the 'avant-garde' and the place for 'forward-thinking people' to be. This kind of hype characterized many analyses of the Internet in the 1990s (e.g. Dyson 1999; Dyson et al. 1994; Kelly 1997; Negroponte 1995;

Rheingold 1994), which also tended to debunk criticism of the new technologies (Postman 1993; Robins and Webster 1999; Sale 1995; Stoll 1995). This early 'polarization between narrow suspicion and uncritical enthusiasm' (Woolgar 2002: 3–4) that characterized new media studies in the 1990s has to some extent given way to more empirically grounded research into new media, its uses, and impacts (Flew 2001; Livingstone 2005; Silver 2000; Wellman 2004).

The **dot.com crash** of 2001 also revealed very starkly the dangers of investing too much in the new media hype of companies that rested on fatally flawed business plans. At the same time, the hype that surrounds new media remains pervasive, partly because it helps to boost share prices, to persuade politicians, and to sell product, but also because it taps into what Vincent Mosco (2004) refers to as the 'digital sublime'. Mosco describes the extent to which cyberspace possesses not only technical, political, and economic properties, but also how it is a form of cultural myth and as such, offers possibilities of transcending the limits of contemporary society and the material world.

Popular writing about the Internet and cyberspace in the mid-1990s had no shortage of pronouncements regarding the utopian, almost transcendent nature of the implications of the new media. Nicholas Negroponte's *Being Digital* (1995) was one of the most influential texts promoting this view. As founding director of the Media Lab at Massachusetts Institute of Technology (MIT) and a founder and columnist for *WIRED* magazine, Negroponte championed the idea that digitization had reached a point where the transition from an economy and society based on 'atoms' (tangible physical assets) and the production of goods, to one based on 'bits' (intangible wealth based on knowledge), meant that 'computing is not about computers any more. It is about living' (1995: 6). Negroponte concluded *Being Digital* by proclaiming that 'the empowering nature of being digital' meant that 'like a force of nature, the digital age cannot be denied or stopped and that it has four very powerful qualities that will result in its ultimate triumph: decentralizing, globalizing, harmonizing and empowering' (1995: 229, 231).

Electronic Frontier Foundation (EFF) co-founder John Perry Barlow argued that 'with the development of the Internet, and with the increasing pervasiveness of communication between networked computers, we are in the middle of the most transforming technological event since the capture of fire' (1995: 36). George Gilder (1994: 49) predicted that the Internet would mean the death of television, which he saw as being 'a tool for tyrants . . . [whose] overthrow will be a major force for freedom and individualism, culture and morality'. In 1994, through the Progress and Freedom Foundation (www.pff.org), Esther Dyson, George Gilder, George Keyworth, and pioneering new media thinker Alvin Toffler (1970, 1980) published *Cyberspace and the American Dream: A Magna Carta for the Knowledge Age*, which found in the Internet both a concrete expression of uniquely American values of entrepreneurship and rugged individualism, identifying cyberspace as 'the land of knowledge . . . civilization's truest, highest calling' and the basis for the 'creation of a new civilization, founded in the eternal truths of the American Idea' (Dyson et al. 1994).

This optimism wasn't confined to academics and industry players. Former US vice-president Al Gore's 1994 speech to the International Telecommunications Union, for example, proclaimed that the US-led Global Information Infrastructure initiative would promote 'robust and sustainable economic progress, strong democracies, better solutions to global and local environmental challenges, improved health care, and—ultimately— a greater sense of shared stewardship of our small planet' (Gore 1994). John Brockman's anthology of interviews with and short pieces authored by the 'digerati'—defined as those who 'evangelize, connect people, adapt quickly . . . [and] give each other permission to be great' (1996: xxvi)—is an excellent primer on mid-1990s 'cyberbole' for readers who did not experience the adventure first-hand.

Not surprisingly, such hype generated counter-hype and a debunking of the claims of the cyberspace advocates, as part of what Knights and colleagues (2002) refer to as the '"emperor's-new-clothes" story'. Former cyberspace advocate Clifford Stoll (1995: 13) had second thoughts about cyberspace, warning that 'life in the real world is far more interesting, far more important, far richer, than anything you'll ever find on a computer screen'. Critics of the digital age such as Brook and Boal (1995) and Sale (1995) reinvoked the spirit of the **Luddite** opposition to industrial technologies of early nineteenth-century Britain to warn of the need to 'resist the virtual life', with Sale going as far as to smash a computer on stage while promoting his book (Silver 2000: 20). Barbrook and Cameron (1995: 1) argued that the new media discourse fostered by *WIRED* magazine was part of a Californian ideology that constituted 'a bizarre fusion of the cultural bohemianism of San Francisco with the hi-tech industries of Silicon Valley', combining political **libertarianism** with a belief in free markets in a world where 'everybody can be both hip and rich'. Postman (1993) critiqued the entire relationship of culture to technology in modern societies as one of technopoly, defined as 'the deification of technology, which means that the culture seeks its authorization in technology, finds its satisfactions in technology, and takes its orders from technology' (1993: 71). When the sharp decline of the NASDAQ index in April 2000 led to the collapse of many of the dot.com enterprises that had started up in the late 1990s, a veritable cottage industry of corporate *mea culpas* was generated about the dangers of attaching too much belief to new media hype (Kuo 2001; cf. Lovink 2002; Malmstein 2001).

Interpreting Hype and Counter-Hype: Methodological Considerations

In their review of the social implications of the Internet, DiMaggio et al. (2001) present a fivefold typology of Internet impacts that identifies positive and negative assessments (see Table 3.1).

Overly optimistic or pessimistic accounts of the impact of new media—cyberbole— have been countered by approaches that seek to identify a middle ground between extreme positions. Some have called for a 'new empiricism' in Internet studies that goes beyond utopianism and critiques and engages with new media users and the environments, both technological and socio-cultural, in which they make use of networked ICTs (Flew 2001; Silver 2000). In other words, the new empiricism—which is not that new any more, being almost a decade old—tries to ground new media studies in real data and the real experiences

TABLE 3.1 Social Implications of the Internet

Internet Impact	Positive	Negative
1. Inequality	New access to information based on computer use and availability (digital opportunity)	Patterns of access, availability and use of ICTs reflect other social inequalities (digital divide)
2. Community	New forms of social interaction and community formation through virtual communities that are not space-bound	Online activities become an obstacle to real-life interactions; declining commitment to locality-based social capital formation
3. Politics	New opportunities for online political engagement, information exchange, and deliberation; a virtual public sphere	Isolation from others in politically effective geographical locales; management of participation by political and economic elites
4. Organizations	Flexible organizations; networked interaction among those within and outside of the organization; more 'horizontal' channels of online communication	New forms of internal surveillance; online communication remains hierarchical; online as a low-trust communications environment
5. Culture	'Demassification' of access to and use of media content; new opportunities for users to become media producers ('produsers' [Bruns 2005])	Hyper-segmentation and 'I media' as a barrier to communication with others; fragmentation and dilution of a common culture

Source: DiMaggio et al. (2001).

of those who use media. As such it is a both a break from the earlier utopian and dystopian approaches and also an implicit acknowledgement that what we are talking about is not a separate sphere ('cyberspace') but rather the online aspects of regular life.

At the same time, there are limitations to such an approach to understanding new media, of trying to identify optimistic and pessimistic accounts of new media and aiming to find a moderate, middle ground between them. We will return to current themes in new media research later in the chapter, however, it is worth noting here three implications of a new empiricism for new media studies.

First, any approach lends itself more readily to some research and theoretical traditions than to others. Empiricism lends itself to statistically-based sociology and quantitative, survey-based, methodologies that are linked to advice for government policy-makers on managing technological change. It is important to remember, however, that these empirical approaches exist alongside others, such as: (i) speculative media theory, which has tended to approach the interaction between technology and culture in more future-oriented terms; (ii) critical political economy, which has questioned whether policy-making organizations possess sufficient distance from the most powerful private interests to be able to act in the public interest; and (iii) online ethnography that looks at the use of new media and the Internet in everyday life (Bakardjieva 2005).

Second, an empirical approach to new media tends to have an 'after-the-event' element to it; it seeks to manage change rather than to make change. This in itself may be a legacy of ways of thinking associated with earlier one-to-many broadcast media systems, such as television. Kress (1997: 78), for example, makes the observation that, just as the binary opposition between producers and consumers of media is challenged by new media technologies, so too is the distinction between design and critique, where 'some individuals set the agenda and others either follow or object'. One of the recurring themes of new media developments is the extent to which critique of existing systems happens through design—such as open source software, open publishing, citizen journalism, and participatory media systems—so that the politics of new media is as often enacted through the relationships between large-scale corporate media and those who pursue alternative forms of digital creativity, as it is between those who analyze the power relations of new media from an academic or research perspective.

Third, it is important to consider the recurring significance of optimism about new media as a form of *myth* that is historically grounded. In his discussion of the 'cyberspace myth', Mosco (2004) notes that his interest in this topic stemmed in part from his experience as a graduate student in 1973 when he looked at claims that multichannel cable television would 'usher in a Wired Society governed by Electronic Democracy' (2004: 1; cf. Streeter 1987). Mosco points out not only how claims about the democratizing potential of cable television now look silly (30 years after the advent of television), but also, that such claims bear a striking resemblance to those made about the transformative impact of the Internet (20 years later). Mosco also draws attention to the pioneering analysis of Carey and Quirk (1992) on the parallels between recent prophecies about the 'electronic revolution' of new ICTs and the late nineteenth century utopian idea that industrial machinery and electrical technology could be harnessed in harmony with nature to provide both material prosperity and social peace.

Approaches to Technological Change: Divergent Perspectives

Many of the utopian propositions noted above (and elsewhere in this book) can be seen as marked by **technological determinism**. While technological determinism is not a theory of technological change as such, it is a way of thinking (or perhaps not thinking) about the relationship between new technologies and society that has been quite pervasive. Technological determinism sees social change as driven by technological change. Williams (1974: 13) defines technological determinism as a view that 'research and development have been assumed as self-generating. The new technologies are invented . . . in an independent sphere, and then create new societies or new human conditions'. The literature on the impact of the Internet is rich with examples of such arguments. In relation to new media, Buckingham (2000: 45) observes that in such arguments, 'the computer is predominantly seen as an autonomous force that is somehow independent of human society, and acts on it from the outside'.

Historical analysts of technology such as Winner (1986a, b), Cowan (1997), and MacKenzie and Wacjman (1999) demonstrate the flawed logic of technological determinist arguments—which would have technology advancing of its own accord, propelled by innovation, free of outside influence—and how these flaws have been highlighted by several real world new media developments:

- the VCR/Beta wars of the 1980s, where the adoption of a common standard for video recorders had less to do with the inherent superiority of one format over another (some suggested that Beta was a superior format), than with the capacity of other video recorder hardware manufacturers to squeeze Sony (the principal promoter of Beta) out of the crucial US market;
- the legal battles between Apple and Microsoft in the late 1990s over ownership of the 'desktop' graphical user interface, which indicated that GUIs did not simply evolve from earlier to newer versions but that they might constitute highly lucrative forms of intellectual property;
- the over-investment of telecommunications companies in 3G wireless broadband spectrum in the early 2000s, driven by an assumption—largely untested—that users sought to access Internet content through their mobile phones; and
- the continued difficulties in developing digital television in many parts of the world, as the implications of a more economical use of spectrum come up against the resistance of incumbent broadcasters to the possible development of new television services (Galperin 2004).

We question the argument that the relationship between new media technologies and society is technologically determinist in nature. In doing so, there are two important caveats to be noted. The first is related to the question of whether a cluster of technologies will, in fact, shape historical development over the long term. Heilbroner (2003), for example, has argued that a particular technological form contains within it implicit forms of social organization that are difficult to reverse. Once it is created and adopted, it is hard to go back. A good example of this is the household washing machine, which carries with it the implicit assumption that clothes will be washed by homeowners, and no longer by servants—otherwise why make it so fancy? And once you have one, why hire someone to wash your clothes? (Rowland 2006). The second caveat to keep in mind is to observe the partial truth of technological determinism, in that once particular technologies are widely adopted and used, they acquire a degree of 'lock-in' that shapes society and culture in a wider sense. Winner (1986a,b) makes this point in relation to what he terms 'inherently political technologies' such as nuclear power, whose very existence requires hierarchical, command-and-control forms of internal organization and high levels of external surveillance. In a different but related vein, Arthur's (1999) example is the QWERTY typewriter keyboard and how it achieved dominance in the early twentieth century, with adoption by large organizations and training among prospective workers, leading to technological lock-in since the costs of change for individuals and organizations became too great to contemplate.

Though these are valid points, we will focus on the **social shaping of technology** approach, the major alternative to technological determinism. This theory argues that social, institutional, economic, and cultural factors shape the choices made about the forms of technological innovation, the content of technological artifacts and practices, and the outcomes and impacts of technological change for different groups in society. This approach stresses the need to analyze 'the socio-economic patterns embedded in both the content of technologies and the processes of innovation' (Williams and Edge 1996: 866). This, in turn, requires a broader understanding of technology than simply its most basic application as the tools and artifacts used by humans. Rather, a definition of technology as simply 'hardware' needs to be extended to consider the uses of such technologies, their contexts of use, and the systems of knowledge and social meaning that accompany their development and use (MacKenzie and Wacjman 1999). This multi-dimensional understanding of technology is apparent in the origin of the word 'technology' in Ancient Greek, combining *techne* (practical or applied arts and skills) and *logos* (systematic reason, knowledge, or discourse) as well as in French and German, where the words *la technique* and *die Technik* convey a meaning of technology that involves the tools, their uses, and associated forms of knowledge (MacKenzie and Wacjman 1999: 7).

The broad framework of social shaping of technology theories has within it three distinctive strands: (i) the diffusion of innovations model; (ii) the political economy model; and (iii) theories of culture and technology. The **diffusion of innovations model** is associated with the communications theorist Everett Rogers (2003), who sought to model the rate of adoption and eventual spread of an innovation in the social system through communication via particular channels—influential individuals, related businesses, social networks—over time. Rogers' model identifies different categories of user (including early adopters) and the adoption threshold at which an innovation becomes a mature technology. In *The Invisible Computer*, Norman (1998) draws on Rogers' work to argue that there is a shift in market focus from the attributes of the technology to its ease of use and ability to solve problems as it evolves through a given diffusion cycle (see Figure 3.1). The 'innovator's dilemma' (discussed in Chapter 8) draws upon this framework to observe the risks of developing more complex technological solutions at the stage in the product cycle where a technological product is becoming a mass-market commodity.

Where the diffusion of innovations approach tends to focus on social uptake of new technologies and has what Rogers acknowledges is a 'pro-innovation bias' (2003: 106), the **political economy approach** focuses much more specifically on the politics and power relations embedded in technological development. MacKenzie and Wacjman (1999) argue that an understanding of how technologies developed both historically and in the present era requires that close attention be paid to dominant economic relations, social relations of production, military priorities, the role of the state, and gender relations.

Critical theories of technology, of which the political economy approach is a part, see technology as part of the interplay of power and domination in society. So, for example, Sholle (2002: 6) points out that 'technologies are . . . processes that structure the world in particular ways . . . we should not see technology and the social as separate domains'.

FIGURE 3.1 Consumer Demand and the Diffusion Cycle
Source: Norman (1998: 30).

The political economy approach and critical theories of technology, more generally, draw attention to the ways in which politics, power, and economic relations are embedded in the process of scientific and technological research itself. This can occur directly, through the capacity of large corporations, government agencies, and the military to shape the research and training priorities of academic research through large-scale funding at a time when government funding and other traditional sources are being squeezed. Indeed, Schiller (2000) argues that this has become increasingly central to Internet and other new media research.

Less directly, but perhaps more profoundly, it is argued by Feenberg (2003) and others that 'technological development is constrained by cultural norms originating in economics, ideology, religion, and tradition'. These kinds of constraints are often obscured by an underlying technological rationality, or what Feenberg terms a 'technical code'. Technical code—often in the form of software for programmable machines—is 'not merely a belief, an ideology, but is effectively incorporated into the structure of machines' (2003: 657, 658). Thus the computer that uses Windows software presents the user with a vast array of established relationships, mainly commercial, between the user and their computer.

Picking up on Feenberg's critical theory of technology, Sholle (2002: 7) argues that:

> A technology such as the computer is a product of social processes from the beginning. The particular construction of knowledge in institutions of science and engineering, the economic interests of companies, the cultural patterns of consumption, the spatial arrangements of communities and nations, the political motifs of government policies are inscribed into the technology from the very beginning.

This technical code does not always constrain freedom. More recently, Flanagin et al., building on Feenberg's concept of the technical code, argue that 'the Internet's technical design supports interoperability and open access, while suggesting an enormous capacity for personalization and innovation' (2010: 179). A key feature of the design and a factor in much of the recent excitement about new media and Web 2.0, is the way in which web users are able to take control over their configuration, use, and re-use of the Internet, which results in 'a sense of individual empowerment achieved through enhanced agency' (Flanagin et al. 2010: 179).

Technology and cultural studies

Feenberg's (2003) observation that technology and culture are interdependent has also been developed in work from a cultural studies perspective. Cultural studies theorists view new media as *cultural technologies*. In other words, they are interwoven collections (sometimes called 'assemblages') of technology, content, context, power relations, and social knowledge.

Berland (1992: 40) proposes that media as cultural technologies produce not only content (media texts), but also spatial arrangements and modes of consumption that 'are material practices with their own structural effects and tensions'. The concept of 'technocultures' has been used by Penley and Ross (1991), Menser and Aronowitz (1996), and Green (2002) to refer to 'tools of mediated communication through which cultural material is created and circulated' (Green 2002: xxx–xxxi). Green makes the important point that, while all technologies have cultural impacts (think, for instance, of the myriad cultural implications of the automobile), media technologies have a particular significance in this regard because they carry both explicit and implicit messages. A website, for example, delivers its explicit content (the words and images on the screen), as well as a message about its creator (and the society in which it was created), delivered implicitly through elements including design choices such as colour and font styles, set-up and configuration, and the level of language used. Via these implicit messages, media technologies enable the circulation of what Thompson (1991: 132) terms 'symbolic forms . . . by virtue of which individuals communicate with one another and share their experiences, conceptions and beliefs'.

The significance of this conception of culture as communication mediated through technologies becomes apparent when recognizing that, just as the concept of technology has multiple levels of meaning, so too does culture. On one level, culture can be understood in terms of *aesthetics*, which equates culture with the arts. Cultural studies, however, have drawn attention to a more *anthropological* definition of culture as the whole way of life, or forms of lived experience, of people, communities, and social groups. Such an expanded definition of culture draws attention to the significance of forms of communication, social relations, and practices of everyday life. As Raymond Williams observes in *The Long Revolution*:

> Culture is the description of a particular way of life, which expresses certain meanings and values not only in art and learning but also in institutions and ordinary behaviour . . . Such analysis will . . . include analysis of elements in the way of life that to followers of the other definitions are not 'culture' at

all; the organization of production, the structure of the family, the structure of institutions which express or govern social relationships, the characteristic forms through which members of the society communicate. (1965: 57–8)

In addition to artistic and intellectual activity and the ways of life of communities or groups, culture can also be understood as derived from what Thompson (1991: 136) refers to as the *structural conception* of culture. This conception of culture 'emphasizes both the symbolic character of cultural phenomena and the fact that such phenomena are always embedded in structured social contexts'. Noting the observation of the famous semiotician Umberto Eco (1976: 9) that 'every act of communication . . . presupposes a signification system as its necessary condition', this structuralist approach to culture draws attention to the ways in which individuals are 'produced' as social beings within a given system of social, cultural, linguistic, and psychological relationships, which possess an underlying structural 'code' not necessarily accessible to outsiders. Drawing out the implications of this for new media studies, Poster (2005: 136) observes that 'computer-mediated communication fundamentally shifts the registers of human experience as we have known them in modern society . . . Time and space, body and mind, subject and object, human and machine are each dramatically transformed by practices carried out on networked computers'. It is clear that, from a cultural studies perspective, these different ways of looking at culture can be equally applied to technology. Table 3.2 provides a summary of these perspectives.

Political economy and cultural studies

Cultural studies, while important for understanding new media, benefits from being considered along with a study of the political economy of new media (Flew 2007). New media, after all, are a business, and their economic implications are important factors in whether or not and how widely they are deployed. Political economy approaches tend to start from the perspective of economic and industrial dynamics. They focus on the extent to which access to resources at various levels influences the directions that new media developments take (or do not take, because those proposing them lacked sufficient resources). These resources include access to investment capital to participate in new media ventures, access to political

TABLE 3.2 Defining Technology and Culture: A Three-Level Approach

	Definition of technology	Definition of culture
First level: 'common sense' definitions	Technology as physical objects, tools, artifacts	Culture as 'the arts' and aesthetic excellence
Second level: 'contextual' or user-based definitions	Technology as content or 'software', defined by how it is used	Culture as 'ways of life' or the lived experience of peoples, communities, or groups
Third level: 'communicative' or 'structural' definitions	Technology as systems of knowledge and social meaning	Culture as an underlying 'structural system'

influence on the basis of economic power and significance as a decision-maker, and access to the technologies themselves on the part of potential users, with the focus on inequalities of access across all of these levels. These are seen as relating to various indicators of social inequality, such as class, gender, race, ethnicity, and other markers of disadvantage.

Theorists such as McChesney (1999, 2000, 2002), Schiller (2000; cf. McChesney and Schiller 2003), Mosco (1996, 1997, 2000, 2004), Gandy (2002), and Murdock and Golding (2004) are among the most influential contributors to developing a political economy approach to new media. For the most part, this work is skeptical about claims that new media have led to fundamental changes in the socio-economic structures in which they are embedded. In an essay refuting claims that the rise of the Internet promises new forms of democratic media politics, McChesney (2000: 33–4) observes that 'despite its much-ballyhooed "openness" . . . [the Internet] will likely be dominated by the usual corporate suspects. Certainly a few new commercial players will emerge, but the evidence suggests that the content of the digital communications world will appear quite similar to that of the pre-digital commercial media world'. Similarly, Kumar (2005: 154) argues that developments associated with new media and the knowledge economy have not produced a radical shift in the dynamics of capitalist societies since 'the imperatives of profit, power and control seem as predominant now as they have ever been in the history of capitalist industrialism. The difference lies in the greater range and intensity of their applications . . . not in any change in the principles themselves'.

While political economy theories start from the perspective of economic power, cultural studies approaches start from the perspective of communications and culture, and examine the complexities and power relations that emerge in the relationship between the production, reception, interpretation, and use of messages arising from technologically mediated forms of communication like new media. While cultural studies approaches have a common lineage with political economy in their historical relationship to neo-Marxism and critical theory, the tradition within this field to see audiences as *active* (having minds of their own and able to make decisions about the worth of those messages) has seen it tend towards more positive assessments of the transformative potential of new media. Jenkins (2006a) captures the extent to which, from a cultural studies perspective, the relationship between producers and users of new media constitutes a contested space where positive outcomes *can* occur. This is akin to earlier work in cultural studies on the relationship between popular culture and power relations in society (cf. Flew 2007: 39–43; Hartley 2003):

> We are entering an era of prolonged transition and transformation in the way media operates. Convergence describes the process by which we will sort through these options . . . Media producers will only find their way through these current problems by renegotiating their relationship with their consumers. Audiences, empowered by these new technologies, occupying a space at the intersection between old and new media, are demanding the right to participate within the culture . . . The resulting struggles and compromises will define the public culture of the future. (Jenkins 2006a: 24)

Those working from a more cultural studies-oriented perspective have tended to be more optimistic about the potential of new media. By contrast, those working from a more political economy-based perspective have tended to be more skeptical about the transformative capacities of new media, stressing more strongly the continuities between old and new media. At the same time, this correlation is complicated at several points.

From a perspective grounded in Marxist political economy, Graham (2006: 16) argues that the current phase of what he calls 'hypercapitalism', has transformed the dynamics of capitalist economies so fundamentally that 'use-values and exchange-values are not necessarily separable in a knowledge economy'. In other words, the traditional categories for understanding capital—labour, capital, and exchange—get blurred in a **knowledge economy**, making analysis difficult and traditional assumptions about workers and bosses either irrelevant or worth reconsidering. When you work at home, using your own computer, and do some blogging on the side as a hobby, are you a labourer?

Similarly, Tiziana Terranova describes the 'cultural politics of information', which breaks with conceptions of information as mere communications content that requires subsequent critical decoding, or as 'immaterial' and of lesser importance than the dynamics of industrial production (2004: 3). In Terranova's view, information is important *because* it is not all powerful, convincing people to make decisions they would not otherwise make, nor is it entirely subject to interpretation by the receiver. Instead, there is a dynamic at work that must consider both the material force of information (who owns it, who buys it, who controls the sale) and the messages contained therein, including the potential for creativity and change.

At the same time, there has been debate within cultural studies over its relationship to new media. Bassett (2007) examines how a focus on both the politics of signification (acknowledging that the encoding of messages cannot be value free) and the sender–text–message–receiver relationship often effaces the significance of the media technologies themselves as drivers of systems of meaning in their own right. Bassett proposes that a cultural studies practice oriented towards new media needs to consider the forms of political engagement that are specific to digitally networked media, such as 'tactical media' (Cubitt 2006) and 'hacktivism' (Dyer-Witheford 2002; O'Neil 2006), while also requiring the '(re)incorporation of the political economy of new media into cultural studies' (Bassett 2007: 234).

Pioneer Media Theorists: Marshall McLuhan and Raymond Williams

The relationship between new media technologies and media content raises a series of complex issues about the social and cultural impacts of media themselves. While the new media discussed in this book have largely been developed and popularized since the 1990s, it is important to consider that the question of whether media technologies have the power to transform society and culture has a much wider and more longstanding provenance (cf. Lister et al. 2003: 72–92). Two of the key thinkers from the 1960s and 1970s were the Canadian communications theorist Marshall McLuhan and the British cultural theorist Raymond Williams. In many ways, their respective approaches to the question of how media technologies relate to the wider society and culture have constituted the two competing poles of thought about new media that we have been discussing—technological determinism and social shaping theory.

Marshall McLuhan was a controversial and eclectic theorist whose work stressed the extent to which cultural content was embedded within specific technological forms, meaning that media influence not only *what* people think but *how* people think. His work, developed in key texts such as *Gutenberg Galaxy* (McLuhan 1962), *Understanding Media* (McLuhan 1964), and *The Medium is the Massage* (McLuhan and Fiore 1967), has always polarized opinions, with his advocates arguing that 'his was the first coherent interpretation of the electric world' (McLuhan and Zingrone 1997: 6), while his critics have maintained that his writings assumed 'an importance which has nothing to do with their worth' (Ricks 1968: 59). McLuhan's ideas became unfashionable during the 1970s and 1980s, particularly in light of the critique of technological determinism levelled by Raymond Williams and others (see below), but the rise of the Internet saw McLuhan championed as a visionary (see e.g. de Kerckhove 1998; Levinson 1997; Wolf 1996).

Central to McLuhan's theory of communications media is his well-known aphorism that 'the medium is the message'. What this means is that technologies are first and foremost extensions of human selves, human capacities: 'The personal and social consequences of any medium—that is, of any extension of ourselves—result from the new scale that is introduced into our affairs by each extension of ourselves, or by any new technology' (McLuhan 1964: 23). At the same time, the impact of any medium on the conduct of human affairs is neither transparent nor obvious. For McLuhan, the key to understanding electronic culture is not in the technologies themselves, such as machines or computers, nor in the uses of their content or alleged effects, but rather, in the ways in which they subtly alter the environment in which humans act and interact. He proposed that the logic of the 'electric age' can be found in electric light, since it is pure information, 'a medium without a message', which can only have content when it is used in conjunction with another medium, for example the use of electric light to spell out a neon sign:

> The electric light escapes attention as a communication medium just because it has no 'content'. And this makes it an invaluable instance of how people fail to study media at all . . . The message of the electric light is like the message of electric power in industry, totally radical, pervasive and decentralized. For electric light and power are separate from their uses, yet they eliminate time and space factors in human association exactly as do radio, telegraph, telephone and TV, creating involvement in depth. (McLuhan 1964: 24–5)

One implication of McLuhan's analysis is that 'the impact of the communication media on sensory perception influences not only what we think but how we think' (McPhail and McPhail 1990: 69). For McLuhan, the 'grammar' of a medium structures human sensory responses to it, fundamentally altering perceptions of social reality: 'All media work us over completely. They are so persuasive in their personal, political, economic, aesthetic, psychological, moral, ethical and social consequences that they leave no part of us untouched, unaffected, unaltered . . . Any understanding of social and cultural change is impossible without a knowledge of the way media work as environments' (McLuhan and Fiore 1967: 26).

In contrast to McLuhan's focus on how media technologies reshape society and culture, Raymond Williams was primarily interested in the question of how technologies *are shaped by* social, cultural, political, and economic forces. This stress on the social shaping of technology meant that Williams focused on the social forces, power relations, and conflicts between competing interests that lead to some (technological) options being pursued while others are not developed or are actively foreclosed upon. For Williams, a failure to focus on the social dimensions of how technologies are developed and how they are used is an example of technological determinism, which he accused Marshall McLuhan of and which Williams believed was an ideology used by the powerful to support their own interests:

> If the effect of the medium is the same, whoever controls and uses it, and whatever apparent content he may try to insert, then we can forget ordinary political and cultural argument, and let the technology run itself. It is hardly surprising that this conclusion has been welcomed by the 'media-men' of the existing institutions. (Williams 1974: 131)

Using the historical development of television as his principal case study, Williams argued that the medium's development needed to be understood as arising from a series of primarily commercial investment decisions in the technologies of mass broadcast communication, which had been shaped by the development of radio and which promoted a relationship between technology and the wider society based around 'centralized transmission and privatized reception' (1974: 24). Media both shaped and was shaped by a wider set of developments in industrial capitalist societies, such as mass production, the rise of consumer society, large-scale commercial investments in communications technologies, and the development of suburban housing, which saw a spatial separation of home from places of work. Williams also noted the significance of different institutional forms for the broadcast television content that emerged and placed particular emphasis on the contrast between the American commercial broadcasting system and the role played by the BBC as a public service broadcaster in the United Kingdom.

In the context of new media, the frameworks developed by Williams and McLuhan generate important differences in focus. The social shaping of technology approach that Williams championed draws attention to how people, groups, and social institutions have the power to make decisions about the development and adoption of new media technologies and the possible alternative uses of these technologies (cf. Winston 1998 for an extension of such themes). It thus draws attention to the political economy of communications media and technology. By contrast, McLuhan's approach stresses the extent to which societies and cultures become so immersed in modes of being and behaving that are shaped by their wider technological environment that the very ways of being human are inherently linked to the technological forms through which people extend their capacities and senses. Such an approach, therefore, questions the extent to which culture can be understood independently from the technological forms through which it is always, already mediated.

Social Psychology: Identity and Interpersonal Relations Online

There has always been a strong interest in the social psychology of new media use, or what is also termed '**computer-mediated communication**', or CMC. Reasons for this range from the well-established interests of corporations in how best to target marketing activities to new consumers, to government interests in managing concerns about access to new media, and those who see CMC generating new forms of community, sociality, and identity. A curious feature of debates about new media and CMC is the tension between ensuring that children, in particular, have access to the new media, while navigating moral panics about the dangers of online pornography, violent video games, cyber-stalkers, and so on. While concerns about the adverse impacts of a new medium on children have been common (see Critcher 2006 for an overview of this literature), new media debates have also been marked by a visionary utopianism (Buckingham 2000: 46), whereby the young—variously termed the 'N-Gen' (Tapscott 1998), the 'screenagers' (Rushkoff 1996), and the 'digital natives' (Prensky 2001)—are seen as already immersed in a digital environment that promises a better world—more interactive, democratic, and communicative—than that of one-way broadcast media. This highly positive spin on the social psychology of the Internet has deep roots in the most influential literature of the 1990s.

Two of the most influential books of the 1990s on the social psychology of Internet use were Howard Rheingold's *The Virtual Community* (1994) and Sherry Turkle's *Life on the Screen: Identity in the Age of the Internet* (1995). For many people, one or both of these books were their introduction to thinking about the world of CMC in a systematic way. Previously, communications specialists had viewed CMC with skepticism, concerned that the absence of visual and other non-verbal cues in online communication when compared to face-to-face interaction would make CMC a risky business (Baym 2005). What both Rheingold and Turkle brought to bear was a perspective that saw CMC as playful, fun, interactive, socially progressive, and very possibly a better world than that of real or offline social experience. Moreover, both developed their arguments from intellectually well-grounded and theoretically sophisticated positions that were, nonetheless, readily accessible to the lay reader.

In perhaps the most famous early account of CMC-based online cultures, Rheingold defined virtual communities as 'social aggregations that emerge from the Net when enough people carry on those public discussions [using the Internet] long enough, with sufficient human feeling, to form webs of personal relationships in cyberspace' (1994: 5). While recognizing that the origins of the Internet lay in the US military-industrial-governmental complex, Rheingold observed that the democratic potential of CMC lay in the decentralized nature of such networked communications. They present, in a way very different from one-to-many mass media, the possibility to 'piggyback alternative networks on the mainstream infrastructure' and to 'use CMC to create alternative planetary information networks' (1994:

14). Rheingold was enthusiastic about the development of virtual communities, seeing in them the possibility of a reinvigorated sense of community-building and citizen participation in public life. This potential arose from three interrelated attributes of CMC: (i) the building of social networks and social capital; (ii) the sharing of knowledge and information; and (iii) the enabling of new modes of democratic participation in public life. With an optimism that was drawn from experiments in virtual community, Rheingold emphasized the elements of social choice and political activism that would be involved in the achievement of such outcomes:

> The technology that makes virtual communities possible has the potential to bring enormous leverage to ordinary citizens at relatively little cost—intellectual leverage, social leverage, commercial leverage and, most importantly, political leverage. But the technology will not in itself fulfill this potential—this latent technical power must be used intelligently and deliberately by an informed population. More people must learn about that leverage and learn to use it, while we still have the freedom to do so, if it is to live up to its potential. (1994: 4–5)

Turkle (1995) identified virtual communities as sites of play and performativity through the creation of online identities that were indicative of the transition from modernity to postmodernity. Turkle presented a detailed argument about how participants in various forms of online communications—most notably MUDs (Multi-User Dungeons) and MOOs (Multi-User Object-Oriented Domain)—were engaged in forms of performativity online that differed significantly from their personas in real life. Drawing on psychoanalysis, Turkle found that participants in virtual communities increasingly came to view real life as simply one 'window' through which a personality is developed and expressed, and that CMC constitutes a constructive and potentially liberatory space through which 'the obese can become slender, the beautiful plain, the "nerdy" sophisticated' (1995: 12). Turkle found in this multiplicity and performativity of identities in online environments a parallel to: (i) postmodernist and post-structuralist arguments about the fluidity and fragmented nature of contemporary personal identity; and (ii) developments in human–computer interface interaction that promote 'surface' interaction over deep engagement with the technology. Turkle argued that through both identity play within CMC and the simplification of GUIs seen with Apple and Microsoft Windows, 'we are moving toward a culture of simulation in which people are increasingly comfortable with substituting representations of reality for the real' (1995: 23).

Like many of the prophetic enthusiasms of early Internet culture, the passage of time has seen the puncturing of some of these speculative balloons in favour of more empirically nuanced accounts of the nature of community and identity in CMC. It must be noted, too, that CMC has also had it critics. To take one example, Lockard (1997: 225) argued that 'cyberspace is to community what Rubber Rita [an inflatable sex toy] is to human companionship'. The novelty of CMC has also decreased over time, Herring (2004: 33) observes, in that many current students 'do not relate to the utopian and dystopian speculations of earlier decades, and find the debates of the 1990s about online democracy, identity and virtuality hyped and vaguely silly'. This point is not simply technological or generational. It also reflects a strong tendency in the 1990s Internet literature to counterpose the virtual to the real, understanding the two as almost parallel universes into which people entered and left with varying degrees of personal commitment and intensity. In the present age, this distinction is blurred, with many younger people not even comprehending how the two could be seen as distinct. Life proceeds, with both its online and offline aspects.

Wellman and Haythornthwaite (2002) argue that speculative accounts of the Internet in terms of hype and counter-hype, as compared to more everyday forms of communication and interaction, were both poorly grounded empirically and deeply unhelpful in terms of understanding how users integrate either into their everyday lives. Slater (2002: 544) argues that this dichotomy emerged at a transitional stage of new media research more generally and that it is not surprising to find that, since a medium such as the Internet evolves in terms of technologies, user behaviours, questions of access, and legal and commercial environments, there is a 'process of disaggregating "the Internet" into its diversity of technologies and uses, generating a media landscape in which virtuality is clearly not a feature of the media but one social practice of media use among many others'. This is not to reject the importance of research into the social psychology of Internet use and CMC. It is, rather, to make the more modest claim that forms of community formation, civic engagement, and social interaction through CMC are likely to be diverse and contradictory and that 'it is better to ground this understanding of the complexity . . . in research than in speculation and assertion' (Rice and Haythornthwaite 2005: 108).

Case Study: The Tetrad

Marshall McLuhan did not use explicit or easy to follow methods in his analysis of media in our society, and even when he did propose a method it was as quirky and challenging as everything else he did. Nevertheless, the 'tetrad' has become a useful lens through which to view new media and, if nothing else, it is a good basis to start asking questions.

The concept of a tetrad first appeared in *The Global Village: Transformations in World Life and Media in the 21st Century*, by Marshall McLuhan and Bruce Powers (Oxford University Press, 1989). The book is an attempt to make sense of a world increasingly linked by instantaneous video communication (mainly, in that era, via satellite television).

McLuhan was dissatisfied with traditional media analyses, which did not provide sufficient dynamism, in his view. He proposed an alternative method—which he called 'tetradic analysis'—that did not rely on causal relations but instead offered a way to perceive the 'resonances' between effects (see Figure 3.2). The approach called for creating a 'tetrad' (four sides) comprised of explorations of four questions:

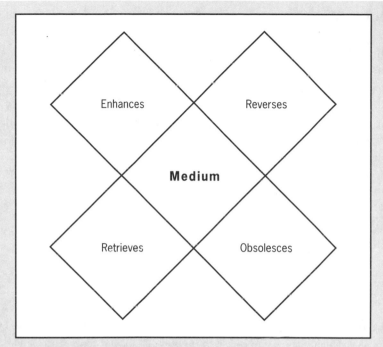

FIGURE 3.2 McLuhan's Tetrad
Source: Wikipedia, http://en.wikipedia.org/wiki/File:MediaTetrad.svg.

- What does the medium enhance or enlarge?
- What does it erode or obsolesce?
- What does it retrieve from the past?
- What does it reverse or flip into when pushed to the limits?

It is important to note that McLuhan believed that these effects were not sequential but simultaneous, in a 'resonant relationship'.[1] In McLuhan's view media forms are extensions of human sensory and expressive capabilities, similar to the way that machines enhance our physical abilities. He described these questions as a tetrad rather than a simple list of 'media effects' to highlight the extent to which they were interrelated and did not have a simple cause and effect relationship.

For McLuhan there were no right answers to the tetrad inquiries. Rather, the concept and its questions were provocations, things to get a discussion going. One of the class activities for this section suggests doing a tetrad analysis on new media (for example the Internet, or mobile phones, or instant messaging). In keeping with McLuhan's view of the usefulness of tetrads, the objective should be to come up with as many possible interpretations for the questions as possible and then discuss the implications of each, rather than seeking to converge on a common interpretation.

Useful Websites

H2O Playlist: Political Economy of New Media
←http://h2obeta.law.harvard.edu/78774→

Compiled by Vincent Reynauld of Carleton University, this is a blog site housed with the Berkman Center for Internet & Society at the Harvard Law School. It has an extensive list of websites, blogs, and other electronic resources relating to political economy and new media.

McLuhan Program in Culture and Technology
←www.mcluhan.utoronto.ca→

This website provides useful resources, and contemporary applications of the work of Marshall McLuhan.

MIT Communications Forum
←http://web.mit.edu/comm-forum→

This website captures many of the leading international contributions on new media, particularly through the papers from MIT's annual Media-in-Transition conferences.

Further Reading

Marshall McLuhan, Douglas Coupland (2010)
This recent biography of McLuhan manages to convey much about his theories in an accessible fashion while fusing a writing style that McLuhan scholars might appreciate. The book is a useful supplement that can be used to better understand the man and his theories, which are enjoying a renaissance of late.

Internet Society, Maria Bakardjieva (2005)
This book provides a comprehensive look at the Internet from a strong 'social shaping of technology' perspective, influenced by critical theory and critical constructivism and with a careful nod to other theories and perspectives. It gives an interesting look into the small details of research and a view on an era (the early days of home Internet use) that has been almost forgotten.

Under Technology's Thumb, William Leiss (2000)
In this wide ranging exploration of technology and its role in society, Leiss probes the power relations behind, implications of, and potential of a technological society. See especially his chapter on the information society, and consider the effects of the rise of social software and tools like Wikipedia on his critique of the information society.

Discussion Questions

1. What has been some of the hype about new media, in terms of the expectation that they are able to change everything, typically for the better? What has some of the counter-hype been?

2. In what ways can identifying the strengths and weaknesses of different approaches to and perspectives on new media bring an understanding of how multiple perspectives/approaches are helpful and when one might, in some cases, be more appropriate or useful than another?

3. What is meant by the term, 'technological determinism' and how is this different from a 'social shaping of technology' approach?

4. Discuss the three-level approach to technology and culture as presented in Table 3.2 on page 61 and the ways in which such an approach can inform your understanding of new media in society and how people engage with new media (or *less* new media, for that matter).

5. In *Being Digital*, Negroponte proclaimed that 'like a force of nature, the digital age cannot be denied or stopped and that it has four very powerful qualities that will result in its ultimate triumph: decentralizing, globalizing, harmonizing and empowering'. What is meant by these four qualities? What are your thoughts on the likening of the digital age to a force of nature that cannot be stopped?

6. Flanagan describes 'a sense of individual empowerment achieved through enhanced agency' derived from recent developments in new media (such as the way in which Web 2.0 users are able to take control over their configuration, use, and re-use of the Internet). Consider both 'empowerment' and 'agency' in this context and discuss.

7. In what ways does the work of Marshall McLuhan and Raymond Williams inform new media studies? Why is it useful to consider the differences between the two?

8. Consider Mosco's description of the 'digital sublime' and discuss how cyberspace possesses not only technical, political, and economic properties, but also how it is a form of cultural myth.

9. What is meant by a 'new empiricism' for new media studies? What are some of the reasons such an approach has been called for?

Class Activities

1. Marshall McLuhan's tetrad of media effects (see case study, above) is a fun way to 'unpack' a new media form. Divide into four groups with your fellow students—one each for obsolesce, retrieve, reverse, and enhance—and come up with an example and/or insight for a series of new media forms. Mobile rich media cellphones, or smartphones, are a good example with which to start.

2. How do you see the Internet today? Discuss how your vision relates to the following quote from Marshall McLuhan (1962): 'The next medium, whatever it is—it may be the extension of consciousness—will include television as its content, not as its environment, and will transform television into an art form. A computer as a research and communication instrument could enhance retrieval, obsolesce mass library organization, retrieve the individual's encyclopaedic function and flip into a private line to speedily tailored data of a saleable kind.'

4 Mobile New Media

Questions to Consider

- In what ways can mobile devices be seen as evolving along the path of earlier technological developments?

- How does the proliferation of mobile devices affect your personal, academic, and/or professional life?

- What are your thoughts on the debate about whether or not dependence on mobile devices (and other new media technologies) has resulted in an unhealthy relationship to these technologies (as suggested by the term, 'crackberry')?

- Are you aware of ways in which mobile phones and networks, like many telecommunication undertakings, are seen as part of the national interest of a country, taking on a national character or receiving special treatment within a home country?

Chapter Outline

Mobile technologies, including but not limited to cell phones, are a vital and important part of new media today. In this chapter we explore the mobile phone and related technologies, such as the tablet computer and netbook, from an historical, technological, and economic basis. Some of the key features of mobile phones are explained and examined with an eye to making this sometimes mysterious technology more accessible to the reader. We also look at how social software such as Facebook or Twitter is deployed on mobile devices, and the implications of location on these services. We examine, as well, some of the cultural impacts (for example on children) as well as social, health, and environmental issues, including surveillance implications.

Many Kinds of Mobile

If this chapter were being written even a few years ago, it would have focused on the mobile phone, perhaps with special emphasis on the **smartphone** (a category of mobile phones that read email, take pictures, and surf the Internet in addition to making and receiving calls). There are now, however, many new media devices that either are not a phone at all—e-book readers, such as the Kindle, for example—or are so multifaceted it is difficult to consider them solely as phones. With the addition of the tablet computer, what has become increasingly significant is not a particular type of device, but rather, the ways of interacting that are now possible while people are away from their homes and offices.

In earlier work on mobile and wireless communication (see, for example, Gow and Smith: 2006) the distinction between 'mobile' and 'portable' seemed important. A phone was mobile because it could be used while the user was moving, in contrast to a laptop, which was portable, since the user could not be mobile when connecting to a network (even a wireless network). This distinction, too, is eroding, as a growing number of laptops offer 3G (and beyond) connectivity, which works while the user is moving. In fact, a growing number of automobile companies provide the ability for cars to be a mobile 'hot spot', specifically to enable the use of computers while driving (presumably by the passengers).

For these reasons this chapter focuses on 'mobile new media' and not mobile phones or even smartphones. It is useful, however, to first consider the origins of the mobile phone in order to better understand where this technology has been and where it may be in the future. As with all aspects of technology in society, with mobile new media there is a surprising amount of path dependence at work whenever things change. That is, technological developments that occur and the social uses of media that arise from those technologies are influenced and constrained by the path along which they evolved and were used in the past.

The Origins of Mobile Phones

Wireless communication has a significant advantage over wired communication in the fact that—in principle—the people connecting to each other do not need to be anchored to a particular place and further, they do not even need to know the precise location of each other. In the early days of radio telegraphy, as Marconi was building his business and finding it difficult to compete with wired telegraphy on land, he took advantage of the limitations of the technology by targeting the ships at sea market. Ships at sea certainly could not be reached by wire and they were large enough to carry the heavy equipment needed to generate the power for a radio signal by the spark method used in the day. Also, because ships carried large quantities of valuable cargo (people and goods), ship owners were inclined to pay Marconi's fees for a radio and radio operator. The safety benefits of having a radio on board a ship became clearly evident when the *Titanic* struck an iceberg and the radio operator was able to call for help.

As discussed in the chapter on the history of new media, radio communication advanced over the course of several decades, including voice communication and better sound quality from less expensive and smaller receivers. Most radio development focused on the broadcasting business model, in which there is one powerful transmitter and many inexpensive receivers. Few people, aside from hobbyists and the military, engaged in transmission and receiving. Gradually, however, the benefits of a mobile two-way communication method expanded from the early niche communities into the business sector. Size and expense remained problems, so the initial portable radio systems were built into vehicles, but by the time of the Second World War, a hand held two-way radio—the walkie talkie—was on the market (Agar 2004; Gow and Smith 2006).

This type of radio had a significant disadvantage for business users, however: it was severely constrained by limited capacity in the system and it was unreliable for calls that went beyond the local area. Capacity problems had plagued radio systems since the earliest days, as the electromagnetic spectrum is very much a shared resource. One way to understand the shared **electromagnetic spectrum** is to imagine it like the water in a lake: radio waves are like waves in the lake and excessive use makes it difficult to know which waves belong to whom; they can become confused or even cancel each other out.

In order to cope with radio interference problems, governments around the world agreed to certain standards relating to the power and frequency of transmissions. These agreements were settled in the early part of the twentieth century (and have been revised every few years at World Radio Congress meetings). As a result, in a typical city, the likely place where a business user might want a two-way radio connection, it was (and continues to be) extremely difficult to get a licence. In New York City in the 1950s and 1960s the waiting list to have a mobile radio-telephone numbered in the thousands; and this was for a service that was very limited by today's standards, as it only worked in a vehicle and in the city where the licence was purchased.[1] The service did have one significant advantage, however: it was connected to the regular phone system, so it could be used to make a call to a telephone.

The solution to the problem of too many people and not enough capacity lay in a radio system design called a **cellular** system, so named because the service is divided into small hexagonal units that look like cells, or perhaps a honeycomb, with a radio tower at the intersections pointing in three directions (see Figure 4.1).

The design of the cellular system was deliberately low-powered. Earlier radio telephones had been built on the same model as the radio broadcasters: a single tall tower was built, reaching the whole city, and every radio would transmit back to the tower. This kept tower building expenses down, but it also drastically limited the number of two-way connections, since each call required a channel or a bit of the radio spectrum that was licensed from the government.

The cellular system was different. Rather than trying to build a radio system that could reach people no matter where they were in the city, the cellular system was deliberately low-powered so that radio frequencies could be re-used over and over again. Instead of one large tower, the cellular system used many little towers that would cover very small areas. The design of the cellular radio system was developed in the 1940s by an engineer at Bell Telephone Laboratories[2] but the first cellular telephones did not arrive until the 1980s. This development may seem to have taken a long time; however, while cellular telephony is elegantly simple in theory, it is incredibly complicated in practice. As it turned out, creating a telephone that could listen to one tower and ignore the others (and especially one that could switch from one tower to another when the phone was mobile)[3] was a much larger and more complicated task than first anticipated. It was, as it turned out, a task that required very fast computers. In the 1940s those computers did not exist. Even in the 1960s and 1970s the computers with sufficient capacity were much too large to consider putting in a vehicle, let alone give to people to carry in their hands.

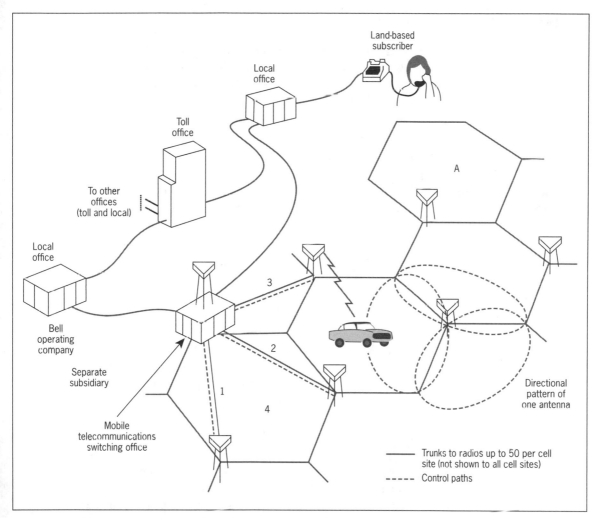

FIGURE 4.1 Advanced Mobile Phone System Service Plan
Source: Adapted from Private Line, www.privateline.com/Cellbasics/AMPSsystemplan.gif.

Gradually, however, the miniaturization of computers resulted in the first cellular telephones (still mounted in cars) and a first boom in sales. Cellular telephone companies soon could be found all over the world, building the devices for both users and operators of cellular telephone networks. These networks got a second boost when hand-held cellular telephones—fondly referred to as 'the brick' in some circles—were made available. These phones were based on an analog transmission and reception technology and as a result were expensive, heavy, and consumed batteries at an alarming rate. The third boost came from digital cell phones, which accomplished the same thing as earlier phones but with far less power and hence smaller size and lower cost. The era of the pocket-sized cell phone, which almost anybody could afford, had arrived.

New Services

With the digital cell phone—called personal communication services or PCS when they were launched in Canada in the mid 1990s—came a number of additional features. At first these features were modest (such as caller identification) and they did not change the user experience in any fundamental way. People still used a mobile phone for the primary purpose of making phone calls. One feature, however, would have an enormous impact from both a business perspective and a social perspective: the short message service (SMS) that is now referred to as **text messaging** or texting (Agar 2004).

The story of how texting came to be added as a feature of mobile phones is an interesting one. According to one of the engineers on the team that worked on the technical specifications of the mobile phone, the initial idea for text messaging was to give the service provider a way to send a message to users, to tell them that they had a new voice mail message, for example (Wray 2002). The decision to allow *users* to initiate messages and send those messages to any other subscriber was (as the story goes) almost an afterthought. What began as an afterthought has become the common practice of texting, as billions of messages are now sent every day (not to mention the billions of dollars they generate for mobile operators) (Katz 2008).

SMS was possible because the terminal device, the telephone, was a kind of special-purpose computer. It had memory, processing power, an input device, and a display. That computing power was needed in order to cope with the challenges of being a mobile device, but once the phone had that computer power, it was reasonable to look at other ways the phone could be used. The phone business then, as now, was intensely competitive and phone manufacturers were always looking for additional ways to attract attention.

SMS was popular because it was, at first, free to use (or at least very inexpensive). Indeed, it seemed economical compared to a high-priced voice call but in point of fact, text messages, at the time of writing, can be very expensive when you compare the price of data in a text message to the price of data in a data plan on a home Internet service or even on a mobile phone, when cost per byte is the deciding factor.[4] Whatever the pricing model, the fact remains that SMS proved to be incredibly popular, especially with young people. This chapter returns later to further discussion about the way in which young people adopted mobile phone technology—first in Northern Europe and then around the world—and how that has changed youth culture, but first, we look at some of the other 'things that are not voice' in a mobile device.

SMS proved not only to be incredibly lucrative in its own right but it also opened the doors to thinking about the mobile phone as a platform for other things. As using text became more popular, people grew to appreciate a larger display, for example. With a larger graphical display came the possibility of non-ASCII (American Standard Code for Information Interchange) text and the opening up of markets outside of Northern Europe and North America. The larger display also enabled games and the phone game era began.

The first game on a mobile phone is widely thought to be 'snake' on a Nokia handset from the early 1990s. According to one industry legend, the designers showed the possible game to their manager who decreed that it would not be included in the phone, but the engineers liked it so much that they added it anyway. While this story may well be apocryphal, it illustrates the extent to which the mobile phone business was driven not only by engineering but also by people (mainly in the Nordic countries of Finland and Sweden) who loved their phones (Ling 2004). The latest features and capabilities were a source of constant discussion among young people, especially employed people in their twenties, who could afford new phones, and people upgraded their phones frequently. A feature like a game also appealed to those who were texting often, since they had their phone in their hand and were looking at it, rather than keeping it in their pocket except when talking (Ito et al. 2005).

From the game that came with a phone when it was purchased, to games that could be installed on a purchased phone (a challenging undertaking, at first), these add-ons were a growing source of revenue for phone companies. In a similar way, competitiveness and a desire to distinguish one phone from another—not to mention the newfound capabilities of memory, computing power, and tone generation to make a game work—led to the practice of building phones with multiple ringtones. The ability to buy and install new ringtones became immensely popular.

For many of these kinds of additional features, SMS was a kind of backbone or enabling technology. A ringtone could be purchased by sending a message. A game could be installed by receiving a special kind of SMS called an MMS (multimedia message) or EMS (enhanced message service). The mobile phone was quickly becoming a multipurpose technology and SMS was acting as the computer network linking phones to each other and to the many businesses trying to reach this market and sell things.

The Internet on your phone

The mobile phone industry grew explosively through the 1990s, just as the Internet was extending beyond government offices and universities and into wider public consciousness. It was clear that these two technologies were going to intersect, but how that was going to happen was not clear at first. Despite the advances in phones made since the early days of analog cell phones, or even the first digital cell phones, mobile devices did not connect to data networks at a very high rate and still had very limited ability to display or process data.

A slight detour: wireless speeds

The simplest radio connection—as Hertz demonstrated more than 150 years ago—is made by creating a spark in one place and detecting that spark in another. The spark creates a disruption across the entire electromagnetic spectrum and contains very little information (other than that a spark occurred and lasted a certain amount of time). This was good enough to get dots and dashes across the Atlantic and to ships at sea but it required a long, slow process of encoding and decoding messages and further, due to interference, was an inadequate way to communicate when there were multiple users needing the airwaves.

One of the key breakthroughs for wireless communication was to create a carrier wave—which is like a single tone in music—and then to encode differences from that wave. There was a double benefit to the carrier wave: (i) it went out on a single frequency (or, more precisely, within a narrow band of frequencies) and others could tune out or tune in; and following from this, (ii) there was an added commercial benefit in that it became possible to have many more radio stations. Of course, the spectrum is not unlimited and not all of it is equally usable, so carrier waves could not solve all capacity problems because it eventually becomes infeasible to use additional frequencies. What then?

Radio operators learned from the telegraph and telephone operators, who faced similar challenges of fitting a growing number of calls into a single wire: the solution was something called **multiplexing**. For the purposes of this chapter, rather than focus on engineering details, consider a simple analogy of a plot of land (from which the goal is to get the greatest possible value). One simple way to increase the capacity of the land is to build many lots on top of each other by building a multi-story building. Each floor can be further subdivided into offices, etc. This is a rough equivalent of the multiplexing process. In the electromagnetic spectrum the techniques of creating these subdivisions are based in software and codes, but the outcome is similar: more useable space/capacity from the same resource. The methods to achieve this are myriad and are growing in complexity and sophistication all the time. All of these things are being done to put more capacity into the airwaves: first to allow additional callers, then to provide a better experience for each caller, and then to add more data for each person with a phone.

Each of these refinements is typically given a technical name and a specification and all of the equipment that is used has to abide by those specifications so that everyone can connect and be understood. When there is a major change in the way that mobile phones work, it is called a 'generation'. The first analog cell phones were the first generation, the first digital cell phones the second generation (or 2G). The current generation is the third and this is why phones are described as 3G phones. Within each generation, there will be refinements and enhancements, especially as one generation approaches the next. The latest enhancement in 3G service in Canada is called 'high speed packet access' (HSPA).[5] The next standard on the horizon is a further refinement, known as LTE, or long-term evolution. LTE is already in operation in a few markets in the world, and is the final bridge before the fourth generation (4G) of mobile communication, which is a fully Internet protocol based network.[6]

Since voice calls have been as good as they need to be for many years (or even decades), most of the recent enhancement efforts have involved building data connections between mobile devices that provide a broadband or high speed experience (and still provide room for other people to use the network), complete with web pages that load quickly, music that arrives in seconds, and video that looks like it does at home or at the office. Prior to the 3G revolution, one of the ways that mobile phone network operators, Internet entrepreneurs, and phone designers tried to bring the Internet to phones was to recreate miniature versions of web pages that were programmed in special languages, with limited amounts of text and graphics (or no graphics at all). These and almost every other attempt to create a simplified, separate Internet for phones proved to be spectacularly unsuccessful and many people wondered if the Internet would ever be available on a mobile phone.

There has been an interesting turn of events, however, spearheaded in part by SMS (of all things). As unlikely as it may seem, the short message service, with its 140 characters and no underline, italics, or bold (let alone graphics), has become one of the dominant ways that people interact with the Internet on their mobile phones. This interaction occurs through intermediaries, however, because the Internet—and the operators of large Internet sites such as Facebook and Twitter—realized the potential of adapting their services to the sending and receiving of SMS, of reaching out to text message users, rather than asking users to reach out to the Internet. So, for example, status updates on Facebook can be made with a text message and alerts from Facebook can be received as simple text messages. The **microblogging** service Twitter is premised on SMS and only offers 140 characters per update, regardless of how the characters are entered. Visitors to the Twitter website get no more space than someone sending a 'tweet' by phone.

From Multifunction Phones to Smartphones

The beginnings of the multifunction or 'feature' phone, with games, ringtones, caller ID, and text messages have already been mentioned. Phone manufacturers did not rest, however, because once they had a device with processor, memory, storage, and user interface, they essentially had the ingredients for a computer and therefore, all of the potential of a computer. Phones have gained the ability to do calculations, maintain address books and calendars, and perform myriad small organizational tasks.

A parallel technology, called the 'personal digital assistant' (PDA), appeared for a short time as though it might take on these sorts of roles, but people quickly tired of yet another gadget in their pockets and purses, and as soon as phones were able to offer those organizational capabilities, interest in PDAs dropped. Small portable game machines mounted a stronger resistance to encroachment by phones. With bright colour displays, graphics processors dedicated to games, and important development resources tied to specific platforms, the Nintendo DS and similar gadgets have continued to do well. That said, mobile phones such as the iPhone have increasingly targeted the gamer with their offerings, their user interface, and their pricing.

As phone usage grows toward unity with population (that is, the point at which every person has a phone) in country after country, the ability of mobile phones to colonize product categories continues unabated. Consider one example: a simple feature that phone designers added very early—time display on the front of the phone—proved to be the death knell for the makers of inexpensive watches. Although watches continue to be sold for older people and as jewellery, many young people have stopped purchasing watches because their phone is their watch, their timer, their alarm clock, and their calendar. It is also, as we will see, their music and video player.

In the past five years mobile phones have moved into the camera and the video recorder market and these are useful examples of how the phone is able to displace better products because the phone is: (i) always in the consumer's pocket; and (ii) much more integrated into the consumer's life. Phone cameras have been steadily improving, and they have begun to approach the features of a dedicated camera but they remain limited. Yet, as the maker of an iPhone app designed to help people with the phone's admittedly limited camera, says:

'The best camera is the one you have with you.' His product, 'The Best Camera', makes some modest improvements to the built-in camera software on the iPhone, but more importantly, it connects the user with a community of photographers who exchange tips and upload pictures into a common space for sharing with others.

These twin capabilities—being always present and being a link to the social use of the technology—are what give mobile phones a key advantage over specific-purpose technologies. These twin capabilities are helping mobile phones become popular devices for recording video and they are even leading users to watch television on their phones. This is not so much because phones perform these functions particularly well, but rather, it is because phones are present and they make it possible for users to share—immediately—what they create, experience, and think.

When Is a Phone No Longer a Phone?

By 2005 a new category of phone was emerging: the phone that included calendar and address book functions, a capable email program, and possibly a camera and a web browser. The so-called 'smartphone' was not for everyone, as it was expensive both to purchase and to maintain. The smartphone depended on a data connection to get onto the Internet and get email, which was very expensive. The larger screen meant that smartphones were bigger, heavier, and ran out of batteries more quickly. Nevertheless, they were popular with business people and politicians. Access to email, in particular, was seen to be essential and a growing number of people became very active users of mobile email, particularly with the ubiquitous BlackBerry devices made by Canadian firm, Research in Motion.

The BlackBerry and similar devices (the Nokia Communicator and E-series phones in Europe, for example) enabled a kind of 'always on' approach to phone messaging, which led to the colloquial term 'crackberry' coming into circulation, drawing a parallel between dependence on drugs and dependence on sending and receiving email at all times of the day or night and in inappropriate times and places. Whether such use constitutes an addiction remains open to debate; however, the growth in non-phone uses of phones, when coupled with the use of a mobile phone as a planner and calendar, as an address and phone book, as a game platform, and as a camera, seemed to herald a transition of the phone from being just a phone to something more like a computer and as a result a 'general purpose technology' (Lipsey et al. 2006).

By 2007 the smartphone had become familiar to most people. It may have been associated with business executives or politicians, but people commonly knew what it was. Those following the technology industry at the time knew that Apple was widely thought to be developing a phone. What Apple would release, however, was not really a phone. Apple had hinted at what they might do with a phone a couple of years earlier when they put a version of iTunes onto a Motorola phone. Apple's iTunes is a software program that runs on personal computers and enables the purchase of music online for playback on computers or Apple's own MP3 player, the iPod. Although the Motorola ROCKR (as it was called) was not much of a commercial success, with it, Apple gave indication of an interest in mobile phones.

As the largest selling gadget on the planet, the mobile phone was both an obvious market for Apple and a threat, since it seemed likely that mobile phones could repeat their colonization of music players, the way they had with cameras and watches. If Apple were to make no attempt to enter the phone market, they would be vulnerable to dwindling returns in the music player market as people began listening to music on their phones. What Apple developed was the iPhone and the iPod Touch, devices similar to each other—especially now that the iPod Touch has a microphone—with a large screen and no keys. Both devices integrate completely with iTunes and all of their features are implemented in software. There are virtually no buttons, aside from a 'home' button, volume control, and on/off, with everything else done by tapping on the screen. These Apple devices have been very commercially successful and—for people who can afford a high-end phone—they have been sought after items for reading email, browsing the web, and talking to people (it is a phone, after all) while moving around.

The key difference between previous smartphones and the iPhone (and iPod Touch), however, is the way that they are integrated into iTunes; in particular, the section of iTunes called, the 'App Store'. Making a clever link to both 'Apple' and 'application', the App Store is the place to go for new iPhone software. Apple recruited and supported—with free development software—an army of software developers in the months leading up to the launch of the iPhone. Further (and perhaps more importantly), Apple agreed to take a modest fee (currently 30 per cent) for retailing the applications created by developers.

Although the App Store and Apple's relationships with its developers have not been without problems since the launch, the overall environment has been spectacularly successful. During Christmas of 2009 Apple announced that more than three billion copies of the 120,000 applications available at the time[7] had been downloaded since the launch on 10 July 2008. That number had grown to over 300,000 by October 2010 and over 7 billion downloads. The number of downloads grows every day and has been such a success that Apple's sales slogan, 'There's an app for that', is widely recognized and poised to enter popular culture.

What Apple has done is redefine the relationship between people and their phone and between people and their phone company. By emphasizing—and delivering on—all the *other* things the phone can do, Apple has created the first example of handheld general purpose technology. Others have quickly followed suit (in particular Google's Android, and the many companies building Android phones) so it is by no means a guarantee that Apple can continue to occupy the position of premiere designer and manufacturer of these mobile new media devices. What they have done, in a way that previous phone developers and network operators were unable to do, is establish a handheld device equivalent to the personal computer. It is a device that takes on a character based on the programs that are loaded into it and is valuable because of that malleability and permutability.

'New' New Media on Phones?

The phrase 'new new media' is courtesy of Paul Levinson, who has written a book by the same name. He takes a stance against calling things Web 2.0 (or 3.0) in favour of the awkward but definitely evocative term 'new new'. In his view, new new media is distinguished from the old media, and even new media, by the ease with which regular folks can participate in the creation of content. Some of these elements are discussed, above, as they relate to mobile phones, particularly the ability of phones to capture sound and video and post updates to sites like Twitter. But what about moving beyond that to something really new, something that could not be done on a regular desktop or laptop computer? What is *really* 'new media' on mobile devices?

One of the most promising—and perhaps over-hyped—technologies to emerge on mobile devices recently is something called **augmented reality**. Augmented reality works by creating an overlay of data on top of what is already visible to the user. Users may be somewhat familiar with this in the form of the 'heads up display' that is featured in movies about fighter pilots or is even now available in some high end cars, pinpointing the location of pedestrians and wildlife through infrared cameras, for example, and projecting them onto the windscreen of the car.

Video and computer game players are familiar with this feature as well, as games commonly have multiple 'gauges' or 'readouts' with important information about what is happening on screen, layered over the action. Sometimes these appear in the lower half of the screen but in many games they float 'above' the screen, augmenting the players' ability by giving instantaneous feedback on the scores and the health and status of the various bits of equipment, monsters, or players that they are controlling, depending on the type of game.

These sorts of augmentations are helpful, however, they do not quite capture the full capability of an augmented reality application on a smartphone. Consider the following example: Imagine that you are walking in an unfamiliar city, unsure of the directions to the nearest coffee shop, or perhaps you'd like to know which of two coffee shops is best. You can, with the appropriate application on your phone (and restaurant recommendations are one of the first places this has been used, as it turns out), flip open your device, launch the application and then look at the places you were considering through the lens of your camera. As the coffee shop comes into focus, comments about it float into view. You can also receive coupons from the shop itself or even access a database that reveals its last health inspection report. More importantly—and this is particularly 'new new' for phones—you can add your own comments if you choose to do so. Your comments 'stick' to that place, courtesy of geographic encoding, image recognition, computer databases, and the wireless networks linking them together. A free application, called 'Wikitude', is available for iPhones and enables this type of interaction with locations and information.

This kind of augmenting of reality is particularly attractive not only to retailers but also for municipalities that might use it for a 'report a pothole' application, or to museums that might use it for guides; indeed any number of still-unthought of public service uses. The key aspect of this is people's interest in—and willingness to—create content and share it online. YouTube and similar sites have shown that user-generated content is enormously popular. Augmented reality applications on mobile phones provide a way to anchor those contributions in space and time and to do so in a way that creates value for people at the moment in which they need information or have some information to share.

Spime, anyone?

Anchoring things in space and time is the responsibility of a whole new range of devices, which science fiction writer Bruce Sterling terms **spime** (Sterling 2005). The term is a blend of 'space' and 'time' and thus devices which exhibit the ability to locate themselves in space and time are spime. These devices seem like the furthest thing from new media since they are often just a 'dumb sensor' or even just a 'Radio Frequency Identification' (RFID) chip that responds with a unique number when it receives a specific radio frequency signal (much like a bell rings in a specific tone when struck).

Rather than dismissing spime as dumb objects, however, it is better to see them as a component of a much larger network that—when working together with all the other components—enables considerable elegance and elaboration (just as the cells in the human body combine to create each unique person). Spime in a user's shoes might connect to spime in their music player to allow the user to run with an inspiring sound track that is responsive to his or her running pace or location (accelerating up a long hill or easing off before returning home, for example). Upon returning home, spime could help in logging a user's runs or to compare statistics, set goals, or track progress in a global database of runners. All of this is not achieved solely by any one component part, and many of them operate completely without user interface, but the combination offers a richer, more elaborated, more interactive experience. Already we are seeing examples of this type of system design, both at the level of manufacturing and distribution and in consumer goods. Many running shoes, for example, come equipped with the Nike+ system, which works with your iPod to enable the running scenario described above. Representatives from Ericsson, a designer of mobile telephone infrastructure, noted that machine-to-machine communication driven by devices such as spime would be the leading driver of mobile connections by 2020, with 50 billion devices connected according to their estimates.

> Machine-to-machine communications, or M2M, will be a key component in the future growth of the mobile industry. For energy companies it could be smart meters that read themselves, increase business efficiency and cut operational expenses. In transportation—tracking solutions improve route optimization and safety for vehicles on the road. Digital signs that can be updated remotely, cameras that can send pictures halfway around the world and even a soda machine that requests restocking when needed are other examples that machine-to-machine technology make possible. (Anonymous 2010)

Kids on Phones

Back in the 1980s and 1990s, mobile phones—expensive, unwieldy, and restricted to workmanlike tasks—were associated almost exclusively with business and government. This changed in the twenty-first century (even earlier in Asia and Europe) as mobile phones evolved and became more affordable. As a result, they have reached a very high level of popularity with young people. This shift is unsurprising: As a group, young people value privacy and independence and are very likely, if given a new device with unexpected capabilities (such as text messaging), to quickly figure out how to use that capability to maximum advantage.

North Americans (and especially Canadians) have seen broad adoption of mobile phones by young people in the last decade. Adoption was slow at first compared to elsewhere in the world, perhaps related to the high prices in Canada, incompatibility between the text messaging systems of the major providers prior to 2002, and the fact that landlines were widely available, with many homes having a 'teen line' as a second phone line. Young people in other parts of the world, in contrast, were early adopters of the technology. Telephone companies facilitated this process with pay as you go plans, inexpensive basic phones, and low prices for text messages. Young people quickly adopted this technology as a way to get in touch and stay in touch, arranging social events, romantic contact, and even arranging homework (and sometimes cheating) via their mobile phones. Although Canada continues to lag other developed (and even many developing) countries in mobile phone adoption, in the last five years Canadians, especially young Canadians, have begun to resemble mobile phone users in the rest of the world, using the mobile as their only telephone and sending billions of text messages.

Children in some cultures, like Korea and Japan, found in the mobile phone a tool for liberation from their parents (Ito, Okabi, and Matsuda 2005) and several writers have gone so far as to consider mobile phone use as part of a revolution in youth culture (Ahonen 2000). The phone has brought mobility to young people, it has contributed to a 'last minute arrangements' orientation, and it has fostered entire linguistic genres and shorthand. Youth slang—or slang among any subgroup, for that matter—is nothing new, but some of the abbreviations adopted in text-speak have migrated into the wider culture and have spread around the world.

Slang is not just a way of keeping messages private from parents, it also allows a form of ad hoc compression, allowing more information to fit into the limited space of a text message. Text slang also aids speed of composition, since messages (especially in the early days) are often composed on the traditional telephone keypad. Early mobile phones did not even have a text expansion capability as is now common on phones (for example, the T-9 system) and as a result, some of the best phone typists still do not use **predictive text**, preferring the old fashioned method.

Although there have been periodic alarms raised that typing short messages full of abbreviations would lead to the downfall of the English language and the inability of the youth of today to make themselves understood, research on the topic has not been definitive and several studies report exactly the opposite: that texting is writing, at least, and encourages people to both read and write. Most students understand the difference between texting and term papers.[8]

The impacts flow both ways, of course. Youth adoption of mobile phones may have been unanticipated at first but both system operators and manufacturers were quick to act upon the perceived needs and interests of young people and provided plans and handsets that suited these new consumers. In this sense the role of youth in the evolution of mobile phones and mobile carriers can be seen as a signal example of the social shaping of technology discussed in Chapter 3.

Other concerns related to texting include health effects ('texter's thumb'), disruption of sleep patterns (staying up late, being interrupted while sleeping by a phone beeping with a new text), contact with inappropriate or undesirable friends, cheating on tests, and the expense, especially when young people who are on a plan that is paid for by their parents go over the limit and incur large bills. As the trend for younger and younger children to have a cell phone continues, inevitably there are some times that children do not fully comprehend the implications and power of the device in their hands (indeed, the same could be said for adults).

While parents are concerned about how the phone might harm their children, the parents are also the ones who are making the purchasing decisions and paying the bills (especially for younger children). It gives parents peace of mind to know that their child could call them whenever required, especially given the declining number of pay phones. Texting also provides a way for children and parents to break through the voicemail wall when parents (or teens) are at work. Parents find that texting, something they might rarely do with friends and colleagues, is an easy way to stay in touch with children. While it is difficult to tell if the technology is feeding on or fuelling the need that parents have to hover over their children, cell phones are definitely implicated in the 'helicopter parents' phenomenon. It is of little surprise, then, that an entire category of kids' phones and kid plans for those phones have been developed by telephone companies eager to serve every niche in the market.

The Business of Mobility

Mobile phones and networks (and other mobile devices, discussed later in the chapter) are big business by any measure. Recent data suggest there are over 5 billion lines in operation world-wide, with some countries approaching 130 per cent penetration rate.[9] In other words, many people have multiple mobile phone lines. With an increasing use of mobile devices for security services, car safety systems, and the like (see spime, above), it is not hard to imagine the numbers going even higher.

Mobile networks are considered —like many telecommunication undertakings—part of the national interest of a country and often take on a national character or receive special treatment within their home country. Mobile networks are inevitably involved in multiple aspects of public safety and even national defence, from the 911 phone call, to the construction of regional and national data networks managing the operations of police and security forces. These networks, therefore, are often regulated, employing large unionized workforces, with close ties to other strategically important industries, such as microelectronics, electronics, software, and computing.

If considering Canada, for example, the mobile device in the pockets of many Canadians could very well have been made by a Canadian company, as one of the leading manufacturers of smartphones is Research in Motion (RIM), of Waterloo, Ontario. RIM is the maker of the famous BlackBerry (so well loved by Barack Obama that he had special steps taken to ensure that he could still use his as President of the United States). At present there are no other Canadian manufacturers of cell phones. Other North American players in the industry include Apple (of California) and Motorola (of Illinois). The other large players are Nokia (Finland), SonyEriccson (Sweden/Japan), LG and Samsung (from Korea), and HTC from Taiwan (maker of the Nexus One, the 'Google Phone').

Of these, Nokia is by far the largest in terms of total units shipped worldwide, employees, and revenue. Nokia may be the largest but it has had some difficulty competing in the smartphone category—the fastest growing and most prestigious—and this is remarkable because Nokia more or less defined the category with its Communicator and N-Series phones. It is unlikely that Nokia will disappear in the near future and their importance on a global level, given the number of people who cannot afford a fancy smartphone, can be expected to remain for some time yet.

Mobile phones would be of little use without a **network operator**, however. Just as a home telephone does not work unless it is plugged into a phone jack in the wall, the modern mobile phone is dependent on a network. Until 2009, there were the 'Big Three' in the cell service in Canada: Telus, Rogers, and Bell. Each also has a subsidiary discount brand that they use to give themselves increased access to the market. So, for example, Telus owns Koodoo, Rogers owns Fido, and Bell operates the Virgin brand under licence from Virgin in the UK. Those living in Manitoba or Saskatchewan may also have access to MTS Mobility or SaskTel Mobility.

These large companies have recently been joined by a group of newcomer companies, the most well-known of which is WIND Mobile. Another (called Mobilicity) launched in 2010. These new companies are part of a group operating on new electromagnetic (radio) spectrum licences that were auctioned off in 2008 with regulatory preference given to new entrants, virtually ensuring that some of the spectrum would go to new companies. This strategy of encouraging new entrants has been pursued in the past by the Canadian regulators: when the first digital cell phone licences (PCS) were allocated, preference was also given to new companies. Of the two that actually launched a service, Clearnet was purchased by Telus and folded into their existing service, and Fido was purchased by Rogers and kept alive as a parallel and complementary brand. It is too early to see if a similar fate awaits WIND, Mobilicity, and the others.

A cell phone company provides service to end consumers both through monthly plan and pre-paid (pay as you go) options and to business customers (typically, large accounts, who pay on a monthly basis). Phone costs may be subsidized in order to entice users into signing longer contracts (typically two or three years), during which time the phone will be locked to the carrier from which it was purchased. Until recently there were some fundamental technical differences between the network operated by Telus and Bell (which used a CDMA network, referring to the kind of division scheme used for handling multiple calls within a single frequency; see above for our description of multiplex) and that of Rogers/Fido (which used GSM). At present all three of the big companies in Canada use a GSM-based system and even the new entrants are using a compatible system. In theory, users can roam from one network to another, although agreements are not in place in all cases.

Service from a mobile carrier typically includes the purchase of a service bundle with a certain number of minutes of voice calls, some text messages, and (perhaps) some Internet/data access. A bundle, before taxes, can range from $15 to $50 per month for a typical consumer. Another $30 or more would include added data features such as email and web browsing. If users exceed the amount they have paid for, extra charges are applied, by the minute, by the message, or by the megabyte. These overage charges can be quite high.

Mobile companies in Canada build their own radio towers and maintain their own links back to switching, interconnection (to phones from other companies), and billing operations. There is some tower sharing and the regulator has mandated that, in future, towers be shared equitably in order to lessen the proliferation of towers and to ensure that the newcomers are able to build their networks in a reasonable length of time. Roaming agreements are similarly mandated to ensure that a new company does not have to build a whole country-wide network just to get started. Any use of a competitor's tower or network, of course, has to be paid for by the newcomer. In other countries towers are actually a separate business and mobile operators typically just lease space on the towers. There is some concern that this practice has been limited in Canada in part to make it harder for new entrants in the Canadian market (see Townsend 2004).

The mobile phone industry is represented by the Canadian Wireless Telecommunications Association (CWTA). The CWTA publishes industry statistics regularly, as does Statistics Canada. The box below offers some details on the size of the industry in Canada.

The Mobile Phone Industry in Canada

- Wireless communications generate a total economic value of some $39 billion for the Canadian economy.
- Canada's wireless carriers invest more than $1 billion in mobile phone communications infrastructure each year.
- The members of CWTA pay licence fees in excess of $150 million each year—more than two-thirds of the total fees collected by Industry Canada from all spectrum users.
- Over 294,000 people are employed in Canada as a result of the wireless industry. The wireless sector offers high value employment—it has an average salary level of $59,000, compared to a Canadian average salary of $42,640.

- Wireless phones are among the fastest growing consumer products in history.
- At the end of December 2009, Canadian wireless phone subscribers numbered 22.8 million.
- 75 per cent of Canadian households have access to a wireless phone.
- Canadians send 122 million text messages per day.
- Each year, Canadians place more than 6 million calls to 911 or emergency numbers from their mobile phones.
- Wireless revenues in Canada totalled $15.9 billion in 2008.
- Half of all phone connections in Canada are now wireless.

Source: The Canadian Wireless Telecommunications Association, www.cwta.ca/CWTASite/english/industryfacts.html.

What Matters with Mobile?

Although the mobile phone industry is large, it is changing rapidly and with these changes there are also significant challenges ahead. The remainder of this chapter examines some of those changes, issues, and why mobile is important to society in Canada and elsewhere.

Probably the most notable shift in mobile phones from a new media perspective is that just as the mobile phone is becoming a full player in the new media space, by virtue of its user interface and ability to display and record full motion video and audio, it is also being joined by an army of other mobile devices. One category of these new devices includes a crop of special purpose products that are wirelessly enabled, such as game players and e-book readers. In another category are laptop and netbook computers that have either built-in or plug-in cellular data connections, which make them not only portable but, in fact, truly mobile. Some of the devices that appeared to be under threat by mobile phones—cameras, in particular—are getting wireless capability either built in or through memory cards with WiFi capability. The tablet computer is even more flexible and appears poised to compete significantly with the phone, the laptop, and e-book readers. The distinguishing feature of phones—the ability to make high quality voice calls—is being usurped by many of these other devices, now able to make voice and video calls through services such as MSN and Skype.

The former dividing line between mobile and portable—a mobile being something you could use as you move around, and a portable being something you can move around and then use—is being broken down by a combination of ever-spreading wireless local area networking, via WiFi and the growing availability of mobile hotspots on planes, trains, and even automobiles. These hotspots gain Internet access through some other technology, such as satellite or wide area wireless (for example, WiMAX) or just the local 3G telephone data networks, then redistribute it via a local area network (LAN) that is wireless and mobile.

The net result is an interesting combination of blurred lines (increased mobility for previously generic and non-mobile computing devices and increased capabilities on mobile devices like iPhones and Android devices) with sharp lines drawn by the addition of wireless Internet access to very specialized devices like home audio equipment, e-book readers,[10] cameras, bedside clocks, televisions, and a vast array of sensor devices.

Health implications

In these turbulent market conditions, there are significant controversies related to the health, environmental, and social and cultural impacts of any new technology. Wireless and mobile devices such as smartphones are implicated in a variety of health concerns. Because of the nature of the electromagnetic energy used for almost all consumer technologies—it is very weak and non-ionizing—there is little in the way of a proven link to direct health impacts on humans. In other words, if there is harm being done (which is not at all clear), the mechanism of that harm is unknown.

On the other hand, because so many people use wireless mobile devices and use them so heavily and from such an early age, the companies that manufacture and regulate these devices would be sensible to take a prudent approach. Concerns about the health impacts of mobile devices have prompted numerous studies and a review of those studies was completed by the Royal Society of Canada in 1999. Their conclusion reflected the findings of most of the science that has been done on mobile technologies over the past couple of decades: there is minimal risk.[11] Nevertheless, health concerns persist and new studies may yet support a more restrictive use of these technologies. For those who are concerned, the general advice is to limit use, to use a (wired) headset, and to consider texting rather than talking.

Surprisingly, the most significant vector of harm from the use of mobile devices is not the radiation, but rather the tendency of mobile devices to divert users' attention from what they are doing while using a mobile device (driving, walking, etc.). A recent US study linked mobile phones—texting or talking—to an astonishing 28 per cent of all traffic accidents. These findings include more than just vehicles: evidently people also bump into things or even walk into traffic or fall into holes when texting while walking. A growing number of jurisdictions now ban the use of mobile phones while driving or at least restrict use by requiring a headset.

A secondary area of concern—although not something about which any direct health linkage has been proven—is the impact of cell phone towers on people living nearby. In Canada, as in many other countries, decisions about the sites of cell phone towers is a nationally regulated and mandated undertaking and when a tower is planned for a sensitive area—such as near a school—people in the area quite often object strongly. In most cases these objections can be overcome through moving the tower, but there have been cases where issues related to cell phone towers have caused considerable anxiety and threats of lawsuits due to perceived health risks.

Since a physiological link is difficult to identify at the low power that mobile devices use, it is quite challenging to find evidence of how harm may be occurring and so far the only way to study these sorts of issues has been through indirect means. These have typically been population health measures, which look for statistically significant increases in health concerns across a broad spectrum of people over a long period of time. The problem with evaluating these studies is that there are so many other variables (work, home, diet) that can affect human health that it is difficult to identify correlations if they are at low levels. It is not surprising that this is also an area for considerable amateur opinion and conjecture, which does not tend to include sound, scientific research.

Environmental concerns

Mobile phones are implicated in an array of environmental concerns, many of which are linked to health issues. These span a considerable range and include direct and indirect impact. At one level, mobile technologies factor in an ongoing erosion of the aesthetic aspects of the environment, both natural and human-made. Despite the best efforts to disguise the towers that bristle from the top of almost every major building in an urban area, they can be seen as detracting from the horizon, the skyline, and even the building design envisioned by an architect. Yet, since many of the people that those towers hope to reach with their signals are on the ground, the antennae have to be visible, for the most part.[12] The towers are even more obtrusive outside of urban centres, despite some attempts to camouflage them as faux trees or church steeples.

Cell phone and other radio towers also have an impact on wildlife, especially birds, which become entangled in wires or confused by blinking lights (or to a lesser extent, electrocuted in power supply circuits). Cell phone antennae are somewhat less prone to these things as they are not as large as the old TV and AM/FM towers, but in rural areas cell antennae are typically affixed to tall towers (sometimes abandoned radio and television broadcast towers) and in these situations they are disruptive to the local and migrating bird populations.

While the harm done to natural and architectural beauty, as well as wildlife, should not be underestimated, by far the most serious impact of mobile phones comes from their impact on the soil, water, and air, due to the manufacture and disposal of the devices. Mobile phones have a considerable environmental impact in this regard for a host of reasons. These include:

- Mobile phones include electronic components manufactured from rare earth elements, which are sourced in so-called conflict zones and as such subject to significant concerns regarding human rights and environmental regulation in the mining process.
- Mobile phones are made in factories all over the world and as such have a very high carbon load in the form of transport energy that goes into moving parts to factories and finished products to customers.
- Manufacturers of mobile devices have moved increasingly toward a fashion mentality in which phones are an element of style and are replaced (sometimes more than once a year) for reasons that go well beyond functionality or features. And, of course, the features change regularly in any case. This means more phones, more components, and more transportation than would otherwise be necessary.
- The eventual disposal and (hopefully) recycling of mobile phones is not only at a very early stage in most countries, but it is difficult, dangerous, and dirty work that is inevitably farmed out to people in developing countries, if it is done at all. If not properly disposed of, the phone enters the waste stream, where it has not (until recently) been well designed for biodegrading.
- Even during use there are environmental implications. Mobile phones are typically plugged in at night and sit all night in a charger, when they probably only need an hour or two at most. The charger itself is typically left in the wall, consuming power even when not charging the phone. The wasted energy is considerable and has prompted European governments to issue new regulations for the design of cell phone chargers.

Almost all of the concerns linked to mobile phones or wireless devices generally have to be viewed in light of the fact that these are devices that—in a very short time—virtually every person on the planet may well be carrying. Even though mobile devices are small, they do, in their ubiquity, have a significant impact on the environment.

Social and cultural impact

One further area of concern for those looking at the impact of mobile phones and other wireless technologies on society are the social and cultural impacts. Some of these are common to new media generally and apply to both wired and wireless activities in society, and others are specific to mobility.

The impact on youth and youth culture has already been mentioned but this bears repeating because the increased independence and autonomy accompanying mobile technologies has been linked—if only in the popular media—to numerous anti-social trends such as mobs of young people gathering for impromptu events, the spread of sexual communication (sending salacious text messages—'sexting'—or posting nude photos via cell phone camera), or simply as a vehicle for bad manners, cheating, and escaping from school and other responsibilities. Certainly the injuries and deaths resulting from texting while driving have had a disproportionate impact on youth, as well.

Mobile phones are blamed for the erosion of traditional separations between men and women in more traditional societies, which may be less of an issue in Canada than elsewhere but it is a concern in countries that have long kept the sexes apart prior to marriage. While increased freedom might be a concern for some people, the mobile phone is also implicated in some significant declines in freedom.The extent to which parents are able to use mobile phones to keep tabs on their children was noted earlier. This phenomenon has a much more significant impact on a global basis because of the general surveillance capabilities that mobile phones enable (see Chapter 10 for more on surveillance and new media). In part this is because of cell technology: cell phones are effectively mini tracking devices, by design. In order to create a system that was manageable in terms of completing and charging for calls, the designers of cellular phone services have to know where the phone is and what it is doing. In fact, cell phones engage in a constant silent dialogue whenever they are powered up. They send out a short, silent, pulse of code to the cellular network, and receive back a code. That code contains the cell phone number and it is duly entered into a database, along with the tower that received the best reply. When a call comes into the system for that phone—whether from another mobile phone or from a land line—the location is looked up in the database and the ring is sent out to the cell where the mobile phone last checked in. That incoming call is then completed (assuming it is answered) and another set of entries is posted in the database—the start of the call, the end of the call, and who called whom. This information is not specifically designed for surveillance, but rather, it is part of a billing system. But it is a very useful tool for both law enforcement and government agencies that would like to keep track of people, where they are, and to whom they are talking.

Employees may also be subject to tracking from systems like this, as services exist—most notably in the UK—whereby the phone location can be determined based on a lookup system available through the web. The phone has to have this feature enabled and there is a cost for lookups, but in a workplace scenario these requirements are readily turned into requirements of the job: to keep the phone with you and keep it turned on. The delivery person or travelling salesperson who diverges from a known route can be called to account or, in a less sinister use, would be dispatched as the nearest person who could provide service (e.g., for a taxi or repair).

Being constantly connected—even when location is not part of the reported information—affects a vast number of people, who increasingly use a smartphone or laptop as a way of keeping in touch with things at the office. This can lead to the feeling that work is becoming all pervasive, invading personal lives, and vice-versa. This kind of impact, as Ladner notes, is not strictly an outcome of the technology but is also part of the social relations and expectations of the workplace (Ladner 2008).

Other uses of these tracking systems include locating people in emergencies. These situations may happen when individuals are away from home, making it difficult to dispatch emergency services to an unfamiliar location. Again, the cell tower information (especially when combined with information from other towers that might be slightly further away, but can sense a signal) will allow for pinpointing a phone (and user's) location for fire, ambulance, or police. In Canada this is called Enhanced 911 or E911.

Case Study: Canada's Smartphone: The BlackBerry

The BlackBerry—a smartphone made by Research In Motion (RIM) from Waterloo, Ontario—is a major player in the global market for advanced wireless devices. Having a long association with the University of Waterloo, the company has been expanding its offerings and capabilities since its first products—digital sync devices for film and then two-way pagers—back in the late 1980s.[13] Since then, RIM has continued to hold their ground in the face of considerable competition from Apple's iPhone, myriad Android devices (powered by Google's Android operating system), and of course, industry leader Nokia's line of smartphones.

The BlackBerry is in many ways the quintessential smartphone. First, it combines a number of functions (such as a camera, a personal digital assistant, and a GPS) that once required additional devices. The result is not just convenience for individuals but a social impact as more and more people have these capabilities with them all the time. As well, BlackBerrys are connected to the Internet via a data network and thus connect the user to a global network in a way that less advanced phones—even those with text messaging—did not ever achieve because of the high cost of international calls and texts. BlackBerry Messenger, which is included for free with the phone, also includes free picture messaging, an added cost feature on a regular cell phone. Although the BlackBerry app store, known as 'App World', is not nearly as well populated as the Apple or even Android app stores, it contains a broad range of solutions and coverage in all major categories.

Overall, the BlackBerry displays the three features—capabilities, connectivity, and extensibility—that combine in smartphones to make them a key player in the social media revolution of the twenty-first century. Applications for social media tools such as Facebook, Twitter, Foursquare and Flickr provide the means for rapid creation and sharing of content from the hand held device.[14] This capability is proving to be enormously popular and smartphone sales are growing rapidly: 23 per cent in 2009 alone (Ahonen 2010).

That a Canadian company is a major player in this realm is perhaps a surprise, but we might remember that the largest manufacturer of mobile phones also comes from a northern country with a small population. Finland, home of Nokia. Also, although Nortel has all but disappeared in the wake of its 2009 filing for bankruptcy, Canada does have a long tradition of excellence in telecommunications, and wireless technologies in particular. In fact, in the early days of RIM, when they made wireless two-way pagers, one of their major competitors was Glenayre Electronics, of Vancouver. Proximity to and connections with the University of Waterloo[15]—both founders are alumni—has no doubt also led to some of the strength of their technology offerings.

Research In Motion did not start in the mobile telephone business. In fact, their first unit with voice capabilities did not come until 2002 (the breakthrough 5810 model). Their email device—the first BlackBerry—was tightly integrated to corporate email systems (it arrived prior to widespread use of email in the general population) and offered the speed and security that big corporations demanded. It became so popular in government, industry, and business circles that it garnered the name 'crackberry' in reference to its purportedly addictive properties. Sweeny describes the extensive use of the BlackBerry in the corporate and government world:

> Today the BlackBerry monopolizes the world of work—nobody else comes close. An astounding 85 percent of public corporations are supplying staff with the devices, and more than 175,000 BlackBerry Enterprise Servers are installed worldwide. The US Congress was RIM's first big client,

and Uncle Sam is still the biggest consumer of BlackBerrys. Today, more than 500,000 devices are installed in every department of the US government and throughout the US Senate and House of Representatives. (2009:2)

Although Research In Motion became embroiled in some high-profile patent litigation—most notably a suit with patent-holding corporation, NTP, which resulted in a judgment of $23.7 million that was then appealed only to be settled years later for more than USD $670 million—RIM has continued to expand its offerings and market share, even as Apple's iPhone has taken over the lion's share of 'cutting-edge' notoriety. Perhaps most surprising of all, the BlackBerry's image as a business phone has been expanded, with the result that they are increasingly popular among younger people, who appreciate the ability to create and consume large numbers of text messages. In this regard, BlackBerry has another advantage over other mobile device manufacturers that typically do not supply any infrastructure software. As with the integration tool for corporate email systems (BlackBerry Exchange Server), there is a separate—and free to the user—messaging platform, called BlackBerry Messenger (BBM). The software comes pre-installed on most new BlackBerrys and has been a surprise hit among certain groups of young people especially, who are sometimes burdened by expensive text messaging bills. Another feature—anonymity—has been proving popular in countries where pre-marriage conversations between men and women is discouraged. BBM has provided a safe and untraceable way of connecting with others, as BBM messages are not linked to your phone number.

The privacy provisions go even further than that, and with even more serious national security and crime implications. BlackBerry's enterprise services provide for user-created encryption keys with the result that snooping on email passed through the system is not possible, even with the cooperation of RIM or the telecommunications provider. The Indian government, in 2008, delayed approval of sales of BlackBerry services by telecommunications company Tata on the basis that they would not be able to monitor email sent through the BlackBerry Exchange Server. In 2010 the Indian government threatened BlackBerry, as well as Skype and Google, with exclusion from the Indian market if some sort of back door to their encrypted services was not provided to the security services in that country.[16]

Research In Motion was the fastest growing company in the world in 2009 (according to *Fortune Magazine*[17]) but its stock slumped in early 2010 in the face of fierce competition from Android devices—especially on the Verizon network in the US—as well as the iPhone (Poletti 2010). Still, sales of BlackBerrys remain strong (more than 11 million handsets in first quarter of 2010, compared to 8.75 million iPhones) and the company continues to push forward into touch enabled devices as well as their signature QWERTY style keyboards. With more than 12,000 employees (worldwide) and revenues of almost $15 billion, the company that was briefly in 2007 the most valuable company in Canada[18] remains a significant force in the Canadian technology landscape and a major player in the global smartphone business.

 # Useful Websites

Blogspot
←http://cemore.blogspot.com→

Kingsley Dennis, at the University of Lancashire, keeps this blog up to date with the latest on mobilities, with lots of current events and commentary from an academic perspective. The Centre for Mobilties Research (CeMoRe) studies and researches the newly emerging interdisciplinary field of mobilities: the large-scale movements of people, objects, capital, and information across the world.

Smartmobs
←www.smartmobs.com→

Howard Rheingold started this blog while writing his book of the same name (2004), but the blog continues on and includes both news and commentary about the mobile world, with a strong emphasis on the social aspects of mobile technologies. The website tag line is, 'The next social revolution: Mobile communication, pervasive computing, wireless networks, collective action'.

Open Gardens
←http://opengardensblog.futuretext.com→

Open Gardens is more focused on the mobile and wireless industry than the other two sites listed above, but it provides excellent coverage on a global basis for everything relating to mobile, especially on how the web is mobile and on movements toward a more open mobile environment (in contrast to the largely proprietary mobile landscape we have had up to now).

Further Reading

Mobile Information Society, Gordon Gow and Richard Smith (2006)
The book provides a blend of technical and socio-cultural explanations of mobile technologies that tries to balance the 'how does it work' and 'what does it mean' questions.

Smart Mobs: The Next Social Revolution, Howard Rheingold (2002)
Howard Rheingold was not the first scholar to tackle the social implications of mobile technologies but he brought much greater attention to the topic and provided both a wide ranging and insightful look at trends and issues many years before they were well understood outside of Europe and Asia. The book remains useful

eight years later (see also the website, above, for on-going contributions).

Mobile Nation: Creating Methodologies for Mobile Platforms, Martha Ladly and Philip Beesley (eds), (2008)
This is an edited collection from a conference that brought together Canadian social and technical researchers, with designers, developers, and investors to imagine ways in which they could better connect sociological insight to the commercializers of mobile technologies. It includes contributions from a wide variety of participants and some very interesting and novel research projects.

Discussion Questions

1. In what ways is path dependence evident in the development and social uses of mobile technologies?

2. How did the cellular system present a solution to the capacity problem of earlier radio and telephone systems?

3. What capabilities give mobile phones or mobile general-purpose devices a key advantage over specific-purpose technologies?

4. Several aspects of telecommunications policy are discussed in this chapter. What are these and why are they significant?

5. In what sense was the advent of short messaging service (SMS) an important turn in the evolution of mobile communication?

6. What is the significance of the way(s) in which the operators of large Internet sites such as Facebook and Twitter seized the potential of adapting their services to the sending and

receiving of SMS, of reaching out to text message users, rather than asking users to reach out to the Internet?

7. What are some of the favourable and unfavourable implications of the 'always on' capability of mobile devices? In what ways are these becoming almost default characteristics in personal and professional life, and what are the consequences?

8. Mobile phone use is considered by some as part of a revolution in youth culture. Discuss what this means and in what ways such changes are evident in varying degrees across generational (and/or other demographic) lines.

9. This chapter notes that there are significant controversies related to health, the environment, and the social and cultural impacts of mobile technologies. Discuss these (and any others) and what could be done to address the concerns raised.

Class Activities

1. In small groups with other students, take out your phone and trade it to the person beside you. Take some time to reflect on, and share with the class, how you feel about giving someone else access to your phone. Discuss the implications of such a personal device.

2. Explore the various price plans and services (minutes, texts, data, voicemail, features) both for the mobile device(s) you have and (perhaps) the one you wish you had. What sacrifices do you make, if any, to afford this plan?

3. Break into small groups and create a re-enactment or skit that portrays the many things that people do while they are using their mobile device (for example, consuming other media, eating dinner with family, visiting with friends, driving, etc.). Comment on the implications of this task switching or interruption.

5 Social Networks and Participatory Culture

Questions to Consider

- What does it mean to live in a network society?
- What kinds of issues and questions arise when considering participatory culture?
- In what ways are social capital and social media linked?

Chapter Outline

This is a chapter in two parts. In the first half of the chapter we consider the concept of social networks and how these enable a culture of mass participation—a participatory culture. We also examine how these networks enable and enhance many other social processes. Although networks are not new phenomena, they are enhanced and extended by new media and we explore this process in more detail. Networks are economic and political as well as social phenomena. Given their importance, it is not surprising that new research methods have arisen. One of these, social network analysis, is considered in detail from both a practical and an historical point of view. We will also discuss social network theories, as well as some of the criticism of these theories. In the second part of the chapter we look at social production and the participatory culture that has emerged in social networks, boosted by information and communications technology.

Networking for Fun and Profit

The ability of electronic communication networks to foster collaboration in the production of media has been evident for more than a century. Our earlier discussion of the effects of the telegraph on newspaper chains and news associations illustrates how quickly businesses recognized and capitalized on the ability of networks to reuse materials. Until fairly recently, however, the ability to create and take advantage of networks was limited to professional and commercial settings, due to the high cost and relatively complex nature of the required infrastructure. The computer era has reduced those costs dramatically and in the process has enabled an enormous outpouring and sharing of media works by professional and non-professional users, uploading literally millions of songs, photos, videos, and blogs every minute—thus using the physical, technical networking of modern computers to create intangible networks of shared experience.[1] Computers have also made it possible to more easily study the social connections embedded in those networks ('social networks') and to better understand the power and capabilities that a network makes possible. We will first explore the academic research on social networks and then turn to some of the uses of those networks, in the form of participatory or user-generated media.

The Nature of Networks

Human beings are social creatures and exist in a vast array of social networks including kinship, friendship, neighbourhood, and community. The first electronic networks—the telegraph and the telephone—provided important enhancements to those social networks by speeding up and extending the reach of our connections to one another. As a result, communications networks are a central factor in social theories and particularly social theories of new media. A key feature of networked electronic communication, in contrast with other earlier forms of communication, is the ability to connect, directly, with almost any other person in your various social networks. You do not have to make an appointment or navigate an assistant or servant, in order to send an email. In fact, the telephone was a bit of a shock to nineteenth and early twentieth-century British culture, apparently, because of the possibility that 'just anyone' could call you (Rowland 2006: 127–8). Communications networks are central to the organization and operation of twenty-first century society and culture. The speed and reach of these networks and our ability to reach directly into rules and systems, as we do when we arrange travel by directly accessing an airline database, means that we start doing things without intermediaries, we do things in different ways, and we come to rely on a very tightly coordinated system of interconnected networks.

Computers have propelled networking—in both a communications sense and a social sense—further than might have been imagined in the early days of even the telephone. Of course, social networks are not just a recent phenomenon. In their 2009 book, Christakis and Fowler provide vivid and compelling examples of how social networks result in extraordinary outcomes—good and bad—in the real world, and have done for millennia (Christakis and Fowler 2009: 3–32). But online networks have sped up and expanded these existing social organizations to a degree and breadth previously unimagined (Christakis and Fowler 2009: 253–86).

Elaborating on the link between the Internet and the network as social morphology, Wellman (2001) argues that a computer network is part of our **social network**. Proposing that both individuals and organizations socialize into communities through networks rather than groups, Wellman identifies the many social advantages that the Internet and related ICTs provide for sustaining both geographically specific community ties and enabling new and potentially global networked ties. A key distinguishing feature between a network and a group, in this context, is that in a group everyone knows everyone, but in a network you might "know someone who knows someone". In other words there are indirect connections. These are seen as part of a general process of modernity 'away from place-based inter-household ties [toward] individualized person-to-person interactions and specialized role-to-role interactions' (2001: 231). Finding that 'cyberspace fights against physical place less than it complements it', Wellman observes that the relationship of new media to social networking is that it 'has increased the importance of network capital in the fund of desirable resources, along with financial capital, human capital, and cultural capital' (2001: 247, 248).

The growing importance of computer networks as a part of social networks can be understood from (at least) two angles. One emphasizes the growing significance attached to networks in areas of social, cultural, political, economic, and, indeed, military relations. The other considers how the Internet as a technological form that is fundamentally grounded in networks comes to permeate all aspects of society in terms of the form as well as content of social relations.

Networking, politics, and terrorism

The growing significance of networks to politics has long been documented. It has had clear manifestations since the 1960s in the rapidly declining membership of major political parties, declining participation in electoral politics, and a growing sense of popular alienation from formal political institutions and processes (see e.g. Castells 1998: 342–53). Miller draws attention to the rise of network campaigns pursued by social movements through loosely organized representative agencies and coalitions, outside of traditional political channels, and how this is enabled by new media:

> Network campaigns allow a diverse grouping of organizations and individuals to participate through commitment to a shared purpose, while remaining autonomous individual agents. In this way, it is possible to gain additional leverage over decision-making bodies through the 'multiplier effect' of a coherent message and more efficient deployment of resources and effort, while maintaining the flexibility and energy that more bureaucratic forms of co-ordination tend to squander (2004: 208).

The specific characteristics of network campaigns that generate such advantages include having a shared goal; being 'structure-light'; mobilizing a diverse coalition of skills and resources around shared goals; advanced use of new media technologies; embracing diversity and openness; the ability to draw upon and develop media celebrity; the ability to use media spectacle around specific targets; time-limited strategies; high levels of media visibility; and the ability to act cheaply and quickly (Miller 2004: 208–13).

Miller had in mind network campaigns conducted by peaceful means, such as the Jubilee 2000 campaign for debt-reduction for nations with developing economies or the role played by environmental organizations such as Greenpeace. It is also the case, however, that network strategies are tactics used by terrorist organizations such as al-Qaeda and leaders such as Osama bin Laden.

Al-Qaeda's stated goal of the elimination of Western power and influence from Muslim states would have had peripheral influence on world events had it been conducted solely from the mountains of Afghanistan and northern Pakistan. What has given al-Qaeda its enormous significance in current world events is the alignment of such a goal with aspects of network politics. These include:

- the capacity to use new media to disseminate messages widely to current and potential supporters;

- the high level of visibility attached to events such as the terrorist attacks on the World Trade Center and the Pentagon on 11 September 2001, as well as subsequent terrorist attacks in Bali in 2002, on the Madrid subway in 2004, and the London Underground rail network in 2005; and
- the inherently 'structure-light' nature of this organization, which maintains itself through a dense and seemingly amorphous network of agents and activists.

Al-Qaeda has continued to operate in spite of the massive growth in surveillance in the aftermath of 9/11, the war in Afghanistan to depose the Taliban government, and the war in Iraq. Friel (2002) observes the extent to which bin Laden exemplifies the network logic of developing and running a global organization:

> He decentralized decision-making authority and created a flat management structure to quickly respond to changes in his operating environment. He overcame turf battles by creating an overarching sense of mission and doctrine. He used the Internet and the globalization of news and the revolution in telecommunications to advance his organization's goals worldwide. He developed a complex organizational network in which information gets only to the right people at the right times. In his network, connections between individuals and groups are activated at key times to get work done and severed when they are no longer necessary.

Social Network Analysis

Social network analysis is a methodology developed in the social and behavioural sciences to map interpersonal linkages using statistical and graphical techniques. Wasserman and Faust identify the distinctiveness of **social network analysis** in that 'the social environment can be expressed as patterns or regularities in relationships among interacting units' (1994: 3). Understanding forms of self, activity, and behaviour as being related is fundamental to this approach. Four key elements of social network analysis are identified by Wasserman and Faust:

1. Actors and their actions are viewed as interdependent, that is, formed through relationships to others.
2. Relational ties, or what are referred to as linkages, are channels for the flow of resources, which may be material (capital, commodities, etc.) or immaterial (power, influence, information, etc.) in nature.
3. Network models view the network structural environment as providing opportunities for, or presenting constraints upon, individual behaviour.
4. Network models conceptualize structure (social, economic, political, etc.) as lasting patterns of relations among actors. (1994: 4)

Social network analysis characteristically works from the bottom up, in that it aims to identify relationships that exist in a particular place and time, the mapping of which can

Networks and Organizations

Podolny and Page (1998: 59) observe that 'every form of organization is a network', since the nature of an organization—whether a business or other not-for-profit type of organization—requires ongoing processes of exchange between more than two social actors. At the same time, one of the distinctive features of a social network is a set of ethical orientations around behaviours such as trust, reciprocity, goodwill, and mutual obligation that differ from the contractual nature of purely market-based transactions and the notion of authority that characterize businesses. Moreover, the focus of network analysis is as much on relations between organizations as it is on relations within organizations. Benefits of social network forms of organization include:

- the capacity for collective learning among agents across the network;
- accrual of legitimacy or status for individual agents from being part of a larger network;
- greater adaptiveness to unanticipated changes in the wider socio-economic environment; and,

- minimizing forms of vulnerability arising from resource dependency upon others (Podolny and Page 1998: 62–6).

In considering why the reliance on networking as a basis for an organization's activities will vary, Podolny and Page note three key variables:

- the importance of power relations to the interactions between organizations—the more power is exercised to achieve organizational goals, the less significant network forms will be;
- the age of an organization—older organizations are typically less imbued with a networking culture than newer ones; and,
- national cultural and legal differences—network forms of organization tend to be associated more with collectivist cultures than with more individualistic ones, they are, for example, more characteristic of Asian countries than they are of the US or the UK (Doremus et al. 1998; cf. Hofstede 1980; Podolny and Page 1998: 67–8; Scott 1986).

contribute to wider hypotheses about social structure. Wasserman and Faust identify seven core concepts (1994: 17–21):

1. Actor: an actor is a discrete unit of decision-making and action, which may be an individual, but may also be a corporation, a government agency, or some other form of organization such as an association, a trade union, or a university.
2. Relational ties: this refers to the establishment of links between actors, which can include mutual admiration, shared membership of associations, regular meetings and other forms of communication, movement of actors between places, formal relationships of authority, and biological relationships based upon kinship.

3.   Dyad: this is the information used to establish a relational tie between two actors, so that they can be seen to constitute a pair.

4.   Triad: this identifies probabilities of relationships between three actors based on knowledge of dyadic relationships.

5.   Subgroup: if identification of the existence of dyadic relationships can be established, and these can be triangulated to the potential for triadic relationships, then this will form the basis for the existence of a subgroup of actors.

6.   Group: the group in social network analysis is 'the collection of all actors on which ties are to be measured' (Wasserman and Faust 1994: 19). Such a group should be finite in its nature (i.e. the set of actors involved is already established) and there is a need to establish that these actors constitute a group as a bounded set.

7.   Relation: this refers to the evidence of interaction and relationships among members of the group that indicate both durable ties and the capacity to act in response to a situation in the social environment.

Social network analysis has its origins in the development of the 'sociogram' as a way of illustrating the nature of interpersonal relations within a group. Two of the core elements of what was termed 'sociometry'—as a precursor to social network analysis—were the use of visual representations of group structure, and a probability-based model of structural outcomes.

Another important approach to social networks is the one pioneered by Bruno Latour. Called **actor-network theory**, this approach places not just people in a network but also things. Both ideas and technologies, for example, can be seen as 'actants'. A social network analysis of a network such as Facebook would have to include not just the participants, but the software and servers that enable that network, as well as the concept of a friend as used in that context. Importantly, for actor network theory, these relationships are in a state of constant evolution, being remade each time the actors interact (Latour 2005).

Particular questions within the social sciences and, more recently, theories of the creative economy and creative industries, have acted as trigger points for social network analysis. One long-standing question for social network analysis has been whether it can be used effectively to prove the existence of a ruling class in capitalist societies (what C. Wright Mills [1956] referred to in the American context as a *power elite*). Identifying that there are rich people who derive wealth from the control of economic property is only part of the story; what is required is the ability to demonstrate that such a group may be able to act cohesively and collectively in order to pursue shared interests. Social network research aims to provide this type of evidence, by examining the effects of interlocking corporate directorships and their relationship to other ties, such as those based on corporate share ownership and investment financing. Research on these kinds of questions has been critical in clarifying some of these issues and in establishing points of difference between different capitalist models (e.g. comparisons between the American, Japanese, British, or German models) (Scott 1986, 1991; cf. Stokman et al. 1985).

Researchers are also interested in the linkages that the Internet creates between our various forms of personal or face-to-face social networking using the interconnections established through technology. Wellman's point that 'we find community in networks, not in groups' (Wellman 2001: 227) draws attention to the way in which forms of interaction that constitute the basis for social networks are increasingly developed through mediated communication (e.g. email correspondence) and provides clear points of intersection between the analytical concerns of social network analysis and the capacity to map 'data transfers' that the Internet enables. A good example of this is the blogging process, as bloggers often provide a 'blogroll' of those other bloggers they consider to have opinions that are worth looking at.

A third question within the social sciences relates to the attention given to interpersonal networks or what is referred to as 'soft infrastructure' in the literature on creative industries and creative cities. Charles Landry (2000: 133) defines soft infrastructure as 'the system of associative structures and social networks, connections, and human interactions that underpins and encourages the flow of ideas between individuals and institutions'. The process of uncovering such interconnections is the basis of social network analysis and Wellman's (2001) work on the social networks at play in emerging online communities in Toronto suburbs was a pioneering effort in this regard.

Social network analysis is rapidly moving from the academic world to the business world with the growing recognition of the importance of social networks. Facebook, with over 500 million members, is among the most compelling examples of this phenomenon. Mark Zuckerberg, the founder of Facebook, coined the term social graph[2] to describe 'the global mapping of everybody and how they are related'[3] on Facebook. The term has been expanded to include all of the social networks and connections a person has on sites such as Facebook, Twitter, and foursquare—anywhere that you have 'friends' or 'followers'. The distinction between the social graph and social networks is that the social graph is strictly about online relationships. The problem with this distinction is that many of those online relationships have parallels in the real world. For businesses, the potential represented by the social graph is to take advantage of the value of those relationships, for example by selling you things that your friends or followers are also buying.

Networks and the Economics of Social Production

Much of the work on the socio-economic role of communications networks has focused on the ways in which they transform organizational relations, as seen in the literature on network enterprises (Barney 2004: 83–90; Castells 2001: 64–116; Thompson 2003: 111–48). In *The Wealth of Networks* (2006), Yochai Benkler argues that the impact of networks runs deeper than this. He says that the early twenty-first century has brought the rise of a networked information economy, whose core characteristic is that 'decentralized individual action—specifically, new and important cooperative and coordinated action carried out through radically distributed, non-market mechanisms that do not depend upon proprietary strategies—plays a much greater role than it did, or could have, in the industrial information economy' (2006: 3). The key driver of such development is the generalization of the Internet and networked personal computing, whose degree of connectivity continues to grow as the costs of accessing ICTs continue to fall, and the capacity of each networked computer to produce, retrieve, and store data of all sorts continues to rise. For Benkler, this 'removal of the physical constraints on effective information production has made human creativity and the economics of information . . . core structuring facts in the new networked information economy' (2006: 4).

The rise of the Internet and networked ICTs provides a necessary but not a sufficient explanation for the rise of the networked information economy. Benkler's work points to three subsidiary conditions. First, there is the rise of information, knowledge, and creative industries themselves, which even at their most industrialized—as they were in the second half of the twentieth century—needed to be more flexible and more reliant on non-market motives than traditional manufacturing industries. Second, the existence of the Internet itself has given a major boost to all non-market forms of production and distribution of information, knowledge, and culture, as there are coordinate effects to a multiplicity of individual actions that greatly enrich the networked information environment. When one superimposes the information retrieval capacity of an Internet search engine such as Google on the billions of web pages that exist on the Internet, it is possible to see what Benkler terms the '"information good" that . . . is produced by the coordinate effects of the uncoordinated actions of a wide and diverse range of individuals and organizations acting on a wide range of motivations—both market and non-market, state and non-state' (Benkler 2006: 5). Third, there is the rise of peer production of information, knowledge, and culture through large-scale cooperative efforts. The conceptual and practical origins of this rest in the free and open source software movement, but the rise of Web 2.0 and social software has seen effects across a range of domains. Peer production—or user-generated content as it is often called in the Web 2.0 world—is the basis for the business model used in notable sites such as Flickr, YouTube, and Facebook. No corporate media production department exists for these sites. Instead they rely almost entirely on the productive efforts of their users (this phenomenon is explored in greater detail below).

This draws attention to the rise of **social production** and the rise of models of information, knowledge, and cultural production that are loosely collaborative, not necessarily driven by market criteria, and not directly proprietary in terms of who owns and controls the use of the final product. Observing that individuals have a variety of motives to act, to make information available to others, and to cooperate, Benkler argues that social production rises to prominence in the networked information economy from the confluence of two factors: the fact that knowledge as a uniquely valued input to production is always possessed uniquely by individuals, and that the majority of these individuals 'have the threshold level of material capacity [i.e. networked computers] required to explore the information environment they occupy, to take from it, and to make their contributions to it' (2006: 99). Given that in any society an excess of useful human knowledge and creativity exists relative to what is required economically, Benkler identifies two features of those projects that can most successfully harness the human resources necessary for effective social production.

The first feature is modularity, or the properties of a project that determine 'the extent to which it can be broken down into smaller components, or modules, that can be independently produced before they are assembled into a whole' (2006: 100). At one extreme, development and management of a nuclear power plant is extremely difficult to modularize, as the centre needs to be sure not only of the quality of all work (in order to avoid nuclear accident) but of the loyalty and commitment of all staff (because of the dangers of trafficking nuclear products to third parties). By contrast, Wikipedia demonstrates successfully the degree to which the assembling of an online encyclopedia can occur through the agglomeration of a vast and diverse range of independent inputs.

The second feature identified by Benkler is that of granularity, or the size of the modules, in terms of the time and effort that an individual must invest in producing them, which sets 'the smallest possible individual investment necessary to participate in a project' (2006: 101). Wikipedia is again a good example, as the investment of time and resources involved in making a single contribution is relatively small, or, in Benkler's terms, fine-grained. As an illustrative example, Table 5.1 indicates not only the growth in the number of contributors to Wikipedia between 2001 and 2005, but also the degree of granularity that exists between those who have been occasional contributors and those who maintain an ongoing relationship to the site and its contents. Two notable features of the table are that while the number of contributors of all types grew exponentially over the period, the fastest rates of growth were in the number of occasional contributors (reflecting granularity) and the number of non-English language contributions (reflecting the globalization of the Internet):

TABLE 5.1 Contributors to Wikipedia, January 2001 to June 2005

	Jan 2001	Jan 2002	Jan 2003	Jan 2004	July 2004	June 2005
Contributors[1]	10	477	2,188	9,653	25,011	48,721
Active contributors[2]	9	212	846	3,228	8,442	16,945
Very active contributors[3]	0	31	190	692	1,637	3,106
No. of English language articles	25	16,000	101,000	190,000	320,000	630,000
No. of articles, all languages	25	19,000	138,000	409,000	862,000	1,600,000

[1] Contributed at least 10 times
[2] Contributed at least 5 times in last month
[3] Contributed more than 100 times in last month
Source: Benkler (2006: 72).

Recent research on Wikipedia (e.g., Suh, Covertino, Chi, and Pirolli 2009) suggests that the period of exponential growth may have slowed or plateaued. This is particularly pronounced among those who are not insiders to Wikipedia but instead make casual or infrequent contributions. Part of the problem—if it is a problem, as growth in contributors need not necessarily continue upward at such a rapid pace—may be that the governance mechanisms for Wikipedia have failed to keep pace with changes in the community. In fact, complaints about cliquish behaviour among Wikipedia's elite—and that there even is an elite—dogged the service during 2008 and 2009. Recent changes in the governance structure may address this, but these are early days yet in terms of the impact of these revisions.

Like Castells, Benkler believes that the combination of the Internet and the network form marks a seismic shift in the socio-economic order of the twenty-first century as compared to the twentieth. The title of his book, *The Wealth of Networks*, alludes to the foundational text of market economics, Adam Smith's *The Wealth of Nations*, published in 1776. Smith and other classical economists identified the expansion of markets and trade as being at the core of new forms of wealth creation (on Smith, see Dobb 1973). In the late nineteenth and twentieth centuries, free-market economics was somewhat usurped by the rise of the large corporation—what James Beniger (1986) termed the 'control revolution' and what Alfred Chandler (1977) referred to as the 'visible hand'—where the combination of corporate control over resources on a large scale and scope, the capacity of planning to enable control over the external environment, and the combination of rewards and sanctions over individual employees that ensured loyalty and identification over time, made the corporation the superior form of economic organization. Benkler's argument is not that social production through networks will quickly supplant both markets and corporate hierarchies as the dominant form of economic organization. Indeed, he acknowledges that 'the rise of social production does not entail a decline in market-based production' (2006: 122). For many businesses, the principal change is in 'the relationship of firms to individuals outside of them . . . [as] consumers are changing into users—more active and productive than the consumers of the industrial information economy' (2006: 126).

Social production will have the greatest effects on the areas of economic life that lend themselves most readily to its core characteristics, such as the industries connected to information, knowledge, communications, culture, and creativity. At the same time, as the size and significance of these sectors is growing, particularly in advanced capitalist economies, the impact of social production will have a considerably wider resonance over time. As a general rule, the more important non-contractual factors are to an economic relationship—such as gifts, reciprocity, and trust—the more significant social production will be. This will in turn generate conflicts and contradictions at the heart of the core sector of the networked information economy, as 'social production in general and peer production in particular present new sources of competition to incumbents that produce information goods for which there are now socially produced substitutes' (Benkler 2006: 122). Copyright law has very often been the flashpoint at which these conflicts have been played out. Chapter 9 will explore in more depth the nature of these conflicts and the role of authors such as Benkler, Lawrence Lessig, and others associated with Creative Commons as a socio-legal response to these debates.

As we now turn to a discussion of participatory media cultures, it is important to keep in mind that without the content and the culture that is embedded in media exchanges, social networks are little more than empty webs. In fact, when social networking is seen as empty of meaning it often becomes the object of ironic criticism, such as the early, scathing critiques of Twitter. People network in order to accomplish something and in so doing they add meaning to their messages and in this meaning, culture is born. The remainder of this chapter examines participatory culture in more detail.

Participatory Media Cultures

One of the great promises of new media has always been that it could create a more participatory media culture. Early writers such as Rheingold (1994) envisaged the rise of a virtual public sphere, while Turkle (1995) saw identity as something that could become much more fluid and changeable in the virtual world of cyberspace. The scope for new media to be more participatory arose from its apparent structural differences from the forms of mass communication that dominated twentieth-century society. Authors such as Thompson (1995) and McQuail (2005) identify some of the key features of these earlier models of mass communication:

- the use of media technologies which enable large-scale production and distribution of informational and symbolic content to reach the largest audience possible, who in turn possess technological devices for reception of such content;
- institutional separation of the producers/distributors and receivers of media content, arising from both the costs of access to technologies of production and distribution, and the role played by various media gatekeepers as determinants of what constituted professional media content;
- an asymmetrical power relationship between producers/distributors and receivers of media, with the latter having little scope to respond to a largely one-way communications flow;
- relations between producers/distributors and receivers/consumers of media that were largely impersonal, anonymous and, in most instances, commodified through the reliance of large-scale commercial media industries upon advertising revenue (i.e. the audience was viewed as a target market); and,
- tendencies towards standardization of content, as the desire to maximize aggregate audiences (market share) created dynamics that promoted media content with the broadest possible appeal (i.e. limited scope for market segmentation through product differentiation).

The mass communication paradigm rested on the transmission model of communication which—allowing for factors such as feedback, noise, and signal failure—saw communication primarily in terms of a one-way flow of messages from senders (typically few) to receivers (typically many). While this model was certainly being challenged conceptually from the 1970s with cultural studies and its focus on the complexities of decoding and the activity of audiences (Hall 1982; see Bassett 2007 for a recent evaluation), and was eroding as a model for an understanding of media industries from the 1980s, it was the rise of the Internet and networked ICTs in the 1990s that heralded claims of a decisive break from mass communications. This argument typically had two components, one relating to the capacity of new media to enable greater participation in politics and political communication, the other relating to new media's potential to enable more and more people to become media producers and distributors as well as consumers. Many have identified the possibility of new media and ICTs enabling greater democratic political participation, and fostering a new, more egalitarian and participatory form of citizenship and political engagement. The factors commonly cited as enabling ICTs as a force for broadening and deepening democracy have been identified by several authors (Blumler and Coleman 2001; Clift 2000; Hague and Loader 1999; Tsagarousianou et al. 1998) and include:

1. the scope for horizontal or peer-to-peer communication, as distinct from vertical or top-down communication;
2. the capacity for users to access, share, and verify information from a wide range of global sources;
3. the lack of government controls over the Internet as a global communications medium, as compared to more territorially based media;
4. the ability to form virtual communities, or online communities of interest, that are unconstrained by geography;
5. the capacity to disseminate, debate, and deliberate on current issues, and to challenge professional and official positions; and,
6. the potential for political disintermediation, or communication that is not filtered by political organizations, spin doctors, or the established news media.

The second, related conception of this rise of participatory media through the Internet and networked ICTs is their capacity to promote do-it-yourself (DIY) media production. Blogs and other Web 2.0 technologies are substantive manifestations in a digital environment of what McKay (1998) terms—in the context of protest activities in 1990s Britain—DIY culture. McKay defines DIY culture as 'a combination of inspiring action, narcissism, youthful arrogance, principle, ahistoricism, idealism, indulgence, creativity, plagiarism, as well as the rejection and embracing alike of technical innovation' (1998: 2). Picking up on McKay's suggestive proposition, Hartley (1999a) developed the concept of DIY citizenship, which relates the decline of deference and a growing reluctance to accept the authority of established institutions of the media as well as government, to a demand for speaking rights, meaningful interaction with authority figures, and what Hartley (1999a: 186–7) terms semiotic self-determination or the right to determine one's own identity. Although new media is not at the centre of either McKay's or Hartley's analysis of DIY culture and citizenship, it certainly is significant in relation to tendencies in the wider media and public culture where, as Deuze argues, 'people not only have come to expect participation from the media [but] they increasingly have found ways to enact this participation in the multiple ways they use and make media . . . the Internet can be seen as an amplifier of this trend' (2006: 68).

Participatory media

The concept of participatory media predates the rise of the Internet and networked ICTs. The Hutchins Commission on Freedom of the Press, set up in the US in 1942, argued in its final report in 1947 that a responsible press needed not only to have full, truthful, and comprehensive reporting of events, but should also 'serve as a forum for the exchange of comment and criticism' while providing 'a representative picture of constituent groups in society' (McQuail 2005: 171). The sense that mainstream commercial media have failed to meet such objectives acted as a stimulus to the development of various forms of community media or alternative media in the second half of the twentieth century. In some countries these took the form of party-political or openly partisan forms of media (print media examples in Canada might include *Canadian Forum* (1920–2000), *Canadian Dimension*, *Alberta Report* (1973–2003), and the *National Post*), to very locally based newspapers and monographs, and the community broadcasting sector.

In Canada, community broadcasting got a dramatic boost with the emergence of cable television in the 1960s. In order to gain permission to set up a cable television service, many operators promised—and eventually it became seen as a condition of licence—to set up and fund a community channel, complete with studios, cameras, and a few paid staff to support the volunteer-run community television activities. These stations were designed to promote access, participation, and openness to perspectives not covered in mainstream media, and such activity was at the cornerstone of the PBS in the US (see Rennie 2006 for an overview). Community radio, often in association with low-powered stations set up on university campuses across Canada and the US in the 1970s and 1980s, also provided other important alternative voices in media in North America.

Atton (2001, 2002, 2004) draws attention to the extent to which confusion about what constitutes 'community', 'alternative', and 'radical' media may in the past have understated the significance of these forms of media to the contemporary media landscape. This leads Atton to define alternative media as being characterized by:

1. de-professionalization: the capacity to write, publish, and distribute news, ideas, and comment that is not contingent upon a set of professional skills, values, and norms that make a potential contributor 'qualified' to disseminate such material;
2. de-institutionalization: the ability to get such material into the public domain, which is not contingent upon the decision-making practices of large-scale media institutions, whether in the commercial or public sectors; and,
3. de-capitalization: the willingness to distribute media in all forms through mechanisms that require low up-front investments and low recurrent costs, so that the capacity to disseminate media content is not thwarted by the prior need for market viability of the distributing venture. (2002: 25)

A different way of understanding participatory media emerged from cultural studies and the observations made from within this theoretical framework about how the circuit of mass communication was never complete and always contested, since the personal, political, and emotional meanings and investments that audiences made in the mass-distributed products of popular culture were frequently at odds with the intended meanings of their producers.

Cultural studies theorists (e.g. Fiske 1987, 1992; Hall 1986; Turner 1990) questioned the claim that the dominant meanings of popular media reflected the class interests of those who own and control the institutions that control the means of production and distribution. They drew attention to the complex and contested nature of the politics of meaning through use of the Italian Marxist Antonio Gramsci's concept of hegemony (1971). This work discussed the extent to which readings of popular cultural texts rarely duplicate the preferred reading of their producers, but are instead commonly characterized by 'negotiated' or even 'oppositional' readings; and textual polysemy or the ways in which the meaning of a text is never limited only to the intentions of its author, but rather, is subject to a wider social negotiation and interpretation.

One important implication of such work, made most explicit in the work of John Fiske (1987, 1992), was that there were two economies in mass media: a financial economy, driven by the profit maximization strategies of commercial media institutions, and a cultural economy, where the popularity of media texts is determined through 'the exchange and circulation of . . . meanings, pleasures and social identities' (Fiske 1987: 311). Since success in the former is contingent upon success in the latter, it followed that popular media needed to be open to multiple interpretations by a socially diverse and mixed population, in order to be both popular and commercially successful.

This brief detour through active audience theories in cultural studies is relevant to our discussion about participatory media in the new media context because it draws attention to arguments that have been central to what Jenkins (2006a) terms **convergence culture**. For Jenkins, contemporary phenomena associated with Web 2.0 activities such as blogging, and sites such as YouTube, MySpace, and Flickr, need to be understood in the context of the history of fan cultures that have developed with popular media over a number of years, which include fan interest as diverse as fanzine reinscriptions of the *Star Trek* series, engagement with scripts of the HBO series *True Blood* through virtual community fan fiction sites, and the engagement of game developers, as well as the developers of reality TV programs such as *Lost* and *Survivor,* with their online user communities (Jenkins 2006a, b). Following earlier insights from cultural studies, Jenkins proposes that convergence is a cultural as well as a technological phenomenon and both a top-down and a bottom-up process:

> Media companies are learning how to accelerate the flow of media content across delivery channels to expand revenue opportunities, broaden markets, and reinforce viewer commitments. Consumers are learning how to use these different media technologies to bring the flow of media more fully under their control and to interact with other consumers. The promises of this new media environment raise expectations of a freer flow of ideas and content. Inspired by those ideals, consumers are fighting for the right to participate more fully in their culture. Sometimes, corporate and grassroots convergence reinforce each other, creating closer, more rewarding relations between media producers and consumers. Sometimes, the two forces are at war and those struggles will redefine the face of . . . popular culture. (2006a: 18)

The struggle that Jenkins refers to is both visible and invisible. The struggle over media content is visible when community members take video from popular films and mash it up with their own content. A good example of this is found in the numerous 'Hitler has a meltdown' videos that can be found on YouTube. The use and re-use of professionally produced media sometimes stirs a backlash, however, and sites are forced to remove community member submissions when they are found to contain copyrighted material. Other times, the reuse is permitted and even encouraged by savvy media companies that know that it ultimately promotes their own product, at the risk of losing some control.

The struggle over media content is less visible in other cases. Sometimes the very popularity of completely amateur content more subtly undermines the broadcast model of popular culture. In other words, if people start to ignore the mainstream media and create their own media content and culture they are being just as subversive—and perhaps even more so—than when they repurpose existing content. Below, we explore how participatory media work and how its widest expression, these days, can be found in what is widely described as Web 2.0.

Participatory media and Web 2.0

One of the issues that has arisen with second-generation new media technologies, referred to under the general rubric of Web 2.0, is whether they have provided significantly more opportunities for people to produce and disseminate creative work and to demonstrate their creativity to a wider community. In noting the growing capacity of new media technologies to enable the capturing and sharing of digital content in its various forms, Lawrence Lessig observes:

> This digital 'capturing and sharing' is in part an extension of the capturing and sharing that has always been integral to our culture, and in part it is something new. It is continuous with the Kodak model, but it explodes the boundaries of Kodak-like technologies. The technology of digital 'capturing and sharing' promises a world of extraordinarily diverse creativity that can be easily and broadly shared . . . Technology has thus given us an opportunity to do something with culture that has only ever been possible for individuals in small groups, isolated from others. Think about an old man telling a story to a collection of neighbours in a small town. Now imagine that same story-telling extended across the globe. (2004: 184–5)

In the context of Web 2.0 and the websites and technologies associated with it, this has of course become a reality. Lessig's example of photography draws attention to the shift away from what he refers to as the 'Kodak model', where photos become easy for all to take, but where their processing remains reliant on specialists. The Kodak model also presumes that distribution is largely contingent on the ability of the photo-taker to show people their photos in face-to-face situations (e.g. the photo album or slide night). In contrast, a completely new model is emerging with sites such as Flickr.

Digital cameras (including those embedded in mobile phones) and their link to computers make it easy for photographers of all levels of skill to take pictures and upload them onto their personal computers. While the camera and computer remove the necessity of processing pictures, the computer and a website like Flickr changes the distribution process. If, for example, you have a series of baby photos that you would like to share with your extended family, but that family is geographically dispersed, you can use Flickr's site capabilities to share those photos. If, however, you are a budding professional photographer and wish to have your work available to a wider community of users (including potential clients and buyers of your work), the Flickr site allows your work to be subject to peer ranking systems that provide ongoing feedback about your work and expose it to very wide communities of interest.

The significance of these kinds of changes to models of media content production, distribution, and access is taken up in the context of various discussions in the research literature. Burgess (2006) draws upon the work of Atton (2002) and Couldry (2003) on media democratization, which identifies the capacity of 'hybrid forms of media consumption-production . . . [to] challenge the entrenched division of labour . . . that is the essence of media power' (Couldry 2003: 45).

Leadbeater and Miller (2004) refer to this as the **Pro-Am Revolution**. Defining 'Pro-Ams' as 'innovative, committed and networked amateurs working to professional standards' (2004: 9), they identify activities as diverse as: rap music and music sampling; the Linux open source software program; the Jubilee 2000 campaign around Third World debt; user modifications of 'The Sims' online computer game; and the activities of Muhummad Yunnus in alleviating poverty in Bangladesh through micro-credit schemes, as examples of how, 'when Pro-Ams are networked together, they can have a huge impact on politics and culture, economics and development' (2004: 12). Arguing that 'Pro-Ams work at their leisure, regard consumption as a productive activity, and set professional standards to judge their amateur efforts', Leadbeater and Miller (2004: 23) distinguish the Pro-Am from both the casual leisure enthusiast and the accredited professional through the following typology:

FIGURE 5.1 Pro-Ams in the Wider Participatory Community
Source: Leadbetter and Miller (2004: 23).

Leadbeater (2007) proposes that modern capitalism is, as Benkler (2006) also argues, based on systems of social production that blur historical lines of demarcation between commercial production, public sector provision, and the community/non-profit sector. The rise of Pro-Am production models and the scope for mass distribution with continuous feedback through networked new media technologies, generate 'a huge challenge to the established organizational order and the professions who design, control and lead them':

Consumers turn out to be producers. Demand breeds its own supply. Leisure becomes a form of work. A huge amount of creative work is done in spite, or perhaps because, of people not being paid . . . They embody a new ethic of collaborative, shared effort, not often motivated by money . . . The truth is that most traditional commercial organizations do not want their consumers to become collaborators. They quite like them passive and so dependent . . . The idea that you might be able to lead more effectively in a far more open, transparent and conversational way ruins all the fun. *The irresistible force of collaborative mass innovation is about to meet the immovable force of entrenched corporate organization.* (Leadbeater 2007; emphasis added)

Leadbeater seems skeptical of the ability of corporations to take advantage of social and participatory media; however, for those firms that do adapt, there can be advantages in collaborating with consumers. Many new businesses have been founded on these models and many existing businesses are adapting their practices to take advantage of the interactivity and creativity that working closely with a community offers. Sometimes this creativity is contained within a site—as is the case with the reader reviews that make shopping on Chapters.indigo.ca such a worthwhile process—and sometimes the creativity of the users is found beyond the confines of a site and extends across communities. A savvy media organization will participate in both and take note when, for example, a blogger is writing about their product or service.

Blogs as participatory media and social software

Web logs, or blogs, are user-generated websites where entries are made either by individuals or by groups, in an informal journal style, and are displayed in reverse chronological order. Blogs are typically interactive and networked. They solicit and respond to the commentary of others on the material posted on the blog and they characteristically offer links to the blogs or websites of others with related interests (what is known as a blogroll), and—while mainly text-based—blogs can provide links to other media resources, such as video and photos (a video-based blog is called a vlog, while a photo-based blog is a photoblog). The term blog refers to both the online artifact created and to the act of maintaining such an online resource, or blogging. The social network of blogs and bloggers is referred to as the blogosphere and it is through this network that 'the social networking of blogs and the potential for collaboration . . . [provide] a decidedly human dimension to the publishing and publicizing of information' in ways that 'represent for authors an opportunity to reach out and connect with an audience never before accessible to them, while maintaining control over their own personal expressive spaces' (Bruns and Jacobs 2006: 5). Blogs have been a vitally important component of social software and Davies has argued that:

> The principle of social software is to break down the distinction between our online computer-mediated experiences and our offline face-to-face experiences. It is software that . . . seeks to integrate the Internet further into our everyday

lives, and our everyday lives further into the Internet. It is software that seeks to eradicate the gulf separating two such separate social networks. (2003: 7)

The significance of **blogging** as social software must also be considered in light of its popularity. In November 2006, there were 57 million active bloggers worldwide (BBC 2006). A 2006 survey of US bloggers conducted through the Pew Center's Internet and American Life (Lenhart and Fox 2006) project found that about 12 million Americans over the age of 18 (or 8 per cent of the US Internet-using population) kept a blog and that blogs were viewed by 57 million Americans over the age of 18 (or about 38 per cent of the US Internet-using population). The survey found that bloggers are considerably younger than the Internet population overall, with 54 per cent being under the age of 30, compared to 24 per cent of Internet users. Indeed, 19 per cent of Internet users 12 to 17 years of age kept a blog. In terms of general online media and communications practices and habits, bloggers overwhelmingly have a home broadband network connection, consume a large amount of other online media content (particularly news), are highly engaged with other forms of technology-based social interaction, and tend to source material more widely than other media users (Lenhart and Fox 2006: 4–6). In terms of what motivates people to establish and maintain a blog, the Pew Internet survey found that making money was the least important reason and that about one third of bloggers saw the content of their blog as a form of journalism, with creative expression, documenting of personal views and experiences, and keeping in touch with friends and family being the most important motives (see Table 5.2).

TABLE 5.2 Motives for Developing a Blog: Pew Internet Survey of US Bloggers

Reasons for developing a blog: US bloggers survey 2005–06	Major reason %	Minor reason %	Not a reason %
To express yourself creatively	52	25	23
To document your personal experiences or share them with others	50	26	24
To stay in touch with friends and family	37	22	40
To share practical knowledge or skills with others	34	30	35
To motivate other people to action	29	32	38
To entertain people	28	33	39
To store resources or information that is important to you	28	21	52
To influence the way other people think	27	24	49
To network or to meet new people	16	34	50
To make money	7	8	85

Source: Lenhart and Fox (2006: iii).

In placing the rise of blogs in Internet history, Clay Shirky argues that they are part of a 'third age' of social software (GBN 2002; Shirky 2003). The first age began with email and, particularly, the 'cc' tag line, which allowed one-to-one or one-to-few communications. The second age came with the rise of virtual communities, as discussed by Rheingold (1994), Turkle (1995), and others. For Shirky, one of the key limitations of the technology and how it was used in this period (the mid- to late 1990s) is that both the software and the modes of web content development tended to be static, had limited interactivity, possessed a central-ized mechanism of content control, and operated on a largely 'broadcast' model; whereas the participation in chat rooms, online discussion forums, and so on was not occurring through the web, but instead, through conduits such as email. As a result, there was a lim-ited sense of community in the latter (which lent itself to flame wars, discontinuation of subscription, information overload, etc.) and a lack of interactivity in the development of web pages. By contrast, the 'third age' of social software has evolved around the principles of Web 2.0, which place a particular emphasis on collaboration, community-building, simpli-fication of software and access points for users, 'light touch' regulation of site content, and relative ease in producing, distributing, accessing, and responding to the full range of forms of digital media content. In cases where such principles have been extended to collaborative publishing models, such as Wikipedia, this also includes collaborative editing (Bruns 2005).

Participatory Media, Social Software, and Social Capital

One question that arises from the development of participatory media such as blogs and other forms of social software is whether their development contributes to the growth of social capital and in particular, to new forms such as virtual social capital. In his well-known work on the significance of **social capital**, Putnam (1995: 665) defines social capital as 'features of social life—networks, norms, and trust—that enable participants to act together more effectively to pursue shared interests . . . Social capital, in short, refers to social connections and the attendant norms and trust'. Woolcock (2001: 13) defines social capital as 'the norms and networks that facilitate collective action' and Davies (2003: 11) defines it as the 'value of social networks'; this is 'a resource which we can invest time and money in, and which pays returns'.

The promotion, nurturing, and maintenance of social capital is seen as critical to over-all economic performance, to the avoidance of adverse social consequences (crime, drug abuse, public health concerns), and to the emergence of new forms of social entrepreneur-ship that fill gaps between market-led solutions and government-driven reform programs (Davies 2003; Leadbeater 2000; Putnam 1995; Woolcock 2001; World Bank 2003). In addressing such questions, Aldridge and colleagues (2002) distinguish between three main types of social capital:

1. bonding social capital, characterized by strong social bonds between individuals, for example members of a family, a local community, or an ethnic community;

2. bridging social capital, characterized by weaker, less dense but more cross-cutting ties, for example with business associates, links across ethnic groups, links between families and communities; and,

3. linking social capital, characterized by connections between those with differing levels of power or social status, for example between political elites and the general public, policy-makers and local communities, and individuals from different social classes.

Early commentaries on the relationship between the Internet and social capital identified a positive correlation between the decentralized and inclusive nature of the Internet and the revivification of civic engagement and a sense of community (e.g. Rheingold 1994; Schuler 1996; Sclove 1995).

Putnam himself, however, does not fully embrace the idea that Internet users would be more civically engaged and he expresses concerns about unequal access to the new technology and 'cyber-balkanisation' (2000: 177). There are related concerns about the adverse effects of Internet use on family life and on other offline activities (Nie and Erbring 2000), and the tendency towards group polarization and heightened political conflict among those with divergent points of view (Sunstein 2002). There was empirical work emerging during this period that showed the Internet acting, on balance, as a positive stimulus to community engagement and civic and political participation; however, there was also a need to recognize that the Internet was changing such forms of engagement and participation and that new metrics were needed for new media (Wellman et al. 2001). In a similar vein, Aldridge and colleagues (2002: 48–9) conclude that the Internet was promoting a transformation of forms of civic engagement, particularly among younger users, where sustained engagement with globally networked organizations was becoming more important than traditional, locality-based forms of participation in community organizations (such as sporting teams, local churches, or Rotary clubs).

An important question that remains is whether social software and its facilitation and promotion of large-scale, public, online participation is changing the nature of engagement and participation and their relationship to social capital. Using the definitions of social capital provided above, blogs are clearly a use of social software to develop new forms of social capital that are bridging and, to varying degrees, bonding and linking. The function of permalinks within blogs, which establish a permanent link to other blogs and the documents posted on them even as they change (and as the URL changes with them), is one of the many indicators of the desire of bloggers to maintain an ongoing sense of community, not only with their readers, but with the wider community of bloggers with whom they coexist. By a variety of indicators, it would seem that the rise of blogging and other forms of social software are having positive effects on the development and maintenance of social capital, even if they may also represent to their critics (e.g. Keen 2007) a new form of narcissism on a global scale.

Another key issue with blogs is whether their moment has peaked. While the number of daily blog posts grew from 500,000 at the time of the US presidential election (October 2004) to 2.5 million at the time of the Israel–Hezbollah conflict in southern Lebanon (June 2006), there was subsequently a notable plateau (Doctorow 2006). The Gartner Group estimated that the number of blogs worldwide would level off at approximately 100 million. There are also an estimated 200 million abandoned blogs or blogs that were started, but whose creators have long since ceased to post on the site, including celebrities such as Lindsay Lohan, Melanie Griffith, and Barbra Streisand (Australian 2007). It may well be that some former bloggers have moved on to other forms of social software and it is also the case—as often occurs in the age of the global Internet—that the fastest rates of growth are outside the English-speaking world. For example, as tensions escalated in the Middle East, the Farsi or Persian language—the majority language of Iran and Afghanistan and a significant language through Central Asia and the Middle East—became one of the top ten languages of the blogosphere (Doctorow 2006).

Downsides of Networks, Social Media, and Participatory Media Culture

It is important to conclude this chapter—which has emphasized the beneficial and transformative capacities of networks for social, economic, cultural, and political relationships—with some consideration of the potential downsides to the network form, both in terms of its internal logic and its wider socio-economic impacts. The first is that, at a purely technical level, networks frequently fail. Servers crash, infrastructure systems fail, and website access becomes overloaded and hence unavailable. There are also concerns related to what contract lawyers term 'force majeure', which can range from a power blackout on a particular location because of an overloaded electricity grid, to an act of war or terrorism that decimates core communications infrastructures almost instantaneously, as happened in the Downtown Manhattan district of New York in the immediate aftermath of 9/11.

Second, it is important to be conscious of the insider/outsider dimensions of networks. At a global level, Castells draws attention to the inclusion/exclusion dimensions of access, involvement, and participation that arise in a networked global economy and are based on geographical location and the geopolitical significance of that location in the global space of flows (see e.g. Castells 2000: 70–165). In relation to the creative industries, McRobbie (2005) argues that a form of 'network sociality' in these sectors has generated a form of 'PR meritocracy' whereby familiar patterns of social exclusion on the basis of gender, race, ethnicity, social location, and other factors continue to occur, but they are based less upon overt discrimination than upon the question of who has the time and capacity for after-hours social networking. Gill's research (2002) on participation in project-based new media work and the very significant barriers confronting women and people with young children (again, mostly women) is pertinent in this context.

A third, notable concern is that networks have historically been associated with corruption and crime. As we have noted, al-Qaeda and similar organizations, for example, use the innovative capabilities of networks and social media in ways that are massively damaging to populations worldwide both in terms of wider geopolitical implications and in how they affect populations at a very local level (e.g. shopkeepers, tourism service operators, and restaurateurs in Bali seeking to maintain tourist-related trade after the 2002 and 2005 bombings). The popular television program *The Sopranos* offered a useful fictional example of how bonding social capital can be used to serve anti-social purposes (Lavery 2002) and there are comparable cases in the (real world) family-based and ethnically structured nature of criminal organizations such as the Sicilian mafia, the Colombian drug cartels, the Russian *mafiyas*, the Chinese Triads, and the Japanese Yakuza.

In a different way, high levels of bonding social capital in particular have been associated with racial intolerance and conflict between communities. One example includes the Catholic/Protestant divide in Northern Ireland, where there is a great deal of bonding social capital within the sectarian communities, but what is missing are forms of social capital that bridge these community divides. Whether or not the rise of the Internet, ICTs, and social networking media provide new forms of virtual social capital that can effectively work across such divides remains to be seen.

Beyond these serious criticisms, participatory media is also vulnerable to the accusation that the 'immaterial labour' (van Dijck 2009) of participants is being co-opted by owners of websites without any meaningful control over how it is being used. In part this is fostered by End-User Licensing Agreements (the notorious EULA) that assign blanket rights to the owner of the site. As well, user behaviour is meticulously tracked and, along with preferences and 'likes', becomes data that can be sold to third parties for marketing purposes or other surveillance related activities. We return to a discussion of these and other economic questions in Chapter 8 following an examination of games, the games industry, and creative industries in general in the next two chapters.

Case Study: Digital Storytelling

Digital storytelling has emerged since the mid-1990s as an important use of new media technologies that enables ordinary people to tell their own stories in a compelling format that is readily available to others. Digital storytelling frequently involves short, auto-biographical films (usually no more than eight minutes in length) with an interactive element that can be distributed through the web or television. Here in Canada, the National Film Board—which in the 1960s pioneered storytelling through film in its Fogo Island project—has been collaborating on digital storytelling initiatives across the country as part of the 2010 Olympics (Matlin 2009).

Importantly, this form of new media is not simply about enabling access—as found with web pages, web cams, social networking sites, and so on—but rather, it involves a facilitated process whereby those who have specialized knowledge in the use of these digital technologies provide training to relatively new users, not only in how to use the technologies, but also in how to tell stories in ways that have strong underlying narratives and are emotionally compelling for an audience (Burgess et al. 2006; Lambert 2002). This commitment to community engagement and empowerment differentiates digital storytelling from related new media forms such as interactive journalism, narrative-based games, or personal blogs or home pages.

Two broad developments mark the conceptual as well as practical origins of digital storytelling. First, a production workshop was developed in 1993 by the American artist and media producer, Dana Atchley, at the American Film Institute. This served as a catalyst for

Joe Lambert and others to develop training workshops in the San Francisco Bay Area, which constituted the basis for the Center for Digital Storytelling (CDS), established in 1994. Inspired by a vision of cultural democracy and community arts activism, the Center's focus is on grassroots initiatives, personal narratives, and the empowering of those unfamiliar with the use of digital technologies. The CDS is a 'non-profit training, project development, and research organization dedicated to assisting people in using digital media to tell meaningful stories from their lives', with a focus on personal voice, thoughtful and emotionally direct stories, and facilitative teaching methods that enable knowledge-sharing and knowledge transfer (CDS 2007).

The second major digital storytelling initiative has come from the BBC and its decision in 2001 to commission the Capture Wales project, led by Daniel Meadows from Cardiff University's School of Journalism, Media, and Cultural Studies (Meadows 2003). In 2002, the BBC undertook an initiative called 'Telling Lives'. Digital stories produced with the assistance of the BBC are now distributed across many of their sites, including dedicated websites (www.bbc.co.uk/wales/capturewales; www.bbc.co.uk/tellinglives), through BBC television, BBC satellite television, and BBC Radio in the case of audio stories. The BBC has further developed its resources for online DIY storytelling and media participation through its Create site (www.bbc.co.uk/create), which offers a plethora of tools and sites from which to develop digital content in the form of films, stories, music, artworks, reviews, journalism, and family histories. There is also the BBC Action Network (formerly iCan) which has promoted grassroots community political activism (www.bbc.co.uk/dna/actionnetwork).

While the BBC initiative shares obvious features with CDS, it is also overlaid by elements of the BBC's goal of promoting citizenship and representing experiences from across the United Kingdom. In the BBC Charter Review process that commenced in 2004 and was completed in 2007, the six core principles for the BBC in the twenty-first century were identified as: sustaining citizenship and civil society; promoting education and learning; stimulating creativity and cultural excellence; reflecting the United Kingdom's nations, regions, and communities; bringing the world to the United Kingdom and the United Kingdom to the world; and Building Digital Britain (DCMS 1998). Digital initiatives such as digital storytelling serve this new active citizenship agenda in the digital age by creating opportunities for people to become more active citizens, particularly at the local and regional levels, and stimulating the creativity of audiences by giving them a chance to tell their own stories and make their own programs (BBC 2005). Initiatives in digital storytelling and related manifestations of everyday creativity support the proposition of Burgess and colleagues that:

> Communication policy around networked media should not only be concerned with ownership, content regulation and controls, but should also try to 'do no harm' to, and even support, platforms, technologies and practices that enable the flowering of the unpredictable forms of everyday and ephemeral creativity and engagement that make up active participation in the networked cultural public sphere. (2006: 13)

Useful Websites

Augmented Social Cognition
←http://asc-parc.blogspot.com/search/label/wikipedia→

This website is a guide to 'understanding how groups remember, think, and reason' from the Augmented Social Cognition Research Group at the Palo Alto Research Center (PARC). This group maintains a regular watch on Wikipedia, among other social media.

BoingBoing: A Directory of Wonderful Things
←http://boingboing.net→

This is a lively website committed to aggregating and publicizing the most interesting things to come from blogs and other forms of social networking software.

BBC Create
←www.bbc.co.uk/create→

Designed for users of all ages, this is a comprehensive do-it-yourself media toolkit, with more than 50 sites from which users can access tools to assist in producing and distributing everything from music and short films to news stories and family histories.

Center for Digital Storytelling
←www.storycenter.org→

Established in the San Francisco Bay Area in the mid-1990s, the Center for Digital Storytelling has been a pioneer in enabling people without digital media skills to develop online stories that reflect on their life experiences.

Confessions of an Aca-Fan: The Official Weblog of Henry Jenkins
←www.henryjenkins.org→

Professor Henry Jenkins practises what he preaches concerning participatory media in this lively blog where he posts daily with the aim of bridging the gap between academic media research and a general public trying to make sense of these emerging forms. Jenkins covers everything from computer games to censorship to professional wrestling.

International Network for Social Network Analysis
←www.insna.org→

This website is dedicated to gathering and distributing academic research on social networks. The INSNA was founded by Barry Wellman in 1978 and the professional society has over 1,000 members worldwide.

Technorati
←http://technorati.com→

This website aggregates blog contributions and provides data on hit rates for blogs and other forms of social software. It also provides analysis and commentary on developments in the blogosphere.

Further Reading

Internet Galaxy, Manuel Castells (2003)
Although Manuel Castells' *Information Age* trilogy may be too much reading for an undergraduate course reading list (Volume 1, *The Rise of the Network Society*, is almost 600 pages), the smaller *Internet Galaxy* provides some of the same concepts as well as a condensed history of the Internet.

Convergence Culture, Henry Jenkins (2008)
This book, along with Jenkins' other two books—*Fans, Bloggers, and Gamers: Exploring Participatory Culture* (2006) and *The Wow Complex* (2007)—reveals the breadth, depth, and complexity of a popular culture that is rapidly emerging from the top-down era of the twentieth century and both regaining its participatory elements as well as new digitally enabled versions of commodification and distribution.

Linked: The New Science of Networks, Albert-László Barabási (2002)

Studies of social capital are most commonly linked to Robert Putnam or Pierre Bourdieu but this text helps explain the science behind social capital in a lively and engaging way and makes it accessible to the general reader. The book is well worth reading for those who want to have a better sense of the underpinnings of social capital and social networks.

Discussion Questions

1. What are the benefits of networked organizations as identified by Podolny and Page? What examples of these can you give in terms of your knowledge or experience with organizations in your personal, academic, or professional life?

2. Social network analysis is based on the understanding that forms of self, activity, and behaviour are relational. Discuss the four key elements and seven core concepts of social network analysis identified by Wasserman and Faust.

3. What is meant by the terms 'social production' and 'participatory media culture' and why are these significant in terms of understanding new media? Discuss not only the promise but also the peril of networks, social media, and participatory media culture.

4. Within the different kinds of networks that are central to globalization there are clear dynamics of inclusion and exclusion, as well as a diverse range of oppositional movements based on resistance identities and project identities. Why is this significant and what are some possible consequences?

5. Aldridge and colleagues (2002) distinguish between three main types of social capital. Discuss these, identify examples of these in your own work and life, and consider the implications for you (and others).

Class Activities

1. Do a 'degrees of separation' experiment so see how many links connect you to your classmates, and from each of you to a famous person. Discuss how you use social media to enhance or take advantage of those links (e.g., Facebook Friends or LinkedIn connections). Discuss the use of social media for professional (rather than personal) use. What are the differences?

2. As a class, compile a list of how your group both consumes and produces 'participatory' media (e.g., YouTube, Flickr, Facebook) using a show of hands or simple poll. Keep in mind the following statistics—that the general population typically includes 90 per cent who only consume, 9 per cent who contribute comments or stars or votes, and only one per cent who contribute content.[4] Compare your classes participation with participation more broadly.

6 Games: Technology, Industry, Culture

Questions to Consider

- In what ways are technology, industry, and the culture of games linked?

- What is the significance of marketing and branding practices, immersive play, and interactive experiences in gaming?

- In what ways do the games industry and game culture have implications for issues such as identity, the experience of childhood, and intellectual property?

- How do the values encoded into game cultures reflect offline cultural values? Conversely, how do games offer a chance to emphasize alternative or subjugated values in the name of fantasy and play?

Chapter Outline

This chapter offers a broad examination of games, game play, and the game industry as a prime example of new media in the twenty-first century. We examine games as a significant part of popular culture, extending beyond their notable economic impact. We also look at how the immersive nature and rapid pace of change places online and computer games at the centre of debates relating to gender, cultural impact, childhood experiences, and intellectual property. We then consider how the performance of games has ramped up steadily over the past several decades as game platforms compete for higher resolution, speed, and richer, more demanding game play. We take a look at the economics of the game industry including its dependence on subcontractors and its rather diffuse economic model—the need for smash 'hits' to finance the many 'misses'—followed by a consideration of the value chain and the tension between the creative side of the business and the investment side, as well as the complex relationship between production and distribution. The last part of the chapter looks at some of the most significant gaming developments in the first decade of the twenty-first century, such as the role of producer-consumers 'modding' games, and the issues arising from that, including the question of who owns the subsequent content. The chapter concludes with a discussion of the political economy of the game industry, as well as a section on the game industry in Canada.

Game On

The global interactive games industry is large, growing, and at the forefront of many of the most significant innovations in new media. While measures of industry size vary, global revenues in the games sector were estimated to be at least USD $30 billion in 2006 and in the US, the Entertainment Software Alliance, which represents the major players in the games industry, reported USD $7.4 billion in sales of computer and video game software in 2006 (ESA 2006). Games are most commonly purchased as: (i) a stand-alone package and played on consoles commonly attached to the television (video games); or (ii) online **multiplayer games** (sometimes also called massive multiplayer online games or MMOGs), which are played on personal computers that have broadband connectivity and are accessed on a subscription basis. In 2005, video games accounted for over 85 per cent of the total games market (ESA 2006: 10). There is also growth in gaming undertaken through handheld mobile devices such as mobile phones and personal digital assistants (PDAs) and this will develop further with advances in wireless telecommunications.

The significance of interactive games to new media development extends substantially beyond their economic role. As *The Economist* (2005) has observed:

> Games are widely used as educational tools, not just for pilots, soldiers and surgeons, but also in schools and businesses . . . Anyone who has learned to play a handful of games can generally figure out how to operate almost any high-tech device. Games require players to construct hypotheses, solve problems, develop strategies, and learn the rules of the in-game world through trial and error. Gamers must also be able to juggle several different tasks, evaluate risks and make quick decisions . . . Playing games is, thus, an ideal form of preparation for the workplace of the 21st century, as some forward-thinking firms are already starting to realize.

Kline and colleagues identify interactive games as 'the "ideal commodity" of a post-Fordist/postmodern/promotional capitalism—an artifact within which converge a series of the most important production techniques, marketing strategies, and cultural practices of an era' (2003: 24). The games industry itself identifies direct spin-offs for technological innovation and consumer demand relating to computer processing, demand for broadband services, mobile telecommunications, and digital content, and indirect spin-offs and technology transfer to sectors as diverse as real estate and travel, military training, health care, intelligence testing, and corporate training (Crandall and Sidak 2006).

The convergence of continuous technological innovation, dynamic corporate marketing and branding practices, and the intensity of immersive play and interactive experiences place this sector at the leading edge of new media innovation and central to debates associated with the cultural appropriateness of digital content, gender identities, the experience of childhood, and intellectual property. Moreover, the rise of games and gaming culture (and particularly the development of MMOGs), where players are increasingly the creators of the game's content and form themselves into online virtual communities, brings to the fore a series of debates about participatory media culture and user-led innovation, as users increasingly become the creators—and not simply the consumers—of their own media. At the same time, as critical work by authors such as Kline and colleagues (2003) and Terranova

(2004) reminds us, there are significant disputes about issues ranging from the ownership and control of user-generated content in proprietary online games, to poor working conditions and burn-out among those working in games production.

Games History

Early computer games were developed by the military-industrial-academic complex, which also originated the Internet, with researchers involved in the US nuclear program at the Massachusetts Institute of Technology (MIT) Artificial Intelligence unit creating games in their spare time, such as the joystick-based 'Spacewar' (completed in 1962) and the paddle-and-ball game 'Tennis for Two' (first created in 1958, but patented in 1968 by Ralph Baer). These would be prototypes for the games that would find mass-market success in the 1970s, such as 'Pong' (released by Atari in 1972) and 'Space Invaders' (released by Midway in 1978). These games—and later, games such as 'Monaco GP' and 'Pac-Man'—were primarily arcade-based games, played on coin-operated machines in public places, although console-based games systems, played at home through the television, were becoming increasingly significant. In 1982, worldwide home sales of video games were estimated at USD $3 billion and arcade games grossed USD $8 billion in revenue; this compared to international sales of popular music of USD $4 billion at the time (Kline et al. 2003: 103–4). The industry experienced a bust in the mid-1980s, however, partly triggered by the development of too many poor quality games, and Atari (the giant of the industry at this time) incurred massive losses for its parent company, Time-Warner.

The second half of the 1980s was dominated by Nintendo, as the crash of the North American video game market coincided with the launch of the Nintendo Entertainment System (NES) in 1985, accompanied by the remarkably successful 'Super Mario Bros.' game, which had gross sales of USD $500 million by 1990. Learning from the Atari experience, that quality of games and not simply volume was the key to success, Nintendo games were marked by dramatically improved pacing, visuals, sound, and dynamism, thus greatly enhancing the experience of play. Nintendo also developed a way to outsource the development of games content to third parties, while retaining quality control over the games through strict licensing procedures, thereby starting the process of separating the game engine from the game content. Importantly, Nintendo developed a sophisticated marketing strategy, which gave information and support to players and consequently nurtured a gaming subculture, while also using this infrastructure to gain player feedback about the games. The Super Mario brand also provided the basis for spin-offs into other media, including a successful children's television cartoon and a less successful Hollywood film, as well as merchandizing in the form of t-shirts, comic books, removable tattoos, lunch boxes, etc.[1]

The 1990s were marked by the entry of Sega into the games environment with the 16-bit Genesis console, with micro-processing capability to generate bigger animated characters, better backgrounds, faster play, and better sound. While not initially successful against Nintendo, the strength of Sega was in its ability to attract game developers, in particular from the gaming company giant, Electronic Arts. Sega worked from the proposition, identified by economists Carl Shapiro and Hal Varian (1999: 196), that to develop new markets, 'you need to offer performance "ten times better" than the established technology' and, in 1991, Sega introduced 'Sonic the Hedgehog' as their flagship game. Sega also developed riskier content, such as 'Street Fighter' and 'Mortal Kombat', marketed strongly to teenage boys and criticized for being excessively violent (Kline et al. 2003: 132–5). While Sega made significant market inroads, particularly in Europe, Nintendo responded by developing the GameBoy, a miniature, portable, handheld console that would, among other things, transform the thumbs of a generation of users (it also prepared them for mobile phones!). The nature of the console wars changed again in 1994, when the giant media conglomerate, Sony, launched the PlayStation, which capitalized on both Sony's high-profile brand identity and the shift in games storage devices from cartridges to CD-ROMs, which were much less costly to produce and distribute.

This period also saw computer-based gaming, which had long been the sleeping giant of the sector, rise in prominence with the development of 'Wolfenstein' (1991), 'Myst' (1993), 'Doom' (1994), and 'Quake' (1995). Building on new graphics capabilities in the personal computer, strengthened by the emergence of the dedicated graphics processing unit (GPU) in graphics cards, games on a PC started to rival the capabilities of dedicated console games. These games were less juvenile than standard gaming fare and, as importantly, exploited the possibilities presented by the Internet to generate player-developed content. The makers of 'Doom', id Software, released their source code online, thereby allowing players to develop their own levels of the game, and thus extend and modify the game itself.

By the early 2000s, the console-based games industry was organized as a large number of games producers, a smaller group of games distributors or publishers, and a very small group of games hardware producers. The games hardware industry was dominated by: Sony, which released PlayStation 2 in 1999; Nintendo, which produced GameCube in 2001; and Microsoft, which launched its Xbox amid much fanfare in late 2001. For companies such as Sony and Microsoft, in particular, involvement in the games industry was at the forefront of their efforts to establish their media content platforms at the centre of the emerging broadband Internet environment.[2] Key players in games distribution or games publishing include Acclaim Entertainment, Atari, Capcom, Eidos, Electronic Arts, LucasArts, Midway, Namco, and Take-Two Interactive Entertainment. Sony, Sega, Nintendo, and Microsoft also established themselves as significant games publishers as well as platform distributors.

The dynamics of the games industry and games development reveal a bewildering and changing array of digital software production houses, which maintain a range of subcontracting, licensing, and fee-for-service arrangements with the games publishing houses. As an industry characterized by inherent risk, where five per cent of successful titles effectively subsidize the 95 per cent that do not break even in sales, the sector exhibits the classic risk profile of the creative industries, where hits are greatly outnumbered by misses (Cutler and Company 2002: 18). Games distributors nonetheless seek out a range of titles in order to ensure a diverse portfolio of creative product that is either in the market or under development, and games developers learn to live with chronic insecurity, high upfront costs, and the need to develop market savvy in dealing with games publishers/distributors.

The 2000s have been dominated by the growth of MMOGs (sometimes known as MMORPGs for 'massively multiplayer online role playing games'). 'Ultima Online' was launched in October 1997 and by early 2001 had almost 250,000 subscribers. Its success would in turn be overtaken by the striking rise of the online role-playing game, 'EverQuest', released in July 1999 by Verant Interactive, a division of Sony Entertainment Online. 'EverQuest' is an online role-playing game, or what Edward Castronova (2005) terms a massively populated persistent world (MPPW), where players adopt avatars (online personas) and undertake a range of activities such as trading, exploring, producing items, and engaging in combat, in the fantasy world of Norrath. The growth in MMOGs has been further stimulated by the emergence of games such as 'Dark Age of Camelot', 'The Sims Online', and 'Star Wars: Galaxies'. In Asia the game 'Lineage' had attracted over four million subscribers by 2002 and it is estimated that 17 million South Koreans are regularly gaming in PC Baangs (Internet café-style online game rooms), with up to 17 million engaged in 'e-sports' more generally, particularly around games such as 'StarCraft' (Cho 2006; Herz 2002; Rossignol 2006). Notably significant in the MMOG market has been 'Blizzard's World of Warcraft' (also known as WOW), which launched in 2004 and by January 2007 claimed eight million subscribers worldwide. Recently merged with Activision, WOW reported over 11 million players in 2008, a number that has held steady since (CBC 2010; Grey 2008). It has successfully entered the Asian market with more than 3.5 million subscribers in China and more than two million US subscribers. WOW has become something of a legend for surviving in an industry and category that had previously seen regular turnover and switching, as MMOG players shifted alliances to try the next big thing.

China is both a source of enormous growth for Blizzard and a continuing operational challenge, as China is home to numerous 'gold farmers': large groups of players who are recruited and (poorly) paid to 'play' by working in sweatshop conditions, grinding through levels and acquiring 'gold' (game currency). The gold is then sold to other players (who want to gain advantage or otherwise avoid the boring or difficult parts of the game) for real currency in unwelcome and unsanctioned but difficult to control online markets such as eBay. Blizzard also has a practical challenge in providing continuing service to their Chinese customers as the game is distributed and managed in that country through a Chinese partner company and there have been outages and shutdowns of the service by the Chinese government for both political and social (typically claims of combating 'game addiction') reasons.

Consoles have moved to capitalize on online environments with Microsoft's Xbox Live and Sony's Playstation3 both having online connectivity and networked gameplay. Voicechat is also available, meaning that players in disparate locations can communicate with each other by talking rather than typing. This move away from keyboard controls is extended even further by Sony's Playstation Portable (PSP), Nintendo's Wii, and Microsoft's Kinnect. The Wii has introduced game controllers that incorporate motion sensors and integrate players' movements with on-screen action. The Wii is marketed especially to those outside of the traditional gaming community.

Games Industry: Integrating and Disintegrating the Value Chain

Over the past 30 years, the games industry has evolved a multi-layered structure in which games development, distribution, platforms, and users have found themselves in shifting and interconnected arrangements. What is important to players is access to the gaming experience, but different players seek different experiences. One of the ways that both game developers and players have coped with the diversity of possible games is the creation of genres. Just as there are Mystery and Romance sections in the bookstore, so too have games evolved into categories that provide familiarity and predictability for producers and consumers of. For example, there are the high adrenaline games such as first person shooters or driving games, strategy games, social games, and casual games. And, games frequently blend these genres, with social strategy games, strategic first person shooter games, or multiplayer games with one-on-one aspects.

Industry profitability is typically tied to the software (i.e. the games), with hardware sold at minimal, sustainable costs and often at a loss. More recently, games development has been dominated by the rise of middleware, which straddles the hardware/software divide. Middleware involves the development of game engines, including physics engines that can be repurposed for different games, renderware which turns mathematical models of shapes ('wire frames') into shapes with colour, shadow, and texture. There are also other software tools that assist with the production of the game software. These middleware tools reduce the amount of time that developers need to spend on programming for each game and represent a move towards some standardization within the industry.

What is most highly valued in the games industry is the creative abilities or intellectual capital of those involved in the development of games, in areas such as creative design and scripting, software programming, project management and production, and systems development. Yet, this can in turn generate familiar tensions in between the creative people, the technology developers, and corporate interests, those responsible for the mass marketing of commercial games products. The video games industry crash of the mid-1980s and the meltdown of Atari, in particular, was triggered in part by the incompatibility of the creative ethos of game designers and the corporate environment, by expectations of traditional media giants such as Time-Warner, as well as the pressure to rush poorly designed titles to market in order to meet marketing deadlines. This in turn generated a consumer backlash to what Kline and colleagues (2003: 105) refer to as the 'suck factor' or 'software pumped out without quality control [which] failed because the experiences it offered were simply not worth the investment of time or money'.

More recently, Electronic Arts (EA) has been criticized for rushing products to market that still contained significant bugs and for overworking employees. In 2004, EA paid USD $30 million to settle class action suits undertaken by both game artists and programmers for alleged non-payment of overtime and other benefits, after it was claimed on sites such as the famous 'EA Spouse' blog that it had become mandatory for staff to work 80 hours per week at all times (Feldman and Thorsen 2004). Within the games industry there is widespread criticism of reliance on 'crunch time' in the period leading up to the launch of a game, when staff are expected to work in excess of 80 hours per week, leading to sleep deprivation, poor productivity, high levels of staff turnover (also known as 'churn'), bugs and other errors in the games, employee burn-out, and adverse effects not only on the employees themselves, but also on their spouses and families (Robinson 2005). Chris Taylor, the founder and CEO of Gas Powered Games and lead designer of the PC-based real-time strategy (RTS) game 'Supreme Commander', drew attention to this when he argued at the 2007 Game Developers' Conference that staff who worked regular hours produced considerably better games than those subject to crunch time regimes:

> You make better games when you work regular hours. You're more creative—when you go home at night you're still thinking, because you're creative people. So when you get back at the computer, you have all these ideas and you get them down anyway . . . We don't want people to live in the office at Gas Powered Games. (Quoted in Ramsay 2007)

Kline and colleagues (2003: 200) have argued that 'management harnesses youthful technophilia to a compulsive-obsessive work ethic, one-dimensional character formation, and a high rate of burnout'. The extent of this burnout and the impact it has had on family members was highlighted in the 'EA Spouse' case, in which the partner of an overworked game industry worker posted an open letter to a blog about the experience of living with the Electronic Arts work environment:

> [The letter describes how] . . . initial enthusiasm for a job with a company listed as one of *Fortune*'s '100 Best Companies to Work For' had evaporated, as seven-day, 85-hour work weeks, uncompensated either by overtime pay or time off, became routine. It told of EA's 'put up or shut up and leave . . . human resources policy'; of its dubious invocation of California labour-law exemptions on 'specialty' employees to avoid paying overtime; and of creativity decomposing in a 'money farm' churning out commercially safe game designs. Describing an industry pressing its workers 'to individual physical health limits' EA Spouse wrote of how 'the love of my life is coming home late at night complaining of a headache that will not go away and a chronically upset stomach, and my happy supportive smile is running out'. (Dyer-Witheford and de Peuter 2006)

Notably, Dyer-Witheford and de Peuter do not simply paint the life of a video game employee as that of an exploited worker. They give full acknowledgement to the agency and intent of those workers in choosing and continuing in their jobs. Using a formula that they call 'enjoyment, exclusion, exploitation, and exodus', Dyer-Witheford and de Peuter describe a workplace that is a site of struggle and while people do enjoy working on video games and in the 'game culture', they do not simply put up with anything and everything to remain there.

It has been argued that the creative industries have long exemplified a **post-Fordist** business model, where the generation of creative content is structurally separated from its distribution and marketing (Aksoy and Robins 1992; Caves 2000; Christopherson and Storper 1986; Garnham 1987), and this certainly characterizes the games industry. Just as the 1980s industry fallout marked the realization that games hardware should be developed separately from games software, the 1990s marked a further break-up between games development and games publishing or distribution. The games industry today is characterized by a complex and recursive game development value chain in which some companies are building tools, some companies are doing nothing but special effects, and some companies specialize in motion capture or physics engines or faces. Sawyer (2002) argues that the games industry value chain can be seen as having six distinct but connected layers:

1. capital and publishing layer, involved in investing in new titles, and seeking returns through licensing for those investments;
2. product and talent layer, which includes developers, designers, and artists, who may be working under individual contracts or as part of in-house development teams;
3. production and tools layer, which generates content production tools, game development middleware, customizable game engines, and production management tools;
4. distribution layer, or the publishing industry, involved in generating and marketing catalogues of games for retail and online distribution;
5. hardware layer, or the providers of the underlying platform, which may be console-based, personal computer-based, or accessed through new generation mobile devices; and,
6. end-users layer, or the users/players of the games.

Sawyer further identifies significant trends in the games industry in the first decade of the twenty-first century as follows:

- a shift from 'shrink-wrap'-based distribution in which games are marketed and sold as physical goods on cartridge or CD-ROM, to online distribution, which will make it much easier to upgrade games through online expansion packs;
- increasingly simultaneous releases of games and associated products, such as music or movies, enabling greater marketing coordination in multiple markets;
- the global growth of pervasive gaming experiences, as games products increasingly span platforms (console, computer, television, handheld device) and use mobile and wireless technologies to reach people wherever they are, and whenever they want; and,
- the rise of game players as fourth-party developers of game content, which will accompany more open source models of game design, development, and engineering.

It is the last of these that is of particular interest, since it places the games industry at the centre of the shift from mass media models based on producer-defined content where users are consumers of the already defined product, to a new media model, the possibility of an endlessly recursive loop between producers and consumers. Sawyer observes that the modification of game content by online user communities—known as **modding**—has been a characteristic of computer-based games since the mid-1990s. Games such as 'Counter-Strike', for instance, are a user modification or 'Mod' of an earlier computer-based game, 'Half-Life'. While this community of modifiers may only make up about one per cent of a particular game's user base, the number of those involved will clearly grow as both the international community of gamers grows and as more games offer modifying opportunities. Sawyer (2002) estimates that this could generate as many as 600,000 established online game community developers by 2012 and that 'for the industry value chain, this foretells the rise of an entirely new component to the gaming industry. If user-led development continues to mature, it will begin to integrate itself into the overall industry, but it will also seek tools and services specific to its role in the development process'.

In the online games environment, the emergence of user-led games development has been associated with a new dialogue between the games industry and game players, where the latter increasingly constitute a community interacting with games developers about the nature of a game. Total conversion of an existing game—as in the case of 'Counter-Strike'—is uncommon and is often in breach of the original developer's copyright. More common are what are known as partial conversions or the addition of new items, such as weapons, characters, enemies, models, modes, textures, levels, and story lines by the players themselves (Wikipedia Contributors 2007). Very popular games such as 'World of Warcraft', the 'Star Wars' games, the 'Doom' series, 'Command & Conquer', and 'Battlefield 1942' actively promote and assist user modification and very lively online user communities exist to provide tools and software to assist. This of course draws attention to the question of who owns the subsequently modified content, as most games also have End-User Licensing Agreements (EULAs) that assign the ownership of that content to the game's creators. A key issue arising from game players becoming content co-creators is therefore that of control over the game itself and associated ownership of the player-created intellectual property that resides both within the game and in associated fan-based media such as websites, blogs, and other forms of online user community formation.

The Game Industry in Canada

Canada is home to numerous game companies, including branch offices of major players such as Electronic Arts and Ubisoft. Studios exist in most major cities in Canada, with concentrations in Vancouver, Toronto, and Montreal (Smith 2004, 2006). Canada also has its share of superstar game developers, the most famous of whom is probably Don Mattrick, associated with a variety of games, including 'Evolution' and 'Test Drive'. He became a legend in the Vancouver game scene when his company became part of Electronic Arts (EA) in 1991 and he became an instant millionaire.[3]

Many of the EA sports titles continue to be produced in the EA Canada studios in Burnaby, British Columbia, which have become well known for cutting edge technologies developed in the EA research and development labs, also based in Burnaby. Soccer, baseball, and football are all realistically recreated on computer screens using motion-capture technology developed there. Star athletes come to the studios and wear special suits equipped with sensors, acting out their key moves, which are then embedded in the game for a greater sense of realism.

Employment in the gaming industry is seen as an important outcome of policy initiatives particularly in British Columbia, Ontario, and Quebec. Various incentives are put in place to encourage companies to locate their studios in those provinces, including tax breaks and other programs for game employers. Ontario has the Ontario Interactive Digital Media Tax Credit, for example, which provides up to 40 per cent of wage expenses as a tax credit to eligible companies. British Columbia has a similar program, providing a 17.5 per cent tax credit for labour expenses on interactive media.

Some analysts have been critical of parts of the game industry for developing a type of share cropper mentality in which game developers are set the task of creating games using licensed assets (typically spin-offs from Hollywood films and television programs), using standardized tools, leaving them with no intellectual property but only a fee for their service (Smith 2006). Small game companies sometimes turn to these contracts as a way to build revenues while they are starting out, but unfortunately are unable to break out and develop their own games and end up folding or being bought by larger game companies. A Vancouver firm, Radical Entertainment—ironically developed as a breakaway boutique firm from the Electronic Arts mother ship—now develops games exclusively for its new media conglomerate owner, Vivendi (Smith 2006). The Ontario tax credit system recognizes the dangers of this approach and encourages those with their own intellectual property by offering a higher rate of tax credit—40 per cent versus 35 per cent—for products developed under a 'fee-for-service' arrangement.[4]

Game Cultures

Playing games can be a solitary pastime but it is more often something done with other people. Digital games are proving to be increasingly social—a trend that works against the mainstream media's portrayal of players as isolated (usually adolescent) boys, hidden away in darkened bedrooms, failing to engage with the social world. Recent statistics show that between 40 and 50 per cent of computer game players are women and that the average age of players is increasing and is now between the late twenties and early thirties (Brand 2007; ESA 2006). Digital games are played in many different and often very social and public settings. Consoles and computers may be located in the living areas of domestic homes, where people often play with friends and family. Local area network (LAN) parties, where people get together in larger public spaces and create networks of computers to play with each other, have been held for many years now. Large gatherings of dedicated game fans have assembled at events like the 'EverQuest Fan Faires', where several thousand players of 'EverQuest' come together for weekends of socializing and playing. In these ways people create communities around their game-playing activities, much as they have done around sports, hobbies, and other pastimes.

In South Korea, the phenomenon of PC Baangs online game rooms is widespread.[5] South Korea has one of the highest rates of broadband penetration in the world, which has connected domestic spaces and enabled people to play online games together. The main game played is the strategy game, 'StarCraft', which is 'not just a game in South Korea, it is a national sport . . . Five million people . . . play. And three cable stations broadcast competitive gaming full-time to a TV audience' (Herz 2002). South Korea also had the largest online role-playing game for many years, 'Lineage', which has more than three million subscribers ('World of Warcraft' has exceeded this figure recently). Players of 'Lineage' often play together in PC Baangs, talking to each other across the room, as they play together in the virtual space.

The PC Baangs are a particularly illustrative example of the ways in which online and offline spaces can be seen as merged rather than separate. The high rate of broadband connectivity and the specific cultural mores of Korean society may mean that other countries do not develop public game cultures in the same way, but the potential is there (Rossignol 2006). Even when players are not physically located in the same space, they are often involved in socializing together. This is particularly so with the online gaming communities. In many of the online games, whether they are FPS games like 'Quake', action games like 'Counter-Strike' or role-playing games (RPG) such as 'World of Warcraft' and 'EverQuest', play is organized around clans or guilds. Players will form or join groups that persist over many sessions of play, sometimes for years. Clans and guilds can be made up of people who know each other offline (friends and families often play together), people who have never met in person, or a combination of these. Clans and guilds vary in their styles and functions. Some exist in order to fight or raid together, while others exist for more social purposes, providing an online family for players. Like sports teams, clans and guilds can create an experience of belonging and of cooperative teamwork, as well as competition. People learn to carry out particular roles within groups and organize themselves into joint projects (slaying dragons, completing quests, fighting other clans, raiding, building cities or empires, or whatever else the game environment enables).

Like any other social formation, these groups are both self-regulating, creating their own social norms, and subject to regulation and constraint through the code of the game and sometimes through the policing of the game by owners, administrators, and publishers who run the game. The values that are policed vary from game to game. Many of the values encoded into game cultures reflect offline cultural values, but games also offer a chance to emphasize alternative or subjugated values in the name of fantasy and play. Real-world law also comes into play in the regulation of games spaces. Players and publishers enter into EULAs or Terms of Service agreements and this is where some of the terms of game-play are encoded.

It is often argued, particularly in the mainstream media, that digital games cause violence. The effects-based research, which gives rise to the 'computer games cause violence' discourse, is mostly psychology-based research, often linked to moral panic discourses, particularly after horrific events (such as the shooting of schoolchildren at Columbine High School in Littleton, Colorado in 1999).[6] Cause-effect models of relationship between game-play and real world violence have encountered criticism and the evidence that games cause violent behaviour has been challenged and regarded as highly contestable (Vastag 2004).

Cause-and-effect models often take insufficient account of the relevance of cultural contexts and the ways in which media are actually implicated in the circulation of meanings in our cultures. Also, differing contexts of media consumption must be taken into account, which include the particularities of players and how and why they play.

Games are also frequently cited as a source of anti-social behaviour among (mainly) young people, and especially boys because of their supposed addictive properties. These addictive properties are most often ascribed to role-playing games, but all computer games have been tarred with this brush from time to time. As with debates linking gaming to violence, the debate rages back and forth between those who dismiss concerns and those who describe games as sharing certain properties with drug addiction. Chee and Smith have argued that rather than seeing games as akin to an addictive substance, it is more useful to look closely at the role of the community of gamers and the place they occupy in the players' lives.[7]

Questions of identity often arise in relation to digital games. Key concerns related to issues of identity and games have focused on the representations offered to players (in the forms of avatars), the question of how players identify with or relate to their avatars, and the styles of play suggested and enabled by games and whether they are gender-biased. Representations of gender in digital games are often sexist, with hard-bodied muscled men and soft-bodied nearly naked women being common. Bryce and Rutter (2002: 246) find in their research that 'female game characters are routinely represented . . . as princesses or wise old women in fantasy games, as objects waiting on male rescue, or as fetishized subjects of male gaze in first person shooters'. These roles emphasize female passivity and highlight a dominance of masculine themes. Not all games are like this, but enough are to make it notable as a general characteristic. Access to the machines to play games may also be gendered. A further argument on gender and games is that people of different genders have different gaming styles or preferences and that these differences are not catered to by the market (Cassell and Jenkins 1998); however, this is much disputed.[8]

The context of play is a significant factor for identity in games. It is important to recognize that the game-world, rather than being completely separate from the real world, is embedded in a real-world context that determines game experience (Chee, Vieta, Smith 2006). Issues of identity also need to be considered in terms of the choices that gamers make. Players use games and their enabling representations in many ways. For instance, a player may choose (or not choose) to play a stereotypical female avatar for different reasons: Some women enjoy adopting what they feel to be an image of femininity more acceptable or desirable than their real-world body, while other women may feel completely alienated by what they see as an offensive or unreal representation of femininity. Some women may choose to play as a male character instead. Men may choose to play as female characters because they expect that they will be given more gifts by the male characters. Some men will play using a female avatar for quite instrumental reasons: if the female character has different abilities than the male, what the avatar looks like does not matter; what matters is what it can do (Newman 2002). Some people like to experiment with cross-gendered play out of their own curiosity. Identity tourism, as Nakamura (2000) notes, tends to perpetuate and accentuate existing stereotypes, as people adopt alternative identities based on understandings gleaned from other media representations. As Sherry Turkle notes, there is considerable 'plasticity' when it comes to identity and the role that games play in both enabling and shaping our identity remains an important area for social research (Turkle 1997).

Games are also a serious issue for those who have concerns about the increasing commercialization of childhood and the role that computer games and online games in particular play in this process. There is a growing trend to link games to television programs and children's toys such as Webkinz (www.webkinz.com), for example (Grimes 2008). This connection has, as one might imagine, stirred up a considerable controversy both in the academic world and in public and policy circles. Club Penguin —one of the most successful independent online games for children—was developed in Kelowna, British Columbia, and from a financial perspective is a remarkable Canadian success story. It was recently purchased by the Disney Company, anticipating a link between Club Penguin and Disney movies, theme parks, and merchandising. (See Case Study).

Games and the Academy: Game Cultures and Game Studies

As the computer games industry has grown exponentially as both an employer and as an influence in the lives of millions of gamers, game studies has become a significant area of academic research in research associations, research centres, journals, and scholarly texts. The Canadian Game Studies Association (http://contagion.edu.yorku.ca/cgsa) and its companion journal, *Loading: A Journal of the Canadian Game Studies Association* (http://journals.sfu.ca/loading) was an early entrant in the field, as was DIGRA, the Digital Games Research Association (www.digra.org). Other academic journals include *Game Studies* (www.gamestudies.org) and *Games and Culture* (http://gac.sagepub.com). Games research is conducted at sites such as the Experimental Game Lab at Georgia Tech in the US (http://egl.gatech.edu) and the Center for Computer Games Research at the IT University of Copenhagen (http://game.itu.dk). Some of the key texts in the field include *Digital Play* (Kline et al. 2003) and *Game Cultures* (Dovey and Kennedy 2006). While computer games have been studied from computer science perspectives, and their impact on players from medical and psychological perspectives, the game studies literature is distinctive in aiming to bring insights from critical humanities traditions to the study of computer games, without subsuming their distinctive forms and properties into existing film, media, or cultural studies paradigms.

Some of the distinctive features of digital games that have drawn the attention of the research community are user interactivity, immersion in a virtual environment, social interaction within the game, and the capacity of players to become co-creators of content, especially in multi player games. While none of these are unique to games, they suggest an interesting and more productive relationship between the players and the game text than is characterized by other media. This relationship involves more than active interpretation of the text or identity construction through consumption: it is a form of engagement that serves to *create* the text each time a person engages with the game.

Early game studies debates were concerned with the ways game texts work and a particularly intense debate arose between those who held that narrative is the key organizing structure of a game (the narratologists) and those who subscribed to play theory (the ludologists). Authors such as Murray (1997) and Bolter and Grusin (2000), for example, discussed how computer games employ aspects of narrative and they identified games as emergent forms of story-telling or 'cyber-dramas', in which there would evolve greater narrative complexity over time. By contrast, ludologists such as Aarseth (2001) and Juul (2003) argued that there was a quite different relationship of the player to the game, since the goal-driven nature of games brings an emotional engagement with the text derived not from appreciation of characters and events (such as occurs in conventional narratives), but rather, because the players are actors themselves, seeking a goal. The engagement is derived from the player being a performer and the game evaluates the performance and adapts to it. As a result, argued some ludologists, there is a need to incorporate elements of play theory as an alternative to traditional models of literary theory and the applied humanities (Juul 2003; Liestøl 2003) in game studies research.

Two further developments can be noted in this rapidly changing field. One has been the growing awareness that games are big business and need to be taken seriously as such. Political economists of media, and game studies in particular, need to engage more systematically with the unique political economy of the games industry. There has been some movement in this direction lately. Kline et al. (2003) and Kerr (2006), in particular, give close attention to the changing economic dynamics of the global games industry, a concern that is also discussed in detail by Dovey and Kennedy (2006). Four features of the political economy of games are prominent in this literature. First, the games industry sector is subject to strong dynamics of concentration and consolidation, despite the large number of games titles available. This is most apparent in the console-based games market, where the big three console providers—Sony, Microsoft, and Nintendo—can exert substantial control over games publishers and developers, but it is also a characteristic of the PC-based and multiplayer online games markets (Kerr 2006: 54–61). Second, games production increasingly occurs through global production networks, although production in emergent countries remains very much tied to the distributional relations controlled by the big console and publishing companies based in the US, Japan, and to a lesser extent, Europe (Kerr 2006: 76–9). Third, as noted above with the case of EA Spouse, workplace relations in the games industry are notoriously harsh, with long hours, extended crunch times, job insecurity, and a sense of forced 'workaholism' leading to high rates of labour turnover and burn-out among those employed in the sector (IGDA 2004).

Gill (2002, 2006) also identifies how this work environment is particularly incompatible with family or parental responsibilities and how many women in new media sectors intensely dislike this combination of a boys-club type culture and a lack of interest in social skills or self-care; employment rates for women in the games industry are well below those of most other sectors (Dovey and Kennedy 2006: 61–2). Fourth, as the sector seems to clone a certain type of worker—young, male, and with limited responsibilities outside of work—and since males aged 13–25 represent the market best understood in the sector, it is highly likely that 'the prospects for widespread innovation become very limited . . . [as] a minority of gamers with a particular set of tastes command a large cultural space which is disproportionate to their actual numbers' (Dovey and Kennedy 2006: 62).

Dyer-Witherford and Sharman's review of the political economy of Canada's game industry (2005), provides an excellent introduction to both recent research—they report on a three-year study—and to key data on firms, labour relations, and government interventions.

The second major development has been the growing presence and popularity of so-called 'emergent' games. Rather than dictating the direction of play, emergent games offer environments and sets of rules, but not a hard-and-fast direction in which play must proceed. What results is an endless variety of unexpected play directions emerging from players' own decisions about what to do within that environment. Many multiplayer online games take this form, to a greater or lesser extent. A role-playing game like 'EverQuest' or 'World of Warcraft' provides a world for players to log into and they play with each other within that world. There is a system of 'leveling up' that gives a sense of progress to players, but the particular ways in which they achieve that progress are not set and some players may choose not to progress and to do other things instead, such as focusing on more social aspects of the game. Structurally, the text is added to and changed by the player, rather than being finished by the developer. In this model, publishers rely on players to continue the cycle of development. Thus, a game can be seen as the result of a combination of paid and unpaid labour, whose features arise in a variety of new media contexts, but are particularly marked in relation to games. It is clear that player creativity is part of the game production cycle in a number of ways. Emergent games are based on a recursive model of production whereby players create various iterations of the text. Players can also become part of the production cycle as modders or people who make new objects for games, new levels or artificial intelligence for games, or even whole new games (like 'Counter-Strike', as mentioned earlier).[9]

The computer games industry

The games industry is currently faced with choices about how much they will embrace the player creators or mod-communities as part of their structure. Some industry leaders are openly encouraging of such communities, releasing the source code and tools for creating content. Others have chosen instead to enclose their games in heavily policed copyright or intellectual property regimes, which precludes the creation of derivative works by fans. As models, the former seeks to leverage the R&D capacities of the player communities and harness the creativity of players, while the latter holds to more conventional production and intellectual property rights (IPR) management. These choices in licensing in the new production models hold opportunities for innovative new industry structures—structures that fully embrace the recursive and fluid features of the networked, interactive technology and the passion of the gamers. It is here, too, that work must be done to determine what the rights of this passionate productive community might be. Who should own the intellectual property rights of player-created content? How can IPR be managed such that these practices do not become exploitative? Is property even the most appropriate model to be using? Intellectual property is much better suited to conventional texts that are fixed or finished, rather than to ongoing collaborative creations like games made through the joint effort between developers and players.

Games need to be understood as exemplary and illustrative of the possibilities and challenges presented by online interactive environments. The networked nature of the game production cycle is one that will become more prevalent with time. Some of the key issues arising in the games industry and game studies are not restricted to games, but rather, are indicators of structural changes that give rise to broad-scale concerns related to existing regimes of the management and regulation of new media. The more that interactive applications are created and used in our increasingly connected and networked environments, the more issues of regulation, ownership, and service will arise and need to be looked at in light of the differences inherent in these interactive texts.

Online social environments such as multiplayer online games present the challenges not only of resolving issues of IPR management, but also, of community management. What governance regimes are instituted by media corporations that have as their main goal the generation of profit rather than social equity? Should there be any checks and balances on corporate behaviour in this respect or should it be left to the marketplace to regulate? These are questions that will rise in importance as more and more people live parts of their lives inside proprietary spaces and contribute to the economic well-being of media corporations. Although the media publishers may not have financial obligations to the player-creators, they may instead incur social obligations. Issues such as the terms of access to environments, freedom of speech, and privacy are all currently determined through EULAs or Terms of Service Agreements, which in most cases are heavily weighted in favour of the publishers. Such imbalances may come to be the source of struggle and negotiation in the same way as has been the case with the ownership of player-created intellectual property.

Computer games were successful interactive entertainment applications long before other applications. They have shown the way forward with structural design and technological innovation generating engaging and often profitable environments. The position of computer games at the forefront of innovation in the digital world has meant that they often indicate where change, negotiation, and controversy will arise in much broader arenas. It is well worth attending to the issues that arise from computer games: the structural changes to the nature of the text; the reorganization of the relations of production and the impacts on industry; the reshaping of the role of consumers and the effects on social relations; and the new configurations of authorship and the consequences for intellectual property are just some of the areas that have wide significance and justify academic attention.

Case Study: Club Penguin

If you thought a simple web-based game (using Adobe Flash technology) about penguins living in igloos (never mind the North and South Pole confusion) and aimed at pre-teens seemed like an unlikely success, you would have been wrong. Club Penguin, launched in October 2005 by an independent game company based in Kelowna, British Columbia, grew to almost 700,000 members before being purchased by the Disney Company in 2007 for USD $350 million (Barnes 2007). The game has remained in Kelowna, with its 130 employees, and has continued to flourish under the new management. With more than 6 million members from 190 countries worldwide in 2010, it is the largest online computer game for children in the world. The runner-up, Webkinz, has just 3.8 million members (Barnes 2010). The Club Penguin site carries no advertising, relying on subscriptions ($5.95 a month at the time of writing, June 2010) for revenues. A free version is available for those wishing to try out the service.

Club Penguin was created by a group of three men, all parents, who sought to create a safe place for children to interact online. The game emphasizes fun, through little mini-games and modifications you can make to your penguin character (avatar) and his or her home (typically an igloo). Participants can also chat with each other, but with a high degree of control on what can be said and to whom, something that parents are concerned about. Players can play on a computer or, as of June 2010, a Wii game console (Businesswire 2010).

The founders have been very careful with the tone and style of the game, sometimes to the chagrin of Disney executives who hoped for more tie-ins to other Disney brands and theme parks (Barnes 2010). There is a strong global awareness focus to the game and the founders have devoted 10 per cent of their initial purchase price to a foundation dedicated to child-focused charitable work (Stueck 2007). Members of the site can also donate their virtual money to the Coins for Change program inside the site. The patterns of donations helped shape the fund's operations into three categories: kids who are sick, kids who are poor, and the environment.

Still, games designed for children is not an uncontroversial topic, despite the best intentions of the founders of the site. Critics worry about excessive time spent indoors, excessive time spent in virtual rather than face-to-face play (Levitt 2008), the possibility of stalkers or others who prey on children, and the commodification of children's play (Grimes 2008).

 ## Useful Websites

Game Studies
←www.gamestudies.org→

This is an online academic journal dedicated to developing cross-disciplinary research into games. It has been a leader in developing the play-based approach to studying games.

Canadian Game Studies Association (CGSA)
←http://contagion.edu.yorku.ca/cgsa/index.php→

CGSA is an association supporting the work of Canadian researchers, graduate students, artists, game designers, programmers, theorists, and others working in the interdisciplinary study of digital games. CGSA also has a journal: *Loading: A Journal of the Canadian Game Studies Association*.

International Game Developers Association
←www.igda.org→

This is the website of the premier international game developers' association. It includes particularly interesting resources on quality of life issues for those working in the games industry.

WomenGamers.com
←www.womengamers.com→

This website is for women who play computer games, who work in the games industry, and for anyone interested in questions around gender and gaming.

TerraNova
←http://terranova.blogs.com→

This is a must read site for both academic and industry observers of the virtual worlds aspect of games and for those working in the game industry. Founded by four prominent game scholars, it contains well-written and insightful commentary by a rotating group of practitioners and academics.

Further Reading

For The Win, Cory Doctorow (2010)
Doctorow's novel about unrest in the 'gold farmer' ranks in a near future world presents an eloquent portrayal of game culture and the issues and the economics of virtual economies. Available as a Creative Commons download or as a printed book, this would make an excellent supplement to those interested in knowing more about life for non-Western gamers as well as those who play games but are not familiar with the back room decisions that go into the economic aspects of games with virtual currencies.

Learning with Digital Games: A Practical Guide to Engaging Students in Higher Education, Nicola Whitton (2010)
One of the interesting developments in the past few years has been the use of games for learning, premised on the notion that people are both used to learning through games (of course, they are learning game-related concepts), and that games, being fun and engaging, will help people with the repetition or exploration that is required to learn new material. Games can also bring in a competitive aspect that motivates some players/learners. Whitton's book examines this phenomenon in the context of higher education and discusses both using existing games and developing new games.

From Barbie to Mortal Kombat: Gender and Computer Games, Justine Cassell and Henry Jenkins (eds.), (1998)
Although this collection is a bit dated now, it lays the groundwork for what has become a considerable scholarship on games and gender. The book is worth a read, if only to dispel some of the old stereotypes of games being something that only boys play, or that girls do not play action games.

Additional games titles include: *The Business and Culture of Digital Games: Gamework and Gameplay* (Kerr 2006), *Computer Games: Text, Narrative and Play* (Carr et al. 2006), *Understanding Digital Games* (Rutter and Bryce 2006), and *Worlds in Play: International Perspectives on Digital Games Research* (de Castell and Jenson, eds. 2007). Each of these provides additional insights into games and gaming from an industry-insider perspective (Kerr), semiotic analysis (Carr et al.), and game research overview (Rutter and Bryce, as well as De Castell and Jenson's edited collection).

Discussion Questions

1. What are the different roles (and their corresponding communities of professionals) in the games industry and what are some ways of describing the dynamics among them?

2. What are some of the shifts in the games industry described in this chapter?

3. There is an ongoing debate about whether or not digital games cause violence. Discuss both the legitimate concerns and justifiable objections in this debate.

4. What is meant by the term, 'game culture', and in what ways are people creating communities around their game-playing activities, much as they have done around sports, hobbies, and other pastimes?

5. This chapter draws attention to how the values encoded into game cultures reflect offline cultural values but also how games offer a chance to emphasize alternative or subjugated values in the name of fantasy and play. What are the implications of this and why are they significant?

6. Discuss the concerns related to issues of identity and gender-bias and games, as they are related to: the representations offered to players (in the forms of avatars), how players identify with or relate to their avatars, and the styles of play suggested and enabled by games.

7. Why do you think that the following distinctive features of digital games have drawn the attention of the research community: social interaction within the game, the capacity of players to become co-creators of content, and the relationship between the players and the game text?

Class Activities

1. Building on the notion of games in education (see the Whitton text, in Further Reading, above), create a game version of this course. How would points be awarded? Would the assignments be like 'quests' or 'kills', or something else? Do you think you would be more engaged by this experience? Create a paper version of the game, or discuss the rules, and then debate the expected outcome. You might take a look at the article from the *Chronicle of Higher Education* on Lee Sheldon's course in which the course itself is a game: http://chronicle.com/blogPost/At-Indiana-U-a-Class-on-Game/21981.

2. Online games, such as 'Second Life', frequently provide a free trial account that can be used by anyone. Hold a class discussion inside the game, with fellow students either logging in from their own laptops, from home, or from terminals at your school. Test the requirements (sometimes a game requires that software be downloaded, making it difficult to do on public computers), and if necessary, adjust to a virtual tour or demonstration by students who already have accounts. Consider a virtual tour of a particular type of game (e.g., a children's game such as Club Penguin). See Case Study, above, for more on Club Penguin.

7 Creative Industries

Questions to Consider

- What has been the significance of creative cities, historically? How do cities today work to remain part of this tradition of creative industry?

- What are the creative industries? How can the dynamics of these industries be characterized?

- In what ways are knowledge and information different from each other? Why is this relevant to understanding both the knowledge economy and creative industries?

- In what ways do policy initiatives undertaken in Canada and different parts of the world affect cultural industries?

Chapter Outline

In this chapter we consider the industrialization of creativity, something that was not initiated by new digital media—mechanical reproduction of works of art famously preoccupied Frankfurt School member Walter Benjamin in the first half of the twentieth century—but the process has accelerated, broadened, and deepened with digital media. We begin with an examination of the concept of creativity itself and especially the question of under what circumstances it can flourish. We next consider the notion of a creative industry and how and why this has become a policy objective of cities, provinces and states, and countries around the world. The reasons for the rise of a creative economy, creative cities, and the creative class both as realities and as visions or ideals, are considered and debated.

Creativity in Question

The first decade of the twenty-first century has seen a surge of interest in creativity that shows few signs of abating. The popular business literature exhorts corporate managers to unlock the creative potential of their staff, while there is also an extensive self-help literature on how to realize personal creativity (see de Bono 1995; Flew 2004a for discussion; Gary 1999; Nussbaum 2005; cf. Osborne 2003). Tim Berners-Lee (2000), a key figure in the development of the Web, notes a critical flaw in its commercially driven evolution since the mid-1990s—that interactivity is promoted ahead of intercreativity— while the legal scholar, Lawrence Lessig (2004), identifies the suppression of creativity as a critical flaw of current intellectual property regimes. In his highly influential, *The Rise of the Creative*

Class, Richard Florida (2002: 5) describes creativity as 'the decisive source of competitive advantage' in the twenty-first century global economy. Leadbeater (2007) proposes that the twenty-first century social-economic system is one that will be based on mass creativity.

Creativity, however, is a famously slippery conceptual category. In one highly influential understanding, which has its origins with both Plato and nineteenth-century Romanticism, any harnessing of creativity to organizations or to policy agendas is anathema, as creativity arises from the 'free, wakeful play of the imagination' (Negus and Pickering 2004: 7). In this tradition, creative people are seen as special people (the troubled genius persona), with creativity closely linked to the arts and not to business, science, or technology; further, the creative process is understood as essentially spontaneous, with the implicit assumption that creativity cannot be formally taught, since it is a gift that some have and others do not.

Bilton observes that although artists have come to be somewhat more circumspect about such understandings of creativity and increasingly interpret their activities through frameworks such as performative research or practice-led research (Gray 2006; Haseman 2006), the notion of creativity as the wild play of imagination has found new champions in the business community. This leads to assumptions that 'creative people need to be protected from commercial realities, that budgets and deadlines might interfere with the eccentric, child-like world of pure inventiveness . . . [and] managers are warned from "meddling" in the creative process because their rules and rationality have no validity in the world of art and innovation' (Bilton 2007: 8).

Such discourses in turn invoke skepticism about the value of the whole notion of creativity. In the context of debates about the creative industries, Donald (2004: 236) remains unconvinced that creativity is 'anything other than a conceptual black hole' and that trying to teach creativity is 'absurd and self-defeating' since demonstrated creativity is 'invariably a by-product of learning to do other, more concrete . . . things'. In a similar vein, Osborne (2003: 510) opposes the idea that creativity, as a feel-good concept, 'as a combination of doctrine and morality . . . can be captured by business gurus and management writers, Californian lifestyle sects, new age groups, post-identitarian philosophers, literary critics turned cultural theorists, intellectuals, postmodern geographers, anti-globalization protestors, whoever'.

Yet Clay Shirky, in *Cognitive Surplus: Creativity and Generosity in a Connected Age* (2010), describes how new digital technologies and especially social software and Web 2.0 technologies, are enabling forms of creativity that are not directly tied to making money but in fact are part of larger amateur contributions to the creative output of society. These amateur offerings are not just pale imitations of the professional side of creativity but something else entirely, created specifically and solely to be shared (2010: 78).

Going even further, authors such as Robinson (2001), Bilton and Leary (2002), Negus and Pickering (2004), and Bilton (2007) address some of the conceptual vagueness that has surrounded the concept of creativity, and move the debate beyond the Platonic conception of creativity as a unique individual gift. Robinson (2001: 116, 118) defines creativity as 'imaginative processes with outcomes that are original and of value' and asserts that 'creative ideas are more than novel; they are valuable'. Bilton and Leary (2002) argue that the criterion of value is as central as that of newness or innovation, even if it is recognized that the value of a new idea, concept, or product may not be appreciated at the time and place in which it is presented to the world. Negus and Pickering (2004) draw attention to several aspects of creativity: (i) the need for creative activities to demonstrate extrinsic value and for creative acts to be not only expressed, but also, effectively communicated; and (ii) the need to draw upon symbolic and representational systems that can be understood and appreciated by a wider audience, whether a relatively discrete community of scholars or practitioners, or audiences in the wider sense of the general public.

One study that illustrates how conceptual understandings of creativity have been usefully extended into the policy realm is the 'Beyond Productivity: Information Technology, Innovation, and Creativity' report for the US National Research Council of the National Academies (Mitchell et al. 2003). 'Beyond Productivity' makes much of the importance of domains of creativity, recognizing that 'no intellectual domain or economic sector has a monopoly on creativity' (2003: 18). The report acknowledges that creativity manifests itself differently across the scientific, technological, economic, and cultural domains, in diverse forms such as patents and designs, entrepreneurship, and artistic product. Identifying information technologies as a unifying factor that can bring these domains of creative practice into a closer collaborative set of relationships, the report maps these interconnections in the manner set out in Figure 7.1.

The specific focus of 'Beyond Productivity' is the extent to which developments in information technology and creative practice can be mutually reinforcing, generating dynamic forms of IT-related creative practice (ITCP) and new modes of research, collaboration,

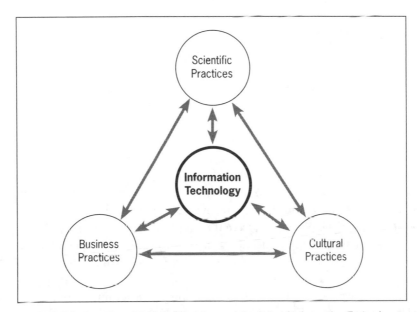

FIGURE 7.1 Domains of Creative Practice and the Role of Information Technology
Source: Mitchell et al. (2003: 25).

education, and wealth creation that bring together the fields of art, design, and information technology. Arguing that 'to work within the realm of information technology and creative practice . . . individuals or groups need to be fluent in multiple disciplines' (Mitchell et al. 2003: 30), 'Beyond Productivity' goes on to identify the main institutional and policy challenge as being how to better facilitate such cross-disciplinary interaction.

In the education context, Seltzer and Bentley (2000) seek to identify the implications of a growing stress on creativity in the knowledge economy for learning and for educational institutions. They reject claims that creativity is primarily associated with brilliance, a unique artistic sensibility, innate talents, or even acquired skills, arguing instead that:

> [creativity] requires the ability to solve problems progressively over time and apply previous knowledge to new situations. Creativity is also bound up with context—it can only be defined and assessed in relation to the context in which it is achieved. It must be developed through the interaction of the learner, her underlying goals and motivations, and the resources and context in which she operates. (2000: 19)

Seltzer and Bentley identify four core characteristics of creativity, which they associate with creative problem-solving:

1. the ability to formulate new problems, rather than depending on others to define them;
2. the ability to transfer what one learns across different contexts;
3. the ability to recognize that learning is incremental and involves making mistakes; and,
4. the capacity to focus one's attention in pursuit of a goal. (2000: 19)

For these writers, the paradox of the creative age for education is that the rapidly changing socio-economic environment requires individuals to be increasingly adaptive, however, adding more and more content into course curricula so that people can formally learn more and more skills (which is a model often used) does not train people for a creative environment. Creativity, understood in this way, is not seen as the unique property of the individual, but rather, creativity is understood as deeply shaped by both the domains in which it is applied (the arts, sciences, business, policy-making, community sector organizations, schools, etc.) and by those who validate creativity by making judgments on it. The nature of creativity in a given field may vary, from the judgments of teachers, professors, assessors, judges, or peers, to the purchasing decisions made by consumers. Given that the realization of creativity necessarily entails an interaction between the person, activity, and task, the domains in which it is applied and the fields through which it is validated, creative outcomes can never be guaranteed by a school curriculum, a government policy, or any single institutional instrument or form. Seltzer and Bentley (2000: ix) argue that creativity is best promoted in environments characterized by: trust, freedom of action, application across a variety of contexts, the balance between skills and challenges, interactive exchange of knowledge and ideas, and the experience of achieving concrete, real-world outcomes.

Burgess (2006) discusses the concept of vernacular creativity, linking it to a growing capacity for ordinary cultural participation—across the amateur/professional divide—with the democratizing and participatory potential of new media technologies. She defines vernacular creativity as 'both an ideal and a heuristic device, to describe and illuminate creative practices that emerge from highly particular and non-elite social contexts and communicative conventions' (2006: 206). The concept of the vernacular is used 'to distinguish "everyday" language from institutional or official modes of expression' and Burgess defines creativity as 'the process by which available cultural resources (including both "material" resources—content, and immaterial resources—genre conventions, shared knowledges) are recombined in novel ways, so that they are both recognizable because of their familiar elements, and create affective impact through the innovative process of this recombination' (2006: 206). In developing a definition of vernacular creativity, it is described as 'a productive articulation of consumer practices and knowledges . . . with older popular traditions and communicative practices' (2006: 207).

In his review of literature on management and creativity in the creative industries, Bilton (2007) draws attention to the phenomenon of 'the genius and the water-carrier'. Drawing on a comment by the former French soccer star Eric Cantona that his team-mate, Didier Deschamps, was 'merely a water-carrier', Bilton argues that it is precisely the existence of workhorse players whose play is characterized by effort and unspectacular endeavour that allows the brilliant but sometimes undisciplined players such as Cantona to flourish. Even if, as is often the case, it is those who are perceived to be creative geniuses who attract the most attention and, no less significantly, sponsorship. But flamboyant, creative individual talents such as Cantona, David Beckham, and others, are only as good as the teams around them. Bilton identifies in this a wider metaphor for the organization of creativity in the media entertainment industries, where creative teams and projects depend on uncreative people and activities:

> Creativity in the commercial creative industries is represented through the branding and packaging of individual talent and the personality cult fostered around stars and celebrities. Yet behind the scenes, a more realistic unit of analysis for creative processes and products is the team or partnership. At the core of this creative team is the double-act of the genius and the water-carrier. Creative thinking, like football, depends upon a union of contrasting abilities and styles of thinking or playing. (2007: 19)

Creativity, however defined, is significant in considering larger social and economic practices and dynamics that are embedded in organizations, networks (as we saw in Chapter 5), and industries. The next section of this chapter gives focus to the role that creative industries play in the economy and how digital new media are making it possible to turn creativity into commerce more quickly and across a wider geographic range than ever before.

The Rise of Creative Industries

The rise of **creative industries** is related to several trends: the growth in cultural production and consumption; the increasing significance of knowledge and creativity to all aspects of economic production, distribution, and consumption; and the growing importance of the services sector. The expansion of creative industries is also linked to the dynamics of knowledge-based, global, and networked economies (Castells 2000), as well as to the renewed attention given to the importance of location and place as drivers of creativity and innovation. This turn to the creative industries arises in part from the ability of ICTs to allow for greater flexibility in production—such as small-batch production rather than long production runs—as well as the increasingly common global separation of research and development activities from commodity production through global production networks (Ernst and Kim 2002). In industries such as film, television, and games, for example, this has been described as the 'Global Hollywood' model, where concept development and content production are increasingly geographically separated (Miller et al. 2001). The rise of creative industries also reflects the growing significance of design and signification, to everything from urban spaces, offices, retail outlets, cars, mobile phones, and indeed, corporations and governments themselves in an era of 'promotional culture' and electronic commerce (Graham 2006).

The rise of creative industries is commonly measured in economic terms. In 2005, Canada's Creative City Network published a series of reports called, 'Making the case for culture'. The lead-off report, titled, *Culture as an Economic Engine*, makes many of these same arguments, highlighting culture's impact on economic growth and jobs, on building linkages between public sector and private foundations, in helping cities become tourism destinations, and noting the link to urban revitalization, attraction of skilled workers, and the creation of spin-off businesses (Creative Cities 2005). The latter is reinforced in Richard Florida's argument on the importance of the **creative class** for innovation and economic development, generally. In the earliest work that used the concept, the Department of Culture, Media, and Sport (DCMS) in the United Kingdom identified the creative industries sectors as being worth £112 billion to the UK economy in 1997, accounting for five per cent of British GDP (DCMS 1998). Globally, John Howkins (2001) estimated the creative industries to be worth USD $2.2 trillion in 1999 and to account for 7.5 per cent of global GNP (Howkins 2001: 114), although it is important to note that this figure has been questioned on the basis of its inclusion of all research and development as well as the software industries into the creative industries (Cunningham 2002). A study from the US estimated that the copyright industries accounted for 7.75 per cent of US GDP and 5.9 per cent of national employment (2002). In the European Union (EU), where there is certainly no shared definitional understanding among its members as to the nature of the sector, it has nonetheless been observed that employment growth rates in cultural occupations were four times the EU average (4.8 per cent growth between 1995 and 1999, compared to overall employment growth in the EU of 1.2 per cent) and that people working in cultural occupations were almost three times as likely to be self-employed as the EU average (40.4 per cent compared to 14.4 per cent for the EU as a whole), and twice as likely to have a tertiary educational qualification (MKW 2001:

84–6). In a recent international survey of the creative industries and their wider relevance to economic development, the United Nations Conference on Trade and Development (UNCTAD) proposed that this sector now accounts for seven per cent of global GDP, with estimates of annual growth of 10 per cent or more per annum, with annual growth in some sectors of 20 per cent or more (UNCTAD 2004).

All these figures on the economic significance of the creative industries, however, draw attention to the question: what are the creative industries? The early approaches of DCMS had a dual focus. Creative industries were defined as 'those activities which have their origin in individual creativity, skill and talent and which have the potential for wealth and job creation through the generation and exploitation of intellectual property' (DCMS 1998). More pragmatically, the Creative Industries Task Force identified 13 sectors as constituting the creative industries (see Table 7.1).

This list-based approach inherently carried a pragmatic element where, in the UK case, the inclusion of sectors such as architecture and antiques was based on the institutional alignment of culture with the heritage industry. Garnham (2005) has argued that the linking of arts, media, and IT sectors has involved an unduly optimistic take on more longstanding problems and issues in the arts and cultural sectors, in order to link arts and cultural policy to the more salient—government—domain of information policy. In a different but related vein, Healy (2002: 101) argues that the evidence for transition towards a new economy that has creativity as its 'axial principle' is at best mixed, and cautions against 'using new economy jargon to give a bullish defence of the arts in economic terms'.

Underpinning these discussions are shifting understandings of culture and its nature, role, and significance. The historical tension between 'culture as aesthetics' and 'culture as everyday life' has been noted in the historical genealogy of the term (Bocock 1992; Williams 1976). What is now apparent is that there are three further overlays on the concept of culture that have significant implications for thinking about the creative industries:

1. culture as mediated symbolic communication, or the interaction between systems of mass-mediated representation of social reality and the everyday reality of lived

---

TABLE 7.1 Creative Industries in the United Kingdom (DCMS study)

Advertising	**Interactive leisure software**
Architecture	Music
Arts and antique markets	Television and radio
Crafts	Performing arts
Design	Publishing
Designer fashion	Software
Film	

Source: DCMS (1998).

experience, much of which occurs through mediated forms (TV and radio, computers, mobile phones, etc.);

2. culture as resource, or the tendency identified by Yúdice (2003: 9) for culture to be 'increasingly wielded as a resource for both socio-political and economic amelioration' across a range of fields, and his associated concept of the expediency of culture, or the growing understanding of its role as being involved in the deployment of specific resources to identifiable ends; and,

3. culture as policy discourse, or the role identified by Bennett (1998) for cultural policy as a mechanism for intersecting governmental priorities into everyday conduct, which have historically revolved around citizenship and the cultural sense of belonging to a nation, but are increasingly concerned with the management of culturally diverse populations.

The creative industries understood in this way become clearly significant for and linked to issues of economic drivers and entrepreneurial dimensions. We look at these issues in the next section.

Economic Drivers of Creative Industries

A mix of economic and cultural factors, with a very significant public policy overlay, has driven the rise of the creative industries. Factors driving the adoption of creative industries policy discourse have included: the re-branding of arts industries and arts policy to emphasize their significance as wealth-generating sectors (see, for example, Americans for the Arts 2007); the more general identification of creativity as a key driver of growth and innovation in a knowledge-based economy; the implications of digital convergence for bringing together the media and communications, cultural content, and information technology sectors; and the turn towards user-generated content in the context of Web 2.0. Hartley argues that 'the idea of the creative industries seeks to describe the conceptual and practical convergence of the creative arts (individual talent) with cultural industries (mass scale), in the context of new media technologies . . . within a new knowledge economy, for the use of newly interactive consumer-citizens' (2005: 5).

A study by the National Endowment for the Arts (2010), reports that 'arts participation through media appears to encourage—rather than replace—live arts attendance. There is a strong relationship between media arts participation and live arts attendance, personal arts performance, and arts creation' (14).

The three key economic drivers of creative industries have been the rise of the service industry sectors, the emergence of the knowledge-based economy, and the culturalization of the economy as services become increasingly central. Arguably the major trend in advanced capitalist economies since the 1970s has been the rise of the services industries as the principal source of employment, wealth generation, and innovation. In terms of both employment and the share of total output, the services industries have grown in significance throughout the twentieth century, and especially in the period after 1970. Castells and Aoyama note that, in 1990, services accounted for 75 per cent of employment in the US and 70 per cent of employment in the UK, compared to 52 per cent in the US and 47 per cent in the UK in 1920 (Castells and Aoyana 1994). Taking even more of a macro-historical perspective, Abramovitz and David (2001) observe that the growth in the share of intangible capital—devoted to knowledge production and dissemination, on the one hand and education, health, and well-being, on the other—has been accelerating in the US economy for the whole of the twentieth century and its share of total wealth has exceeded that of tangible capital (physical infrastructure, equipment, inventories, natural resources etc.) since the early 1970s. This trend can only be partly explained by the movement of manufacturing to lower-wage economies in developing countries. This is increasingly true of many developing countries: India has established itself as a global leader in IT-based services, while revisions in 2003 to how GDP was calculated in China found that the services sector was twice the size (40 per cent of the Chinese economy) as was previously thought. Moreover, manufacturers are themselves increasingly engaged in the services industries. Giarini (2002) observes that the pure cost of production or manufacturing of goods rarely accounts for more than 20 per cent of the final price and that 70 to 80 per cent of the cost is attributable to service and delivery functions undertaken before manufacturing (R&D, financing), during manufacturing (quality control, safety), selling (logistics, distribution networks), during product and system utilization (maintenance, leasing), and after product and system utilization (waste management, recycling). New media and especially the Internet is a key component in the creation and delivery of these services, many of which are themselves aspects of the creative economy.

In *The Age of Access*, Jeremy Rifkin (2000) locates the rise of services industries in a wider pattern of transformation of the nature of property and markets that includes the following shifts:

- from markets and discrete exchanges between buyers and sellers, to networks based on continuing relationships between suppliers and users;
- from wealth based on the ownership of tangible assets (plant, equipment, inventory, etc.), to the outsourcing of production, and wealth creation based on access to intangible assets, most notably goodwill, ideas, brand identities, copyrights, patents, talent, and expertise;
- from the ownership of goods to the accessing of services;
- from production and sales to customer relationship marketing; and,
- from production-line manufacturing and long product cycles to the Hollywood organizational model of project-based collaborative teams brought together for a limited time.

For Rifkin, these changes together marked the rise of cultural capitalism, developing out of new forms of linkage between digital communications technologies, culture, and commerce:

> More and more of our daily lives are already mediated by the new digital channels of human expression. And because communication is the means by

> which human beings find common meaning and share the world they create,
> commodifying all forms of digital communications goes hand in hand with
> commodifying the many relationships that make up the lived experience—
> the cultural life—of the individual and the community. (2000: 138)

The nature of a knowledge-based economy, and the role played in it by networks and clusters, will be explored in more detail in the next chapter. It is nonetheless worth noting several key ways in which the development of a knowledge-based economy has contributed to the rise of the creative industries. The relationship between information, knowledge, and creativity, and the ways in which sustained technological and economic innovation are accompanied by social, cultural, and institutional innovation, is strongly connected to the rise of creative industries. Fundamentally, there is an increasingly significant role for knowledge in all sectors in the twenty-first century new economy, as Leadbeater notes:

> In the new economy more of the value of manufactured products will come
> from the software and intelligence that they embody, and more of what we
> consume will be in the form of services. Across all sectors the knowledge con-
> tent of products and processes is rising . . . Knowledge push and market pull
> have made know-how the critical source of competitive advantage in the mod-
> ern economy. (2000: 39)

The concept of knowledge push refers to the growth in outputs in education and scientific research arising from public and private investment, and the ways in which ICTs speed up the production, collection, and dissemination of such research outcomes, enabling more rapid transformation into new products, services, activities, and processes (David and Foray 2002). Market pull factors that promote the rise of a knowledge economy include economic globalization, increased competition, greater sophistication in consumer demand, and the growing importance of intangible assets, such as branding and know-how, to competitive advantage.

The fact that knowledge is not synonymous with information, as Brown and Duguid (2000) point out, also contributes to the rise of the creative industries. At an epistemological level, they distinguish knowledge from information on the basis of the personal dimensions of ownership of knowledge, the difficulties in disembedding knowledge as content from those who possess it, and that knowledge transfer requires a learning process, which takes time and effort. You cannot simply send knowledge to someone, the way you might send him or her information. Arguing that a knowledge economy is different not only from an industrial economy but also from an information economy, they emphasize how 'the importance of people as creators and carriers of knowledge is forcing organizations to realize that knowledge lies less in its databases than in its people' (2000: 121).

Brown and Duguid's observations about the embodiment of knowledge and learning in people and communities is supported by Andy Pratt's (1998) observation that knowledge in the new economy is characterized not only by its weightlessness but also by its embeddedness in people, locations, networks, and institutions, and the related point that cultural activity and employment is not only growing, but is becoming more tied to places, especially cities. Justin O'Connor (1999) links this to new modes of cultural production and consumption among the young (18–35 years old) in urban centres where:

- making money and making culture are one and the same activity;
- there is an antipathy to distinguishing between work time and leisure time;
- there is a heavy reliance on informal networks for information and ideas;
- there is an emphasis on intuition, emotional involvement, immersion in the field, and an enthusiast's knowledge of the market; and,
- cultural producers desire to work for themselves and outside the nine-to-five routine.

Finally, the culturalization of economic activity over the latter half of the twentieth century has been an important factor in the rise of creative industries. Du Gay and Pryke (2002) and Amin and Thrift (2004) argue that there has been a growing 'culturalization of economic life' and that evidence of this can be found in the increasing importance of organizational culture as a key to economic performance; the rise of the services sector, where there is a 'more or less direct relationship . . . between one or more service provider and one or more service customer' (Du Gay and Pryke 2002: 3); and the growing role played by cultural intermediaries in sectors such as advertising, marketing communication, and public relations. Hauge and Hrac, in a 2010 paper on the link between indie music and local fashion designers in the Toronto area, provide an excellent example of this process at work (Hauge and Hracs 2010).

The creative industries also have their own distinctive dynamics as industries, which authors such as Lash and Urry (1994), Rifkin (2000), Lash (2002), and McRobbie (2005) suggest are increasingly becoming the norm in many sectors in the twenty-first century market capitalist economy. Harvard economist Richard Caves (2000) draws attention to core features of these sectors, whether publicly or privately supported:

1. considerable uncertainty about the likely demand for creative product, due to the fact that creative products are 'experience goods', where buyers lack information prior to consumption, and where the satisfaction derived is largely subjective and intangible;
2. the ways in which creative producers derive non-economic forms of satisfaction from their work and creative activity, but rely on the performance of more humdrum activities (e.g. basic accounting and product marketing) in order for such activities to be economically viable;
3. the fact that creative production is frequently collective in its nature, which generates a need to develop and maintain creative teams with diverse skills, who often also possess diverse interests and expectations about the final product
4. the almost infinite variety of creative products available, both within particular formats (e.g. videos at a rental store), and between formats;
5. vertically differentiated skills, or what Caves terms the 'A list/B list' phenomenon, and the ways in which producers or other content aggregators rank and assess creative personnel;

6. the need to coordinate diverse creative activities within a relatively short and often finite time-frame; and,

7. the durability of many cultural products, and the capacity of their producers to continue to extract economic rents (e.g. copyright payments) long after the period of production.

What these characteristics suggest, for Caves, is major risk and uncertainty about the economic outcomes of creative activities. This uncertainty and risk, and the need to spread risk and provide insurance to creative producers, is one reason for public funding for some creative activities. In commercial terms, risk and uncertainty are also managed through contracts, whereby the various parties involved in the production and distribution of a creative product seek to manage risk and diversify rewards, based on the skills and capacities they bring to the project and the need to ensure mutual obligation to meet commitments. The ongoing management of risks, contracts, and creative production processes is a factor that leads to industrial organization in the creative industries, in forms such as publishing, recording, broadcasting, and film companies commissioning production and managing distribution; guilds, unions, and legal arrangements protecting creative producers; and intermediaries such as agents managing the more commercial elements of a career in creative practice.

Policy Drivers of Creative Industries

Creative industries policy has been taken up enthusiastically in a variety of local, regional, national, and international contexts. While there is a long history of policy-making with cultural objectives—Canada advanced a number of initiatives in the 1920s and 1930s, including the creation of the CBC (Dorland 1996: x)—the concept as a policy discourse has gained momentum since the early 1990s. For example, shortly after its election in 1997, the Blair Labour government in the UK advanced policies that led to a variety of national and regional creative industries development strategies as well as some highly influential sectoral mapping documents. Since then, some of the policy initiatives that have been undertaken in different parts of the world include:

*   Canada: Creative industries strategies have been adopted at both the national and regional level. Some of these date back several decades, including 'Canadian Content' incentives and regulations for film, television, and radio as well as subsidy programs for artists and new media productions. Canada has a Department of Canadian Heritage, which works closely with cultural industry actors, ranging from individual artists to major museums and symphonies, coordinating its activities with Industry Canada. Each of the provinces and many cities have their own culture strategies. A good example of this is the City of Calgary, which has an organization called Calgary Arts Development working closely with the city's economic development office and explicitly linking a vibrant artistic sector with benefits in the broader community, claiming that 'A strong Creative Industries

sector leads to a vibrant culturally rich city that attracts and retains people' (see
www.calgaryartsdevelopment.com/node/512);

- Sweden: The Knowledge Foundation was established by the Swedish government to
  examine the role and significance of what it terms, 'the experience industries', which
  it identified as constituting 6.5 per cent of the Swedish labour market (Nielsén 2004);
- Australia: A creative industries strategy was adopted by the Queensland state
  government in 2001 and there is a proposed national strategy for developing the
  digital content industries, as well as a pioneering national mapping strategy that
  identified the sectors as being 50 per cent larger than was previously understood
  (Cunningham 2006);
- New Zealand: Creative industries are identified as one of the three pillars of the
  2002 Growth and Innovation Framework (with biotechnology and information and
  communication technology);
- Singapore: The Remaking Singapore strategy has sought to redefine the economic
  base of the city-state around creativity and entrepreneurship (Leo and Lee 2004);
- South Korea: The 'Korean Wave' (*Hallyu*)—or the growing international popularity
  of film, music, television, games, and entertainment software from South Korea—
  has been capitalized on by the Korean Ministry of Culture and Tourism, which is
  investing heavily in developing Korea's digital content industries;
- Hong Kong: The 'Baseline Study of Hong Kong Creative Industries', undertaken
  by the Centre for Cultural Policy Research at the University of Hong Kong (CCPR
  2003), identified the importance of creative industries to the image or branding of
  Hong Kong, as well as the opportunities to shift the local economy towards high-
  value-added services as labour-intensive manufacturing shifted to the Guangzhou
  (Pearl River Delta) regions of mainland China;
- China: The Eleventh Five-Year Plan, promulgated in 2005, drew attention to the
  need to develop the creative industries (*chaungyi gongye*) in order to take advantage
  of opportunities in the digital content sectors, which combine knowledge economy
  priorities with the need for enhanced creativity. This is part of a wider set of debates
  about how China can move from being the 'world's factory' ('Made in China') to
  a 'Created in China' agenda, which sees China as a leader in intellectual property
  development (Hartley and Keane 2006; Keane 2004).

Internationally, UNCTAD (2004) has estimated that the creative industries, which it
identifies as lying at the crossroads between the arts, business, and technology, are growing at 10 to 20 per cent annually, or two to three times the growth rates of the global
economy overall. UNCTAD has explicitly linked expansion of the creative industries to five
trends of globalization:

1. deregulation of national cultural and media policy frameworks;
2. increasing average global incomes, which allow for more discretionary expendi-
    ture on arts, cultural, and entertainment products and services;

3. technological changes, particularly the role played by the Internet in the global distribution of digital media content;

4. the global rise of service industries, which place a higher premium on intangible forms of knowledge, and are demand sources for creative industries outputs in areas such as design, advertising, and marketing; and,

5. expansion of international trade generally, and trade in services in particular.

Creative policy agendas have been even more marked at the level of cities and regions. Stevenson (2004: 119–20) describes this as the new civic gold rush in urban planning and cultural policy alike, where strategies are developed for 'fostering strategically the cultures of cities and regions . . . [where] culture and creativity have become . . . forms of "capital" that supposedly can be measured, developed, and then traded in an international market-place comprised of cities eager to compete with each other on the basis of image, amenity, liveability and visitability'. Examples of such strategies can be found throughout Europe, the US, Canada, Australia, New Zealand, and increasingly throughout Asia. The role played by the European Capital (formerly City) of Culture initiative in developing such re-branding of cities has been noted, particularly with the redevelopment of cities such as Barcelona, Glasgow, and Dublin in the 1980s and 1990s (García 2004), and it can also be seen in the competition for cultural leadership between Beijing and Shanghai in China. The boom in public art in the US has also been linked to the role of cultural infrastructure as a lever of new forms of place competitiveness (Weiss 2007). In an evaluation of such initiatives in cities in the Netherlands such as Amsterdam, Rotterdam, Tilburg, and Utrecht, Mommaas (2004) observes that such creative city strategies have been driven by a heterogeneous—and sometimes contradictory—mix of policy priorities including:

- attracting globally mobile capital and skilled labour to particular locations;
- stimulating a more entrepreneurial and demand-oriented approach to arts and cultural policy;
- promoting innovation and creativity more generally, through the perceived interaction between culturally vibrant locales and innovation in other economic sectors;
- finding new uses for derelict industrial-era sites in post-industrial economies; and,
- promoting cultural diversity and cultural democratization, and being more inclusive of the cultural practices of otherwise marginalized social groups.

Two key authors who have influenced these new urban cultural policy agendas are Charles Landry and Richard Florida. Landry (2000: 133) draws attention to the significance of a creative milieu to the development of creativity in modern cities and regions, which he defines as a combination of hard infrastructure (the network of building and institutions that constitute a city or a region) and soft infrastructure (defined as 'the system of associative structures and social networks, connections and human interactions, that underpins and encourages the flow of ideas between individuals and institutions'). In outlining the case for considering London as a creative city, Landry (2005) proposes that culture constitutes a valuable resource for cities such as London in the twenty-first century global economy in six respects:

1. both the historical artifacts and the contemporary practices of a city's population generate a sense of local belonging and civic pride;
2. cultural activities are linked to innovation and creativity, and the capacity of cities to adapt and innovate is the key to their longevity;
3. the cultural sectors are linked to place image and place competitiveness in their ability to attract international capital investment and geographically mobile skilled workers;
4. culture and tourism are inextricably linked, as tourists seek both the high culture of a city (museums, galleries, historic buildings, etc.) and its popular culture (clubs, bars, restaurants, street festivals, etc.);
5. the growing economic significance of the creative industries in the global economy raises the importance of innovative forms of digital content and of networks that promote innovation and creativity; and,
6. culture may be able to promote greater social inclusion and redress economic inequality and social disadvantage, through the ability to provide places where otherwise marginalized groups can engage in collective forms of cultural activity.

Florida (2002) emphasizes the power of place for the rise of what he terms the 'creative class', arguing that creative people attach great importance to being in diverse, culturally vibrant cities with a distinctive identity and a variety of engaging experiences. Florida argues that urban centres with a strong wellspring of cultural creativity will thrive because their economic dynamism is driven, not by government incentives to attract new ICT-related industries, but by what he terms the 'Three *Ts*': technology, talent, and tolerance. This is because 'regional economic growth is powered by creative people who prefer places that are diverse, tolerant and open to new ideas. Diversity increases the odds that a place will attract different types of people with different skill sets and ideas' (Florida 2002: 249). Florida uses American cities such as San Francisco, Boston, and Austin as examples of 'second-tier' cities that can utilize their embedded reputations for diversity, tolerance, and openness to become dynamic new economy hubs. Note, however, that Florida's work has come under increasing scrutiny of late, especially in the post-recession era in which restraint is limiting budgets and tolerance is seemingly in short supply. The advice to create, in some cases from scratch, a 'creative city', is seen as misguided in some instances and far-fetched in others. Florida, who relocated to Toronto in 2007, has responded to his critics in a variety of venues but the overall message is seemingly getting lost in an increasingly testy debate (Ravensbergen 2008).

Recent work on **creative cities** has drawn upon some well-established historical lessons. Hall (2000) draws attention to the historic significance of creative cities, in which he includes Athens in the fifth century BCE, Florence in the fifteenth century, London in Shakespeare's time, Vienna in the nineteenth century, Paris between 1870 and 1910, and Berlin in the 1920s. He argues that what characterized these cities was not simply that they were sites of wealth creation and global trade, but that they were also centres of cultural achievement, large-scale migration, intellectual leadership, creativity, and public dissidence. Jacobs (1994) argues for the centrality of diverse, mixed-use urban centres, and for the contribution of importance of urban villages not only to the quality of life of residents, but also to economic growth, since diverse and concentrated urban zones encouraged the productive cross-pollination of ideas.

Creative Industries and Evolving Arts and Cultural Policy

Public support for the arts, media, and culture has evolved in the past few decades and can be described as going through three stages, culminating in something called the 'creative industries' approach.

The first stage saw arts policy as a distinctive activity, associated with publicly subsidized excellence in the production and exhibition of art forms such as opera, orchestras, live theatre, the visual arts, dance, and literature. Areas that were primarily commercial in their operations, such as the media, were not considered relevant to arts policy, while government-supported activities in these areas—such as public broadcasting and national film production—were understood as being outside the domain of arts policy. Culture in this framework was associated with quality, excellence, national identity, and social improvement: it was by definition outside the domain of the economic. This approach underpinned the development of arts policy in many countries from after the Second World War until the 1980s.

The second stage was that of cultural policy, which brought the media and other forms of popular cultural content production into an expanded policy domain. Cultural policy has been the dominant mode in many European countries, most notably France (since the 1960s) and UNESCO strongly promoted cultural policy development in newly decolonized developing nations (Flew 2005, 2007: 174–8). In countries where more traditional forms of arts policy had prevailed, such as the UK, cultural policy was seen as a way of moving from an idealist conception of the arts that rejected the commercial market, to one that sought to more actively intervene in the cultural industries and cultural markets (Garnham 1987; Lewis 1990; Mercer 1994). It sought to focus the traditional arts on the challenges presented by establishing greater commercial viability (marketing and audience development, value chain analysis, etc.), new forms of advocacy such as 'arts multiplier' studies,[1] and the opportunities presented by new digital media technologies. In the UK, cultural industries development strategies gained momentum from Labour-controlled local councils in cities that had faced the consequences of deindustrialization in the 1980s, such as Sheffield and Glasgow. Such approaches understood cultural industries as being important in terms of their contribution to national economic development and drew attention to the value-adding possibilities arising from effective policy development, particularly in relation to developing the cultural industries value chain, or ensuring that the products and outputs of artistic creativity were better distributed and marketed to audiences and consumers.

While cultural policy was broader in its remit than traditional arts policy, and identified the economic contribution of the arts and cultural industries, it nonetheless retained a certain 'arts-centredness'. To take one example, cultural economist David Throsby proposed a model of creativity that was 'centred around the locus of origin of creative ideas, and radiating outwards as those ideas become combined with more and more other inputs to produce a wider and wider range of products' (2001: 112). Arguing that 'cultural goods and services involve creativity in their production, embody some degree of intellectual property and convey symbolic meaning' (2001: 112), Throsby proposed a 'concentric-circles' model of the cultural and creative industries based on their level of cultural and non-cultural inputs and outputs 'with the arts lying at the centre, and with other industries forming layers or circles located around the core, extending further outwards as the use of creative ideas is taken into a wider production context' (2001: 113).

The third stage, a 'cultural industries' approach, is distinct from both of the first two approaches. The differences between a creative industries policy and an arts policy or a cultural policy can be seen clearly in comparison (cf. Cunningham 2005). First, as we noted earlier in this chapter, it is difficult to sustain the argument that creativity is the exclusive provenance of the arts; in a knowledge economy context it is increasingly seen as integral to sustainability and competitive advantage across a range of sectors (a corollary is that entrepreneurship is no longer seen as the exclusive domain of business, but also exists in the policy, social, arts, and cultural sectors [cf. Leadbeater 2000]). Second, drawing on Howkins' (2001) calculation of the value-adding sectors of the creative economy, it is apparent that the significance of the creative and performing arts is dwarfed by that of highly capitalized and globalized sectors such as publishing, software, design, and the audiovisual industries. Howkins argues that, in 1999, the creative and performing arts accounted for only two per cent of the market value of the creative industries overall (2001: 114). Third, creative industries policies tend to work around the relationship between local initiatives and the global cultural economy, whereas the focus of cultural policy has tended to be resolutely national and relatively autonomous from wider economic policy concerns (cf. Flew 2005). Finally, creative industries policy draws on the impact of digitization and convergence to argue that such policies should enter into the mainstream of national innovation policies, linking the cultural sectors to the knowledge and service industries, presenting the promotion of creative innovation and the digital content industries as a central part of innovation strategies in the twenty-first century knowledge-based economy (Cunningham et al. 2004; PMSEIC 2005).

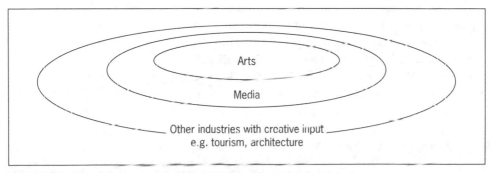

FIGURE 7.2 Throsby's 'Concentric Circles' Model of Creative Industries

There has been some disquiet with regard to the tendency to simply fold arts policy and arts practice into a creative industries policy template. McQuire (2001) expresses a concern that the creative industries model runs the risk of blurring 'the slender but significant difference between being market-savvy and being market driven', running the risk of losing sight of 'the important role that art has assumed in generating a critical space within contemporary culture' (2001: 209, 210). McNamara (2002) notes that the creative industries model may generate an unduly narrow definition of creativity as that which acquires commercial value, arguing instead for 'an expansive rather than a narrowly functionalist approach' (2002: 73). In a more policy-related context, O'Regan (2002) wonders whether the rise of creative industries policy models means that 'even in the domain of "creativity", the close attribute of "the arts", policy-making is no longer being carried out by arts-based cultural policy institutions but by other actors and agents. Even "creativity" seemed too important to be left up to cultural policy institutions and frameworks' (2002: 23). Finally, Rossiter (2006) questions the linkage of creative industries to intellectual property, arguing that it may too readily have attached these sectors to intellectual property regimes that are 'reactionary' and can act to inhibit new forms of creativity (2006: 108–11). We will return to the issue of intellectual property laws in the digital environment in Chapter 9.

The model of creative cities championed by authors such as Landry and Florida has also been challenged. Peck (2005: 763) argues that Florida's creative cities solutions have the potential to destroy what they aim to celebrate, which is culture, uniqueness, and authenticity. He argues that 'rather than "civilizing" urban economic development by "bringing in culture", creativity strategies do the opposite: they commodify the arts and cultural resources, even social tolerance itself, suturing them as putative economic assets to evolving regimes of urban competition'. Kotkin (2006) argues against urban development strategies aimed at attracting a mobile and footloose creative class, observing that cities where the creative economy is strongest—such as Los Angeles, New York, and London—are also those where urban inequality is highest. Kotkin also questions the claims that the most creative US cities, such as San Francisco and Boston, are more economically vibrant than cities such as Phoenix and Denver, or that the case has been convincingly made that creativity needs cosmopolitan urban milieux and cannot happen in new suburban communities. In an astute insider's account, Oakley (2004: 72–3) identifies problems with such generic, cookie-cutter models of creative industries strategies in the UK context: 'Rather than trying to understand the difference between the creative economy of Glasgow and that of Cornwall, we currently seem hell bent on trying to replicate a single creative industries model across the country. It appears that everywhere needs a university, some incubators and a "creative hub", with or without a café, galleries and fancy shops.'

In *The Flight of the Creative Class* (2007), Florida concedes some of these points. He acknowledges that some of the most creative city-regions of the US are also among the most unequal, with San Jose, Washington DC, Raleigh-Durham, Austin, and San Francisco being in the top ten in both the creativity and inequality rankings (2007: 190). He also addresses the criticism that the 'Creativity Index' as developed in *The Rise of the Creative Class* may have been overly focused on the gay population and bohemians and insufficiently focused on other indices of tolerance, such as tolerance of recent migrants, and that the question of openness relates more simply to '"low barriers to entry" for talent . . . from across the entire demographic spectrum' (2007: 53). In doing so, Florida proposes the need to move from thinking about a creative economy to that of building a creative society. He notes the need for reform of social institutions that harness and extend the benefits of the creative economy to those who may otherwise be excluded, in order to overcome the emergent class divide between those in creative sector and service industry jobs, in a manner parallel to the New Deal that Franklin Roosevelt proposed in the 1930s as a response to the Great Depression:

> The creative economy is the Schumpeterian growth engine of our age, and the socio-economic dynamic that it sets in motion is the modern-day equivalent of the divide Roosevelt faced— the growth of two divergent classes; the creative and service sectors . . . We need a strategy that is the modern-day equivalent of the New Deal—one that stimulates the creative economic engine while at the same time extending its benefits to a broad base of people . . . To be effective, a fuller, more creative society will require that a large number of individuals feel they have a real stake in its emergence and expansion. (Florida 2007: 243–4)

Is 'Creative Industries' Still a Useful Organizing Concept?

In light of these various critiques of the creative industries idea, associated policy developments, and related concepts, is it still a conceptually useful organizing category? One influential line of thinking, emanating primarily from the UK, questions this. Linking the shift from 'cultural industries' to 'creative industries' to the shift towards a 'Third Way' for the British Labour Party under Tony Blair, Garnham (2005: 20) argues that this discursive shift constituted 'an attempt by the cultural sector and the cultural policy community to share in its relations with the government, and in policy presentation in the media, the unquestioned prestige that now attaches to the information society and to any policy that supposedly favours its development'. Hesmondhalgh and Pratt (2005: 5) propose that creative industries policy discourse constituted a pragmatic turn for cultural policy advocates:

> Cultural policy, previously on the margins in many areas of government, could be seen to be economically relevant in an era when policy was judged primarily in terms of its fiscal rewards . . . The popularity of such policies was underpinned by an increasing acceptance amongst both neo-liberal conservatives and the postmodernist left that the commodification of culture was not something that could any longer be 'resisted' through arts subsidies and other traditional forms of cultural policy. Moreover, creative industries policy could be portrayed as democratizing and anti-elitist, as opposed to the supposed elitism of arts policy aimed at subsidizing cultural production that could not meet its costs through the market.

Hesmondhalgh (2007) argues against the term 'creative industries', in favour of the concept of 'cultural industries', on the grounds that the concept of creativity is definitionally vague, creative industries policy discourse is too imbued with hype about the creative or new economy, and that strategies to promote creative urban spaces may reproduce established inequalities of access and class-based social hierarchies (Hesmondhalgh 2007: 144–9).

Referring either to 'creative' or 'cultural' industries may be in part a matter of preferred nomenclature. Within the United Nations, for instance, UNESCO (2003) refers to the cultural industries, while UNCTAD (2004) refers to the creative industries, yet both are referring to a broadly similar set of arts, media, and digital content industries. Definitional issues plague the creative industries debate, in spite of the eminently pragmatic solution offered by the Singaporean Ministry of Trade and Industry, which proposed that cultural industries were engaged in the 'upstream' activity of content creation, and the creative industries in the 'downstream' activities of distribution and commercialization (MTI 2003). Both definitions and underlying assumptions about these terms exist within EU member states, ranging from the view in Germany that 'culture' and 'industry' remain antithetical since aesthetic excellence cannot be mass-produced, to the more pragmatic Finnish position that mobile phones can be a part of the nation's cultural output. Longstanding differences can also be identified between the French perspective on the arts and culture as integral components of the state itself, as compared to the alleged British tendency to speak of culture only when it is associated with the media and sport (MKW 2001).

The definitional issues, however, run deeper when they are connected to wider debates about the global cultural economy. Authors such as Hesmondhalgh (2007) broadly adhere to an understanding of the media-cultural system that is identified in the political economy of global media, whereby core–periphery relations continue to operate on a global scale, with 'Global Hollywood' and its adjuncts in other related industries continuing to dominate the flows of capital to creative projects through favourable intellectual property laws, even as they outsource content production to the four corners of the globe (see Miller et al. 2005; Thussu 2006). By contrast, the creative industries perspective has tended to understand the global cultural economy in less zero-sum terms and to see the globalization of media and creative industries as leading to a more matrix-like and mosaic structure. In this approach, new media and creative industries production hubs emerge through processes of 'creative destruction' in which some established production sites decline and others emerge, but where the geocultural space of media and cultural flows has nonetheless become far more complex than was the case in the second half of the twentieth century (see Curtin 2007; Scott 2004).

The latter tendency, it has been argued (Flew 2007), predominates in the twenty-first century global cultural economy, as it is increasingly infused by the dynamics of the knowledge-based economy, multiculturalism, diasporic media consumption patterns, and global production networks. Cunningham (2007) has undertaken an extensive documentary search of creative industries policy statements outside the UK to defend the view (shared with Garnham) that there is much less of a top-down and more of a tentative and explorative trend to identifying both definitions and policy approaches in the creative industries policy literature. The Asian case is instructive in terms of how such discourses do, or do not, travel. In their seven-country Asian study, Kong and colleagues (2006: 191) identify an 'uneven geography of flows of creative economy discourses'. They differentiate between those nations where policy-makers drew upon already established Western notions of the creative industries (Singapore, Hong Kong SAR), to those where more localized understandings of the concept have gained prominence (Korea, Taiwan), to those where the concept either translates into preservation of existing cultural forms (Japan) or has no policy resonance at all (India). They note China as a significantly ambiguous case, where the long-established interest in the cultural industries (*wenhua chanye*) on the part of the state sits alongside a demand for growth and international competitiveness in the cultural sectors, so that there is considerable experimentation at the level of city authorities in how to develop the creative industries (*chaungyi gongwe*).

A new way of approaching these questions has recently been proposed by Cunningham and Potts (2007). They propose four models of the creative industries:

1. the welfare model, where the creative industries are a net drain on the economy (i.e. they consume more resources than they produce), but they receive public subsidy on the basis of their non-economic public good benefits;
2. the competitive model, where the creative industries are like other industries and have a neutral effect on the overall economy, albeit with different industry dynamics to other sectors;
3. the growth model, where the creative industries are experiencing above-average growth in the economy, and are growth drivers in the way that manufacturing was in the 1950s and 1960s and ICTs were in the 1980s and 1990s; and,
4. the creative economy model, where complex new economy dynamics are evolving in the creative industries that have wider resonance throughout the economy, so that they not only evidence above-average growth (as in point 3), but prefigure wider changes in national and international innovation systems.

They argue that while the evidence is not fully conclusive—due in part to the difficulties in agreeing on a single definition, as mentioned above— it tends to strongly support points three and four over points one and two, as measured by indicators such as comparative growth rates, proportionate expansion of the number of firms involved in the creative industries sectors, and average incomes of those working in the creative industries sectors. If this is the case, Cunningham and Potts (2007: 17) argue that 'creative industries are a source of economic growth by their ability to generate and process change in the economic system. Irrespective of the social or cultural value of the creative industries, their economic value properly includes their role in the economic coordination in the face of uncertainty'. An implication of this finding is that 'cultural policy, traditionally based on model 1, may require some critical retooling to adapt to what appears to be a model 4 world [and] cultural and arts policy may work best as an adjunct to innovation policy'.

Case Study: Toronto as a Creative City

If one were to imagine a case study of creativity, creative cities, and cultural industries in Canada it would be difficult not to look to Toronto. The largest city in the country and the home to some of Canada's most significant cultural enterprises—from professional sports to classical music and ballet to the Toronto International Film Festival—Toronto has fully embraced the notion of city as an economic and social force. In his 2006 mayoral re-election campaign, David Miller proclaimed a vision for his city that included creativity as an economic engine.[2] Upon re-election he commissioned a study and a report, which became the Creative City Planning Framework (see www.toronto.ca/culture/creativecity2008.htm).

Toronto's efforts to become a creative city predate this report and include a broad range of initiatives spanning most of the municipal planning, including the 2001 Economic Development Strategy, The Toronto Culture Plan (2003), and the 2006 *Imagine a Toronto: Strategies for a Creative City* (available at www.utoronto.ca/progris/imagineatoronto/home.htm). The latter report, authored by Meric Gertler, Lori Tesolin, and Sarah Weinstock from the University of Toronto's Munk Centre for International Studies, provides an overview of the many faces of a creative city and creative economy policy. For example, the report lists the occupations and employment figures for the creative sector—68,000 by conservative estimate, swelling to almost one million if you use a broader definition, akin to Florida's 'creative class' category; the firms in the creative industries—more than 8,600 in 2005; and the creative spaces used by all these people and firms. While noting seven key strengths and lessons from their review of the Toronto situation, the authors conclude that there are serious challenges, including competition from other centres seeking to become creative capitals in their own right, the underutilization of much of the talented workforce, and the lack of a 'strategic linked-up approach' to support and coordinate activity in the sector.

While Toronto boasts many advantages, not the least of which is a large population that provides the audiences for a diverse range of cultural productions, and a wealthy class of donors and foundations providing financial support where needed (opera, ballet, classical music), it would be unfair to suggest that the cultural industries have this prominence and success merely because of their history. It is clear, when you read the various reports and initiatives, that culture is taken seriously in Toronto, at all levels of government, as well as by local firms and citizens. To have culture as a major platform in municipal elections may be a surprise to voters in other Canadian cities, but in Toronto, it is both expected and respected. The results are clear. To quote the *Planning Framework*:

> Toronto is riding an unprecedented wave of creative and cultural successes, at every scale. Major new and expanded facilities—ROM, AGO, Royal Conservatory of Music, National Ballet School, Gardiner Museum, Ontario College of Art and Design—designed by world renowned architects. The extraordinary success of Luminato—a major new festival created through private sector vision and leadership. The Toronto International

Film Festival—the largest and many argue most influential festival in the world. The Young Centre, the new home of Soulpepper Theatre Company and a visionary new theatre school, a partnership with George Brown College District. The enormous success of Scotiabank Nuit Blanche Toronto. The groundbreaking adaptive reuse of the Don Valley Brick Works and the Wychwood Car Barns. These are only some.

Culture is clearly big business in Toronto but it is also a vital and fundamental part of life for residents and for the growing number of visitors who come purely to experience the magic of theatre, professional sports, ballet, music, festivals, and film.

 # Useful Websites

Innovation Systems Research Network (ISRN) City-Region Initiative
←www.utoronto.ca/isrn/city-region_initiative/index.html→

This site is a network of scholars from across Canada, hosted at the University of Toronto. The research focus is on the role of cities in the social, cultural, and economic health of a region.

Canada's Creative City Network
←http://creativecity.ca→

This website is an outgrowth of a simple mailing list started by members of the Vancouver Office of Cultural Affairs and has emerged as a major initiative helping to coordinate activities and research by member cities across Canada.

Centre for Policy Studies on Culture and Creativity
←http://cultureandcommunities.ca→

The Centre for Policy Studies on Culture and Communities promotes teaching, research, and public outreach on cultural politics, policy, and planning in communities from the local to the global.

Americans for the Arts Policy Research Center: Creative Industries
←www.artsusa.org/information_resources/research_information/services/creative_industries→

This website provides a national mapping of the creative industries in the US, with a strong focus on the creative and performing arts.

Creative Clusters
←www.creativeclusters.com→

This is a website for a UK-based, national, creative economy network.

Creative Economy Online
←www.creative.org.au→

This website provides online news and research on the creative industries, innovation and society. It is hosted by the ARC Centre of Excellence for Creative Industries and Innovation www.cci.edu.au, which is a federally funded Australian university centre for research in the creative industries, with participants from six universities and extensive international collaborative networks.

UNESCO Culture Sector
←http://portal.unesco.org/culture/en→

This website contains a vast database on global resources on arts, culture, and creative industries developed by UNESCO.

Further Reading

Audience Labour: The Asymmetric Production of Culture, Geoff Glass (2006)

Creativity is not confined to the professionals. In this article Geoff Glass shows some of the economic implications of audience creativity as he updates, expands, and extends Dallas Smythe's argument about audience labour (2001) for a twenty-first century understanding of the work we engage in when we participate in web communities such as YouTube or Facebook. The text is available online at: www.geof.net/research/2006/audience-labor.

The Geography of Innovation: Twenty-first Century Cities, David Wolfe (2009)

Wolfe summarizes the key insights and findings from a multi-year study of urban industrial clusters across Canada. Using the data from 15 Canadian cities, this book examines cities as key sites of economic activity—the places where leading-edge innovation generates new ideas, new products, and new industries. Canada, as a highly urbanized nation (though we may not think of ourselves that way), has a particularly keen interest in policies and programs that can help cities enhance and continue their role as hubs for creativity and innovation.

Creative Cities, Cultural Clusters and Local Economic Development, Philip Cooke and Luciana Lazzeretti (2008)

In this volume Cooke and Lazzeretti bring together a collection of essays from around the world that considers the role of culture in local economic development. For students interested in non-North American approaches to culture and economic development, including Asian and European examples, this collection is a useful starting place.

Under Construction: The State of Cultural Infrastructure in Canada, Nancy Duxbury (ed.), (2008)

The cultural industries are dependent on space, equipment, and most of all, people. This report brings together a national profile of those infrastructure resources and argues that merely updating our museums, galleries, and other cultural buildings is not sufficient, given the challenges ahead, particularly in the area of planning and policies for culture. The text argues that we need to invest in the intellectual as well as the physical capital of culture.

Discussion Questions

1. What are some examples of historic creative cities? In what ways were they (and are they still) significant?

2. What is meant by the concepts of 'knowledge push' and 'market pull'? What relevance do these have for cultural industries?

3. What new modes of cultural production and consumption in urban centres among young people (18–35 years old) are discussed in this chapter? Why is this shift significant?

4. In what ways are 'knowledge' and 'information' different from each other? Why is this relevant in understanding the knowledge economy and creative industries?

5. What is the significance of the rise of the service industry sectors in the knowledge-based economy and the 'culturalization' of the economy?

6. What are the four models of the creative industries proposed by Cunningham and Potts?

7. In this chapter, we noted Healy's (2002: 101) caution against 'using new economy jargon to give a bullish defence of the arts in economic terms'. Why is this significant?

8. What is the 'creative class' as discussed in this chapter? In what ways has the concept been challenged?

9. What are some of the creative industries policy initiatives undertaken in Canada? How are these seen as affecting cultural industries?

Class Activities

1. Using the website for your city, locate and summarize the statement on cultural industries. Most large cities, and many smaller ones as well, have such a statement. If available, look for the local cultural industries website (e.g., Culture Montréal) or the ministry of culture for the province (e.g., Ministry of Culture, Ontario). Divide into groups and identify the cultural policy in a selected city (see http://creativecity.ca for a number of useful resources, especially the 'Making the Case' series at www.creativecity.ca/making-the-case/index.html). Identify recent policy statements and consider them in light of the discussion of culture in this chapter. What bias or approach is being taken on the sites you visit?

2. In his March 2009 essay, 'The Art of With', (available online at www.charlesleadbeater. net/cms/xstandard/The%20Art%20of%20 With%20PDF.pdf) Charles Leadbeater addresses the question of whether or not the web is creating a more open, participative, and collaborative approach to culture. Read through the article and then engage with your classmates in a debate on the proposition that 'The web is creating a culture more inclined to thinking, working, acting with providing an alternative to the dominant principle of To and For. The principle of with can apply to art and culture as much as work, politics, and learning. It would draw on a very different tradition of the avant-garde, one that has privileged participation and collaboration as the principles at the heart of modern art rather than shock and separation.' Can you think of examples from your own lives? Can you imagine how a local cultural organization (gallery, museum, orchestra) might transform itself for the 'art of with'?

8 The Global Knowledge Economy

Questions to Consider

- What is meant by the term globalization? Why is it significant for new media?

- What is the knowledge economy? In what ways is it important for new media?

- Why is it important to understand the differences between information and knowledge when thinking about investments in research and education in a global knowledge economy?

- How are creativity and culture relevant to understanding new media as fundamental to the knowledge economy?

Chapter Outline

New media are a powerful force for globalization, as this chapter explores in detail. In Chapter 2 we saw how the telegraph first provided an early version of global communication, but digital media and networks have taken that effect to a new level. This chapter explains the complexity of globalization and reviews some of the main criticisms of these developments as part of an overall knowledge economy. We examine both technological change and its role in the economy as well as more practical matters such as e-commerce strategies and the role that new media play in 'disintermediation' in order to better understand the forces driving the global knowledge economy. We look at the nature of digital goods and how they have disrupted many industries that formerly relied on the expense of reproducing and transporting ideas (news, music, movies, for example) and that now find themselves without that avenue for extracting value. In this context, we return to some of the themes on creativity from Chapter 7 and examine the creative economy more closely from a business perspective, examining topics such as technological innovation and the innovator's dilemma.

The Global Knowledge Economy

Economic activity—making things, providing services, and buying and selling—occurs at a global level these days. We experience this every time we purchase something built in China or consume food grown in Mexico, every time we receive a service call from India. Canada is particularly active in the global economy, with over 30 per cent of economic activity destined for, or originating from, outside our borders (World Bank 2010). As with many developed countries, knowledge—often embedded in services—is a key component of those export and import numbers. This buying and selling of knowledge is called the global **knowledge economy**. Importantly, and to distinguish a knowledge economy from an information economy, knowledge is learned over time and enables action. It cannot simply be purchased. Owning a book is not the same thing as understanding what is in it. As such, for a knowledge economy to succeed it is important to invest in research and education.

The global knowledge economy can be understood as arising from the confluence of three developments. The first is the increasingly ubiquitous nature of new media and globally networked ICTs worldwide. New media are central to globalization because they constitute the border-less technological and service delivery platforms through which flow the images, information, finance, and communication that make up a globalized world. The media industries are also leaders in the push for corporations to expand and integrate themselves globally. Moreover, the media provide informational content and images of the world through which people make sense of events in distant places. The centrality of new media to globalization derives not only from their role as communications technologies that enable the international distribution of messages and meanings, but also from their perceived role in weakening the cultural bonds that tie people to nation-states and national communities (Flew 2007).

Earlier media forms such as radio and television, and even comic books, were similarly criticized for their roles in cultural assimilation and cultural imperialism, (Dorfman and Mattelart 1984). It should be noted, however, that new media are not *necessarily* globalizing forces, or more precisely, they have local, regional, and national manifestations and implications as well. Some aspects of this have been discussed in our review of the creative industries, and Canada's and the provinces' support for new media in this context stems mainly from two impulses: to provide a place for local employment and capital accumulation within a larger global economy, and as a way of presenting Canadian perspectives and culture to that global knowledge economy. Government support for knowledge industries generally, and specifically that subset of the knowledge economy known as the new media industries, often has twin objectives: economic and cultural. So, while new media certainly are implicated in the weakening of cultural bonds, and have been criticized in this context, it is not necessary to see this as an essential aspect of them as media forms.

The second development is globalization. Globalization is a term used to describe and make sense of a series of interrelated processes including:

- internationalization of production, trade, and finance, with the rise of multinational corporations, reductions in cross-border tariffs on flows of goods and services, the deregulation of financial markets, and the rise of Internet-based electronic commerce;
- international movements of people (as immigrants, guest workers, refugees, tourists, students, and expert advisers), the development of diasporic and emigrant communities, and the increasingly multicultural nature of national societies;
- international communications flows, delivered through telecommunications, information, and media technologies such as broadband cable, satellite, and the

Internet, which facilitate transnational circulation of cultural commodities, texts, images, and artifacts;

- global circulation of ideas, ideologies, and keywords, such as the export of Western values, democratic aspirations, and environmental consciousness, as well as counter-discourses such as anti-modern fundamentalist movements;
- the establishment of international regimes in intellectual property, which entrench the enforceability of ownership of knowledge and information;
- the emergence of local resistance to globalization for domestic political and cultural objectives, by both nationalist movements of the political Right, and progressive and anti-colonialist movements of the Left;
- the development of international organizations, including regional trading blocs such as the European Union, the North American Free Trade Agreement (NAFTA), the Association of South East Asian Nations (ASEAN), and the Asia Pacific Economic Co-operation grouping (APEC);
- cultural, professional, and standards bodies such as UNESCO, the World Trade Organization, the World Intellectual Property Organization (WIPO), the European Broadcasting Union, the Asian Broadcasting Union, and the International Telecommunications Union;
- the increasingly significant role played by global non-government organizations (NGOs) such as Amnesty International, Greenpeace, Médecins Sans Frontières, and the Red Cross in domestic and international politics;
- the growing significance of international law to national policies, such as the United Nations Convention on Human Rights, the 'Millennium Round' of the World Trade Organization, and the Kyoto Convention on greenhouse gas emissions; and,
- the globalization of the war on terror after 11 September 2001, which has had many implications for global foreign policy, including its connection to the war in Iraq, the monitoring of citizens within nation-states, the treatment of those seeking asylum from global conflict zones, and the movement of people to and from countries more generally.

There are extensive debates about the extent to which globalization has become the central feature of our times, with positions ranging from those described as globalization enthusiasts (e.g. Friedman 2005) to those who are more skeptical of the extent and significance of trends associated with globalization (e.g. Hirst and Thompson 1996). Overlaid on these analyses of the empirical evidence for globalization are debates between those who believe that globalization should be welcomed (Legrain 2002) and those who are concerned that it erodes local communications and identities (Barber 2000). Among critical theorists and activists, there are those who argue that the rise of global capitalism has reconfigured the entire terrain of political struggle (Hardt and Negri 2000, 2005), and those who argue that globalization is not something qualitatively new, but is rather the latest stage in the development of capitalism as a world system (Callinicos 2001; Curran and Park 2000).

Although economic globalization is arguably more established than political, legal, or cultural globalization; as Held and colleagues (1999) and Held and McGrew (2002, 2003) conclude, while globalization is not completely new and has not eliminated the significance of nation-states and national sovereignty, there have been real and substantive changes in the relationship between political globalization and modern nation-states over the past three decades. This has meant that effective political power is increasingly shared and bartered across agencies at local, national, regional, and international levels, particularly with the emergence of supra-national legal frameworks and authority structures (discussed in Chapter 9). As a result, citizens of all nation-states increasingly find themselves enmeshed within 'overlapping communities of fate' (Held et al. 1999: 81). Examples of the latter relate to matters as diverse as the impact of environmental degradation on climates, drug trafficking, global terrorism, immigration controls, arms trading, and non-renewable resource use. In the cultural sphere, one of the complicating factors in these debates is the duality of culture as both a form of lived and shared experience and as mediated symbolic communication. Much of the discussion of cultural globalization relates to the latter, though Anthony Smith believes that the outcome of common access to global media systems will not be the emergence of a single world culture:

> If by 'culture' is meant a collective mode of life, or a repertoire of beliefs, styles, values and symbols, then we can only speak of cultures, never just culture; for a collective mode of life, or a repertoire of beliefs, etc. presupposes different modes and repertoires in a universe of modes and repertoires. Hence, the idea of a 'global culture' is a practical impossibility . . . the differences between segments of humanity in terms of lifestyle and belief-repertoire are too great, and the common elements too generalized, to permit us to even conceive of a globalized culture. (1991: 171)

The third element prompting the rise of the global knowledge economy is the notion that in a knowledge economy ideas and intangible assets rather than tangible physical assets are increasingly the sources of new wealth creation, and that 'the economy is more strongly and more directly rooted in the production, distribution, and use of knowledge than ever before' (Howells 2000: 51). Such a transition has occurred not only in the so-called 'post-industrial' economies, as the 'information society' theories of the 1960s and 1970s held (see Castells 1999 for a critique), but has been a global phenomenon, particularly driven by the intersection of international economic competitiveness with foreign direct investment and the use of globally networked ICTs. David and Foray (2002: 9) argue that the global nature of the knowledge economy is indicated by the extent to which 'disparities in the productivity and growth of different countries have far less to do with their abundance (or lack) of natural resources than with the capacity to improve the quality of human capital and factors of production: in other words, to create new knowledge and ideas and incorporate them into equipment and people'.

David and Foray observe that the rise of a knowledge economy is both an historical trend of the past hundred years and a process that has accelerated since the early 1990s. In an historical sense, the growth of intangible capital (encompassing both knowledge production and dissemination on the one hand, and education, health, and well-being on the other) has been accelerating in the economy for the whole of the twentieth century, and its share has exceeded that of tangible capital (physical infrastructure, equipment, inventories, natural resources, etc.) since the early 1970s (cf. Abramovitz and David 2001). They attributed the more recent acceleration of knowledge production to:

- the growing diversity of sources from which new knowledge is accessed (e.g. users as a source of innovation);
- the role played by networked ICTs in accelerating the diffusion of new knowledge and the possibilities for collaboration;
- the ways in which ICTs enable new forms of codification of once-tacit knowledge through knowledge management systems; and,
- the importance of knowledge-sharing through cross-institutional and cross-sectoral knowledge communities, of which the open source software movement (discussed in Chapter 9) may represent one of the most globally significant.

Batterham identifies the differences between the old paradigm of economic development, based on the more efficient use of existing physical resources, and the new paradigm, based on continuous innovation and the more effective deployment of intangible (weightless) capital in the new, knowledge-based economy in the terms set out in Table 8.1.

Hodgson (2000: 93) argues that the shift from a manufacturing economy to a knowledge economy, or one that is 'relatively less "machine-intensive", and more and more "knowledge-intensive"', has the following features:

- both production and consumption processes are becoming increasingly complex and sophisticated;
- increasingly advanced knowledge and skills are being required in many processes of production;
- consumers also face increasingly complex decisions about evaluating the quality of goods and services on offer;
- there is an increasing reliance on specialist or idiosyncratic skills;
- the use and transfer of information is becoming increasingly important in economic and social activities; and,
- uncertainty is increasingly central to all aspects of economic and social life.

Hodgson ultimately prefers the concept of a learning economy to that of a knowledge economy, since the latter implies a fixed stock of knowledge to be distributed throughout a society, whereas 'in a complex and evolving, knowledge-intensive system, agents not only have to learn, they have to learn how to learn, and to adapt and create anew' (2000: 93).

TABLE 8.1 The Old and New Paradigms of Economic Development

Old paradigm	New paradigm
1 Key factors: capital, resources, and labour	1 Rising importance of knowledge and creativity
2 More efficient application of existing resources	2 Addition of knowledge-based industry and knowledge-based parts of resource activity
3 Predominant focus on national markets	3 Firms going global and subject to global competition
4 Primary focus on cost competitiveness	4 The imperative to deliver superior value to customers through innovation
5 Relatively long product cycles	5 Trend to shorter product cycles
6 Getting more out of existing businesses	6 Creating new businesses and a new premium on risk-taking and entrepreneurship
7 Reliance on traditional capital sources, such as loans and stock market equity	7 Venture capital as central to new business development
8 Focus on individual achievement	8 Shift to strategic alliances and other forms of collaboration, such as networks and clusters

Source: Adapted from Batterham (2000: 10).

Electronic Commerce

One important aspect of how new media have had effects on ways of doing business has been through **electronic commerce** (e-commerce). While electronic transactions preceded the rise of the Internet, the Internet dramatically broadened the scope for electronic transactions through features such as:

- its open, non-proprietary access protocols based on TCP/IP;
- the development of the Web and its standard coding system based on HTML;
- ease of access to a diverse range of websites using web browsers and search engines;
- falling costs of personal computing and the growing ease of Internet access from the workplace or home; and,
- the ways in which new media technologies based on the Internet allow for both one-to-many communication and direct one-to-one interaction (OECD 1999: 28–9).

Electronic commerce can take a variety of forms, depending on the degree of digitization of: (1) the product or service sold; (2) the transaction process; and (3) the nature of the delivery agent or intermediary. There are varying degrees of physical or electronic commerce in transactions. For example, buying a book through a website (such as Amazon.ca or Abebooks.com) is not pure e-commerce unless one purchases an e-book, because although the agent and the process are both digital, the final product is delivered through physical transportation systems. By contrast, buying software online, acquiring a song from the Apple iTunes site, or purchasing an airline ticket online may constitute pure e-commerce, as the product, process, and agent all exist in digital form. It is also important to distinguish between business-to-business electronic commerce (B2B), which has been estimated to account for 80–90 per cent of all electronic commerce transactions (Lovelock and Ure 2002; OECD 1999) and business-to-consumer electronic commerce (B2C), to which the bulk of the discussion below is devoted, but which is not necessarily at the core of e-commerce transactions (see Figure 8.1).

It has become a commonly held view that businesses have no choice but to develop an e-commerce strategy. Andy Grove, the former chair of Intel, said that by the mid-2000s all companies would become Internet companies, or they would not be companies at all (*The Economist* 1999). The implicit line of reasoning in Grove's remark is that the competitive advantages that accrue to companies from harnessing the Internet are of such significance that neglecting this aspect of operations would leave companies highly vulnerable to losing market share in an increasingly volatile and changing market. The benefits to business of developing an e-commerce strategy have been identified as being:

- expansion of the available marketplace from geographically defined, local markets to national and international markets;
- reduction of the costs of creating, processing, distributing, storing, and retrieving information, both within the organization and between the organization and its clients (both suppliers and consumers);

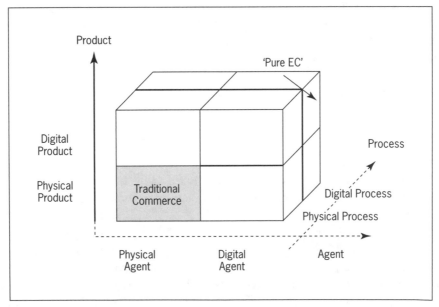

FIGURE 8.1 Dimensions of E-Commerce
Source: Turban et al. (2000: 5).

- ability to develop highly specialized businesses, able to target particular niche consumer groups;
- reduction of inventory and overhead costs, through a move to towards 'pull-type' supply chain management, where processes begin with customer orders and enable just-in-time production; and,
- ability to better customize products and services to client and consumer needs, providing competitive advantages based on 'first-mover' advantages and brand loyalty (Turban et al. 2000: 15).

For consumers, the advantages of e-commerce are:

- the ability to undertake transactions 24 hours a day, all year round, from any networked location;
- a vastly increased range of products and services;
- the ability to compare prices online, and find the lowest-cost provider with minimal search cost;
- quick delivery of products and services, particularly if they are in digitized form;
- the ability to interact with other consumers in virtual communities, and exchange ideas and experiences; and,
- the ability to participate in virtual auctions (Turban et al. 2000: 15–6).

One of the most important implications of electronic commerce for distribution has been related to the processes of **disintermediation** and reintermediation (see Figure 8.2 on page 174). In the manufacturing sector, the relationship between producers and consumers has traditionally been mediated through a supply chain that includes wholesalers, distributors, and retailers. Similarly, in the creative industries, the relationship between the creators and consumers of content has been mediated through those responsible for aggregating, promoting, marketing, and distributing content for final reception by consumers, giving these sectors their characteristic hourglass structure of many producers, many consumers, but a distributional filter that operates through a small and concentrated number of distributors (Hesmondhalgh 2007: 18–24). One consequence of the rise of the Internet and new media has been disintermediation, where a more direct relationship emerges between the creators/producers of content/products/services and their consumers. Another outcome has been reintermediation, where intermediary functions remain, but are conducted by organizations whose operations are driven by the new e-commerce marketing logics, such as a shift towards partnership with consumers, 'permission' advertising, product and service customization, and multiple modes of communication with consumers (Shenton and McNeeley 1997; Turban et al. 2000).

The whole concept of e-commerce suffered a significant setback with the collapse of the NASDAQ share price index in 2001 (the US-based index for high-technology shares). The collapse brought with it the sense that e-commerce and dot.com enterprises had been seriously oversold and that most lacked a credible business plan to match their widely hyped ambitions. The rise and fall of the NASDAQ provides an illustration of the possibility of

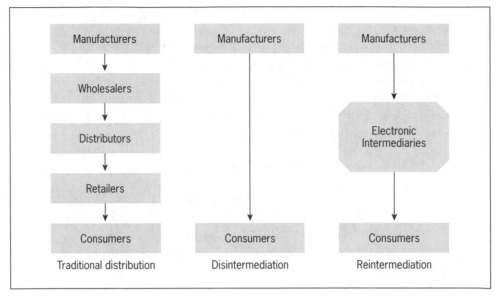

FIGURE 8.2 Disintermediation and Reintermediation
Source: Turban et al. (2000: 64).

dramatic reversals of fortune for companies operating in this environment within a relatively short period of time (as shown in Figure 8.3). It is notable, however, that with the more general share market boom of the 2000s, the NASDAQ has been one of the few global share market indices to reflect that boom.

The companies that have been most successful in the 2000s—such as Amazon, eBay, and Google—have been able to leverage the advantages of what Anderson (2006) terms the '**long tail**'. Anderson argues that digitization of content has completely transformed the distributional models of the media and entertainment industries, as the availability of content is no longer constrained by distributional bottlenecks such as theatres, radio, and television channels, and shelf space in bookstores and record outlets. This challenges the assumption that only mass appeal media content is profitable, as it reveals that when a wider range of content is made more easily available through online distribution and retail, consumer tastes and preferences for books, movies, music, etc. are far more diverse and niche-oriented than the media and entertainment industries have traditionally assumed. With traditional constraints of geography and scale being eliminated, it is niche content that accounts for a rapidly growing proportion of total online sales, meaning that 'popularity no longer has a monopoly on profitability' (Anderson 2006: 24).

Information and Knowledge

The nature and significance of information and knowledge has long been a problematic question in economics. Mainstream economic theories of perfect competition have assumed as a

FIGURE 8.3 Rise and Fall of the NASDAQ, 1998–2001
Source: ABC Four Corners (2001), http://abc.net.au/4corners/dotcom.

simplifying device that both producers and consumers have perfect information and behave accordingly in economic markets. Since this is obviously not the case, an extensive literature has emerged on the economics of imperfect information and related questions, such as information asymmetries (i.e. when sellers know more than buyers or when some agents have privileged access to information that gives participants market advantage [Akerlof 1970]). There is also a tradition of information economics, associated with writers such as economist Don Lamberton, which asks what it means when information is considered not simply as a component of how markets operate, but as a form of capital that 'structures the knowledge base of the economic system' (Potts 2003: 477). As Lamberton noted in an early essay, 'identifying information with the cost or time of transmission, and not with the value of a message, may be misleading' (1971: 10).

The concerns of Lamberton and others about thinking of information as a form of capital that is central to the structure of all economic relations, rather than simply a factor in market exchange relations, have become more pressing as innovation has become more central to economic growth and corporate competitive strategy, as ICTs become more central to the economy as a whole, and as knowledge flows proliferate with the emergence of the Internet (David and Foray 2002; Giddens 1998; Haltiwanger and Jarmin 2003; Lamberton 1999; OECD 2003). Two research questions have been central to these discussions. The first concerns the nature of **digital goods** in the new economy. Quah (2003) defines digital goods as 'bitstrings, sequences of 0s and 1s, that have economic value', which includes 'ideas and knowledge, computer software, digital images, music, databases, video games, blueprints, recipes, DNA sequences [and] codified messages' (2003: 289, 293). Quah argues that digital goods possess five characteristics that challenge conventional understandings of the economics of goods and services. They are:

1. non-rivalrous: use by one agent does not degrade its usefulness to other agents;
2. infinitely expansible: every user can make and distribute as many copies of the digital good as they choose;
3. discrete: they show indivisibility, so that only the whole digital good contains all of its value (i.e. the whole of a film has value over and above that of its component parts);1
4. a-spatial: they exist in cyberspace, and are both everywhere and nowhere on the digital network simultaneously; and,
5. recombinant: they arise in part from drawing together existing elements in new forms that have features that were absent from the original, parent digital goods.

These features have profound implications for those who founded their businesses on scarcity of information and the challenges of moving it around: the media industries in particular. As Clay Shirky (2010) points out, when anyone can press a button that says, 'Publish!', there are by necessity considerable implications for publishers, whether they are in the newspaper, book, music, or film publishing business. Digital goods are infinitely and easily copyable and given this, it is not surprising that people are inclined to share them, as it would seem churlish to not share something if it costs almost nothing to do so.

Recombinant forms of new media are particularly popular, since they are so easy to create and engage an audience's desire to participate, but without the training required to make things from scratch. In this vein, you see the 'mashup' type of content that is so popular on video sharing sites, such as YouTube, or even the silly captions over pictures of cats (LOLcats) on http://icanhascheezburger.com. While LOLcats might seem like a trivial and ridiculous example, as Shirky (2010) notes, this type of engagement with media is far different from the passive stance often taken with broadcast media. Importantly, these low-stakes sharing sites can become a gateway to fuller and richer creative activities, given the capabilities of the tools. As a growing number of people are discovering that YouTube offers simple editing capabilities, annotations, and the ability to add a soundtrack (though, a legal, copyright-free or licensed soundtrack), they are also discovering that if you can watch YouTube videos, you can *make* YouTube videos.

A second key set of issues concerns the rise of **endogenous growth** theory or new growth economics. Economists from Stanford University such as Paul Romer (1994, 1995, 2007) and Paul David (1985, 1999) have argued that technological change and economic growth need to be seen as intrinsically connected, in contrast to the conventional approach that treats technology as an 'exogenous variable' to growth models. An exogenous variable is something that has influence on a system—such as an economy—but originates from outside the system. Romer (2007) proposes that 'economic growth springs from better recipes, not just from more cooking', in other words, that it arises not from the discovery of new resources (labour, capital, or physical resources), but rather, from those occasions where 'people take resources and rearrange them in ways that are more valuable'. Growth, according to this way of thinking, is possible from internal (endogenous) activities. Romer argues that the central economic change of the past two decades has been the shift from people being primarily involved in the production of physical objects to the discovery and design of ideas and new ways of doing things, so that 'the whole economy will start to look like Microsoft, with a very large fraction of people engaged in discovery as opposed to production' (1995: 70). David (1999) argues that it may take up to a generation for the longer-term economic impacts of new technologies to become apparent, not least because the nature of what needs to be measured changes as the structure of economic production and consumption changes, and as growth becomes increasingly driven by the hard-to-measure sectors of services and information.

The Internet makes many of these issues more pressing, as it is the largest repository of information gathered through a networked infrastructure in human history. It is estimated that there were about 30 billion web pages in existence on more than 108 million websites in February 2007 (Boutell.com 2007), all of which may lay claim to providing at least some information that is of interest to someone. Not long afterward, in July 2008, Google engineers announced that their indices contained a trillion unique URLs (pages).[2] Even that is an underestimation by a significant degree since much of the Internet is behind authentication systems. So, for example, Facebook, which is approaching 500 million users, is mainly 'dark' to Google's searches.

The Internet has also begun to bring forth more than just the professional knowledge embedded in the people who work in large organizations. Once it becomes possible for people to share the ambient or embedded knowledge that they have about the things they care about, they are often very willing or even excited to do so. A perfect example of this is Wikipedia. In his examination of what happens when people have access to a **cognitive surplus** (spare time, used effectively) and a way to share their thoughts and ideas, Clay Shirky (2010) reveals the power of Internet-connected hobbyists. A particularly telling example is his rough calculation of the number of person hours represented by Wikipedia (approximately 100 million, apparently) compared to the number of hours spent watching television (200 billion hours annually, in the US alone). In fact, Americans watch 100 million hours of advertising on an average weekend (Shirky 2010). Even a small percentage of this, switched from watching television to participating on the Internet, can have profound implications. Not all this spare time is spent well, but some of it is dedicated to online discussions, updating web pages, doing research, and many other things that contribute to a substantial change in our information and knowledge environment.

Not every commentator is excited about the prospects of this mass participation or of the quality of the results. Andrew Keen, in his 2007 book, *Cult of the Amateur*, takes aim at the demise of professionalism and the inevitable (in his view) dilution of quality journalism, music, and even movies in the face of a deluge of poorly conceived and poorly executed amateur work. Nicholas Carr posed a provocative question with his 2009 essay for *The Atlantic*

Monthly magazine when he asked: 'Is the Internet making us stupid?' Carr followed up on that theme with a book titled, *The Shallows* (2010), in which he takes on the challenge presented by too much information that is of poor quality, combined with the inability (or time) to sort the wheat from the chaff.

This same argument was made more than two decades earlier, by William Leiss in *Under Technology's Thumb* (1990), which provided a wide-ranging examination of the role of technology in our society. In a chapter on the information economy and **information society**, Leiss—writing well before the Internet was widely known outside of research labs—made the point that we were not asking the most basic question of our information technologies: what did we *want* them to bring to our society? Should we not be expecting them to make us more knowledgeable (and not distracted)? And should we not be better able to deploy this knowledge to address the serious issues of the day?

Leiss argued that when we try to extract value from these new sources of information we are met with three considerable challenges: misinformation, disinformation, and excess information. Misinformation is when you wind up with the wrong information by accident. Disinformation is when you have been purposefully misled. Excess information is when an online search turns up 100,000 results and you are not sure where to start. The solution to these information challenges is better education but Leiss was skeptical that the population as a whole was up to the task. Both Keen and Carr have similarly dreary views of the potential of free information and widespread sharing: they see us drowning in a sea of our own mediocrity. Will the world blossom with a hundred Wikipedias as the population takes full advantage of their cognitive surplus, as Shirky imagines? Or will we soon dissolve into a group of imbeciles unable to tell fact from fiction because we have become inundated by misinformation, disinformation, and excess information? Clearly the stakes are high, and there is evidence on both sides (Shirky, Carr, and Keen have their critics, including strong criticism of each other).

The embodiment of knowledge in people and practices as distinct from its capture and storage in databases becomes more significant when considering the distinction between explicit and tacit knowledge. **Explicit knowledge** is knowledge that is codified (i.e. written or recorded in some form as data), that can be formally taught and learned, and readily transferred from one context to another. The Internet is a remarkably cost-effective means of codifying, reproducing, and distributing explicit knowledge worldwide. As the Internet makes explicit knowledge more readily available, however, this has implications for tacit knowledge. **Tacit knowledge** is knowledge derived from direct experience and the processes through which it is acquired are often intuitive, habitual, and reflexive, best learned through practices of doing something and the trial-and-error processes associated with learning-by-doing. Both Leadbeater (2000) and Romer (2007) refer to the significance of cooking in this respect, as an activity that involves both the application of explicit knowledge (codified in the form of recipes) and forms of tacit knowledge, such as knowing when pasta is al dente, or the quantity of a dab of butter or a pinch of salt. Leadbeater (2000: 28–30) sees celebrity chefs such as Jamie Oliver as paradigmatic knowledge entrepreneurs in this sense, because they trade in both formal knowledge, which is acquired by purchasing their recipe books, and tacit knowledge, acquired by watching them cook these recipes on television. By contrast, the challenge for large organizations, in both the public and private sectors, is that their strength in the production, dissemination, and use of explicit knowledge, and the factors that work to their advantage with the handling of information—such as a large-scale ability to preserve information over time, and the capacity to distribute it across large distances (all of which are exponentially enhanced with the Internet)—make the capture of tacit knowledge so difficult.

A third important issue is found in the distinction between incremental knowledge creation and radical knowledge creation. Incremental knowledge creation is knowledge that is embodied in organizations. Those who become part of the organization are inducted into this embodied knowledge and gradually add to it. Within a company such as Disney, whose theme parks are the largest single-site employers of labour in the US, there is a strong emphasis on the induction of new staff, who are not only trained in skills required to do their jobs, but in understanding the 'Disney way', which the company believes to be service that exceeds consumer expectations. Workers therefore bring both explicit and tacit knowledge to the performance of their roles in Disney, but the knowledge comes in forms that have been pre-packaged by the Disney Corporation for mass distribution. By contrast, radical knowledge creation is based on extensive experimentation and testing, and explicit recognition of the likelihood of ideas failing. Leadbeater argues that large companies will find it difficult to dominate sectors such as computer software, communications, and bio-technology, because the speed with which new ideas are being generated exceeds the capacity of such large companies to adopt new processes and unlearn previous practices.

The relationship between the four forms of knowledge described by Leadbeater is outlined in Table 8.2. Although this is, of course, one of many taxonomies of knowledge, in considering Leadbeater's categories of knowledge, what becomes apparent is that, radical knowledge creation based on tacit knowledge and unproven assumptions is unlikely to thrive within large organizations, but is increasingly important to competitive strategy in the new economy, particularly in knowledge-intensive industries. In Leadbeater's view (2000: 105): 'Big companies in knowledge intensive fields will resemble a mother ship with a

TABLE 8.2 Forms of Knowledge and Organizational Strategy

	Formal knowledge	Tacit knowledge
Incremental knowledge creation	Organizational training	Induction into organizational culture
Radical knowledge creation	Promotion and distribution of 'best practice' knowledge	Informal knowledge networks

flotilla of smaller companies around it. To be creative a big company needs to be linked into a knowledge-creating network outside it, which gives it access to the places where counter-intuitive, unconventional ideas are being created.'

Innovation and the Innovator's Dilemma

The significance of both tacit knowledge and radical knowledge creation is drawn into even sharper focus when considering the changing nature of **innovation** or the application of new knowledge to new products, processes, and services. Dodgson and colleagues (2002) refer to a fifth-generation innovation process, linked to the rise of **disruptive technologies** that undercut established products, management practices, and industry players (Bower and Christensen 1999), and the greater role that is played by both global markets and end-users in the innovation process. In contrast to ideas-push or demand-pull models of innovation, or the recent focus on national innovation systems, fifth-generation innovation processes stress the links between suppliers and consumers, strategic integration through research and partnership networks, and technological integration through both the fusion of different technologies (e.g. the linking of electrical and mechanical technologies to develop the hybrid car), and the development of new ICT-based toolkits that promote global collaborative knowledge networks (Dodgson et al. 2002: 54–7).

Indicators of the increasing importance of innovation can be seen in shortened product development cycles, reduced product life cycles, a greater range of products to cater to discrete market segments, and the high 'market-to-book ratios' of many of the world's largest companies. Companies such as Microsoft and Apple possess few physical assets relative to their market valuation as measured in their share capital, when compared to established manufacturers (such as General Electric, General Motors, or Boeing), since much of their wealth creation arises from product innovation. The challenge of innovation, however, is not simply that it is both more complex and more vital to a firm or an organization's survival in increasingly competitive global markets. The challenge rests also in what Clayton Christensen (2003) famously referred to as the 'innovator's dilemma' or the traps that exist in following two long-established business orthodoxies: working to your established strengths and listening to your customers.

The innovator's dilemma arises from the confluence of two factors that are common to products and services based on new technologies. The first, which is derived from Everett Rogers' (2003) model of the **diffusion of innovation**, as well as from Donald Norman's (1998) work on technology users and their needs and expectations, leads to the model of the technology S-curve (Figure 8.4).

The technology S-curve takes the shape that it does for two reasons. First, from the point of view of technological innovators, early applications of the technology may possess significant bugs or faults, or the relationship between the technology and its applications may remain unclear, but there is a threshold point where improvements are rapidly made to the technology as dominant standards emerge with the coalescence of product characteristics and consumer preferences, until the technology matures in a mass market stage as most

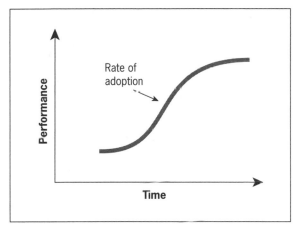

FIGURE 8.4 The Technology *S*-Curve
Source: Sood and Tellis (2005: 153).

users find its performance to be good enough and the energies of researchers go to other, newer technologies. For example, the television would now be considered a mature technology, as most people now have one that is good enough for their purposes, but developing mobile and wireless devices from which you can access television content is at an early development stage. The second factor in the technology *S*-curve relates to users and the fivefold distinction between enthusiasts, early adopters, mainstream adopters, late adopters, and laggards, where, again, the bulk of the user population tend to sit in the middle rather than at either end of the spectrum, generating a bell-curve distribution.

The technology *S*-curve sits alongside the development of new technologies in terms of performance over time as identified by Bower and Christensen (Figure 8.5 on page 182).

If these two diagrams are mapped onto one another, they illustrate the innovator's dilemma, which is the risk on the one hand of providing a product or service that underperforms in terms of the expectations of early adopters in the early stage of the product life cycle, and the concern, on the other hand, of providing a product or service that exceeds the needs of most users in the later stages of a product life cycle (Figure 8.6 on page 182).

The innovator's dilemma in the first case results from new products often containing bugs or design flaws, to which early adopters are particularly likely to draw attention. What is known as first-mover advantage can become first-mover disadvantage, or second-mover advantage as competitors who subsequently enter the market learn from the first mover's mistakes (Tellis and Golder 1996). For example, Apple's attempts to capture the PDA market with the release of the Newton in 1993 suffered from such problems, and second mover products such as the Palm Pilot and Pocket PC took advantage of Apple's popularization of the PDA concept, but with more stable products.

The second case of innovator's dilemma is a more complex one and is linked to the growing disjuncture over time between the trajectory of performance improvement for technologies, and the expectations of users over time as products and services become more mass-market

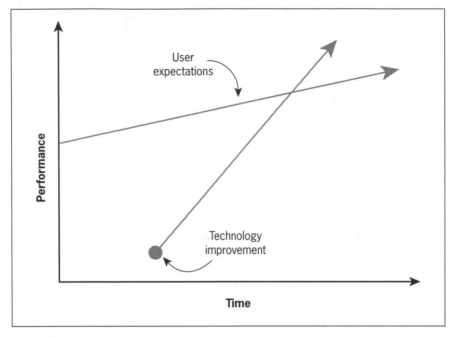

FIGURE 8.5 Assessing Disruptive Technologies
Source: Bower and Christensen (1999: 149).

FIGURE 8.6 The Innovator's Dilemma

commodities. It is quite clear, for example, that 95 per cent of the functionality of a software program such as Microsoft Excel is unlikely to be used by 95 per cent of its users, who are not specialists in statistics, finance, or such areas, and tend to use the program for a small number of basic tasks. The extent to which this matters depends in part on whether competitors can identify an opportunity for a product or service that is less sophisticated and less expensive than that of the established market leader, and on whether they can tap into this unmet demand for a pared-down Excel-type program.

One of the most well known instances of this is in budget airlines, such as WestJet, Porter, and JetBlue. They identified that while incumbent airlines such as Air Canada or American Airlines were continually improving the quality of their in-flight service (better meals, more in-flight entertainment, complimentary drinks etc.), there was a very large class of potential airline users who had little interest in the quality of the in-flight experience, as long as they could get from one place to another more economically. As a result, these new companies were able to create a new market segment of airline travellers who sought low-cost flights with lower expectations of the quality of the in-flight experience than the incumbents had assumed. The opening in the market arose because the incumbents sought to improve what they were already good at and to respond to the needs of their existing customer base, whereas the newer, disruptive, innovators sought to fundamentally change the assumptions underpinning airline travel. Similar observations could be made in the personal computing industry by comparing Apple, which has continuously sought to innovate with the quality of its product, serving a sophisticated user community with high expectations of their personal computers, with a company such as Dell, which largely does not innovate with the quality of its computers, but rather has focused its innovation strategy on developing new, lower-cost distribution channels through the Internet that enable it to deliver PCs economically and quickly.

There is a variant on these innovation theories, one that is finding a growing place in an Internet-connected world. This is called 'lead user' innovation, named by Eric von Hippel, of MIT. His *Sources of Innovation* (1988) describes a world in which new generations of products seem to be emerging, not from the engineers and scientists who create them, but from their most demanding customers. These folks modified the products, enhancing and extending their capabilities to solve specific problems or to go beyond their original specifications. Savvy businesses started to pay attention to this process and actively encouraged these people, helping them to form groups and working with them to design new versions of the product. Finding these people, helping them organize, and staying in touch with them was a herculean—and very expensive—task in the 1980s.

The Internet changed this dramatically. A new book, von Hippel's *Democratizing Innovation* (2005), describes how **lead user innovation**, which involves manufacturers adopting and adapting ideas from their users by bringing the users back into the company, is being transformed into **user-centred innovation** processes. In this scenario, users are no longer simply a source of ideas but are actively engaged in designing and creating products that they want and need. Von Hippel uses an example of windsurfing equipment, but recent examples have included kites and cars as well. The people engaged in these activities are passionate and often—but not necessarily—have a high level of expertise and have the ability to express themselves through tools such as 3D modeling software. The results of their imagination and dreams are posted to online forums and blogs, voted on by a community, and then produced for those who have placed orders.

A Creative Economy?

We noted in the previous chapter that the rise of the creative industries has drawn new attention to the relationship between creativity, innovation, and entrepreneurship in the new economy. While much policy attention in the 1990s was directed towards information policy, the need to develop skills and infrastructure for the ICT sector, and the promotion of electronic commerce, there is now a renewed focus on creativity and the unique skills and talents of individuals. Moreover, with the imperative to innovate becoming ever stronger, but with established models of research and development, based on incremental improvements and direct response to existing customers proving vulnerable in the face of phenomena such as the innovator's dilemma, there is renewed interest in creativity and the creative process as a way of unlocking the potential for new knowledge to generate new and innovative products and services.

John Howkins, author of *The Creative Economy*, captured this shift in thinking from an information society to a creative economy and society in a 2002 presentation to the London Development Agency:

> The information society that we've been speaking about and living in for 30–40 years, and which is symbolized by the boom in information technology, telecoms, media and financial services, is losing its grip on our imaginations and may, indeed, be coming to an end. I define an IS as a society characterized by people spending most of their time and making most of their money by handling information, usually by means of technology. *If I was a bit of data I would be proud of living in an information society. But as a thinking, emotional, creative being—on a good day, anyway—I want something better . . .* I am talking about a change of perspective, a shift of emphasis. Ideas and information are symbiotically intertwined. But when I say I have an idea I am expressing a more personal view, and making a different claim, from when I say I have some information . . . We need information. But we also need to be active, clever, and persistent in challenging this information. We need to be original, skeptical, argumentative, often bloody-minded and occasionally downright negative—in one word, creative. (Howkins 2005: 117–88; emphasis added)

The new economy literature, from economics and other areas of the social sciences, views the dynamics of the new economy as increasingly driven by creativity and culture. For 'new growth' economists, creativity and economic dynamism are best promoted by institutional and policy frameworks that promote a culture of innovation and entrepreneurship (PMSEIC

2005). Castells proposes that the dynamics of the new economy are cultural as much as they are technological or economic, not only in the sense that economic growth is increasingly associated with the development and diffusion of new ideas, but also in the more anthropological sense that the dynamics of ICT development will be dependent on 'the culture of innovations, on the culture of risk, on the culture of expectations, and, ultimately, on the culture of hope in the future' (Castells 2001: 112). Mitchell and colleagues (2003) argue that this requires a shift in the focus of policies, to promote ICT development and measure its influence to move beyond productivity-based indicators, and to understand more fully the relationship between ICTs and new forms of creative practice. Venturelli argues that culture and creativity are increasingly the gold that nations possess in the global information economy:

> Culture can be seen as the key to success in the Information Economy, be-
> cause for the very first time in the modern age, the ability to create new ideas
> and new forms of expression forms a valuable resource base of a society . . .
> Cultural wealth can no longer be regarded in the legacy and industrial terms
> of our common understanding, as something fixed, inherited and mass-dis-
> tributed, but as a measure of the vitality, knowledge, energy, and dynamism
> of the production of ideas that pervades a given community. (2005: 395–6)

Such arguments have been developed most strongly by Richard Florida, in *The Rise of the Creative Class* (2002). Florida proposes that, if the nineteenth and early twentieth centuries were the heyday of industrial capitalism and the factory system, and the mid- to late twentieth century was dominated by organization and bureaucracy, the twenty-first century marks the rise of the creative class, whose core values are a commitment to individuality, meritocracy, mobility, diversity, openness, and the self-formation of identities. The shift towards creativity becoming 'the decisive source of competitive advantage' in the global economy has further implications since 'creativity has come to be the most highly prized commodity in our economy—and yet it is not a "commodity". Creativity comes from people. And while people can be hired and fired, their creative capacity cannot be bought and sold, or turned on and off at will' (2002: 5).

Tracking employment trends in the US over the course of the twentieth century, Florida notes that the creative class has grown from 10 per cent of the US workforce in 1900, to 21 per cent by 1970, and 30 per cent by 1999, thereby making it a larger group than the traditional working class (2002: 73, 330). Moreover, he points out that the creative sector accounts for 47 per cent of wealth generated in the US economy, so the creative class makes a disproportionately large contribution to contemporary economic growth (2007: 29). Defining creative work as that which 'produces new forms and designs that are readily transferable and widely useful' (2002: 7), he distinguishes between a super-creative core—which consists of scientists and engineers, academics, writers, artists, entertainers, cultural figures, researchers, and 'thought leaders', who now make up about 12 per cent of the US workforce—and creative professionals who perform support work in knowledge-intensive or creative industries to facilitate and promote the creativity of others.

Despite criticisms of Florida's analysis and the policy implications derived from it (see e.g. Kotkin 2006; Peck 2005), one reason Florida's work has been so influential is that the notion of creative cities and regions can be linked to arguments about the embodied nature of knowledge that is valuable in particular people and their skills and talents, and the embeddedness of particular forms of knowledge in certain geographical places. Theories of dynamic economic clusters aim to capture the correlation between agglomerations of related firms, industries, or sectors and the economic success of particular cities and regions. Porter (1998) argues that successful geographical clusters generate sustained competitive advantage for the firms and institutions within them, by increasing productivity through access to specialist inputs, labour, knowledge, and technology, promoting innovation by making information about new opportunities more widely available, and promoting new business formation in related sectors through distinctive access to necessary labour, skills, knowledge, technology, and capital. Based on his study of different types of Quebec high technology firms, Shearmur observes that 'there is increasing evidence that innovation is also a spatial phenomenon: the propensity of establishments to innovate also varies with their location relative to major and minor metropolitan areas, independent of local context' (Shearmur 2010). Storper (1997) proposes that the interaction between new digital technologies, organizational changes such as networking, and competition among cities and regions to capture economic rents, means that sources of distinctiveness between cities and regions have become more, not less, relevant in the global economy. Scott (2004) argues that the creative industries (or what he terms the 'cultural-products industries') demonstrate particularly strong tendencies towards location-based clustering due to:

1. the importance of specific forms of labour input, and the quality of such specialized labour and associated forms of tacit knowledge;
2. the organization of production in dense networks of small- and medium-sized enterprises that are strongly dependent on each other for the provision of specialized inputs and services;
3. the employment relation in creative industries, which is frequently characterized by intermittent, project-based work, meaning that recurring job-search costs can be minimized through co-location in particular areas;
4. the indirect, synergistic benefits that result from the interaction of individual creativity with collective learning, tacit knowledge, and historical memory, through the coexistence of people and enterprises engaged in interrelated activities; and,
5. the development of associated services and institutional infrastructure, and the priority that the relevant industry sectors have in the thinking of local and regional governments.

The implication may well be, as Florida argues, that the world is becoming 'spiky'. What he means by this is that rather than globalization and new media generating a levelling or equalizing effect—the 'world is flat' argument proposed by Friedman (2005)—there is instead a clustering of innovation around a small but growing number of urban and regional centres. Because concentrations of creative, talented people become increasingly important to innovation, and because innovation is the principal driver of growth in a global knowledge economy, the phenomenon of clustering around innovation centres becomes ever more significant:

> Creative people cluster not simply because they like to be around one another or they prefer cosmopolitan centres with lots of amenities . . . They and their companies also cluster because of the powerful productivity advantages, economies of scale, and knowledge spillovers such density brings . . . Because globalization has increased the returns to innovation, by allowing innovating products and services to quickly reach consumers worldwide, it has strengthened the lure that innovation centres hold for our planet's best and brightest, reinforcing the spikiness of wealth and economic production. (Florida 2007: xxii)

We are therefore presented with the paradox of place in relation to globalization and new media. While new media in principle allow more and more activities to occur anywhere, the geographical dynamics of clustering and the changing nature and value of knowledge promote new forms of embeddedness of economic activity in a relatively small number of urban and regional centres. As a result, there is uneven development between cities, regions, and nations, and heightened inter-place competition.

Case Study: YouTube

Over the course of the 2000s, far more people acquired access to high-speed broadband Internet connectivity than in previous decades. In many cases this was not due to their home service subscription decisions, but rather, to the availability of high-speed broadband access in workplaces, schools, universities, and other institutional sites. One consequence of access to high-speed broadband Internet was that access to audiovisual content became much more readily available, yet major film studios and television networks were reluctant to put much of their content onto the Internet. The two main reasons for this were concerns about piracy and copyright infringement, and the potential for 'channel conflict' with their traditional distribution sites, such as cinemas, video and DVD outlets, and television channels, from which the bulk of their advertising revenue was derived. Yet it has been increasingly apparent that users are keen to access their media content through personal computers, particularly when they are able to rate, reuse, and distribute this content among their peers. It was in this context that YouTube (www.youtube.com) was launched.

YouTube is a video-sharing site, where users can upload, share, rate, comment on, and distribute audiovisual material. Created in February 2005, it was ranked by *Time* magazine as the 'Invention of the Year' for 2006, and was subsequently acquired by Google for USD $1.65 billion. YouTube was a disruptive innovation in the sense discussed by Bower and Christensen (1999), because its developers identified that the Internet had made it far less costly to distribute audiovisual content, but this was not being exploited by established film and television industries because they had to recoup the high costs of production of their content through managed distribution via their existing channels. Drawing on the Pro-Am Revolution identified by Leadbeater and Miller (2004), we can see that the production costs of making video had fallen, but that this was not recognized at the higher levels of the film and television industries, so YouTube encouraged the multitude of video producers to put their material up for distribution through the site.

The rise of user-generated content has sparked criticism as well as enthusiasm. José van Dijck's 2009 article 'Users like You: Theorizing Agency in User Generated Content' suggests that we have insufficiently theorized the contributions that millions of amateurs and semi-professionals are making in the media landscape. As he points out, 'agency' (the independence of action and reaction that individuals exhibit in their consumption of media) has until recently been tied to the medium being examined. So, for example, it is different to watch a film than it is to sit down in front of the television and that is different than listening to the radio. As the audience becomes users and even 'prosumers' or 'produsers'—implying considerably more potential for action and independence—we need to reconsider many of our theoretical positions. Nevertheless, it is too simplistic to deem the television viewer as passive and the person with a YouTube account as active. A more fine-grained and nuanced perspective needs to be put forward, and in particular we need to take into account the fact that—for most participants, at least—this participation is wholly voluntary and unrewarded.

It was estimated in 2007 that 100 million videos were downloaded through YouTube each day and its audience was about 20 million people worldwide each month, with younger people (median age of 33) comprising a large majority of users (see Figure 8.7).

YouTube also has an increasingly important function as a feedback loop into the mainstream media. In November 2010 the most viewed YouTube videos were music videos: Justin Beiber's 'Baby' (over 374 million views), and Lady Gaga's 'Bad Romance' (just over 300 million views). Home video continues to have a place in the top ten, however: 'Charlie bit my finger', with 244 million views, was third.

Copyright infringement remains an ongoing issue for YouTube. In the case of some of the most popular material uploaded to the site, such as excerpts from television programs such as *The Simpsons* and *South Park*, this is clearly more of an issue for the owners and distributors of the content, such as Viacom and News Corporation, than its own producers, who have long accepted that their material is accessed virally through the Internet community. Nonetheless, the US media company Viacom initiated a USD $1 billion lawsuit against YouTube for breach of its copyright in February 2007, on the grounds that 160,000 video clips that were produced and initially distributed through Viacom have been collectively viewed more than one million times on YouTube without Viacom's permission (Kedrosky 2007). In June 2010 it was reported that Viacom lost their case, but the company vowed to appeal.[3]

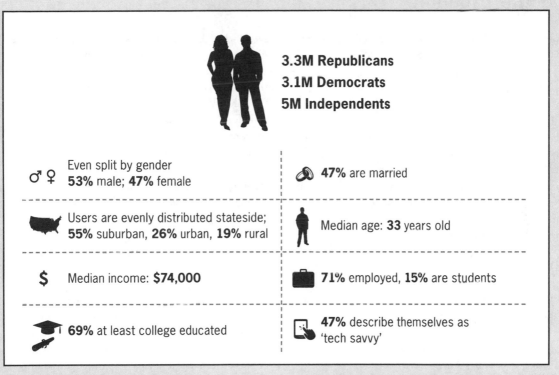

3.3M Republicans
3.1M Democrats
5M Independents

♂ ♀ Even split by gender
53% male; **47%** female

💍 **47%** are married

Users are evenly distributed stateside;
55% suburban, **26%** urban, **19%** rural

Median age: **33** years old

$ Median income: **$74,000**

💼 **71%** employed, **15%** are students

🎓 **69%** at least college educated

📱 **47%** describe themselves as
'tech savvy'

FIGURE 8.7 Who Is the YouTube User?
Source: Adapted from http://willvideoforfood.com/wp-content/uploads/2009/07/Picture-1.png

 Useful Websites

E-marketer.com
←www.emarketer.com→

This website aggregates international trends in e-business and online marketing trends, drawing from over 2,800 worldwide sources.

Knowledge Assessment Methodology
←www.worldbank.org/kam→

This website was developed by The World Bank as part of its 'Knowledge for Development' program, which aims to benchmark countries in terms of their positioning in a knowledge economy. Interestingly,

it found in 2006 that the five most advanced countries were Scandinavian (Denmark, Sweden, Finland, Iceland, Norway).

The Work Foundation—The Knowledge Economy
←www.theworkfoundation.com/futureofwork→

This website provides a major investigation into the nature of the global knowledge economy—with a particular focus on developments in Europe—that commenced in 2006.

Further Reading

Here Comes Everybody: The Power of Organizing Without Organizations, Clay Shirky (2008)

In this book Shirky explains how new technologies are making collective action online—through sites like Wikipedia—possible. Importantly, he begins with why this ability to form groups is a) desirable and b) significant. Humans are social animals, Shirky reminds us, and we form groups to get things done that we cannot do (easily) on our own. In the past the ability to form groups beyond a small number has been hampered by logistics, and as a result we have long resorted to bureaucracies to get larger projects done. The promise of information and communication technologies is to have the advantages of large groups without the burden of bureaucracy. How this works, and how it is most successful, is explored with numerous examples and case studies, including one of the most famous Canadian contributions to social media: Flickr.

Cognitive Surplus: Creativity and Generosity in a Connected Age, Clay Shirky (2010)

In a follow-up text to the 2008 book, Shirky examines the impact of 'free time' (time formerly spent watching television, mainly) that is deployed for collective action. While the first book examined how and why social action online was possible, the second book suggests what the outcome(s) might be, given that we might actually find the time to contribute to our collective well-being. While this might sound hopelessly optimistic, it is important to remember that many of these collective acts are not something we have never done before but in fact the retrieval of behaviours that humans commonly engaged in during a pre-industrial, pre-anonymized society.

Everything Is Miscellaneous: The Power of the New Digital Disorder, David Weinberger (2007)

Weinberger's book is a consolation for those of us who can never get our lives in order. Drowning in bits of paper, and the flotsam and jetsam of everyday life, we wonder how we can cope. The answer is to embrace the messiness of life and see it instead as an opportunity. Conceding that we can never get things into perfect order, but applying the growing power of search engines, Weinberger argues that by learning from the pioneers (digital music is one of his examples) we can all benefit from the shift to digital forms of knowledge and information. In particular, his prescription for greater use of search engines as a bridge between information and knowledge, suggests economic opportunities in the knowledge economy.

Discussion Questions

1. The term globalization is defined in this chapter in terms of a series of interrelated processes. What are these processes and what evidence or examples of them can you identify in your own living, working, or educational spheres?

2. What is meant by the term 'knowledge economy'? What are some of the features, processes, and dynamics involved?

3. What is an e-commerce strategy, what are some of its benefits, and why is it important for new media?

4. This chapter describes the global knowledge economy as arising from the confluence of three developments. What are these and what are the dynamics that link them?

5. This chapter presents both old and new paradigms of economic development. What are the characteristics of each of these paradigms? Why are they significant to new media studies?

6. What are the two examples of the innovator's dilemma given in this chapter? What are some real world examples of this dilemma?

7. This chapter takes up some discussion of the difference between information and knowledge. For example, the notion that knowledge is embodied in persons and practices, whereas information is captured and stored in databases and is readily accessible and increasingly reproducible through the Internet. What significance does this have for understanding the knowledge economy in terms of both creative and cultural aspects?

Class Activities

1. As a class, attempt to discover the country of origin for the collected electronic and fashion items present in the room. Try to account for raw materials and multiple points of origin for complex items with embedded components such as laptop computers. If you can, see how much—if anything—was 'Made in Canada'. What do your conclusions suggest to you about Canada's role in a knowledge economy?

2. Use the World Bank's Knowledge Assessment Methodology tool (see Useful Websites, above) to compare Canada to a selected other country. How do we compare? What are our strong points and what are our weak points?

9 Internet Law, Policy, and Governance

Questions to Consider

- What are some examples of the domains covered by cyberspace law? What are the complications and issues specific to this type of law?

- How do policy initiatives or interventions taken by the Canadian government affect new media?

- Why is it important to consider the distinctions and balance between private ownership and public use of intellectual property when thinking about new media?

Chapter Outline

In this chapter we examine the interesting and sometimes difficult issues that have arisen in a world in which two of the foundational principals of law—property and the state—have been significantly altered by digital and global information flows. We look at some of the major domains of law as they pertain to cyberspace and some of the legal implications that have arisen as that space has changed and expanded. That digital goods are ephemeral and easily cross borders is challenge enough but a further pressure comes from the fact that there is little if any cyberspace law at all currently—the Internet is self-policing but only in a loose sense and mainly at the level of technology standards. Beyond that, only national and local law can be applied—and that, as we will see, is oft-times very difficult to do. Nations have attempted to establish priorities, programs, and policies designed to boost the power and role of their own citizens and corporations in information and communication technologies—first with computers and then networks. Given the origins of the Internet in Western democracies such as the US, sometimes the laissez-faire attitude adopted online is incompatible with local standards elsewhere around the globe. We examine these issues along with implications for copyright and property rights, and the open source software movement.

Internet Law, Policy, and Governance

It takes little more than a cursory glance at the range of legal issues raised by the development of the Internet and networked ICTs to recognize that they are enormous in their scope, domain of application, and implications for different individuals and groups within societies. Examples of some of the domains covered by cyberspace law include:

- cyberspace and business: e-commerce; online contract law, online financial law, online gambling, cyberfraud;
- cyberspace and medicine: telemedicine, online prescribing, online pharmacies;
- cyberspace and equity: broadband development and access, educational uses of the Internet, gender and race online, poverty and unequal access to the Internet (the digital divide);
- cyberspace and education: plagiarism, use of computers in schools, content filtering for minors;
- freedom of speech issues: freedom of expression, obscenity, pornography and online indecency, protection of children, cultural rights;
- intellectual property issues: copyright law, patent law, trademark law, gifts and online exchange;
- privacy issues: cryptography and privacy protection for online transactions, employment privacy, personal information privacy, data security; and,
- security issues: cybercrime, spamming, cyberstalking and online harassment, hacking, identity theft, the Internet and terrorism.

This is a lengthy list and more could easily be added to it. The legal implications of the Internet's rapid development are rendered even more complex by the way(s) in which the Internet is situated in relation to existing laws, regulatory frameworks, and the ideas that underpin them. First, there are the unique characteristics of networked information, in that it is intangible, geographically distributed, recombinant, and continually changing in its form and character. These characteristics confront the legal tradition, where 'existing legislation depends upon clearly demonstrable, localizable and liable legal persons and ownership titles. Information and evidence have to be, or must be able to be, set down on a data carrier that has still to be comparable to printed paper' (van Dijk 1999: 116). The contrast between the need for fixity and tangible links to applicable subjects on which the legal system operates and the fluidity of the online environment is compounded by the difficulties that arise in implementing laws, since activities in networks are frequently non-transparent, communication can be anonymous or very hard to trace back to an original source, and evidence can be destroyed, hidden, erased, or altered by computer users and systems operators.

The second set of factors that greatly complicates Internet law arises from the global nature of the Internet and its network infrastructure, and the predominantly national basis of laws and legal systems. Froomkin (1997) observes that the transnational nature of the Internet as a communications medium promotes regulatory arbitrage, whereby people and corporations can, in certain circumstances, 'arrange their affairs so that they evade domestic regulations by structuring their communications or transactions to take advantage of foreign regulatory regimes' (1997: 129). The problem of Internet users and Internet service providers being able to evade national laws by accessing content or undertaking transactions through other territorial domains—or, as others might see it, the enhanced freedom of Internet users to evade domestic laws that they may deem inappropriate—is compounded by the uncertainties related to legal and territorial jurisdiction in cyberspace. There have been many instances of jurisdictional conflict over content, ranging from attempts by the Chinese government to close down websites hosted in Taiwan and Hong Kong that promote the ideas of the Falun Gong movement (which is banned in China) (Kalathil and Boas 2003), to attempts by the French government in 2000 to pressure the Yahoo! search engine into blocking access by French citizens to Nazi memorabilia on its English-language auction sites (Stein and Sinha 2002).

The third issue is that Internet law, in a sense, does not exist. Just as the Internet marks out a convergent space between computing, telecommunications, and media, what is termed 'Internet law' is in truth rarely more than the application and extension of laws developed for other media and communications technologies, such as print, broadcasting, and tele-communications. The legal issues linked to the Internet have also extended, in a largely unplanned and incoherent manner, to areas of civil, criminal, and corporate law that were developed to address quite different issues from those presented by networked and convergent media. Similarly, what constitutes Internet policy in many countries is often an uncomfortable amalgam of policies developed for traditional media industries (most notably broadcasting), telecommunications policies, and policies to promote production in media content sectors, with defence and national security making an occasional appearance in the policy mix. The problem is not simply one of law and policy lagging behind technological developments, since this, inevitably, will be the case to some extent. Rather, as van Dijk (1999: 117) observes, legal and policy responses have largely been fragmentary and ad hoc adjustments that remain based on outdated assumptions: 'There is no internal readjustment. Instead, detailed alterations are made to existing legislation including technical definitions that will soon be outdated . . . Fragmentary adjustments to legislation are not suitable for the regulation of large-scale networks and their far-reaching consequences to individuals and society at large.'

In the plethora of national information policy statements that emerged in the 1990s, there was also often a curious dualism. On the one hand, there was a confidence that the freely operating commercial market provided the best means of allocating resources and promoting technological development. The Global Information Infrastructure proposed by the Clinton-Gore US administration in the 1990s prioritized private investment, service development driven by free markets and competition, flexible regulatory systems, and the removal of barriers to foreign investment. In tandem with this, new international regulatory organizations such as the World Trade Organization (established in 1995) actively promoted the privatization of public telecommunications monopolies and fostered the promotion of competition policy and free trade, with an underlying view that communications companies were market-based service providers with sharply delimited universal service obligations (CRTC 1995; Flew and McElhinney 2005; Winseck 2002b), linked to the idea of Internet access as a human right (see below). At the same time, through national information policies, many governments heavily funded the ICT sectors in the hope of developing 'national champions' in global markets and promoting a networked society and a Web-savvy population.[1] Melody (1996) observed at the time that, in many of these programs, there was a misplaced primacy given to development of information infrastructure as an end in itself, which was often accompanied by generous subsidies to multinational ICT corporations to produce locally, with insufficient attention being given to the relationship between content applications, user demand, and skills acquisition that would have provided a more sustainable, equitable, and democratic basis for Internet development policies (cf. Breen 2002).

Perspectives on Internet Governance

It has been proposed that, rather than understanding the various attempts at Internet regulation in terms of law (which raises the question of the origins of current laws) or policy (which presumes a national territorial jurisdiction, as well as government stewardship of a global, predominantly commercial medium), Internet regulation can be understood in terms of **governance**. The concept of governance recognizes links between the public and private sectors or between the market and the state: markets themselves can constitute powerful governance structures and governments act as often to promote markets and private sector interests as they do to regulate and constrain them (Jessop 1998, 2000). Moreover, from the perspective of governance, there is an understanding of the various roles played in Internet law and policy—by non-government and non-corporate institutions and by organizations of civil society and social movements, alongside state/public and corporate interests—as well as the ways in which such processes increasingly cross territorial jurisdictions (Murphy 2002).

The concept of Internet governance is useful as an alternative to strong notions of **cyber-libertarianism**, commonly found among key user communities (particularly in the US), which view the infrastructure of the Internet as essentially manageable by self-governance. Cyber-libertarianism was a key tenet of Internet pioneers such as those associated with the Electronic Frontier Foundation (EFF), which saw in the Internet a 'platform which will allow every person to speak their mind and query the world to create their own point of view' (EFF n.d.). The non-hierarchical, decentralized, and networked nature of the Internet presented groups such as the EFF the opportunity to develop self-governing online communities which, being finally free of state interference and censorship, could realize the freedom of speech principles of the First Amendment of the US Constitution. John Perry Barlow (1996a) declared in his 'Declaration of the Independence of Cyberspace': 'We believe that from ethics, enlightened self-interest and the commonweal, our governance will emerge ... The only law that all of our constituent cultures would recognize is the Golden Rule'. In 1996, in one of the first high level court decisions to rule on the distribution of materials via the Internet, the US Supreme Court cited the First Amendment ('Freedom of speech') when it struck down provisions of the US Communications Decency Act that it deemed went too far in restraining the communication rights of adults. The case helped establish the Internet as different from broadcast television and radio, for example, where stronger protection of the public was justified.

Mike Godwin (1998: 23), counsel for the EFF in the case, argued that:

> Give people a modem and a computer and access to the Net, and it's far more
> likely that they'll do good than otherwise. This is because freedom of speech is

itself a good—the framers of the [US] Constitution were right to give it special protection, because societies in which people can speak freely are better off than societies in which they can't.

The cyber-libertarian perspective is no longer articulated as strongly as a model for Internet governance as it was in the mid-1990s. One reason for this has been that as the Internet has grown exponentially and as the user base has become more diverse, the notion of a shared ethos that underpinned early forms of virtual communities is less applicable (Davies 2003). More significantly, the cyber-libertarian perspective was also deeply ambivalent about corporate power on the Internet. Authors and activists such as Lessig note the danger of the cyber-libertarian position and its neglect of questions of corporate power, observing that Internet activists operating from a cyber-libertarian position run the risk of 'winning the political struggle against state control so as to entrench control in the name of the market' (Lessig 2001: 267). Early critics of cyber-libertarianism such as Barbrook and Cameron (1995) noted how an anti-statist vision of Internet self-governance (what they termed the 'Californian Ideology') was likely to experience deep ambivalence in determining its relationship to the rise of corporate power on the Internet and associated neo-liberal ideologies that critique state power in the name of the commercial global market (e.g. Dyson et al. 1994).

A very different perspective on Internet governance emerged from critical political economy. For Mosco (1997), McChesney (1999), and Schiller (2000), the early promise of the Internet as a democratic and decentralized alternative to commercial mass media was quickly swept aside as governments around the world deregulated or eased their regulation of communications systems in the 1990s to give greater power to dominant commercial interests. These writers see the emergent pattern of Internet governance as largely resembling that of the societies in which it operated, meaning that in corporate-dominated societies, it would be these powerful interests that most effectively shape government policy to suit their interests. McChesney argues that 'if certain forces thoroughly dominate a society's political economy they will thoroughly dominate its communications system . . . and so it is . . . for the most part, with big business interests in the United States' (1999: 124–5). Schiller argues in *Digital Capitalism* (2000) that the development of the global Internet is best understood as being driven by the demands of transnational corporations and the US government for a globally integrated computing and communications network that could promote the expansion of operations and markets worldwide, minimizing the capacity of national governments to regulate such activities in the public interest.

As the Internet has developed as a global, decentralized network it continues to challenge the two core tenets of nation-state sovereignty: sovereignty over territory and sovereignty over citizens. Not only will cyberspace always exist apart from national territories and borders (unlike air space, for example), but the Internet itself not only enables, but actively promotes, communications activities and transactions that cross territorial boundaries (Kleinwächter 2002: 56–7). One attempt to develop a framework for global Internet governance has been the Internet Corporation for Assigned Names and Numbers. ICANN was established in 1998 to address a very new problem: how to govern the allocation of Internet domain names, or the addresses that people, organizations, and governments adopt to direct people to their sites on the Web.

Before the mid-1990s, the allocation of Internet addresses had been a largely technical matter, undertaken by individuals or small groups with little discussion or controversy, and with little international consultation. As the Internet grew however, this structure became inadequate. Commercial interests increasingly saw their domain name as a part of their branding and marketing strategies, and they sought to ensure that their brand, as embodied in their domain name, was protected in cyberspace. This was exacerbated by the phenomenon of cybersquatting, where people buy up potentially popular domain names, sometimes in the hope of profit, sometimes to use them for culture-jamming, in which critics of consumerism use mainstream media and advertising to critique popular culture (Lasn 2000). Kalle Lasn's Vancouver-based Adbusters Media Foundation, which produces a magazine and website that contain anti-consumer articles and advertising as well as the annual 'Buy Nothing Day' event, is an example of culture-jamming. Others exploit domain names for less positive ends, directing unsuspecting users to pornography sites, or simply capturing an asset that they could then profitably sell. This was clearly problematic for commercial and other users, and a range of powerful interests collaborated to put in place a more cohesive structure for domain name governance: Internet Corporation for Assigned Names and Numbers, ICANN.

ICANN is a private, not-for-profit agency representing both the global Internet community and the global Internet business community, which includes both those involved in domain name registration and those seeking to register online domain names in order to pursue electronic commerce. While governments clearly have an interest in the outcomes of ICANN decision-making, ICANN seeks to maintain an advisory, back seat function for governments (Kleinwächter 2002: 66). ICANN has also developed an approach to dispute resolution that is non-legalistic, based on a quick and low-cost resolution premised on whether a domain name registrant can be considered to have acted in bad faith.

Paré (2003) and Froomkin (2003) find, however, that both the structure and the conduct of ICANN have, in practice, been heavily influenced by the US government in representing business interests in trademark and intellectual property protection. They question the claim that ICANN has developed a new form of decentralized global Internet governance that transcends national interests and appeals to the distinctive ethos of a global Internet community. Indeed, Paré argues that the consensus-oriented politics of ICANN have in fact generated a crisis of legitimacy for the organization, because it is seen as 'a private organization which is exerting global public authority over a key information and communication resource in a manner that appears to be inconsistent with both the way in which decisions have traditionally been made in the public domain and the traditional norms and values associated with internetworking' (Paré 2003: 169). This crisis of the legitimacy of ICANN was identified at the World Summit on the Information Society (WSIS) in Geneva (2003) and Tunis (2005), where developing countries and civil society organizations in particular argued for an alternative framework for Internet governance over issues such as domain names, one where the organizations of the United Nations would play a leading role (Froomkin 2003; Ó Siochrú 2004; Ó Siochrú et al. 2003).

Canadian New Media Policy

Internet and new media policy in Canada has a long history. As we discussed in Chapter 2, the Internet and other present-day technologies did not emerge wholly formed but rather have evolved from, and in many cases are based on, antecedent technologies. To have an understanding of current new media policy in Canada, it is important to first examine some of the policy initiatives that the Canadian government has taken in these areas. Policy interventions can come in the form of laws and regulations but also in the form of public inquiries, investments, subsidies and tax benefits, and even decisions *not* to regulate at a particular time or in a particular area.

Public inquiries

As with the establishment of the national radio broadcasting system, put in place as the result of a Royal Commission—a government-sponsored inquiry into a given issue in order to support informed decision-making, policy-making, and governance—the Canadian government has often initiated public inquiries into issues of national concern. Just such an inquiry was established in the early 1990s, when the 'information superhighway' (as it was then known) loomed on the horizon. In early 1994, Canada's Information Highway Advisory Council (IHAC) was formed to consider the implications and recommend actions for the government on concerns related to the arrival of digital information into homes and businesses in Canada.

IHAC provided advice to the Federal Minister of Industry in a series of reports, which followed an issues document published in April 1994 under the title, 'The Canadian Information Highway—Building Canada's Information and Communications Infrastructure'. The issues document laid out the main concerns for the government in three broad areas: jobs, sovereignty, and access. The initial report set out four principles as important for a Canadian information highway: (1) interconnections and interoperability between networks; (2) mixed public and private sector investment in infrastructure; (3) competition in services, content, and equipment; and (4) adequate protection of privacy and network security. A series of public meetings and a wealth of commissioned research followed, with a series of reports published through 1995 and a final report at the end of that year. The following year (1996), the government issued an action strategy under the title, 'Building the Information Society: Moving Canada Into the 21st Century'.[2]

Although the type of network that seemed imminent at the time of the IHAC report—a system more dominated by media giants than by the information and interaction-driven Internet that actually evolved—has not entirely come to pass, the country's policy response to the Internet has been shaped and informed by IHAC. The Internet of today, as it is accessed from Canada and contributed to by Canadians, is largely interconnected and open, despite threats to that openness that occur from time to time. Whether this openness has been sustained because of recommendations by the Government of Canada and IHAC or because it makes business sense (see Chapter 2 for a discussion of network economics), members of the public benefit, as they are able to use one network connection to reach all of the potential sites in the world.

Archival Policy

On publication, the Information Highway reports were released online—a novel and radical initiative back then—but today they are difficult to locate except in paper form. A thorough search of available websites in January 2010 failed to locate any current copies on Government of Canada web servers. The 'wayback' service provided by the Internet Archive can be used as an alternate route to locating documents, however, and the archived report can be found by going to http://web.archive.org and searching for the original URL for the report (which was http://strategis.ic.gc.ca/SSG/ih01650e.html)—the resulting complete URL is: http://web.archive.org/web/19990117001335/strategis.ic.gc.ca/SSG/ih01650e.html.

While this service makes the document available, it raises an interesting policy question: should government documents be allowed to go stale and disappear from public view? Was the decision to remove these documents made consciously or were they simply relegated to archive status when Industry Canada upgraded their website or server? Is Canada relying on an Internet archive service to maintain access to its

digital documents? Certainly, it is difficult to imagine a government directive that would remove a document like this from the many libraries around the world that maintain print copies. Yet a digital version can disappear completely. This case illustrates the complexity and subtlety of new media policies and in particular the challenges relating to aging digital documents.

Not only are there problems of deletion of records, but also, the unknown viability of various storage mechanisms. How long does a CD-ROM or DVD last? In 2050, will we be able to read a hard drive that was stored in 2010? What about file formats? Can we count on being able to read documents in Microsoft Word for ten years? Twenty? Information on paper has the advantage of being immediately accessible in and of itself; digital files, on the other hand, will always be dependent on intermediary technology.

It is clear that questions relating to the archiving of digital documents extend far beyond the federal government, to other levels of government, universities, private industry, and even citizens. Every agency and institution is grappling with these issues in different ways.

Public consultations

In recent years, the Canadian government has added a slightly different approach to their information gathering, experimenting with wide-ranging public consultation initiatives. The hub for this, Consulting with Canadians, is housed at its own dedicated website (www.consultingcanadians.gc.ca) and links to initiatives in the various departments. Some of the experiments, such as the recent Digital Economy Consultation (May to July 2010) allow citizens who register on the site to submit an idea, and also to vote (up or down) the ideas of others, similar to sites such as Digg (http://digg.com).

While there have been controversies surrounding these initiatives, particularly on the question of whether the government will or will not follow the advice of Canadians who participate,[3] there is a strong sense that these new tools for public engagement with government, long championed by the proponents of Internet democracy, are finally being tested and trialed.

Public investment and regulation of infrastructure

Internet infrastructure, while at times subsidized (especially at public institutions), remains a strong mix of private and public investment. On the public side, throughout the late 1990s and through 2010, the Government of Canada and several provinces have invested heavily in extending broadband networks to rural and remote communities as well as building a research network (Canarie) across Canada, linking universities and other research institutions. Often times these are not outright government owned projects but rather subsidies to private operators or lease arrangements.

Despite continuing government involvement, there are concerns that the balance may have tipped too far to the side of private investment, leading to lawsuits and challenges relating to the shaping and filtering of the network by Internet service providers that may have a commercial interest in promoting one form of content over another. In most parts of Canada there is competition in the provision of Internet access, although this remains a challenge in rural areas and smaller cities and the prices remain uncomfortably high in places. Another concern is related to the ongoing challenge of the protection of privacy and safety online (see Chapter 10 on surveillance and new media). Agencies of government, including the Privacy Commissioner of Canada, have been able to require significant changes to how organizations handle personal and private information online. A celebrated case from 2009 saw Canada's Privacy Commissioner negotiate notable changes to the privacy settings on Facebook, the giant social networking site used by many Canadians and hundreds of millions of people worldwide.

Public investment in underlying technologies

Governments also influence new media policy through investments in underlying technologies such as computers and networking protocols and the Internet in Canada has benefited significantly in this regard. As early as the late 1940s and early 1950s, the Canadian government was an early customer, through the Air Force and the Navy, of computers from Computing Devices Canada (Mussio 2007: 74). In the 1980s, the Government of Canada, through the Communication Research Centre and the Department of Communication, helped pioneer a technology for the distribution of small text messages as part of a television signal. The technology, called Telidon, was a form of 'teletext' and a pioneering service for the time.[4] It worked with televisions and cable television connections, somewhat like the crawl of information on a cable news channel, but with more interactivity in that users could choose from streams of messages in a branching menu format.

The service was not a success in a commercial sense, but it did contribute to the building of capacity among content providers (firms were set up to create digital content) and manufacturers (that made the encoding and decoding devices), and perhaps most importantly, awareness among Canadians. As such, this serves as a good example of Canada's early investments in the development of digital broadcast satellites, of government investment in new media, and as direct intervention in a media form. This type of intervention in the economy is less popular today and governments by and large do not make direct investments in particular technologies. The business of picking winners is criticized by economists, who suggest that this is not the best role for governments, but rather, that governments should work to create the conditions for business to flourish.

Subsidies and tax incentives

Subsidies and tax incentives are another way that governments can influence technology development and use. In the era of Free Trade, and particularly in the case of Canada in the North American Free Trade Agreement (NAFTA), it is sometimes difficult for governments to give local industries an advantage over companies in other countries. Quite often this favouring of local firms is explicitly forbidden under the rules of such international agreements. Nevertheless, jurisdictions do what they can to attract business and encourage investment, especially in growing areas like new media.

Culture is often one of the exceptions in these agreements and national, regional, and local governments have taken advantage of the inherent cultural content in new media products to justify tax breaks for firms working in those fields. This has resulted in a wide array of tax incentives, subsidies, and rebates for the producers of animation, films, and even computer games. Recent examples include the Ontario Computer Animation and Special Effects Tax Credit[5] or the Canada New Media Fund (through Telefilm Canada). These types of incentives often provide exceptional tax breaks, subsidies on labour, or financial assistance for the distribution of products. New media industries are seen as environmentally beneficial, future-oriented, and as creating products with a high percentage of intellectual property, thereby contributing to job growth and economic growth for the country. In 2009–10, the Department of Canadian Heritage provided $14.3 million dollars for the New Media Fund (now known as the Canada Media Fund), for example.[6] This program, and especially the 'Experimental Stream' division, 'supports the creation of innovative Canadian interactive digital media content' (CMF 2010).

Declining to regulate

It might at first seem to be an odd assertion, but declining to regulate (which is called **forbearance** in legal terminology) is also a policy option for governments. In Canada this has had significant effects in two new media domains in particular: mobile phones and the Internet itself. When mobile phones were first developed they were seen as an extension of the existing telephone system and as such logically subject to regulation by the Canadian Radio-television and Telecommunications Commission (CRTC). Mobile phones were also transmitting and receiving devices, which had implications for another regulatory body, the Department of Communication, now known as the Spectrum Management and Telecommunication division of Industry Canada. At first mobile phones were considered a luxury item and were rarely seen except in the hands of the wealthy or people with exceptional—and perhaps tax deductible—reasons to have one. As cell phones became a more common item, and particularly at the 2G or 'personal communication system' stage (essentially, the small, digital cell phones we have now), the CRTC had to consider how they would regulate these devices.

Would cell phones be regulated as part of the telephone system and subject to all of the requirements and obligations of justifying revenues, or would they be regulated as a separate, competitive business that would have modest oversight? The CRTC, following government policy as well as the economic thinking of the day, decided on the latter stance: they would forbear from making significant regulations and allow a more competitive open market, as with automobiles or home furniture or computers.[7] There remain significant technical regulations, of course, especially because of the need for radio spectrum in order to operate, but on issues of how cell phones are priced, what services they provide beyond some basic needs like emergency access and so on, the regulator has decided to take a hands off approach. This is a significant policy decision.

A similar decision was reached in the case of regulating the Internet.[8] Although Internet access is typically provided through the infrastructure of existing regulated businesses (usually a cable or telephone provider), the CRTC decided to not regulate Internet services beyond a few basic aspects. Importantly, they decided not to get involved in the content on the Internet. While content regulation was never a part of telecommunications regulation—the law is explicitly designed to ensure carriers are not liable for and need not monitor what people say on the telephone, apart from criminal prosecutions that are dealt with in other parts of the law—content regulation is common in radio and television.[9] Both radio and television in Canada are required to have minimum amounts of Canadian content, they have obligations regarding hours of service and coverage areas, they have to abide by codes of conduct with regard to adult entertainment, and so on. The Internet, being full of content (websites, video, music) could have been seen as an object for regulation (how that would be accomplished, of course, is another matter), but in the end the CRTC—which did hold hearings and has considered the matter seriously on at least two occasions—decided on a position of forbearance. The Internet—like mobile phones—has been allowed to evolve largely without regulatory oversight. This, too, is an important policy decision, which has significant implications for other domains. As a simple example, how people use the Internet to copy and share music or movies is considered a civil matter between individuals and not something in which the regulator is willing to get involved (or punish the Internet service provider for).

Next Generation New Media Policy

As Christopher Yoo (2008) has argued, the way in which broadcasting and telecommunications networks are becoming one and the same—with people making phone calls and watching video over the same Internet connection—has profound implications for countries such as Canada and the US, which divide their new media regulation into content and carriage regulatory groups. In Canada, for example, there are the Broadcasting division and the Telecommunications divisions of the CRTC. The latter, based on regulation of telegraphs and telephones and the former, based on regulation of radio and television, have struggled to come up with meaningful oversight of the Internet, as it seems to slip through their grasp at every opportunity.

Yoo's prediction, that content delivery networks, multicast protocols, and much more aggressive traffic management will affect network neutrality debates in the US (2008), has already come true in Canada. In 2009 there was a request—ultimately unsuccessful—from small Internet service providers (ISPs) who argued that the CRTC should take action again against **traffic shaping** by Bell Canada.[11] Traffic shaping is a method of managing different protocols (the web is a protocol, as is email, for example) on the Internet, differently. Bell, and other large ISPs, have reserved the right to restrict some protocols—mainly because of what they claim is exorbitant use of the network by users who are sharing media files using software such as BitTorrent. Smaller ISPs, who were selling unrestricted packages to these users, but who had to buy their Internet connections wholesale from Bell, were not able to deliver truly unrestricted service. They sought a ruling from the CRTC that would force Bell to offer unshaped Internet connections, under common carriage rules. The CRTC denied their request.[12]

Despite this setback, mass media content continues to grow in importance on the Internet and the days of being able to govern the Internet purely as a telecommunication service, or ignore the content side of the Internet, are dwindling. How regulatory regimes will be restructured or recreated remains to be seen, however.

Copyright and Intellectual Property Law: An Overview

Copyright and intellectual property law has become, in many respects, the crucible for many of the issues and challenges that new media poses to law and policy. These legal and policy issues are being played out in a variety of national and international forums and are at the core of how the global knowledge economy or creative economy will develop. Among the issues raised are:

1. the balance between public good and private benefit criteria for use of, and access to, information;
2. the balance between individual rights of ownership and social use for common benefit;
3. the nature of knowledge as both a commodity for commercial exploitation and as a public good for common use; and,
4. the best ways in which to promote and equitably share the benefits of creativity in an age of digital networks for people, communities, nations, and global humanity.

Copyright law as it is understood today was first enacted in Britain in 1709 with the Statute of Anne, which established a term of protection (of fourteen years) for the author of an original work as an incentive to produce new works, and set a limit (of twenty-one years) to the time before which control over the rights to previously published works was ceded from publishers to the public domain. The US Congress, in one of its first legislative acts after the Declaration of Independence, passed the Copyright Act of 1790, to 'promote the Progress of Science and useful Arts, by securing for limited Times to Authors and Inventors the exclusive Right to their respective Writings and Discoveries'. This legislation both provided protection to the creators of original works ('Authors and Inventors') and set statutory limits to the time before such rights passed into the public domain. James Madison, one of the original authors drafting the US Constitution, saw in this an outcome where 'the public good fully coincides . . . with the claims of individuals' (quoted in Vaidhyanathan 2001: 45).

Copyright presumes that original forms of creative expression can belong to individuals, who have both a moral right to ownership and a legitimate economic right to derive material benefit from the use of these ideas and works by others. It also presumes that the use of their original ideas and works should be subject to the laws of free and fair exchange, that there should be adequate compensation for use by others, and there should be safeguards against misuse. At the same time, copyright recognizes that original ideas and works are drawn from an existing pool of knowledge and creativity, and that there is therefore a need to guarantee that such ideas and works exist in the public domain for **fair use** (or fair dealing in Canada) by others. Moreover, since such information is the lifeblood of democracy, commerce, and the development of future knowledge, broad access by the community to the widest possible pool of information, knowledge, and forms of creative expression is a valuable end in itself, as a condition for participation in public life and the development of new knowledge. In order to balance these competing claims on knowledge, copyright law divides up the possible rights in and uses of a work, giving control over some of these rights to the creators and distributors and control over others to the general public (Litman 2001: 16).

The neat distinctions that copyright law seeks to make between private ownership and public use have often been difficult to sustain in practice. Three areas of distinction have been particularly contentious. First, facts, ideas, and concepts are not themselves copyrightable—they cannot be owned by individuals. What copyright protects is original forms of creative expression of such facts, ideas, concepts, and so on, or the ways in which they are expressed, selected, and arranged by individuals through physical works such as books, publications, artistic works, etcetera. Second, what the author or creator has an exclusive right to is the creative expression contained in a work, not the physical form in which that work is produced and distributed. In the case of a book, for example, the original author retains exclusive ownership of the forms of creative expression that constituted that book, but is assumed to have contractually assigned the rights of reproduction of that book to a publisher, and in turn derives subsequent benefit from that publisher's activities in distributing the book, in the form of royalties or other forms of financial remuneration.

Finally, there has developed alongside copyright law a series of exceptions where it is deemed to be in the public interest to make material more widely available at no cost. These fair use or fair dealing provisions for private, non-commercial uses without authorization, have been typically applied to the photocopying of works in public libraries, but are now extensively applied in the copying of software applications, and the placing of materials on the Web (e.g. sections from books and academic journals used for teaching purposes).

Embedded within copyright more generally are two competing visions of intellectual property, as something that can be privately owned as property, and as something that is central to the principles of freedom of speech, equitable access to public information, and economic efficiency (see Table 9.1).

It is notable that the US Copyright Act of 1790 constructed issues relating to copyright upon what can be described as a horizontal axis of content creators, distributors, and users, where each was a broadly equal player in terms of power resources. Subsequently, in a process tracked by authors such as Bettig (1996), Vaidhyanathan (2001), and Perelman (2002), this horizontal axis has been overlaid by a vertical axis, whereby those who have established ownership of copyrighted works—who are, by the nature of contracts in the creative industries, typically the distributors of creative content rather than its originators—have constituted themselves as a powerful group whose interests sit over and above, and frequently in opposition to, the much larger, but far more dispersed, group of end-users of copyrighted or copyrightable material (Figure 9.1 on page 206).

Copyright law is derived from the principle that neither the creator of a new work nor the general public should be able to appropriate all of the benefits that flow from the creation of a new, original work of authorship. In Canada this has taken the form of a balance: '. . . between promoting the public interest in the encouragement and dissemination of works of the arts and intellect and obtaining a just reward for the creator . . .' (Supreme Court of Canada 2002).

Canadian copyright law is similar to US and UK copyright law and contains many of the same provisions and characteristics. In some areas the law is stricter, and in others it is more relaxed. As with US and UK law, Canadian law preserves a right of fair dealing, which has been interpreted broadly in recent court decisions.[13] Indeed, as copyright law is an area of considerable importance in an information and knowledge economy, there has been a fair bit of pressure from US groups who would like to see Canadian laws more restrictive. Changes to the Copyright Act were proposed in 2009 and 2010, with many of the new provisions seemingly inspired by US law. One of the most controversial aspects of the present

TABLE 9.1 Two Visions of Intellectual Property

	Information as public resource	Information as private property
Normative starting point	Free speech and free circulation of ideas and information in society	Individual property rights and rights of personal privacy
Vision of production of ideas	Draws primarily upon existing materials	Individual creativity and originality
Economic perspective	Information and efficiency	Innovation and incentives
Principal concern	Inequitable access to information in society	Denial of individual rights and creativity

Source: Adapted from Boyle (1997: 156).

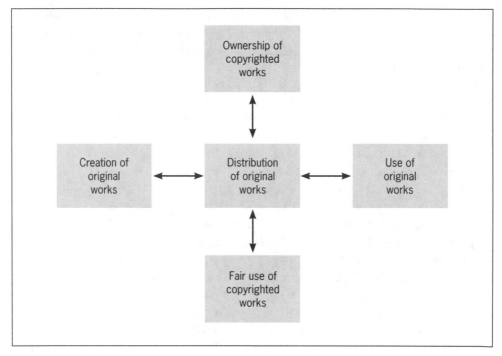

FIGURE 9.1 Relations Within Copyright and Intellectual Property Regimes

proposed law is the provision to legally protect **digital locks**, even when a fair dealing/fair use right may exist. Digital locks—also known as copy protection—are technical ways of preventing people from copying material or otherwise infringing on the rights of copyright holders. The controversy over protection of digital locks arises when users have rights—to back up their DVD, for example—but cannot exercise those rights because in order to do so they would have to break the digital lock and the lock itself is protected by law.

Importance of the public domain

Another way of looking at copyright has been suggested by a group of European academics working on topics related to the digital public domain. Known as COMMUNIA, this group has created a statement focused on those things that are *not* covered by copyright, encouraging people to ensure that as much material as possible goes into and stays in the **public domain**. They lay out a number of principles that help clarify why the public domain is so important and how it can be protected.

- The Public Domain is the rule, copyright protection is the exception.
- Copyright protection should last only as long as necessary to achieve a reasonable compromise between protecting and rewarding the author for his or her intellectual labour and safeguarding the public interest in the dissemination of culture and knowledge.

- What is in the Public Domain must remain in the Public Domain.
- The lawful user of a digital copy of a Public Domain work should be free to (re)use, copy, and modify such work.
- Contracts or technical protection measures that restrict access to and re-use of Public Domain works must not be enforced.

It is unclear whether this initiative will gain the recognition necessary to shift peoples' thinking about copyright, but it provides an important alternative perspective, given that the language is quite often heavily weighted by the groups and organizations with the most to gain from an expansive interpretation of copyright: the owners and distributors of copyrighted movies, music, and books.

Copyright and New Media

Of the many issues that render copyright law ever more complex and significant in an age of new media and the Internet, there are four particularly worthy of attention. First, the rapid development and mass dissemination of technologies that enable low-cost reproduction of data and information has dramatically changed the issues associated with copyright law. Whereas copyright law developed at a time when the reproduction of a work bore significant costs (e.g. the costs of reprinting a book), the development of low-cost duplication technologies readily available at home, work, or school/university has meant that more and more people have the ability to copy materials at near-zero cost. With the development of the Internet, email, and file-sharing technologies, these copies can be distributed to any number of people across electronic networks.

Second, the rise of a knowledge-based or creative economy has seen intellectual property rights become a key source of new corporate wealth. The commercial creative industries are characterized by high costs of production of original material, a high failure rate for new commercial product, and near-zero costs of content reproduction (Caves 2000; Hesmondhalgh 2007). As a result, a very high premium is attached to successful creative product that is likely to accrue economic worth over time. The value of Mickey Mouse to the Disney Corporation, or the value of The Beatles' back catalogue of songs, remains high decades after the content was originally produced. Associated with the enhanced economic value of intellectual property rights has been the rise of the copyright industries, which are defined as those industries 'engaged primarily in the generation, production, and dissemination of new copyrighted material' (Siwek 2002: 9).

Third, copyrighted products are now a part of global popular culture to a historically unprecedented degree. Corporate trademarks are reproduced and often parodied, musical fragments are sampled, references to other pop-culture forms are frequently made in television programs such as The Simpsons and South Park, films and television programs increasingly draw on generic conventions established in other films and television programs, and advertising undertakes a relentless co-optation of cultural referents derived from other media. Coombe (1998) observes that the growth and extension of legal protections to intellectual property has occurred at a time when 'the texts protected by intellectual property laws signify: they are cultural forms that assume local meaning in the life worlds of those who incorporate them into their daily lives' (1998: 7).

Finally, copyright and intellectual property law has been progressively globalized over time. The European states agreed on a common framework for copyright law through the Berne Convention for the Protection of Literary and Artistic Works (1886), although the US was a conspicuous non-signatory to this convention (Drahos and Braithwaite 2002: 34–5). In more recent times, the US has been a leader in promoting international intellectual property regimes, not least because its copyright industries are seen as most at risk from product piracy. The US-based Software Protection Agency estimated in 1994 that as much as 98 per cent of software used on computers in China was pirated, as was 95 per cent of computer software used in Russia and 92 per cent of that used in Thailand (Baase 1997: 174–5), and the International Intellectual Property Alliance estimated that the cost to the US economy of intellectual property piracy has been about USD $40 billion annually (Boyle 1997: 121). As the world's leading net exporter of intellectual property rights, the US has been the principal driver of the Trade-Related Aspects of Intellectual Property Rights (TRIPS) Agreement, signed by more than one hundred nations in 1994 after agreement by the signatories to the General Agreement on Trade in Services (GATS). The entry of China into the World Trade Organization is perhaps particularly significant in this regard, as China has been seen, particularly by US interests, as the nation that is most frequently in breach of copyright and intellectual property law (Montgomery and Keane 2006; Zhang 2006).

Cyber-libertarians such as John Perry Barlow predicted the collapse of copyright law under the weight of new media, arguing that 'Intellectual property law cannot be patched, retro-fitted or expanded to contain the gasses of digitized expression . . . We will need to develop an entirely new set of methods as befits this entirely new set of circumstances' (Barlow 1996b: 10). However, copyright and intellectual property law have not only proved more resilient, they have been strengthened since the rise of the Internet, raising the question of how best to manage the balance of interests (identified in Figure 9.1 on page 206). Litman (2001) observes that the problem with applying old rules to new media is that they are likely to inhibit the development of new technologies in the short term and to fail completely in the medium term.

At the same time, the call for a generalized copyright exemption for new media developments, which follows from the cyber-libertarian position, is unlikely to satisfy the creators of copyrightable content, who are concerned about who would pay for their work and their ability to continue in creative or intellectual pursuits, if content were made more freely available to users. Litman instead proposes that there is a need for more direct dialogue between the creators and users of copyrightable content, or between creative people and the wider public, because their interests are less clearly opposed than is presented to be the case by content distributors. Initiatives such as the Creative Commons digital content licensing scheme (see Case Study) have sought to address such concerns, in ways that are legally robust, readily understood, and applicable to producers of original content in the creative industries and related sectors.

Others have drawn attention to the position of institutions such as public libraries, accepted and honoured for the role they play in education and the furtherance of the objectives of a democratic society. In a satirical blog posting about the 'cost' of libraries in the United States, Eric Hellman writes:

> As soon as I got off the train, I was surrounded by even more of this crowd. Calling themselves 'Librarians', they talk about promoting literacy, education, culture and economic development, which are, of course, code words for the use and dispersal of intellectual property. They readily admit to their activities, and rationalize them because they're perfectly legal in the US, at least for now.[14]

The 'at least for now' closing line is a not-so-subtle reference to the ever widening scope of copyright extension and inclusion.

Recent Developments in International Copyright and Intellectual Property Law

The 1990s saw two very significant extensions in both the scope and the domain of copyright law. In the US, the Digital Millennium Copyright Act was passed by Congress in 1998, along with the Sonny Bono Copyright Term Extension Act 1998, which extends the term of copyright protection for copyright works from the life of the author plus 50 years to the life of the author plus 70 years. Despite widespread criticism of these legislative initiatives from both a legal and policy perspective (see e.g. Litman 2001; Perelman 2002; Rimmer 2003b; Vaidhyanathan 2001), their impact has been significant within and outside the US. Cases such as Eldred *v.* Ashcroft were unsuccessful in challenging the extension of copyright, despite 17 leading American economists, including five Nobel Laureates, arguing that such copyright extension was not in the nation's economic interest (Moore 2005). Rimmer (2003b) terms the Sonny Bono Copyright Extension Act the 'Mickey Mouse Bill' because it arose at a time when Disney's copyright on Mickey Mouse and its other famous cartoon characters was about to expire, but the resultant legislative changes have guaranteed that Mickey Mouse will not pass into the public domain until 2023.

The second major development was the passing of the Trade-Related Aspects of Intellectual Property Rights (TRIPS) Agreement in 1995, at the conclusion of the Uruguay Round of trade negotiations that led to the formation of the World Trade Organization (WTO). The TRIPS Agreement was signed by more than one hundred countries in April 1994, with all members of the WTO bound by the conditions of the agreement, including recent members such as China (Braithwaite and Drahos 2000: 57). Unlike previous multilateral conventions governing intellectual property, such as the Paris and Berne Conventions struck by the European powers in the late nineteenth century, TRIPS is not based on the setting of minimum standards and mutual adjustment of national laws over time. Rather, it establishes a global framework for the protection of intellectual property to which significant legal and economic sanctions can be applied to nations that fail to comply with its highly prescriptive standards to protect the rights of those holding patents, copyright, trademarks, and trade secrets. Sell describes TRIPS as:

> A stunning triumph for commercial interests and industry lobbyists who had worked so tirelessly to achieve the global agreement. TRIPS institutionalized a conception of intellectual property based on protection and exclusion rather than competition and diffusion. By extending property rights and requiring high substantive levels of protection, TRIPS represented a significant victory for US private sector activists from knowledge-based industries. (2002: 172)

One of the factors that links US legislation and developments through TRIPS and the World Intellectual Property Organization (WIPO) is the impact of bilateral free-trade agreements. TRIPS established an important beachhead for uniformity in international patent legislation through the Patent Cooperation Treaty, which enables developers of patentable products to file an international patent application through the WIPO. This has force for 136 member nations as of 2007, which agreed that, if the application is accepted, the patent is binding in all of those nations. Bilateral free-trade agreements between the US and other nations have typically involved the extension of US-based forms of copyright protection to the signatory nations. Canada has so far not completed a rationalization of its copyright laws to coincide with US law, much to the concern of the US, as signaled by Canada's placement on a piracy blacklist in April 2009 (Koring 2009). The pressure for Canada to amend its law has been considerable, but progress has been slow and there have been significant countervailing pressures, both from activists and scholars, such as Michael Geist as well as representatives from Internet industry groups concerned about the costs of implementing some of the measures.

Two critical questions arise from these measures to extend copyright protection into the indefinite future and to establish a legally binding global intellectual property regime. The first is whether or not it is beneficial to society as a whole. The economic argument for copyright protection has revolved around the rights of content creators to receive remuneration for the expression of their ideas and concepts, and the idea that such returns provide incentives for future development of new ideas. Critics have argued that while these are valid arguments in principle, the extension of copyright protection through recent legislation not only shifts the balance too far away from other users and therefore heightens the possibility of inadvertent copyright infringement, but also, is a hindrance to economic and social innovation. Given the capacity of the digital media environment to promote collaboration, content sharing, content reuse and repurposing, and P2P file-sharing, which is arguably 'both the origin and the future of the Internet' (Haussmann 2002), the case can be made that the media and entertainment industries would be better served by fostering such networks, rather than seeking to restrict or criminalize such activities (Benkler 2006; Lessig 2004; Perelman 2002; Vaidhyanathan 2001, 2004).

Moreover, the economic case for extending copyright protection is considered weak: the extension of copyright protection to 70 years under the Sonny Bono Copyright Extension

Act only provides an increase in compensation to creators of less than one per cent (cited in Moore 2005: 74). This needs to be balanced against the economic costs of extending copyright protection and extending the capacity to extract monopoly rents for existing copyright holders over time, in ways that would likely be detrimental to the creation of new works. In its criticism of these changes, the US Committee for Economic Development emphasized how copyright law can inhibit the capacity of 'follow-on' and 'second' innovators to build upon copyrighted innovations, thereby dampening the overall scope for innovation by artificially restricting the public domain (CED 2004). Perelman (2002: 178) argues that information is not only a public good and hence, warranting government oversight of how it is produced and distributed, but is in fact a 'metapublic' good, which generates positive benefits to a community when it is freely available in ways that cannot be calculated, since 'information is not scarce, except to the degree that society allows agents to create artificial scarcity through secrecy and property rights . . . as the economy becomes increasingly dependent on information, the traditional system of property rights applied to information becomes a costly fetter on our development'.

The issues that arise from the global application of US-derived copyright and intellectual property laws, as pursued through agreements such as TRIPS, are considerable (see e.g. Bannermann 2006; Shanker 2006). These tend to involve debates about the equity of such arrangements between economically developed and developing countries, for two reasons. First, the vast bulk of intellectual property rights are held in a small number of countries: in 2004, five patent offices (Japan, US, South Korea, China, and Europe) accounted for 75 per cent of patent applications and 74 per cent of patents granted worldwide (WIPO 2006). Second, the near-zero costs of reproduction of digital goods enabled by new media technologies create strong incentives in lower-wage countries to make illegal copies of such materials (DVDs, computer software programs, etc.) and resell them at substantially lower prices than those offered to consumers in higher-wage nations.

Drahos and Braithwaite (2002: 188–9) draw attention to this paradox, which is that strong protection of intellectual property rights may lead to monopolies, while weak protection may lead to 'free-riding' on the innovations of others, and underinvestment in innovation. Drahos and Braithwaite also identify a positive correlation between democratic societies and efficient intellectual property rights, but note that this is in turn dependent on: (1) an inclusive policy culture, where all relevant interests participate in negotiation of the final outcomes; (2) full provision of information to all relevant parties; and (3) the absence of coercive power by one party over others. Significantly, they find all of these to be absent from international negotiations about the TRIPS Agreement: developing countries were largely excluded from the forums in which TRIPS was debated, awareness of possible adverse consequences of TRIPS (e.g. on the availability of low-cost generic drugs to address the AIDS crisis in Africa) was low, and the US, in their view, threatened trade sanctions and foreign aid withdrawals for nations that did not share its views on the merits of a uniform multilateral agreement on intellectual property rights (Drahos and Braithwaite 2002: 189–92).

Using the public goods framework derived from economic theory, Drahos and Braithwaite conclude that current tendencies on copyright and intellectual property law have the potential to lead to information feudalism on a global scale. They characterize information feudalism as involving the use of intellectual property rights to inhibit competition (e.g. through the patenting of basic business processes); the withholding of valuable information about diseases and suitable treatments from poorer developing nations; and the locking up of basic research outcomes from institutions that once treated knowledge as a pure public good for social use, such as universities.

Some countries, most notably Brazil, have made strong statements that attempt to balance the rights of consumers with the rights of authors in copyright statements. In a recent proposal from that country, initiatives such as digital locks are permitted as long as they do not hinder fair use/fair dealing rights (e.g., using a work for education, research, or criticism). Canada has similar fair dealing rights (as do most countries), recently reaffirmed in the CCH case by the Supreme Court of Canada. In that case, the Law Society of Upper Canada was accused of copyright infringement for allowing students and members of the society to make copies of decisions that were held in the library. Three large publishers of legal materials, led by CCH Canadian Limited, sued for copyright infringement. In a unanimous decision, the court ruled that this form of copying was fair dealing in that it constituted research or private study and as such was protected under Canadian law.

There have also been concerns that proposals in this country relating to digital locks would trump users rights. In other words, you might have a right to use something but not the right to remove the lock that would let you have access, effectively negating your right of access. At the time of writing, Canada's proposed changes to the Copyright Act (Bill C-32) retained these protections of digital locks, despite widespread criticism of the provision.[15]

The more recent Anti-Counterfeiting Trade Agreement (ACTA) can be expected to have significant consequences for new media law and policy. Even before being finalized, the negotiations for the trade agreement, conducted mainly behind closed doors in countries around the world, stirred up considerable debate in 2009 and 2010. In a sense, the way in which ACTA has been negotiated in secret is itself a challenge to many of the principles of open source and the free exchange of information. The agreement, which covers a broad range of topics including the way in which countries are expected to control the production, sale, and export of counterfeit goods (e.g., the fake Rolex, the fake Gucci handbag), also covers 'piracy over the Internet'.[16] Piracy is a term that is widely (mis)used to refer to copyright **infringement**, however, and its use there is inappropriate: no ships have been commandeered, no goods are missing, no one has been deprived of the use of their movies or music or books.

There is a law of piracy in Canada (R.S., c. C-34, s. 75; 1974-75-76, c. 105, s. 3.) but it is entirely related to ships and their cargo. The lobby groups for those who make their money distributing copyrighted material (mainly movies, music, and books) use the term piracy in order to equate copyright infringement with the more loaded concept of piracy, with its long history and considerable cultural reference points. Using such language also serves as a tactic to conjure images of swashbuckling pirates on the bounding main or present-day pirates off the coast of Somalia, in order to garner support for a cause. Effective as it may be, it should be understood as a tactic of persuasion by lobbyists and not a legal term when speaking of copyright.

ACTA began as an initiative between the US and Japan, in 2006. It has since been expanded to a growing number of countries, in part because the US has begun to encourage countries that it trades with to sign the agreement as a way of harmonizing regulation over copyright and intellectual property around the world. The proposed trade agreement has not yet been ratified and the terms of the agreement remain both secretive and far from finalization. The objectives of the agreement, however, have been broadly referenced in a document released by the US Trade Representative and includes the following opening statement:

> The ACTA initiative aims to establish international standards for enforcing intellectual property rights in order to fight more efficiently the growing problem of counterfeiting and piracy. In particular, the ACTA is intended to establish, among the signatories, agreed standards for the enforcement of intellectual property rights that address today's challenges by increasing international cooperation, strengthening the framework of practices that contribute to effective enforcement of intellectual property rights, and strengthening relevant enforcement measures. The intended focus is on counterfeiting and piracy activities that significantly affect commercial interests, rather than on the activities of ordinary citizens. ACTA is not intended to interfere with a signatory's ability to respect its citizens' fundamental rights and civil liberties, and will be consistent with the WTO Agreement on Trade-Related Aspects of Intellectual Property Rights (TRIPS Agreement) and will respect the Declaration on TRIPS and Public Health.

Section 4 of the proposed agreement covers 'intellectual property rights enforcement in the digital environment' and presumably will have the most impact on new media productions. Where such details are concerned, however, according to the document released by the US Trade Representative, 'no draft proposal has been tabled yet,' as of early 2010. Commentary from those who have been party to the talks and various leaks to the press suggests that a number of the provisions will be controversial.

One of the most controversial elements of the treaty may very well be the 'graduated response' system for people accused of copyright infringement. Graduated response is a type of copyright infringement punishment regime, commonly known as a **three strikes** law, in which people who have three accusations of copyright infringement (as from downloading movies or music) would no longer be permitted to have Internet access. There is some ambiguity about whether an entire household would lose their access to the Internet in the case of infringement by one individual in the family or home (e.g., a child accused of file sharing).

These types of laws are in place in a few countries (France, for example), however, there is little experience with them to date. The most controversial aspect of this type of law is that the punishment is meted out, not for a conviction but for an accusation, which opens the law to possible abuse by malicious or mistaken claims of infringement. In July 2009 a French court struck down this key component of that country's three strikes law when the justices ruled that, 'Under the Declaration of 1789, every man is presumed innocent until proven guilty'. The ruling further stated that, 'The Internet is a fundamental human right that cannot be taken away by anything other than a court of law, only when guilt has been established there'.[17] The law has also been criticized as excessive in its levels of punishment, since banning someone from the Internet could be a serious impairment in their life, especially if the allegation is unproven. Again, there are few accounts of how these laws have been applied. New Zealand, for example, had a three strikes law before Parliament in 2009 but it was withdrawn after widespread public protests. A revised law is now in place but as of this writing (early 2010) there have been no reported convictions.

The Internet as a human right or universal service obligation

Several countries have begun to treat Internet use as a fundamental human right. One of the first to do so was Estonia, which made Internet access a fundamental human right in that country in 2000.[18] Greece has also taken this approach, with Finland[19] and Spain[20] adding service level obligations for the telecommunication carriers to provide broadband access. The Conservative party in the United Kingdom made broadband access for the majority of homes part of their election platform in early 2010.[21]

Canada has long had **universal service** objectives for both telephone and broadcasting services. In urban areas these are non-problematic as the market is prepared and welcomes the opportunity to serve large populations gathered closely together. Canada, with a high percentage of its population in urban centres, in close proximity to the US and its massive Internet industry, generally has excellent Internet service for its urban citizens. Rural Canadians, however, are not so well served and remote and northern residents have either slow service or no service. Satellite services are available in most of the country but they are private, commercial services, which are either slow or expensive or both. For residents of narrow mountain valleys where satellite coverage does not reach, prospects for getting high speed Internet service are even more limited.

Universal access to the Internet was discussed as early as 1995 in the CRTC report, 'Competition and Culture on Canada's Information Highway: Managing the Realities of Transition'.[22] Chapter 4 of that report dealt explicitly with 'Public Spaces in a Digital World' and considered universality as a key element. While the commission supported the idea of public access as being important, it declined to impose a cross-subsidization scheme on telecommunication providers:

> While basic telephone services can continue to be supported in part by subsidized rates, the Commission considers that decisions on funding and priorities for infrastructure development on the information highway in high-cost areas should be made by governments (CRTC 1995).

Since the time the report was released, the Government of Canada has, at various times, initiated a number of programs that provide funding, subsidized access, access for community drop-in centres, training, school access, health service access, and a number of other programs. Some of these have persisted for many years, such as the Community Access Program, which provides computers, training, software, and Internet access for community centres, libraries, and other places where the public can have access to and learn to use the Internet.

Although universal service is a policy objective for telephone service in Canada, as noted earlier, there is not yet an equivalent obligation on the part of telecommunications providers to deliver subsidized or universal Internet service, and in particular, there is no obligation to deliver broadband speeds. Whether or not and when a neighbourhood is served with high speed Internet is a business decision being made by telephone companies or cable providers. It should be noted that this business decision has become easier in recent years as the Government of Canada and the governments of several provinces has stepped in with subsidy programs for rural and remote Internet initiatives (Smith 2009).

Digital Gatekeepers and the Open Source Movement

While the challenges of copyright in a digital age have generated different responses both within and across the creative industries, responses in the media and entertainment sectors have often been reactive and defensive. These responses have frequently involved legal action against those perceived to be transgressors of copyrighted material, as seen in the recent USD $1 billion lawsuit lodged by Viacom against YouTube (Viacom *v.* YouTube [2007]) (cf. Butt and Bruns 2005; O'Brien 2007), as well as in heavy lobbying efforts. In the lawsuit, Viacom sued YouTube (and its corporate parent, Google) for allowing users to upload material—largely clips from television programs—that were owned by Viacom. Lobbying for increased terms of copyright by copyright owners associations—typically the recording industry, the television industry, and the movie industry—is both ongoing and effective, as in the case of the Sonny Bono Act we discussed.

At the technological level, there has also been a focus on the development of Technological Protection Measures (TPMs) generally, and Digital Rights Management (DRM) in particular (Flew 2005b; Flew et al. 2006). DRM can be defined as the set of technical and legal mechanisms applied to help control access to, and distribution of, copyrighted and other protected material in the digital environment. Development of DRM systems are technically complex, requiring client rendering devices with trusted processing, input, and output paths, as well as modifications to current personal computing architecture. A key question arising from DRM strategies as a means to regulate access to digital content is whether or not the costs of DRM, and the more general strategy of defence-in-depth of the current copyright regime, justifies its status as the primary solution to the current dilemma. The DRM-driven approach is criticized as an insufficient solution, as it has at least three adverse consequences:

- diminished consumer privacy, as DRMs generate significantly increased functional capability to monitor online user behaviour;
- reduced innovation potential, as the development of new methods to attack peer-to-peer file-sharing networks and applications can inhibit the capacity for 'follow-on' or 'second' innovators to build on copyrighted innovations (as noted above); and,
- greater imbalances in the relationship between copyright holders and users of copyrighted materials; it is impossible to program fair use exceptions into DRM

systems, since fair use is a complex legal mechanism, with outcomes dependent on individual aspects of each case.

An important alternative paradigm and one that is very much grounded in the collaborative, DIY ethos that has underpinned the Internet from its inception (Castells 2001; Flichy 2007), is the paradigm arising from the **open source** movement. The open software and free software movements[23] have pioneered decentralized, networked, and collaborative initiatives to develop new forms of software, licensed through non-proprietorial General Public Licences (GPLs). This means not only that users can acquire the software without cost, but they also can acquire access to the source code, which they can in turn apply, modify, or reconfigure. The influence of open source thinking can be seen throughout the Web 2.0 environment, with the idea that 'back-end' systems should be relatively open and flexible.

Underpinning the emergence of this large community of software developers, from which software such as the Linux operating system has emerged as a major alternative to proprietary systems such as those developed by Microsoft, are a series of broad principles whose domain of application moves well beyond the realm of software. The first is a general belief in freely available content. This is not, as Lessig notes in *Free Culture* (2004), 'free' as in 'free beer' (no one having to pay for anything), but rather, free in the sense that creativity and innovation are best served by information and culture that is as widely available as possible. In this respect, belief in the intrinsic value of an 'information commons' or a 'creative commons' is threatened by recent initiatives to strengthen the intellectual property rights regime, which is seen as presenting the danger of creating 'a "permission culture"—a culture in which creators get to create only with the permission of the powerful, or of the creators of the past' (2004: xiv).

Second, there is a belief that collaborative, non-proprietorial initiatives ultimately generate better product, and that open source has a compelling commercial as well as a moral logic. Eric Raymond contrasts the 'cathedral' model of corporate- or government-controlled initiatives to that of the 'bazaar' model, or initiatives generated by cooperating autonomous communities such as software developers. Raymond (1998) argues that 'perhaps in the end the open source culture will triumph not because cooperation is morally right or software "hoarding" is morally wrong . . . but simply because the commercial world cannot win an evolutionary arms race with open source communities that can put orders of magnitude more skilled time into a problem'. Third, there is an implicit belief in the value of a gift economy, whereby people will freely choose to participate in a collaborative initiative on the basis that sharing and collaboration are good things to do, and that the benefits they derive from such participation can be principally non-material in form (Best 2003).

The rise of the open source movement has focused attention on different possible Internet futures and on the varying layers of control—over physical infrastructure and code as well as over content—in digital communications networks. This attention has sharpened the distinction between a policy moment that could reproduce the old ways of broadcast media with its high barriers to entry for new competitors and its sharp demarcation between content producers and consumers, and an uncertain but potentially more open and democratic future based on the collective empowerment of users of digital media backed by an open and robust public information domain. Yochai Benkler identifies the new public interest in policies to develop open source and an information commons in these terms:

> We are in the midst of a pitched battle over the spoils of the transforma-
> tion to a digitally networked environment and the information economy.
> Stakeholders from the older economy are using legislation, judicial opinions
> and international treaties to retain the old structure . . . As economic policy,
> letting yesterday's winners dictate the terms of tomorrow's economic com-
> petition is disastrous. As social policy, missing an opportunity to enrich our
> freedom and enhance our justice while maintaining or even enhancing our
> productivity is unforgivable. (2001: 90)

Rennie (2003: 56) also terms this a 'new public interest' model that 'involves embracing a range of possible publics that may conflict with or contradict each other. There is no claim to what the "good" is, only a striving for it: more players and more ideas means a greater chance that some kind of progress will emerge, either in the form of economic advancement or the advancement of democracy'.

More generally, the open source movement is characterized by its tendency towards the new and towards innovation. As Lawrence Lessig articulates, 'We as a society should favour the disrupters. They will produce movement toward a more efficient, prosperous economy' (2001: 92). What this debate produces is not Left/Right politics as it has been traditionally defined—the state versus the market, the public sphere versus commercialization, social-ism versus capitalism—but rather, a shifting field of more contingent alliances, which rec-ognizes the capacity of incumbent interests, both public and private, to effectively block innovation in order to protect existing monopoly privileges, and the difficulties in form-ing constituencies for change where the outcomes are uncertain. Arguably, creativity and innovation are best served by information and culture that is as widely available as possible, 'to guarantee that follow-on creators and innovators remain as free as possible from the control of the past' (Lessig 2004: xiv).

Case Study: Creative Commons

Creative Commons (CC) is a worldwide project that aims to make copyright material more accessible and its terms of access more ne-gotiable in the digital environment (Creative Commons 2007a). In order to do this, Creative Commons asks content owners who wish to contribute to the commons to generically give permission in advance to certain types of use of their content, through the labelling of their content with a CC badge and an agree-ment in advance to the terms and conditions attached to this use through a legally binding CC licence. It aims to overcome three bottle-necks that current copyright and intellectual property laws present in the digital environment: (1) the difficulties faced by users of already existing content in locating and negotiating with the initial content creators; (2) the question of rights and conditions attached to use of existing digital content in other domains, for commercial or non-commercial purposes; and (3) the extent to which existing copyright and intellectual property laws circumvent direct negotiation between content creators and prospective users of copyrighted material through the assignation of rights to content distributors, who then manage all legal aspects of content use and repurposing rather than the direct producers of the original content. Creative Commons was founded in 2001 by a series of high-profile intellectual property experts and creative practitioners including Lawrence Lessig, James Boyle, Hal Abelson, Eric Saltzman, Joi Ito, and Eric Aldred, with financial support from the Center for the Public Domain and other organizations. It is currently supported in the US by the Berkman Center for Internet and Society at Harvard Law School and Stanford Law School Center for Internet and Society, and by 2007, Creative Commons licences had been developed in 35 countries outside the US, including Argentina, Australia, Austria, Slovenia, South Africa, South Korea, Spain, Sweden, and Switzerland, with a further 14 countries being in discussion (Creative Commons 2007c). Central to this international expansion of Creative Commons have been initiatives to ensure legally effective harmonization of the Creative Commons licence to the specific national legislation that governs copyright and intellectual property law within different countries. Creative Commons Canada (http://creativecommons.ca) was set up in 2003 and provides English and French versions of the Creative Commons licences, adapted to Canadian law. It is housed at the University of Ottawa and supported by the Canadian Internet Policy and Public Interest Clinic (CIPPIC).

A key aim of Creative Commons has been to simplify the range of choices available to creative people across the artistic, educational, scientific, and digital production domains about how they can designate, in advance and independently of those who distribute their content as commercial product, rights to use and repurpose their work. There are four categories of Creative Commons licence that are available to those who choose to place their content under a CC licence:

1   Attribution: Content developers allow others to copy, distribute, display, and perform the copyrighted work—and derivative works based upon it—but only if they give credit to the original work in the way it was requested.

2   Non-commercial: Others are permitted to copy, distribute, display, and perform a copyrighted work—and derivative works based upon it—but only if it is for non-commercial purposes. If there is an intention to use the work for commercial purposes, then there needs to be a different legal basis for discussion. An example of this would be Alberto Korda's famous photograph of Che Guevara in 1960, which has been made freely available to radical organizations and groups that broadly share Che's ideals. Korda successfully defended the right for this image not to be used by the Smirnoff company to promote its vodka

product in 2000, as he argued that this was clearly at odds with Che's own socialist ideals and Korda's moral rights as the photographer.

3   No Derivative Works: Others are permitted to copy, distribute, display, and perform only verbatim copies of the copyrighted work, but not derivative works based upon it. In this way, the integrity of the original work can be preserved, as well as the moral rights of the original creator.

4   Share Alike: Original content creators allow others to distribute derivative works only under a licence identical to the licence that governs their own work. It should be noted that a licence cannot feature both the Share Alike and No Derivative Works options, since the Share Alike requirement applies only to derivative works.

Creative Commons describes its purpose as providing 'free tools that let authors, scientists, artists, and educators easily mark their creative work with the freedoms they want it to carry' so that creative producers can change 'copyright terms from "All Rights Reserved" to "Some Rights Reserved"' (Creative Commons 2007b). In doing so, the aim has also been to avoid complex and costly legal disputes by dramatically simplifying the plethora of legal questions that face providers of original creative content about how to deal with others who draw upon their creative work. As Fitzgerald puts it: 'Models such as Creative Commons rely on the power of copyright ownership and law to structure access downstream. In this sense CC is not anti-copyright. Rather, it uses copyright as the basis for structuring open access. However, CC is designed to provide an alternative for managing copyright in digital content' (2006: 222).

 ## Useful Websites

OpenNet Initiative and the Citizen Lab
←http://opennet.net and http://citizenlab.org→

The OpenNet Inititive is a collaborative undertaking that involves four major partners, one of which is the Citizen Lab, based at the University of Toronto and led by scholar Ron Deibert. The partners also include Harvard's Berkman Center and the Oxford Internet Institute (see below), as well as Cambridge University. Together, they are pioneering research and interventions in the realm of open and free Internet connections. They study how censorship is being conducted on the Internet, how activists are working to get

around it, and they develop tools to better assist in anonymous and secure use of the Internet.

Berkman Center for Internet Law and Society
←http://cyber.law.harvard.edu/home→

This is a resource site developed at Harvard Law School that is a leader in addressing intellectual property issues, as well as a range of areas of Internet law and policy. It is the host site for a series of major international research initiatives, including the Center for Citizen Media, FreeCulture, and the OpenNet Initiative.

Oxford Internet Institute

←www.oii.ox.ac.uk→

This is a major site for international and interdisciplinary Internet research, based within the University of Oxford. Key research strands include Internet governance and democracy, the Internet and everyday life, and the wider implications of the open source software movement.

World Intellectual Property Organization

←www.wipo.int/portal/index.html.en→

WIPO is a specialist agency of the United Nations responsible for information gathering and promotion of shared international intellectual property standards. The site is a key source of information on what copyright, patents, and trademarks are, how they are distributed worldwide, and how policy and regulation is developing on an international scale.

Further Reading

From *Radical Extremism to Balanced Copyright: Canadian Copyright and the Digital Agenda*, Michael Geist (ed.) (2010)

Michael Geist, a Canada Research Chair in Law, Technology and Society at Ottawa University, will be familiar to many Canadians from his high profile campaign on Facebook relating to the copyright law. He also pens regular columns for *The Globe and Mail* and maintains a blog on various topics relating to technology law. This new book brings together a wide range of authors writing about copyright for a Canadian audience and speaking directly to some of the changes happening currently. See also ongoing coverage of Canadian copyright issues at http://copyright.michaelgeist.ca.

Free Culture: How Big Media Uses Technology and the Law to Lock Down Culture and Control Creativity, Lawrence Lessig (2004)

Lawrence Lessig is a popular and dynamic public speaker (search for his name in the Ted.com website) who famously popularized thinking about the role of free culture and then shifted his work to devote his time to combating corruption and influence in government. His 2004 book, however, lays the foundation for much of what we know and think about the value and importance of free materials in our culture.

Free: The Future of a Radical Price, Chris Anderson (2009)

Chris Anderson, editor of *WIRED* magazine, has penned another book on the concept of free material, though it is more oriented to the business aspects and the prospects and opportunities for companies that want to take advantage of the potential for delivering goods and services for free. All of this sounds too good to be true, but behind the packaging is often another source of revenue, such as the 'Freemium' approach that Flickr uses: give away a basic version in the hope that enough people will upgrade to the Pro account, which is not free. Anderson discusses this and many other models for making money from things priced as free.

Discussion Questions

1. What are some of the domains covered by cyberspace law?

2. What are some of the policy initiatives or interventions that the Canadian government has taken in regard to new media? How are these important to understanding current new media policy in Canada?

3. What are some of the recent developments in international copyright and intellectual property law? What critical questions arise from measures to extend copyright protection and to establish a legally binding global intellectual property regime?

4. In what ways does the Internet, as it is situated in relation to existing laws and regulatory frameworks, complicate efforts to establish binding legal guidelines?

5. Copyright law seeks to make distinctions between private ownership and public use, though these have often been difficult to sustain in practice. What three areas of distinction have been particularly contentious?

6. In the case involving the US Communications Decency Act (1996), Mike Godwin, counsel for the Electronic Frontier Foundation (EFF), argued (1998: 23): 'Give people a modem and a computer and access to the Net, and it's far more likely that they'll do good than otherwise'. How is this view characteristic of cyber-libertarian perspectives and why do you think such views are not now articulated as strongly as they once were?

7. Copyright law is derived from the principle of balanced interests. What are these interests and in what ways have new media and the Internet brought challenges to maintaining such balance?

Class Activities

1. Take a look at the CRTC web site (www.crtc. gc.ca), noting the recent decisions relating to new media. Pick a recent decision that has general applicability (e.g., Net Neutrality, or ISPs as carriers vs broadcasters) and consider how it fits with the concepts and analysis in this chapter. Does the approach of the commission or the tone of the decisions match with the views of this text? Does it match your own views?

2. Consider the implications of making Internet access either a human right or a fundamental right of Canadians. Are these similar to the universal service provisions adopted in Canada (and elsewhere) to ensure telephone service was made widely available outside of urban areas? If you or any of your fellow students are from rural or remote areas in your class, speak about the challenges of getting Internet access at home.

10 Conclusion

Questions to Consider

- What are some of the negative aspects of new media? What aspects of human relations does it disrupt that we would not necessarily wish to have disrupted?

- How can new media be used to go beyond mere entertainment to affecting real change? How can new media—and social software in particular—be used professionally and responsibly, rather than frivolously and hurtfully?

Key Concerns and Future Considerations

As we have discussed in previous chapters, new media is a technical and social achievement with a remarkable history and yet, enormous challenges lie ahead. If new media as a resource is to be made even more broadly available—as recent moves to include access to the Internet as a human right would suggest—how can new media be extended without negating social and cultural boundaries? There are also concerns related to the environment: Will the development, use, and waste from the expansion of information technology continue to weigh more and more heavily on the planet?

Much of the evolution of new media has brought with it an almost gleeful acceptance and adoption of whatever developments come from the minds of software and hardware engineers working in universities and startup companies around the world. Regulation has been light or non-existent and no one has (yet) proposed anything as radical as an 'Internet driver's licence', except as a joke. Yet as new media mature, it may be necessary to consider how more established industries such as automobiles or home construction approach development: as important to the economy, but also with certain risks to be mitigated or inputs and by-products to be minimized or curtailed. In other words, it may be necessary to be more critically aware of and engaged with the changes and consequences of the continued evolution of new media.

As an example, it is estimated that most of the spam in the world is not sent directly from spammers, but instead, travels through 'botnets', or personal computers that have been hijacked and used by others for nefarious purposes. This may at first glance seem to be rather insignificant, however, spam represents more than 80 per cent of the email traffic in the world[1] and computers operating as part of a botnet can be harnessed for tasks even more malicious and dangerous than spam; for example, distributed denial of service (DDS) attacks that periodically rise up to disable even the most well-protected Internet hosts.

This example raises a number of questions. Is this botnet activity something we wish to allow to continue? Should governments require virus checkers on computers? Should we insist that people properly maintain their network-connected device, just as we require periodic safety inspections of cars and trucks? What about an operator's permit, which cannot be obtained without demonstrating a certain level of training and competence? Initiatives such as these would fly in the face of some interpretations of freedom of speech and yet we insist on them for drivers of automobiles, for example, even though there is an equivalent 'freedom of movement' in bills of rights and freedoms.

Similarly, the environmental cost of new media is certain to be an important personal, policy, and corporate decision in the years to come. Just as society began to realize in the 1960s that the unconstrained growth of automobile use—and automobile culture—was having deleterious effects on cities (Jacobs 1961), some of the costs of new media may draw attention. Indeed, there have already been concerns raised about new media, but these have not often taken the form of serious, critical inquiry, rather, new media are more likely to be blamed for some societal malady (game addiction or violence caused by computer games are perfect examples), for which there is very little credible evidence. Alternatively, the mainstream media also tends to run new media stories in which attention is given to little more than new media as a novelty in terms of the angle it brings. These kinds of stories are often about typical human foibles played out, for example, on Facebook or in text messages. This may garner some attention but ultimately, the focus on new media as novelty diverts attention from larger, underlying questions or problems.

This edition of *New Media: An Introduction* highlights the extent to which, in the two decades that the Internet and digital media technologies have established themselves as the dominant media and communication forms, there have been major changes to those technologies and how they are used. Canadians recently passed a significant milestone in this regard: in 2010 a prominent research firm reported that, for the first time, Canadians spent more time on the Internet, on average, than watching television (Ipsos Reid 2010). As Canadians, we are not just *watching* the Internet, however. The rise of social media and Web 2.0 technologies have accelerated the trend of making the users of digital media into new media's primary content producers as well. While the 1990s saw concepts such as convergence, interactivity, and the virtual dominating both popular and academic discourse, in the 2000s there has been an increasing focus on participation, collaboration, collective intelligence, and user-led innovation. This emphasis on participation may partially explain another phenomenon: the co-consumption of media. A recent Neilson study reports that Americans use the Internet, television, and their cell phone all at once, for three and a half hours per week, an increase of 35 per cent over the previous year (Neilson 2010). This 'three screen' activity suggests that there is a modification underway, at least in part, not just in the amount of television being consumed but also in the way it is being consumed. It would appear that Canadians, too, are participating in the 'cognitive surplus' generated by declining television viewing and outlined by Shirky (2010).

At the heart of such changes, the Internet continues to evolve as a dense, ubiquitous, global, socio-technical network. While early Internet studies posed questions about the relationship of this technology to the culture surrounding it, new media is now clearly embedded in global media culture to the extent that people now live in a network society. This has a range of economic, cultural, political, legal, and other implications. In the economic sphere, new media is linked to the shift towards a global knowledge economy, or an economy increasingly driven by knowledge-based and creative industries, and by user-led innovation, rather than industrial production, science-based research and development, and mass consumption. Culturally, new media have allowed participatory culture to flourish through blogs, social media sites, and DIY media production and distribution outlets such as YouTube. Politically, new media presents a challenge to established sites of institutional authority, be they governments, political parties, and indeed the traditional news media, as looser, more fluid and collaborative networks constitute increasingly dynamic sites of innovation and the generation of new ideas, information, and forms of power, resistance, and activism (Milberry 2009).[2] In the legal domain, remix culture and the almost limitless scope for repurposing and remediation of digital content confront traditional copyright and intellectual property laws. Indeed, even issues of personal and professional identities are increasingly located within global networks of information and communication, whether through online affiliations that people have or from the information stored on various databases as a result of their electronic transactions.

The rise of social media, blogs, and social software is linked, as Benkler (2006) describes, to the rise in types of social production that are collaborative in form, strongly motivated by non-market behavioural factors, and over which it is difficult to directly claim ownership or control. Benkler argues that social production models find their most favourable ecologies in industries involved in information, communications, culture, and creativity, meaning that social production models are having their most significant impact in knowledge-based media and creative industries, but that the ruptures they promote in these industries resonate throughout the economic system. This is particularly evident in how information and creativity have become, as authors such as Howkins (2001) and Florida (2002, 2007) argue, the core productive forces of the twenty-first century global economy. Benkler observes that the more important non-contractual factors such as gift relations, reciprocity, and trust are to an economic relationship, the more social production will flourish, and the more of a challenge these new models will present to incumbent producers: the rise of Wikipedia and YouTube are perhaps the most illustrative examples of this. The core challenge, not surprisingly, concerns the status and application of copyright and intellectual property laws in this environment, and it is notable that both the laws themselves have been strengthened over the past decade, and the propensity among incumbent media and information companies to seek their enforcement has increased, even as alternative socio-legal models such as Creative Commons have been evolving.

The copyright wars, or the tensions involving information and creative content as both public resources and private property, are salutary reminders to avoid being overly drawn into new media hype, and that critical analysis and empirically sound investigations of trends in new media are required. This becomes particularly apparent when considering two boom areas in the new media environment: multiplayer online games and new forms of news production such as citizen journalism. In the case of online games, the dynamism of the sector and the pleasurable experiences of gaming need to be considered alongside issues such as exploitative working conditions in the industry and the ongoing debates about ownership of user-generated content in the online games themselves, as well as issues such as identity, pedagogy, and other complex social phenomena linked to gaming.

The online environment has also spawned new forms of journalism and news production, with the shifts in production infrastructures associated with Web 2.0, as well as new patterns of distribution and use, leading to the rise of what has been termed 'citizen journalism'. While citizen journalism emerges in a context where there are growing questions about the professionalism of journalists and their tendency to be subject or beholden to powerful individuals and organizations, who can ruin a journalist by excluding him or her from access to official news or information (Levine and Forrence 1990), there is also the concern that eroding traditional revenue bases for news organizations may see an undermining of news values in the online space, as lower-cost alternatives such as celebrity blogging seem to cater more effectively to the target demographics of marketing divisions. Both instances offer reminders that an understanding of the political economy of new media remains vitally important, even as new opportunities for participatory media culture and the expression of what Leadbeater (2007) refers to as mass creativity are emerging and multiplying.

As new media are currently evolving at the start of the second decade of the twenty-first century, there are several additional topics that are particularly relevant, whether in terms of personal and professional use of new media, the new media industry, or new media policy. The first of these is mobility, which has a number of implications, both for users and providers. The second is the notion of the 'Internet of things' rather than an earlier concept of the Internet as being made up of hosts and people. A third significant consideration involves an understanding of a network as something that is always on and always there. The fourth area worth attention is social media and its implications for social interaction, whether for personal, business, political, or other purposes. Finally, we will look in some detail at the surveillance implications of our networked, digital new media. In concluding the discussion of this text, each of these merits attention, once more, in terms of identifying further considerations.

Mobility

After some false starts, it is clear that one of the accelerating trends in new media is for data and digital content to be accessed from mobile devices. As Chapter 4 makes clear, the rise in mobile phone ownership and use has been astounding since the early 1990s, when phones for the most part functioned as devices for voice communication and simple text messaging, while more complex data, such as web content, continued to be accessed almost exclusively from personal computers. That has all changed in the twenty-first century. The development of third generation (3G) wireless networking and the wiring up of spaces (particularly cities) has been accompanied by the development of devices that fully integrate phone, computing, and PDA functions, such as RIM's BlackBerry, the Android series of phones developed by Google, and the Apple iPhone. At the same time, smaller and smaller laptop computers (netbooks) and the

emerging tablet format suggest that there is a transition away from the desktop for full engagement with the Internet, to Internet everywhere. Or, the Internet in your hand.

The implications of mobile computing becoming a user expectation are only now being
considered. One implication may be that wireless networking access will inform locational
decisions made by people and organizations, as part of the global competition for talent
referred to by Florida (2007). As noted in Chapter 4, studies have shown that employers are
starting to expect that employees will be available outside of work hours or when on the road,
even if their job is white collar or not associated with traditional 'on call' professions (Ladner
2008). Another implication of growing mobile access to the Internet may be further nomad-
ism in terms of when and where people undertake work-related activities. This, too, can be
something that employees take up initially as a source of freedom only to discover the negative aspects of being at work when at home (Ladner 2008). Mobility will also have an impact
on how people consume leisure and entertainment products, with access to information
about major sporting events (cricket scores in India, soccer scores in Europe, baseball and
football information in North America) already proving to be a major driver of demand for
wireless handheld devices. It is also important to consider how relentless access to networked
information affects its users: the BlackBerry has already been referred to as the crackberry
because it facilitates a kind of dependence on email and other forms of text messaging.

Much of the 1990s and early twenty-first century involved adoption of and adaptation to
the ability to have access to people at any time. The mobile phone has transformed everything from movie plots to business meetings with its potential to reach someone at any time,
anywhere. In the coming decades, further transformation can be expected, as people reach
out at any minute to the global knowledge storehouse that is at their fingertips. This raises
different kinds of questions. For example, what are the effects of having constant access
to Wikipedia, when everything from settling bar bets to establishing the location of one's
next meeting is in the palm of one's hand? On one hand, this capacity can offer promising possibilities in terms of communication, knowledge exchange, informing opinions, and
decision-making. At the same time, however, with such changes, life experiences become
increasingly mediated by technology, which suggests hints of the hive mind predicted in
science fiction stories or, at least, raises the question of what is also lost, with such advances?

The Internet of Things

Up until recently, the Internet was understood as comprised of computers used by people.
The unit of analysis was the Internet host computer and the web pages it contained. It was
reasonable, in the earlier days of the Internet, to use measures such as counting the number
of computers and the websites visited, for example, then extrapolate to the people using
them. Gradually, it has become evident that the people—and the relationships among
them—have greater significance than can be measured by counting information housed
on host computers. Now, for example, it is more meaningful to know about the users of
Facebook (and *their use of* Facebook) than how many computers Facebook uses to manage
their site. The next frontier involves not only better understanding the complexity of how

these technologies are used among people (and to what effects) but also, to go beyond people and apply an Internet address to every object that they create using these technologies.

The phrase, 'Internet of Things', was coined in the late 1990s by a group based at MIT known as Auto-ID (Dodgson 2003). In the Internet of things, rather than hosts or even people, what are followed are objects. In this emerging world every—or nearly every—object with any significant value is given an Internet address that is used to locate it, communicate with it, and determine certain pertinent facts about its state. A typical example is in the tracking of shipping containers or pallets in trucks. Instead of the former waybill (or more recently, the barcode), these objects have computer chips with memory and a low power radio frequency identification device (RFID) that allows (typically nearby) receivers to query the object and determine its status. The chip may be connected to sensors that indicate the temperature inside the container or perhaps track memory to indicate past encounters (shocks from being dropped or transit points completed, for example).

At first glance, perhaps assigning an address to an online object or querying the status of the content of shipping containers may not appear to fall under the rubric of new media. Artifacts and their relationship to humans, however, have been central to understanding new media in every era and in fact, form the foundation of archaeology. An enormous amount can be learned about a civilization—long lost or otherwise—by looking at their things, how those things were arranged, and how they were used. In addition, people attribute and derive enormous power from their possessions. Knowing where these possessions are and their status can be very useful: in commerce (stocking shelves, pricing goods, doing inventory, shipping and delivering supplies are all necessary); in war (issues of logistics are one of the most important elements in warfare); in family life (whether there is milk in the fridge and if it is out of date); and so on. Objects have information linked to them, which, if communicated via networks and computers, endow them with greater value

Networks: Always On and Always There

The rise of mobile computing intersects with another major trend in new media, which is increasing access to high-speed broadband services and, at the same time, rapidly diminishing costs associated with Internet access (usage time, network infrastructure constraints, download times, and storage device capacity, for example). As a result, it is becoming the norm for more and more people to leave their computers on at all times, and to consume a growing amount of material—increasingly audio and video material—via their computers.

While this consumption, for now, often consists of downloading (movies or music) and tends to be through software, like BitTorrent, which does not always adhere to or enforce copyright regulations or collect appropriate copyright fees, a growing amount of use does not involve creating a copy but instead is more transient and involves streaming Internet content, as has been popularized by YouTube and Internet music services such as Pandora. Many of the world's broadcasters—for example Canada's national, public broadcaster, the CBC—have adopted this mode as a way of reaching people who might otherwise not bother to turn on a television or radio but still enjoy music and video entertainment.

Even for items of a personal and private nature, some Internet users have given up or greatly reduced their use of local storage. The notion of downloading and uploading content is fading away as the material is no longer anywhere in particular and instead is everywhere by virtue of its presence in the so-called cloud of data in online servers and services. This is most vividly experienced through the collection of software, services, and storage known as Google apps. Here, email does not permanently reside on a computer that the user owns, but rather, is accessed from a variety of terminals or devices, including mobile devices. Photographs, documents, music, and even spreadsheets and computer programs exist either exclusively or largely in the online world. Such a computing and network experience is free from the perils of lost files (backups are part of the service and no longer the user's responsibility), misplaced files (users search for rather than file things), or viruses (virus-checking is done by the service provider).

This vision of the network computer was one of the signature claims of computer and Internet pioneer, Bill Joy, whose company, SUN, had the motto, 'the network is the computer', back in 1980s. In many ways, Joy's vision was almost twenty years ahead of its time: home computers and networks of that era were not up to the task that he saw for them and the sort of dumb network terminals that he envisaged are not likely to be adopted now, but the notion that most of the value of using a computer comes from its network connection is certainly true for many people and is sure to become increasingly true for most people. More recently, Joy was quoted in *The Register*, an online magazine, as saying, 'The answering machine put voicemail by the desk, and then it went back into the network. [. . .] Your iPod is like your home answering machine. I guarantee you it will be hard to sell an iPod five or seven years from now when every cell phone can access your entire music library wherever you are' (Ashlee 2006). In this case Joy might have underestimated how quickly things would evolve, since current iPhones can access an almost limitless variety of streaming music and video already, less than five years later. Although the cost of this level of access has not dropped far enough that people have stopped buying iPods, such affordable access is ever closer on the horizon.

The broader socio-cultural implications of increasing speed and volume of communications or what can be termed 'always on' culture, both for users and for the wider communications ecology, is an increasingly significant research question. For example, as we discussed in an earlier chapter, to be denied access to a network as a result of a court sentence is regarded as draconian and limiting of freedom of speech and association (Kravets 2010),[3] if access to the Internet is understood as a human right. The cost is economic as well: a US District Court ruling turned at least in part on the fact that it was almost impossible for the Appellant to obtain or retain even blue collar work without some access to computers. There are also concerns about far-reaching and profound environmental impacts related to new media, from the building of new media devices, to their use, and how they are discarded. Governments have started to wrestle with some of the challenges relating to electronic waste. Many Canadian provinces have e-waste recycling programs as well as special fees on new electronic devices, similar to what are imposed on new tires and car batteries.

Energy use for new media is one aspect of 'always on' that is becoming increasingly salient as climate change concerns mount. The power consumption of networks and network devices is non-trivial, estimated by some to be equivalent to the global air travel industry. Yet, new media can also bring net environmental benefits: the use of networks can make the movement of goods more efficient and using new media for videoconferencing can take the place of flying to a meeting, for example. Information technology systems themselves can also be made far more environmentally friendly, as is evident in emerging efforts for green data centres. Leading consumers of computing power are looking at creative ways to reduce their burden on the system by shifting computational demands to locations where power is greener or less contested.[4] In fact, there have been efforts to move data centres closer to sources of renewable energy (hydroelectric, solar, geothermal), where power is plentiful and green, rather than pulling the electricity across the country to where the computers are, wasting power as it travels across long distances.[5]

Ubiquitous always-on networks can transform existing businesses and create new ones (and destroy others). One example can be found in the 'long tail' phenomenon identified by Anderson (2006), where businesses can increasingly profit from low-volume sales to niche consumers based on a wider inventory of virtual products (as seen with Amazon and eBay). In this scenario, while it is not profitable or even possible for a bricks-and-mortar bookstore to stock vast inventories of obscure books, centralized inventory coupled with powerful search engines and social features such as commentary and recommendations makes it possible for Amazon to profitably sell books that have very low sales volume. Traditional bookstores have difficulty competing against a network-enabled competitor and have been closing all over the world. Another example of these business transformations can be found in the area of news production, where a 24/7 news cycle is now the norm, rather than the traditional cycles of print or broadcast news production. There are also questions about the quality of communication: if people are receiving more than 100 emails per day and there is an expectation from senders that these will be read and responded to quickly, will the quality of responses deteriorate? How will communication be affected in a society where people lack the time away from work that was previously the basis for leisure and well-being? Will such changed expectations result in more people choosing to downsize by accepting a lower income for reduced workload as a necessary condition for an enhanced quality of life?

Meeting People Made Easy: Social Media

With estimates that there are about 100 million bloggers worldwide and social media sites such as Facebook claiming to have more than 500 million accounts, the critical mass of people involved in online social activities has clearly reached a substantial level. Such trends are consistent with meta-theories such as those of the network society, participatory culture, and social production. There remains a need, however, to continue research on the implications of such a volume of online networkers using social media.

Researchers in the social sciences and humanities are confronted with the challenge of establishing empirical measures for identifying the significance of these trends and developing sound theoretical and analytical frameworks to better understand the implications of these phenomena. Research has shown, for instance, that open source software development is effective because it can produce a powerful operating system such as Linux. What are equivalents for social media? Do bands and musicians that have MySpace sites achieve more sales and downloads of their music than those who do not? Do people with a personal social networking site do better in the employment market? Research in the digital humanities has also opened up discussion about changing forms of texts, discourse, and by extension, knowledge itself. What are the reasons that people have for going into these online spaces and what are the effects of doing so, whether personal, professional, political, or otherwise?

As another example, Facebook has become a force to be reckoned with in political circles. Politicians no longer dismiss user groups and fan groups on Facebook, as they now know that these online manifestations of popular sentiment are not simply virtual. This much was clarified in the winter of 2009–10 when the Canadian parliament was briefly suspended for procedural reasons (prorogued) and more than 200,000 people joined a Facebook group in protest. The group became the hub for real life protests in cities across Canada, with some marches and rallies attracting more than 20,000 people.

Online services are not just for protest and reaction, however: the spring of 2010 saw Canada's prime minister interviewed on YouTube, with the questions coming from an online polling system.[6] In the UK, millions of Britons participated in online polls and other events during the 2010 election, leading politicians in that country to turn to Facebook in their quest for deficit reduction ideas. The initiative, dubbed 'the largest public engagement project' ever launched by the UK government, will be hosted on the Democracy UK Facebook Page and links citizens—there are 26 million Britons on Facebook—to information sources, places to voice their opinions on initiatives, and places to post ideas (Warren 2010).

It is no longer sufficient to see online activities as peripheral or unimportant when the online connections that people have are regarded as an aspect of their full, real, lives. A Facebook friend might be different from a face-to-face friend but many of them are one and the same and more importantly, the real world is being organized to a growing degree by those online tools and connections. Online contacts matter locally but also internationally, as was evident in the summer of 2009, when protests over election results in Iran spilled out onto the Internet through text messages sent to the Twitter service. It is by no means clear that these text messages had any impact in terms of changing the outcome of the elections and many would argue that the texting resulted only in people being identified and targeted for reprisals. Nevertheless these types of services were seen as a legitimate and important outlet for concerns and a way for people involved in the protests to stay in touch with each other.

Surveillance and New Media

New media enables many things for our society, our communities, and for us as individuals. We can coordinate our actions, locate new information, and share aspects of our lives with friends. These capabilities arise in many ways because new media are based on digital electronic technologies and are arranged into systems that facilitate easy exchange and sharing of bits. Mostly, these are beneficial and positive outcomes of the use of digital shared media. Unfortunately, new media also enable an unprecedented—and dangerously unremarked—level of **surveillance** as well. Some of this surveillance is purposeful and targeted and some of it is incidental and a side effect of other features. But all of it results in lives lived under an increasingly sharp lens and an increasingly long memory. In this section we will discuss how this has come about, what it might mean, and how we can cope with this phenomenon.

Watching each other is something that humans are used to and participate in from birth. It is how parents know when their babies need something, how babies learn, and how we know when our clothes are out of style; we habitually watch each other and learn from what we see. Surveillance includes watching, but we nowadays regard surveillance as something a bit more sinister and organized. David Lyon defines surveillance as 'focused, systematic and routine attention to personal details for purposes of influence, management, protection, or direction' (Lyon 2007:14). This definition includes the more benign aspects, and directs our attention beyond merely the gaze of the watcher but further into the myriad other ways in which 'attention to personal details' might occur.

As various commentators have noted, surveillance is deeply connected to the existence and viability of the modern state, and modernity itself (Giddens 1990). We simply could not exist in the modern (or post-modern, for that matter) world without surveillance. We need surveillance for industrial production and distribution of goods, for example. How else to determine that the work is getting done, that the products are being made to specifications, that they are delivered on time to the people who want them, and that the payments are made and distributed to those who participated in the process? All aspects of an automated industrial society are closely monitored for efficiency and effectiveness and all of this is a kind of surveillance.

New media are heavily implicated in that sort of systemic surveillance. We no longer, or rarely, require a boss to be watching the workers or a clerk to be counting inventory. Those tasks are relegated to machines and in almost all cases to digital computers and networks. In consumption, as well, the watching that ensures that our favourite TV show gets the ratings that bring in the advertising that pays for the actors and the producers is almost all automatic, digital, and networked. Using surveillance to ensure the smooth operation of a modern economy seems like a good thing, and often it is. But surveillance is not always benign or confined to accepted industry uses. Surveillance is used to enforce the rules, punish the guilty, identify the perpetrators, and ensure compliance. New media participates in those aspects as well.

What do we think about surveillance? In the aftermath of the Second World War, with the horrors of technology-driven killing machines and the terrible force of totalitarian regimes still felt, George Orwell wrote the chilling novel, *1984*, about a total surveillance state in which Big Brother was always watching (Orwell 1949). This vision came to dominate mid-century thinking about surveillance as a force of government. Later, philosopher and sociologist Michel Foucault theorized the impact that being watched has on society as a whole, applying the concept of a panopticon—a prison design based on the premise that, as all inmates are within view of an unseen guard, they would police themselves because they would never know when they were being watched (Foucault 1975). As it turned out, surveillance by the state and large bureaucratic institutions such as prisons and hospitals has been far eclipsed by the watching being done in the name of consumer capitalism. Throughout the latter years of the twentieth century, elaborate and interconnected systems were developed to optimize both the buying experience and the knowledge that advertisers and marketers were able to deploy to fine-tune their pitches to specific audiences. The fields of demographics (who we are), geo-demographics (where we are), and psycho-graphics (how we think and what we think about) became the powerful tools they are in large part because of the enormous amounts of data and processing power in computers. We played along, using loyalty cards and seeing barcodes on everything we buy, in a kind of passive acquiescence to a system that delivered the goods.

This has changed dramatically in the twenty-first century. We can find the results in two very different places. First, the events of 11 September 2001 crystallized a phenomenon that had been taking place for some time, namely the growing desire to remove risk from our lives and the willingness to give up freedoms in the name of safety (Ericson and Haggerty 1997). A surveillance state, imagined by George Orwell in 1949 and not realized in the 1980s, when he imagined it, grew up in the first decade of the twenty-first century driven by fear and signaled by Orange and Yellow alerts. This policing has taken on a profoundly technological aspect, with a vast array of scanners, cameras, databases, and sensors deployed at borders, airports, and around cities. And many of these tools have their basis in the computers and networks that we see as foundational to new media. For the most part, we accept this imposition in the name of safety and security.

The second way in which surveillance has come into our lives through new media is not imposed at all, but rather embraced and even advanced by our own actions. This is the growing use of new media for social purposes. In almost every case these tools have an explicit or implicit surveillance aspect to them. Take, for example, the photo sharing site Flickr. Here people upload photos from their daily lives. The act of everyday people capturing the events of their life, and sharing them with others, is not new. Amateur painters and photographers have existed for a long time. New media, however, has profoundly changed the depth, extent, quality, and quantity of the capturing since, as we noted earlier in the chapter on mobile technologies, almost half of the planet is carrying a phone and almost all of those have a camera. More importantly, these images are shared to a degree, scale, and scope that is unprecedented. From a surveillance perspective, the photos are not just available but tagged with a rich array of information including where, when, and how they were taken (even the model of camera and its settings are shared).

The ability to embed information in databases and expose them to search engines, even more than the existence of the information, is what makes this type of casual and friendly undertaking re-usable for surveillance. The surveillance can be mundane ('how many pictures are being taken with the new iPhone4?'[7]) or potentially suspect ('who is that person?', 'who is beside them?'), but the fact that we take pictures, upload them, and then tag them, makes it possible to use computers, databases, and networks to use those photos in a focused, systematic, and routine way, in other words, for surveillance purposes.

Many other new media technologies and services discussed in this book have similar or even more significant surveillance aspects. The popular social software site Facebook, for example, has even more users than Flickr, more pictures, and even greater ability to tag people in photos. It isn't just photos, of course. To give some idea on the volume of material going into Facebook, consider these facts from 2010:

- Users spend more than 16 billion minutes on Facebook each day.
- Every week users share more than 6 billion pieces of content, including status updates, photos, and notes.
- Each month more than 3 billion photos are uploaded to Facebook;
- Users view more than 1 million photos every second.
- Facebook's servers perform more than 50 million operations per second, primarily between the caching tier and web servers.
- More than 1 million websites have implemented features of Facebook Connect.[8]

Some services (e.g., Picasa) are experimenting with automated tagging—giving names to the faces in your pictures by recognizing those faces using a computing algorithm. In almost all cases these services have privacy settings that potentially limit the ability of these images and tags to be shared, but in practice a great deal of information is placed online because people want to share it. And much of the surveillance that is done is not malicious but merely commercial (for example a camera manufacturer might wish to see how popular their cameras are among photo sharers on Flickr, or look for trends in the ways photos are taken in order to develop new features to enhance their latest model).

Another important example can be found in the transition to digital cable. Previously, networks had no way of knowing—unless you were a participant in a monitoring project, like the Neilsen Ratings system—whether or not you were watching TV at all, let alone what you were watching. The new cable boxes, however, do not simply provide a dumb pipeline to an always-on stream of content. Instead, they are like little computers that have to be activated on the network, that are addressable by the system operator (thereby enabling pay-per-view features), and request a single channel at a time from the 'head end'. This means that your local cable provider knows when your cable box is on, and what channel is selected. Moreover, they can tell when the channels are being changed and—if they bother to couple this with an analysis of the programs—this could be turned into an incredibly rich data set about what attracts, retains, and repels audiences. This is a fountain of information that cable television companies are only just beginning to take advantage of.

Whether they are related to commercial interests, security, or just curiosity, these surveillance capabilities are both powerful and often misunderstood and it is for this reason that new media developments, especially those that allow or encourage sharing as a default setting, deserve our attention from a policy and regulatory point of view.

Regulating new media is a controversial topic in some ways, since the freedom to innovate and create new media forms without having to seek prior approval is considered one of the hallmarks of the Internet and online media forms in general. Even if we did hope to impose a regulatory framework on new media, the mechanisms for doing that are imperfect and in their infancy, as we discovered in Chapter 9. Nevertheless, there are good reasons to question the automatic approval of new media and a growing trend to question both institutional and personal sharing of information as being unquestionably beneficial. A recent example is the requests—ultimately successful—from the Privacy Commissioner of Canada to Facebook that they revise their default privacy settings, the language used in their instructions, and most importantly the ability of third parties to access information of the site's members through the use of apps. A growing number of people are, on their own, taking advantage of more restrictive privacy settings in services such as Facebook or Flickr and not unthinkingly sharing information about themselves. This is a good first step and through dialogue, consumer demand, and occasional regulator intervention we should see better protection of consumer rights to privacy from potential breaches via social software.

The rapidly changing power of new media, driven forward by the investments in computers and networks being made by manufacturers, systems operators, as well as consumers, is part of the challenge for regulators. Many of our surveillance laws are decades old, having been introduced in an era of film photography and analog telephones. When microscopic mobile cameras can record digitally, on infrared in the dark, in high definition and with excellent sound, and when the results can be linked to databases and analyzed automatically and in real time, you have a technological capability that has far outstripped both our casual understanding and our legal framework.

These capabilities confound both the police and security establishment—who are vexed by the built-in encryption that is available on Skype and in BlackBerrys—and consumers, who don't realize what they are sharing or how much information is really being gathered when they walk down a street covered by cameras with face detecting software. At present the pressure has been on commercial enterprises to greatly improve their protection of personal privacy, but in the coming years we may very well see pressure on states to limit their monitoring so that basic democratic freedoms, such as freedom of speech, freedom of movement, and freedom of association are not compromised. In a simple example, if you worry about who you are speaking to on the street—a person with a pamphlet, for example—because you wonder if you will be tied to them in a surveillance database, then our democracy has suffered a (tiny, perhaps) blow. Agencies around the world, including the Privacy Commissioner of Canada, mentioned above, are working hard to ensure that civil rights are respected and to educate citizens on how to live responsibly in these news times. The recent digital comic, *Under Surveillance*, from European Digital Rights, is a great example of both building awareness and pushing for stronger protection.[9] Ultimately, it is the responsibility of citizens and governments to ensure that these the tiny cuts to civil rights do not devolve into a killing blow for a free and democratic society.

New Media Scholarship: The Next Frontiers

To conclude this edition of *New Media: An Introduction*, it is worth noting two areas of research whose significance and implications warrant further consideration by scholars as new media technologies evolve. The first, a proposal for critical information studies, is something that students in Communication and Information Science programs may be familiar with, although the emphasis here is on new media and a specific proposal by Vaidhyanathan (2006). The second, a call for the de-westernization of new media scholarship, is something that is being taken up to varying degrees by researchers around the world. Issues related to the limitations of the dominant, Western perspective in numerous fields of inquiry are part of a growing discourse to which Canadian scholars are well positioned to contribute (and have been active in), given the diversity of the Canadian population and the strong historical and cultural connections that Canada has to other countries, as well.

Critical information studies

Vaidhyanathan (2006) proposes that the complex set of legal, social, political, economic, and cultural issues arising from new media should be approached from a multidisciplinary perspective that he terms critical information studies (CIS). He proposes that CIS would consider 'the ways in which culture and information are regulated, and thus the relationships among regulation and commerce, creativity, science, technology, politics, and other human affairs' (2006: 293). Identifying how this would translate more specifically into research agendas, Vaidhyanathan proposes examining the following:

- the abilities and liberties to use, revise, criticize, and manipulate cultural texts, images, ideas, and information;
- the rights and abilities of users (or consumers or citizens) to alter the means and techniques through which cultural texts and information are rendered, displayed, and distributed;
- the relationship between information control, property rights, technologies, and social norms; and,
- the cultural, political, social, and economic ramifications of global flows of culture and information (2006: 293).

Vaidhyanathan observes that an interdisciplinary framework such as CIS makes it more exciting to do research in a field such as digital copyright law, as it brings together researchers in debates across cultural studies and political economy as well as law and information studies. CIS also presents the possibility that such scholarly research will engage quite directly with issues that are in the public domain:

> As the sets of cultural producers and consumers intersect, the marginal price of distribution of information and cultural products drops to zero, and global communication networks link disparate bodies of work and people who engage with that work. More people take an interest in the policies that govern how information and information technology get distributed and used. (Vaidhyanathan 2006: 303)

Considerations such as these also link research to the activities of various public interest organizations, legal groups, and policy-makers, as well as providing academic researchers with direct questions about how they wish their own work to circulate in the public domain (for example, should it have a Creative Commons licence? Should it be published in Open Access journals?).

The possibilities of CIS as an emergent field of critical and interdisciplinary socio-legal research are considerable, both drawing from and contributing to a rich range of 'knowledges' from across a variety of other academic disciplines. At the same time, Vaidhyanathan identifies three key challenges for those working within this emergent field. The first is that it is dominated by research from the English-speaking world, in particular from the US. As the Internet has increasingly become a genuinely global domain, he notes that some of the underlying assumptions in the existing research may 'ring flat in parts of the world where liberalism is not taken for granted', pointing to a need for 'CIS [to] get beyond its American roots and consider how every change in the information ecosystem is global' (2006: 306). A second challenge relates to the institutional location of many researchers within universities that increasingly see themselves not simply as the users and providers of information in the public domain, but as significant holders of copyright materials in their own right, from which they extract revenues and develop research commercialization strategies. Finally, there is the question of whether scholars committed to a CIS agenda would practice what they preach by only dealing with publishers and journals that enable more open access to scholarly materials through legal mechanisms such as Creative Commons licences.

De-westernizing the Internet (and Internet studies)

Following Curran and Park's (2000) proposal that there is a need to de-westernize media studies, the data we looked at in Chapter 1 on trends in global Internet use suggest a similar need in relation to understanding new media and the Internet. The fastest growth in global Internet use is happening in Asia, Africa, Latin America, the Caribbean, and the Middle East; with North America, Europe, and Australia/New Zealand moving from a position of dominance in the 1990s to one where they are becoming, or may indeed have already become, a minority of the global Internet community. In fact, as of March 2010 there are more users of the *mobile* Internet in China than there are people in the US.[10] The role of mobile Internet—an emerging phenomenon—is what is largely driving the rapid growth of the Internet outside of its traditional home countries. Mobile access is growing rapidly in North America, Europe, and the developed parts of Asia. Communities in the rest of the world that have not previously had any access to the Internet, now see this access arriving through a phone (or other mobile device). As long as it is useful and affordable, people will make use of it, and the Internet is proving to be both of those things around the world.

Canada has benefited through the early years of the Internet by its close proximity to the US, a common language, and compatible legal and social systems. Being close to both the large consumer base and the major US fibre optic networks has meant that Internet startups in Canada have had relatively low barriers and great opportunities. Sites such as Flickr (and Club Penguin)[11] are premised on very significant bandwidth as well as cultural awareness, such as knowing what would attract people to use a website and how to make it useful and friendly. These offer illustrative examples of how Canada has been able to leverage compatibility with the first major Internet market. Although Canada has not yet leveraged to any notable degree the multicultural and multilingual aspects of Canada's social fabric, it is not unreasonable to expect some of the country's future Internet success stories to be based on being savvy to a Chinese or Indian market (rather than in reaching the US market). The majority of the world's Internet users do not communicate primarily through the English language, yet how this is changing the nature of the global new media ecology is little understood.

Just as Curran and Park note that early paradigms in global media and communications tended to understand much of the world's media as an underdeveloped or state-controlled 'other' to a Western (typically American) norm, Internet studies as a field of inquiry is still strongly influenced by its emergence in the US in the free-wheeling decade of the 1990s. One example of this is the degree of focus on Internet censorship in a number of countries, with China being the largest and perhaps most significant. It is certainly the case that there are varying degrees of censorship, state control, and surveillance of online communication in many parts of the world, and that this may well run at odds to the democratizing potential of new media. Yet this is not the whole picture and it only addresses some aspects of new media use in some parts of the world. Establishing the significance of state control over the Internet in China, for instance, tells little about how the Internet is developing as a new media form in countries such as India, Korea, Brazil, and Russia, to take some examples. It also acts as a filter to more grounded case studies of comparative new media use in different socio-cultural and political-economic environments.

The problems here are twofold. The first arises from the strong historical association of the Internet with libertarian discourses (Flichy 2007). As the Internet was first popularized in the US and the first major political campaigns around the new media tended to focus on questions of free speech, there has been a tendency in Internet studies to focus on the more heroic, political, or resistant aspects of use of the medium, as opposed to more mundane, everyday, convivial, or conversational uses (Burgess 2006).

This is not to say that attention should not be drawn to Internet censorship in different parts of the world, or that support should not be given to those who seek to use the new media to achieve a legitimate right to free expression of opinion and ideas. Rather, that to focus only on these aspects may lead to some significant omissions in understandings of new media use in cross-cultural perspectives. The enthusiasm of Chinese Internet users to vote in televised talent programs, to take one example, may have much to tell about how a popular demand for the right to vote may be expressing itself in that country, if it is given significance as an aspect of new media use.

A second gap is clearly that of language, interspersed with isolation between different research communities, and an associated reluctance on the part of Western new media researchers to learn from developments in other parts of the world. South Korea provides a fascinating case study of how digital media content may evolve where there is near-universal access to high-speed broadband networks, yet published research in English-language new media journals on developments in Korea is patchy and sporadic. To make these points is not to discount what is most valuable in the Western intellectual and political traditions, such as the right to free speech and free expression of ideas and opinions. It is to say that more needs to be done to foster international and intercultural research and collaboration in the new media field (indeed, as in other fields), so that patterns of mutual learning and dialogue can emerge that are more reflective of the dynamics of global new media production, distribution, and use.

Final Words

New media, in the end, are always changing. They are, by their very nature, mutable and changeable in ways that traditional media—tied to a technological form—are not. As such, new media are difficult to define if we confine our view to the physical tools that produce them. Instead, it is more useful to see new media in terms of the outcomes of the exploitation of certain fundamental characteristics, those laid out in the opening chapter, namely: that new media are manipulable, networkable, dense, compressible, and impartial. These characteristics are then expressed in a variety of artifacts, activities, and arrangements (Lievrouw and Livingstone 2005) in such a way as to create an interactive experience.

The nature of those interactive experiences, however, is forever changing and new and different forms emerge frequently. Therefore, a student of new media is well advised to be on the lookout for new forms and new experiences and to consider, as we have done in this book, the underlying characteristics that not only make the existence of new media possible but also, what links them to the past. New media forms are quite often echoes or recreations of previous media forms, but with an interactive element. In trying to understand a new form it can be very helpful to see if there are recognizable aspects or elements, something that may reflect a common human communication pattern or practice, something that recreates a business model or value proposition in a new and interesting way. Although it may be easy to be distracted by the claims of 'new' and 'different', existing knowledge is often a good guide to how these media can be used and how they affect our society, our culture, our economy, and our government.

Case Study: Citizen Lab (http://citizenlab.org)

Political activism is increasingly found not just on the streets but on the online networks of the world. The information sharing and organizing capabilities of computers and networks is unprecedented, but using these tools is dangerous in some countries. A growing number of technologically inclined and politically aware people are engaging in something called 'hacktivism'—the use of computers and networks for an activist agenda (Milberry 2009). One of the most well known of these is The Citizen Lab.

The Citizen Lab is based at the Munk Centre for International Studies at the University of Toronto, Canada. The lab focuses on advanced research and development 'at the intersection of digital media, global security, and human rights'. Their activities have brought international recognition in the form of funding support from large foundations as well as notoriety for their unflinching criticism of the use of information technology to impinge on freedom and undermine liberty. Their research has led to the publication of numerous reports and articles which have documented the ways in which regimes use the Internet to track down dissidents or infiltrate activist computer networks to disrupt and deter them. The Citizen Lab is directed by professor Ron Deibert, of University of Toronto's Department of Political Science (Mitrovica 2009).

In April of 2010 the group published a report, titled *Shadows in the Cloud*, which shows how hackers based in Chengdu, China were able to use a network of malware,[12] botnets, web hosting services, and online social networks to infiltrate computers belonging to the Indian government as well as the Dalai Lama and steal classified and sensitive documents. All of this was released in the form of a lengthy report (Citizen Lab 2010), a press release, and coverage in the media, including *The New York Times*. As Ron Deibert and Rahel Rohozinski point out in an op-ed piece in *The Globe and Mail* released the day the report was published,

> Today, no country is secure in the global sea of information. Preserving cyberspace requires a strategy to address the dark side of the Internet. This requires urgent international co-operation, level-headed judgment and a commitment to preserve our values of freedom of speech and access to information, so as to ensure that in our quest for online security we do not secure ourselves into a new dark age (2010).

The report was completed in collaboration with a private security company in Ottawa (SecDev Group) and a volunteer organization of security professionals known as the Shadowserver Foundation.

This collaboration is typical of Citizen Lab, which has ongoing collaborations with Internet research groups at Oxford, Cambridge, and Harvard (through the OpenNet Initiative, http://opennet.net), and has formed a spin off company, called Psiphon, to market censorship circumvention and managed content delivery systems.

As the exercise of democratic rights, and particularly the organization of protests and civic action, has moved onto computers and online, efforts by governments against such activities has followed. On the other hand, support by organizations such as Citizen Lab has gone beyond pure research and moved into software development. Citizen Lab has helped to develop—and package—software that can help hide or secure the activities of activists by encrypting communications and files as well as get around the growing number of firewalls and filters in place around the world. These tools are made available for free download to help those who wish to protect their communication and to access websites or content previously unavailable to them. Some of the tools are being commercialized by Psiphon, the Citizen Lab's spin-off company.

The lab has also produced a guide to avoiding censorship, titled 'Everyone's Guide to Bypassing Internet Censorship', downloadable from their website.

Glossary

Actor network theory an approach to the study of networks and society that pays attention to both human and non-human (such as technology or organizations) actors.

Augmented reality the use of networks, databases, computers, and sensors (camera, GPS) to overlay location- or time-specific information on top of a 'live' display of the scene in front of the device. A typical consumer application is providing restaurant information over top of a view of the restaurant when a customer holds their camera phone up in front of it and selects the Yelp application.

Blogging (blog, blogger) the web log was initially a simple reverse chronological listing of (typically) web pages encountered in one's daily surfing habits. Elaborated, refined, and expanded with dedicated software that made it easier to start, add multimedia content to, and maintain, blogging became a widespread amateur and commercial activity and a way to not just share links but commentary, photos, and videos.

Broadcasting the practice of sending a signal from one transmitter to many receivers. First done with radio and later television. On the Internet there are some equivalents, such as multicasting, that simulate a broadcast model.

Cellular (phone, radio, system) a method of mobile radio communication that distributes the transmitting/receiving responsibilities into small hexagonal cells that are responsible for a small area—a few blocks in highly populated areas—with participating devices engaging with many different antennae/towers as you move around. When the device moves from one cell to another there is a seamless handoff, without interruption in the call, even when you are travelling at highway (or high speed train) speeds. The small cells require less power on the part of radios, enabling smaller phones, and the reuse of radio spectrum.

Cognitive surplus a term coined by Clay Shirky to describe the human mind-power that is liberated when we stop doing something that has been taking up lot of time (in Shirky's example, it was watching TV) and turn our attention to something else.

Computer mediated communication (CMC) the use of computers to exchange messages, as with email, forums, blogs, wikis, and instant messaging.

Convergence media forms and media businesses coming together, as when America Online (Internet services) bought Time Warner (publishing and cable television); the term is sometimes used to describe technical convergence, as when various media such as music, movies, and magazines are all available on one, Internet connected, device

Convergence culture a term popularized by Henry Jenkins to describe media forms and consumption that cross many different sites and formats and incorporate both professional and amateur aspects.

Creative cities (creative class) a term coined by Richard Florida to describe cities that attract and retain a specific kind of creative people (the creative class), and as a consequence prosper in a world where intellectual property is highly valued.

Creative industries those industries with a heavy emphasis on creativity, including architecture, film-making, fashion, music, and theatre. There is a growing recognition of the role of these industries both for their direct and indirect economic impact.

Critical theory of technology an approach to the study of technology that emphasizes the importance of understanding how power (especially economic power) has and continues to influence the operation and evolution of technology in society.

Cyber-libertarianism see **Libertarian**.

Cyberspace a metaphor for online networks and virtual worlds popularized in the early 1990s first in fiction and then in the mass media. The term is in declining use at present as the online and offline world merge.

Diffusion of innovation model the spread of innovations within a society or market.

Digital made of discrete (usually binary, 1 and 0, on and off) units

Digital divide the gap between those who have access to the Internet and those who do not; the term is sometimes expanded to include gaps related to speed of access as well as capabilities to use the services (as for example when it is not in your native language).

Digital goods items which can be digitized and sold (or given away) through electronic networks, these include music, movies, books, house plans, images, even dress patterns. Importantly these goods are non-rivalous, infinitely and perfectly copyable, can exist in many places at once, and can be easily recombined to form new digital goods.

Digital locks an encryption or other scheme to prevent copying of digital goods. DVDs are often protected by anti-copying codes (widely broken by software available on personal computers), for example.

Disintermediation the ability of buyers to directly connect to suppliers (and vice versa), eliminating the need for wholesalers or other brokers. A simple example is the musician who sells music direct to fans via her website.

Disruptive technologies technologies or services that undermine or overwhelm the value proposition of an existing product or service thereby hastening its demise in the market. They are often unappreciated by suppliers of existing solutions, since they (at first) seem unrefined or unsuited to the task that their customers demand.

Dot.com crash a rapid devaluation of the stock prices in technology companies in late 2000 and 2001, especially those that were based on the Internet. Many people attributed this decline to a rationalization in a market that had become inflated by outlandish expectations and hyperbole.

Electromagnetic spectrum the full range of radiant energy, in the form of electromagnetic radiation, typically arranged from the highest to the lowest frequencies for reference. The higher the frequency, the shorter the wavelength and the more energy they contain. The spectrum includes everything from gamma rays and X-rays at the high end, ultraviolet, visible and infrared light in the middle, and radio waves at the low end. Radio waves range from longer frequencies, used in AM radio, to very high frequencies, used in cell phones, WiFi routers, and microwave transmission systems. This part of the electromagnetic spectrum is very important for communication, and is called the **radio spectrum**.

Electronic commerce (e-commerce) online transactions including consumer (buying via the web) and business to business (ordering new stock from a supplier); the term applies to both physical and virtual goods. For a growing number of industries a fully electronic model is becoming the norm, even for the goods that are consumed (e.g., Apple's iTunes Store).

Endogenous growth a theory from economics that recognizes the importance of innovation in the growth of an economy and, importantly, that it is not outside of the economy (exogenous) but a part of it.

Explicit knowledge knowledge that is or can be written down, shared, and sold; it is usually taught in a formal way.

Fair use (fair dealing in Canada) the principle of copyright law that some users, some times, have the right to use copyrighted material without paying a fee or obtaining a licence. Examples of fair dealing include research and criticism.

Folksonomy a definition or description (tag) for an object (photo, web page) that is generated by users of a web service such as delicious or Flickr, it contrasts with 'taxonomy' or the official naming of things. See **Tag** and **Hashtag**.

Forbearance (forbear) the decision not to fully regulate in an area where a regulatory commission has jurisdiction. The decision by the CRTC not to regulate mobile phones or the Internet has been a significant aspect of new media governance in this country.

Globalization the process by which markets, technologies, cultures, and businesses are homogenizing and becoming accessible everywhere on the planet. The term also refers to the process of moving jobs and capital to the place where they will reap the largest return (as when jobs move to low wage countries).

Governance an amalgam of policy, regulation, law, commercial and consumer practices, and organizational behaviour. In the face of considerable uncertainty as to who has control of the Internet, there is much concern over 'Internet governance', especially as a partial antidote to the free rein of 'cyber-libertarian' notions.

Hashtag a tag prefaced by the 'hash' or pound character (#) to demarcate it as a tag and thereby render it more visible for searches, this usage has been popularized on Twitter.

Hypertext now associated almost exclusively with the blue underlined words that provide links on web pages, the term was coined by Ted Nelson in 1963 for his 'Project Xanadu'.

Information society a society dominated by the movement and use of information, and information and communication technology.

Infringement the act of mis-using copyrighted material (often mislabelled as piracy or stealing) by failing to obtain a licence where necessary. See **fair use.**

Innovation the process by which people or organizations turn ideas into new products and services that are brought to the market.

Innovator's dilemma a choice that confronts those who develop new technologies, of whether to work on new (replacement) technologies, even while the existing ones are doing well in the marketplace. The term was coined by Clay Christensen to describe a trap that many companies fall into, failing to notice the next big thing.

Interactive the ability to contribute to as well as consume media; it is generally reserved for activities that extend beyond merely changing channels. Internet services are almost all interactive

Interface the way a user experiences software or hardware, epitomized by the WIMP (windows, icons, menu, pointer) desktop that has become the standard for computer operating systems.

Knowledge economy an economy characterized by a high level of dependence, internally and in the form of trade, on knowledge creation, distribution, and exports.

Lead user innovation attending to, and adopting if possible, the changes made by your leading customers when they adapt or extend your product.

Libertarianism a political and economic theory that posits the primacy of freedom and especially economic freedom to allow markets to regulate human affairs. Often associated with American author Ayn Rand and also linked to some early Internet activists.

Long tail the large number of items which make up a small sales volume individually but together may account for a non-trivial opportunity for retailers— such as Amazon.com— who can deliver these goods to people who want them. The term was coined by Chris Anderson of *Wired* magazine to illustrate the power of online access to the enormous number of books (and other objects) that wouldn't merit stocking in a brick-and-mortar store.

Luddite a follower of nineteenth-century labour activist Ned Ludd, who advocated smashing the then-new weaving machine. Now often used as a blanket term for someone who opposes all things new, it has been revived as 'neo-luddism' by critics of new technologies in the late twentieth and early twenty-first centuries who have pointed out the rationality in Ludd's resistance to forces that were destroying families and communities.

Metcalfe's Law more of an observation than an actual law of nature, Robert Metcalfe predicted that the value of a network lay in the number of possible connections between the members—or nodes—in the network.

Microblogging posting short messages (typically the length of a mobile phone text message, on which the business was premised, at first) to a website for sharing with others. Twitter is the best known of these, but this would also include the posting of short status updates to your Facebook wall.

Modding the modification, typically by end-users or groups of end-users, of the content or user interface of a game, usually with the tacit approval of the game designers, who make it possible by exposing their game engine to alternative content.

Multiplayer games games that are connected, via computer network, to servers enabling many people to play together at the same time. These are also known as massively multiplayer online games (MMOG), or massively multiplayer online role playing games (MMORPG), such as World of Warcraft. These terms had their origins in earlier multi-user dungeons (MUDs) and MUDs object-oriented (MOOs).

Multiplexing the process of encoding multiple streams of information into a single stream to make maximum use of a scarce resource such as a telegraph or telephone line and more recently mobile phone radio channels and fibre optics.

Network neutrality a principle, borrowed from transportation regulation, whereby the company agreeing to carry goods cannot discriminate between customers who wish to transport similar goods. This is sometimes referred to as the separation of carriage and content. It is widely applied in telecommunications pricing and regulation and most recently in the management of the Internet.

Network operator the provider of service to mobile telephones. The provider arranges for the radio spectrum licences, creates the billing and customer service functions, installs the infrastructure for transmitting and receiving calls and—if necessary— transferring them to other networks (wireless or landline). Network operators also provide additional features such as text messaging, caller identification, voice mail, and Internet service.

Network society a society in which individuals and groups are organized as a type of richly interconnected network rather than a hierarchy, with a resulting emphasis on trust and reciprocity rather than power. Information, and information and communication technology, occupy a special place in such societies.

Open source computer software that is offered with full access to the underlying coding, enabling users to change and adapt the software. It is also known as free software. A variety of licences have evolved for this type of software, covering a range of applications and 'freeness'. In some cases, you are required to keep any derivative works similarly free, in other cases you are free to create a proprietary commercial product.

Packet switching the process by which messages are converted into small bundles (packets), each with its own address information, to permit message passing by simple computers.

Paper tape developed during the days of the telegraph, this was a method of storing messages to be transmitted later, or recording incoming messages for later decoding. Recording was done by punching holes in a paper tape and reading was accomplished by sensing those holes with a light or metal rods. This technique was adapted for use in early computers.

Political economy approach an examination of society that regards law, economy, and the political environment being interrelated and help to establish and sustain the social order. In new media studies this typically focuses on an examination of the regulation and ownership of media.

Post-Fordist a production logic that differs from the classic assembly line factory pioneered by Henry Ford. Post-Fordist production is characterized by multiple small players and independent ownership of the various components and suppliers. The ability to economically manage the complicated relationships in a post-Fordist production chain is dependent on information and communication technology.

Predictive text (also known as autocompletion) a software service embedded in many mobile phones to allow for faster and more accurate entry of words in text messages from a simple numeric or alphanumeric keyboard, it works by predicting, based on a statistical analysis of the entry language, the most likely next character or characters.

Pro-Am Revolution the emergence of 'professional amateurs', people who are producing media content that rivals professional media in terms of quality. This process is often enabled by new technologies such as digital recording and editing that are cheaper, smaller, and nearly as capable as their professional equivalents. It is controversial to the extent that pro-ams begin to siphon funding away from professionals, or lower the prices paid for media (e.g., stock photography).

Public domain works of art (including software, movies, music) that are no longer or have been explicitly removed from copyright protection. Works can be placed into the public domain or they can move into the public domain after a period of time has elapsed.

Radio spectrum see **Electromagnetic spectrum**.

Recombinant the characteristic of digital goods that allows them to be repurposed and reused relatively easily by users with simple tools found on a computer, also known as the mashup.

Remediate in the Bolter and Grusin sense, this describes how new media adopts and extends old media.

Scanning a method of breaking a picture (or later, a series of pictures) into discrete elements for encoding and transmission to a remote location. This process was pioneered with the telegraph (wire photos) and was repurposed for fax machines, television (as a series of pictures), and again for computers.

Smartphone a mobile phone that has the ability to surf the Internet and download and install third party applications. Examples include the BlackBerry, iPhone, and various Android phones.

Social capital an attempt to describe in economic terms the assets one possesses in the form of relationships with others. This takes the form of bonding (strong ties between closely connected individuals, as in a family), bridging (weaker ties, as within a community or group), and linking (connections between different groups or levels).

Social network the face-to-face or electronic relations between people for formal and informal purposes. In the context of this text, this includes especially those aspects enabled or harmed by new media.

Social network analysis (network analysis) a method for the academic study of social networks, with special attention to actors, ties between actors, network structure (patterns of ties), and major influences (such as culture) on the formation and durability of networks.

Social networking (social software, social networking software) websites that are designed around connections between users. A key feature of these sites is the ability to identify friends or followers and to keep up to date with their activities online.

Social production the creation of goods and services, including 'informational goods', in a social or collaborative fashion. Many aspects of user generated content can be included here, but social production is not necessarily outside the market economy. Wikipedia is a classic example of social production.

Social shaping of technology an alternative approach to **technological determinism** that seeks to explain technological change in terms of the influence of key social groups.

Spime a neologism invented by writer Bruce Sterling to describe an object that can be tracked through space and time. The typical application would be inventory control but this is being expanded in all directions as low cost sensors and memory chips (and especially radio frequency identification chips, or RFID) combined with ubiquitous wireless networks make it feasible to embed these capabilities in more and more objects.

Surveillance the coordinated and organized observation of someone in order to control or affect his or her behaviour. Surveillance has commercial, state, personal, and criminal aspects and all of these are greatly influenced by new media. A simple example would be analyzing purchasing trends according to status updates on Twitter.

Tacit knowledge knowledge that is not written down, not codified, and thereby more difficult (than **explicit knowledge,** see above) to share. It is often acquired by learning-by-doing, rather than in a classroom.

Tag (tagging) a descriptive term for a piece of content or a key word, also the act of applying these tags. See also **Folksonomy**.

Technological determinism an approach to technology that posits unmediated outcomes from the use of technology, and in its extreme form, a kind of self-determination and internal logic to the evolution of technology. Often the result of short-hand thinking, e.g., 'Computers are getting faster all the time.' The writer, if pressed, probably does not believe that somehow computers are, on their own, getting faster, but it is easy to slip into saying things like this, given the regular and predictable progress in many technological forms.

Technology S-curve a description of the diffusion of innovations over time, with a few people adopting at first (the bottom of the 'S'), a great number once it is well known (the middle of the 'S') and then gradually tapering off as fewer and fewer new users are found (the top of the 'S').

Telegraph a device developed in the early-nineteenth century for sending coded messages long distances over wires (and later using radio waves). This technology formed the first global network, prompting one writer to call it 'the Victorian Internet'.

Tetrad a mode of inquiry into new media, proposed by Canadian media theorist Marshall McLuhan. McLuhan suggested that when one is considering the impact of a new media form we should ask four questions: what does it enhance? What does it retrieve from the past? What does it change into when pushed to the extreme? What does it erode or obsolesce?

Text messaging (texting, SMS) the process of using mobile telephones to send short messages (140 characters, typically) using a signalling channel built into the phone system. Messages can come from the system operator, or (more commonly) from other mobile phone users.

Three strikes a provision in the copyright enforcement provisions in some countries whereby there is a graduated response to infringing acts (typically file sharing on the Internet). The third accusation results in an automatic punishment of some type, usually being cut off from the Internet. Modelled on three strikes laws in the US that result in mandatory incarceration for some crimes, the provision has been deemed unconstitutional in some countries in part because of the accusation aspect—no conviction is required—and in part because access to the Internet is increasingly seen as a basic human right. The impact on families—where a child may have done the infringing—is also a concern.

Traffic shaping the application of rules to restrict the bandwidth allocated to some protocols on the Internet in order to provide more bandwidth to others. This technique is commonly used to restrict the speed of file sharing and ensure speedy web surfing. It is considered by some to be a violation of **network neutrality** rules.

Universal service a policy objective common in Canada during the early days of telephone service and rural electrification that sought to extend these services beyond their urban origins to rural areas. There has been pressure to apply the same principles to Internet access and even broadband Internet access.

User-centred innovation innovation led by the users, who may build amateur or home built versions of what they hope to use, but which is then adopted, refined, and manufactured by companies.

User-Generated Content the unpaid contributions of the users of a service, which often times constitutes the bulk of the content (over 90 per cent in the case of YouTube). This is also known as peer production.

Web 2.0 sometimes called the 'read write' web, Web 2.0 refers to a website in which the contributions to and evolution of the site happens through the web, by the users of the website.

Notes

Chapter 1

1. The term 'information' is being defined broadly as all forms of message and symbol that are communicated to others, which include those forms that can be considered original knowledge, but also a vast range of other forms that are communicated. One of the difficulties in using the term in relation to new media, such as theories of the 'information society', is that it implies a second, narrower definition, where information is associated with forms of knowledge that advance the understanding of the receiver about their social and physical environment. Any cursory glance at the web, or any other digital media platform, will find an abundance of content that would constitute information in the former sense, but not the latter. The common tendency to conflate access to more information with greater personal and social knowledge has been widely critiqued (e.g., Castells 1999; Graham 1999).

2. The best histories of the Internet have been written by those directly involved in its development, such as Leiner et al. (2003), Berners-Lee (2000), and Gillies and Cailliau (2000), who provide important insiders' accounts of the development of the web. A useful chronology of the development of computers that is very much informed by the development of the Internet can be found in Hirst and Harrison (2006: 207–12).

3. This question is discussed in Rheingold (1994), Hafner and Lyon (1996), Castells (1996a: 41–6; 2001: 39–46), Leiner et al. (2003), and Hassan (2004). Castells (2001) argues that it is more useful to see the culture of early Internet developers as being a techno-meritocratic one, strongly grounded in academic protocols of shared pursuit of science, peer review, and sharing research findings, rather than a culture grounded in military service. The research centres of universities such as MIT, Harvard, and Stanford were central points for its development.

4. The Internet was already changing with the arrival of 'gopher,' but that is a pre-history of the web that is beyond the scope of the present discussion. Those with an interest can do a search and read up on gopher!

5. See the original press release on the Flickr blog: http://blog.flickr.net/en/2005/03/20/yahoo-actually-does-acquire-flickr.

6. You can still watch the video of the trip to the zoo: http://youtube.com/watch?v=jNQXAC9IVRw.

7. Statistics on YouTube are notoriously unreliable as a 'view' is only counted when the video is watched to the end, and a video may appear many, many times on the site and is also referenced in hundreds or even thousands (as this one is) 'response' videos. If you haven't seen 'The Evolution of Dance', here it is: www.youtube.com/watch?v=dMH0bHeiRNg.

8. It wasn't just the news media that solicited and used amateur video. The British police actively encouraged people with cell phone footage to come forward and contribute anything that might help solve the crime. See this story from the BBC, 'Police appeal for bombing footage', available at http://news.bbc.co.uk/2/hi/uk_news/4668675.stm.

9. The description of the Internet as a place to help people 'understand the world around them' came in an interview with CNN, in the fall of 2006, when Zuckerberg was just 22 years old and starting to open the Facebook site up to people outside of its initial target, college students. At that point the site already had 10 million members. See http://money.cnn.com/2006/10/06/magazines/fortune/fastforward_facebook.fortune/index.htm.

10. See this article from *Fortune* magazine: '"FarmVille" gamemaker Zygna sees dollar signs', Jessica Shambora, 26 October 2009, http://brainstormtech.blogs.fortune.cnn.com/2009/10/26/farmville-gamemaker-zynga-sees-dollar-signs.

11. The number of Internet hosts is inevitably less than the number of Internet users, since multiple users will access the Internet from a single host, as seen

in the worldwide proliferation of Internet cafés for travellers. The number of Internet hosts, or sites from which connection to a server is made, is easier to measure than the number of people who access the Internet.

12. See Kate Milberry's 2009 PhD Thesis from Simon Fraser University: *Geeks and Global Justice: Another (Cyber) World is Possible.*

13. Based on an interview with Robert Ouimet, executive producer of three websites (120seconds.com, newmusiccanada.com, and justconcerts.com) that made up the component parts 'Radio 3', a pioneering online initiative created by the Canadian Broadcasting Corporation between 2000 and 2005. The site has evolved, and the three parts have been folded in to one main site (radio3.cbc.ca), but the history of Radio3 is an important milestone in new media in Canada.

Chapter 2

1. This historical approach to new media is presented in much greater detail, and with a warm and eminently readable style, by Canadian scholar Wade Rowland in his excellent book, *Spirit of the Web: The Age of Information from Telegraph to Internet,* (Toronto: Thomas Allen & Son, 2006). Now in its third edition, Rowland's book is an excellent resource in the field of new media and media studies generally.

2. Morse Code was created in the 1840s for Samuel Morse's first telegraph. Although based on 'dots' and 'dashes', there were also different pauses between these elements (which were transmitted as a buzz or click on early systems), resulting in six different discrete elements. An even earlier system for binary encoding of messages, the Braille system for creating letters with raised dots on paper, was invented in 1821 and is still in widespread use today to enable the blind to read by touch. See http://en.wikipedia.org/wiki/Braille for details.

3. Some of these models for revenue sharing and technical standards had already been worked out for the international postal network that existed prior to the telegraph, and in many countries the telegraph was set up as an extension of the post ('PTT', or post, telegraph, and telephone, is an acronym that you still see in Europe).

4. See also James Carey for his important chapter (Chapter 8) on the telegraph and its role in breaking the link between transportation and communication in *Communication as Culture: Essays on Media and Society,* (New York and London: Routledge, 1989).

5. As Briscoe, Odlyzko, and Tilly point out in their 2006 *IEEE Spectrum* article, this 'law' is 'a rough empirical description, not an immutable physical law. See http://spectrum.ieee.org/computing/networks/metcalfes-law-is-wrong/0.

6. The story of the origins of telegraph regulation is told masterfully by Matthew Lasar in an *ars technica* post called, 'How Robber Barons hijacked the "Victorian Internet"', http://arstechnica.com/tech-policy/news/2009/12/how-the-robber-barons-hijacked-the-victorian-internet.ars. Accessed 30 December 2009.

7. Walter P. Phillips, *The Phillips Code, Telephone and Telegraph Age,* (New York, 1879 [1975]). Available at www.radions.net/philcode.htm. Accessed 29 December 2009).

8. Phillips, p. 2.

9. This is chronicled in a fascinating article published in the 17 December 2009 issue of *The Economist.* The article, entitled 'Network effects', appeared as part of a series on newspapers and technology. It is available here: http://www.economist.com/node/15108618?story_id=15108618. Accessed 11 November 2010.

10. Stillman, 'Journalism and Literature', p. 689.

11. Thoreau, *Walden* Vol. 1, p. 84.

12. Anonymous, 'Network Effects', *The Economist,* (17 December 2009, www.economist.com/displayStory.cfm?STORY_ID=15108618).

13. According to the Wikipedia page on 'The Victorian Internet' (a euphemism for the telegraph, and as noted earlier, the title of a book about the Internet), 'besides news reporting, telegraphy, as the first true global network, permitted applications such as message routing, social networks (between Morse operators—with gossip and even marriages among operators via telegraph being

observed), instant messaging, cryptography and text coding, abbreviated language slang, network security experts, hackers, wire fraud, mailing lists, spamming, e-commerce, stock exchange minute-by-minute reports via ticker tape machines, and many others.' See http://en.wikipedia.org/wiki/Victorian_Internet.

14. Although it would seem clear enough that taking the coding out of the telegraph process would make the ability to transmit messages useful for most people, as it happens, the largest operator of telegraph networks at the time—Western Union—turned down a chance to buy Bell's emergent telephone company when given the chance. They did not see the innovation as a viable business and declined to purchase the company.

15. A rival telephone inventor arrived moments after Bell. Eventually, his technology was incorporated into the Bell telephone design via a licence. As we continue to see, new media technologies are often tangled up in patent disputes—the patent war between Apple and Microsoft a few years ago about the 'Windows' interface is an example—and these sometimes delay or distract the inventors in their early days.

16. AT&T's Ralph de la Vega, head of the wireless unit, said (9 December 2009), that 'AT&T is considering incentives to keep [iPhone] subscribers from hampering the experience for everyone else.' See http://blogs.wsj.com/digits/2009/12/09/att-to-new-york-and-san-francisco-were-working-on-it.

17. There are some wonderful old instructional films available on YouTube, showing people how to dial a telephone. See, for example, www.youtube.com/watch?v=CIDw75mUl6c, complete with an example of what 'dial tone,' 'ringing', and 'busy' sound like, along with making a call using the then-usual '5-digit' dialing. These instructional films would have been played at the beginning and end of feature films in theatres, as a way of informing the public of important issues, just as we now have advertisements for popcorn and movie trailers. Cell phone users are unfamiliar with 'dial tone', of course, and quite often never hear a busy signal either, as the cell service provider merely pops up an offer to redial.

18. Early telephones, which relied on a hand crank or buzzer to 'ring Central' (get the operator's attention), did have a crude form of direct dialing to their immediate neighbours—they could buzz or crank a special code to get their neighbours on the line without bothering the operator. This worked for the small number of people who shared that wire, called a 'party line'. Other niceties existed, such as making a small ring when you were done, so others knew the line was available, and a special ring for emergencies. In a way, these practices foretell later uses such as chat rooms and chat lines (commonly used for sex talk these days) that have been recreated using modern technologies. Recreating existing practices is a common occurrence in new media.

19. See Daniel G. Dorner, 'The Essential Services Policy Network: Organizational Influence in Canada's Information Highway Policy Development Process', *The Library Quarterly*, Vol. 72, No. 1 (Chicago: The University of Chicago Press, January 2002), pp. 27–84, www.jstor.org/stable/4309581. See also Glenn Fleishman, 'The Killer App of 1900', *Publicola*, 11 December 2009 (retrieved 15 December 2009 from http://publicola.net/?p=20687). The telephone regulator in Canada, the Canadian Radio-television and Telecommunications Commission (CRTC), issued a call for a review of the definition of 'essential service' in 2006 (see www.crtc.gc.ca/eng/archive/2006/pt2006-14.htm) and issued a decision in 2008 (www.crtc.gc.ca/eng/archive/2008/dt2008-17.htm). In the main, however, these regulations are applicable to telephone companies regarding their wholesale operations and how they are required to share infrastructure ('essential services') to ensure effective competition.

20. See Manovich, *The Language of New Media*, p. 50.

21. See this interview from the CBC archives with the tale of Fessenden's invention of radio: http://archives.cbc.ca/science_technology/technology/clips/10258. Read more about Fessenden at this page honouring the centenary of his achievement (the first broadcast was Christmas Day, 1906): http://blogs.voices.com/voxdaily/2007/01/radio.html.

23. The early history of radio is quite detailed but you can get a nice sense of it from the wonderful chronology, presented in a series of overlapping 'eras', at http://earlyradiohistory.us. The story of Frank Conrad's early radio broadcasts is told there and in a number of books and articles. A useful starting point can be found here: http://en.wikipedia.org/wiki/Frank_Conrad.

24. Godfrey (1982) points out that radio regulation in Canada was 'tentative' and left to a civil servant, variously in the office of Public Works, Fisheries, or the Navy. A Royal Commission on Broadcasting did not take place until 1928 and the first Broadcasting Act did not appear until 1934 (1982: 60).

25. In Britain, with a single government-run broadcaster for many years, there was a form of subscription broadcasting through radio licenses that everyone who owned a radio (and later a television) had to pay. This money subsidized the creation of programs and meant that radio programs were mostly free of advertising. In Canada, the government 'sponsored' the CBC but allowed it to also run advertising. When television came along, the decision was made to remove all advertising from CBC radio.

26. A detailed timeline, not only of television but of radio as well, can be found here: www.hammond-museumofradio.org/dates.html.

27. Details of the coronation, including a copy of the video, can be found in the CBC Archives: Coronation of Queen Elizabeth II, http://archives.cbc.ca/on_this_day/06/02.

28. For more information on the 'media ecology' literature, a good source is the Media Ecology Association (MEA), 'a not-for-profit organization dedicated to promoting the study, research, criticism, and application of media ecology in educational, industry, political, civic, social, cultural, and artistic contexts, and the open exchange of ideas, information, and research' (MEA 2010). The MEA website (www.media-ecology.org) highlights the work of prominent scholars in the field, such as Walter Ong, Elizabeth Eisenstein, Eric Havelock, Jacques Ellul, Harold Innis, Marshall McLuhan, and others.

Chapter 3

1. A marvelous and easy to follow explanation of tetrads can be found on Anthony Hempell's website, www.anthonyhempell.com/papers/tetrad/concept.html. See also the Wikipedia page for the concept: http://en.wikipedia.org/wiki/Tetrad_of_media_effects. Libraries and Archives Canada maintains an 'Innis and McLuhan' page that includes a section on the tetrad as well. You can find it here: www.collectionscanada.gc.ca/innis-mcluhan/030003-2030-e.html, including a variety of multimedia elements and recordings of McLuhan using his tetrad analysis.

Chapter 4

1. This process of licences for wireless devices continues but the design of the cellular system makes so many available that the government issues spectrum in aggregate to the cellular operator (e.g., Bell Mobility) and they manage the process—by having you subscribe to their service—for you. It is completely transparent—and requires no training—to the end-user.

2. "... the best general arrangement of frequency assignments for the minimum interference and the minimum number of frequencies is a hexagonal layout in which each station is surrounded by six equidistant adjacent stations" (p. 3). The original memo, titled 'Mobile Telephony—Wide Area Coverage', is dated 11 December 1947 and authored by D.H. Ring of Bell Telephone. See Ring, D.H. (1947) 'Mobile Telephony—Wide Area Coverage', Bell Laboratories Technical Memo #TA4 47-1 60-37, 11 December 1947.

3. This switching from tower to tower is called 'hand off' and it is a very tricky business. Thankfully the whole process is invisible to users of mobile phones and we can quite happily make a call while zooming along at highway speeds.

4. The price per megabyte is not what people are thinking about when they send text messages, of course. Nevertheless, at 15 cents per 140 characters—current cost for a single message in Canada—that is over $100 per megabyte. By

comparison, data on a mobile phone is available for under $10 per megabyte ($100 per gigabyte) and under $2 per megabyte ($20 per gigabyte) on a home connection.

5. There is even HSDPA and HSUPA (the 'd' and 'u' being 'up' and 'down,' respectively) and sometimes a '+' sign is added to indicate that it is even better for data services. In reality a lot of this is like the specifications for automobiles, great on paper but 'your mileage may vary'.

6. Much of the nomenclature relating to mobile networks is an endlessly confusing array of acronyms and code words. These are made even more confusing because the most widely used terms—like 3G—are little more than marketing terminology or shorthand for engineers. Sometimes there are efforts to more rigidly define the terms, but these inevitably fall victim to 'fast and loose' application of the terminology by vendors keen to sell their technology as the solution to a particular problem. LTE is already being marketed as 4G, for example, although it is not entirely clear that this is justified or that the delivered products fully support the specified capabilities. This is a replay of the situation with 3G, which was delivered by various vendors through various telecommunications service providers at various speeds and prices and continues to be remarkably variable.

7. Current numbers available at http://148apps.biz/app-store-metrics.

8. Similar alarms have been raised about so-called 'L33T-speak' as used in instant messaging programs like MSM and in the chat rooms of games.

9. BBC, 'Over 5 billion mobile phone connections worldwide', 9 July 2010, http://news.bbc.co.uk/2/hi/technology/10569081.stm. Accessed 11 July 2010. See also this analysis of the implications of 5 billion subscribers (and the estimate of 7 billion by 2015): Sam Churchill, '5 Billion Mobile Subscribers', dailywireless.org, 11 July 2010, www.dailywireless.org/2010/07/11/5-billion-mobile-subscribers. Accessed 11 July 2010.

10. The 'war' is ongoing, of course, and things are never as they seem. As this chapter was being written (January 2010), the Amazon Kindle suddenly acquired a 'developer's kit' and news emerged about an 'App Store', making it much more of a general purpose device, albeit one focused on reading, than it was the week before.

11. Royal Society of Canada, 'A review of the potential health risks of radiofrequency fields from wireless telecommunications devices', Expert panel report prepared by the Royal Society of Canada for Health Canada. (Ottawa: Royal Society of Canada, RSC.EPR 99-1, 1999).

12. Modern mobile phone and data services typically use very high frequencies but low power settings. The combination means that the signal is effectively limited to a 'line of sight' and cannot easily penetrate obstructions. This, along with the 'cell' approach to creating capacity, means lots and lots of antennae (unlike the old days of radio and television where one large tower could suffice for a major city).

13. Incorporated in 1984, Research In Motion won both an Emmy and an Oscar (Academy Award for Technical Achievement) for the 'DigiSync Film KeyKode Reader'. See www.berryreview.com/2009/02/12/the-history-of-rim-the-blackberry-smartphone-part-1-the-origins.

14. See the RIM web page on 'super apps' here: http://na.blackberry.com/eng/developers/started/super_apps.jsp.

15. The founders of RIM have donated generously to the Perimeter Institute among other things at the University of Waterloo. Jim Basilie, alone, donated $170 million to the institute.

16. Details of the 2008 request can be found in a PC World article by John Ribeiro, 'RIM Says It Can't Provide E-mail Interception in India', 26 May 2008, www.pcworld.com/businesscenter/article/146306/rim_says_it_cant_provide_email_interception_in_india.html. The 2010 dispute is covered by Mike Masnick of Techdirt, in 'Indian Government Demands Right to Spy on Skype, Gmail, Blackberry Messages', 7 July 2010, http://techdirt.com/articles/20100702/17551510065.shtml.

17. See the story here: Anonymous, '100 Fastest Growing Companies 2009', Fortune, http://money.cnn.com/magazines/fortune/fortunefastestgrowing/2009/index.html. Accessed 7 July 2010.

18. The CBC has a timeline with many milestones in the life of Research In Motion. It is available here: www.cbc.ca/news/background/rim.

Chapter 5

1. For example, over twenty *hours* of video are uploaded every minute to YouTube. See this posting from the YouTube blog: http://youtube-global.blogspot.com/2009/05/zoinks-20-hours-of-video-uploaded-every_20.html.
2. For a useful primer on the social graph, see Alex Iskold's 12 September 2007 article, 'Social Graph: Concepts and Issues', published in The Read Write Web and available at www.readwriteweb.com/archives/social_graph_concepts_and_issues.php.
3. Quoted from CBS News, 'Facebook: One Graph to Rule them All?', 21 April 2010. www.cbsnews.com/stories/2010/04/21/tech/main6418458.shtml. Accessed 12 November 2010.
4. Steve Whittaker, Loren Terveen, Will Hill, and Lynn Cherny, 'The dynamics of mass interaction', Proceedings of CSCW 98, the ACM Conference on Computer-Supported Cooperative Work (Seattle, WA, November 14–8, 1998), pp. 257–64. See also Nielsen's summary of the research here: www.useit.com/alertbox/participation_inequality.html.

Chapter 6

1. Hollywood and the games world have of course had more successful subsequent liaisons, most notably with the *Lara Croft* (Tomb Raider) films, starring Angelina Jolie as the versatile action heroine.
2. It is estimated, for instance, that Microsoft lost USD $1.5 billion in the first 18 months of the launch of its Xbox, but saw this as a necessary condition for its being able to capture market share from more established players like Sony and Nintendo, as well as establishing its credibility in the games development community as an industry player in for the long haul.
3. Industry insight on this and almost any other aspect of the games industry can be found on the MobyGames website. Details on Mattrick and Distinctive Software from this page: www.mobygames.com/company/distinctive-software-inc.
4. Full details on the Ontario program available at the Ontario Media Development Corporation (OMDC) website: www.omdc.on.ca/Page3400.aspx.
5. Florence Chee and Richard Smith, 'Online gamers and the ambiguity of community: Korean definitions of togetherness for a new generation', in M. Consalvo and C. Haythornthwaite (eds), *AOIR Internet Annual*, Volume 4, (New York: Peter Lang Publishers, 2007), pp. 165–84.
6. For a fascinating account of the difficulties in presenting academic research on games to politicians and in the media that does not draw on the 'moral panic' cause-and-effect model, see Henry Jenkins' description of his appearance before the US Congress shortly after the Littleton shootings. Jenkins, Henry. (2006). 'Congressional Testimony on Media Violence', MIT Communications Forum. Available at http://web.mit.edu/comm-forum/papers/jenkins_ct.html. Accessed November 13, 2010.
7. Florence Chee and Richard Smith, 'Is Electronic Community an Addictive Substance? An Ethnographic Offering from the Everquest Community', in S. Schaffer and M. Price (eds) *Interactive Convergence in Multimedia – Probing the Boundaries* (Vol. 10), (Freeland: UK: The Interdisciplinary Press, 2005), pp. 137–56.
8. The pink software movement was a focus of this particular debate. In the 1990s a number of companies were formed to make 'pink' software— games that were designed to appeal to girls. The most notable of these was Purple Moon. However there was much disagreement about whether creating 'special' games for girls had the effect of marginalizing them, and whether a better tactic would be to integrate different styles into more mainstream games. It was also disputed that current games were not appealing to girls (deCastell and Bryson 1998) and that the nature of play was in fact gendered at all. See also Sara M. Grimes, 'Deconstructing the Girl Gamer: From the Girls' Games Movement to Rule of Rose', paper presented at the Canadian Communication

Association (CCA) Annual Conference, University of British Columbia, June 4-6, Vancouver, British Columbia, 2008.

9. For more on this topic see J. Kucklich, 'Precarious Playbour: Modders and the Digital Games Industry,' *Fibreculture* 5 (2005).

Chapter 7

1. The 'arts multiplier' refers to those studies that seek to demonstrate that investment of public funds in arts activities generates economic and on-economic benefits greater than the cost of the original investment (e.g., a tourism industry that benefits from a town that hosts a major festival). Seaman (2000) has argued that such studies are plagued by the problem of double-counting, and the tendency to ignore what economists call *opportunity cost*, or the question of whether the same investment of funds on another activity may have generated greater benefits. The fact that such stud ies are usually linked to advocacy on the part of a particular arts organization or arts funding agency has not helped to diminish their reputation among economists for being a form of industry special pleading that lacks methodological rigour (cf. Madden 2001).

2. The notion that culture is an important part of the mayoral campaign resurfaced in the 2010 campaign as well. See, for example, this review of some of the position statements released in the middle of 2010 by mayoral candidates in Toronto: Shannon Litzenberger, 'Will Toronto's Next Mayor Champion The Arts?', *The Mark News*, 9 July 2010, www.themarknews.com/articles/1837. Accessed 9 July 2010.

Chapter 8

1. This 'discreteness' claim is debatable, since in some cases a small piece is more valuable than the totality. A good example is a six second drum sequence (the 'Amen break') that was included in a forgettable and long forgotten B-side from a 1969 single but since being 'sampled' and included in dozens of other songs has come to be much more

valuable. See the fascinating story of this process explained in Nate Harrison's 2004 YouTube video: http://youtu.be/5SaFTm2bcac. Accessed 15 July 2010.

2. Google Blog, 'We knew the web was big …', 2008, http://googleblog.blogspot.com/2008/07/we-knew-web-was-big.html. Accessed 2 July 2010.

3. See David Kravetz, 'Google Wins Viacom Copyright Lawsuit', *Wired*. 23 June 2010, www.wired.com/threatlevel/2010/06/dmca-protects-youtube. Accessed 3 July 2010.

Chapter 9

1. Among the key national information policy statements of the 1990s were the US government's *National Information Infrastructure Task Force* (1993); the European Union's *Europe and the Information Superhighway* (Bangemann Report) (1994); Singapore's *IT2000-Vision of an Intelligent Island* (1992); the Canadian government's *The Canadian Information Highway: Building Canada's Information Infrastructure* (1994); Japan's *Program for Advanced Information Infrastructure* (1994); the Australian government's *Creative Nation* (1994) and *Networking Australia's Future* (1995) reports; the Malaysian government's *Multimedia Super Corridor* strategy (1995); Korea's *Information Strategies for Promoting National Competitiveness* (1996); and the OECD's *Global Information Infrastructure-Global Information Society* report (1997). See Northfield (1999) for an extended commentary on these; cf. Barr (2000), pp. 169–74.

2. This report was published in *Canada, Industry Canada, Connection, Community, Content: The Challenge of the Information Highway, Final Report* (Phase I) of the Information Highway Advisory Council, Ottawa, September 1995.

3. In June of 2010 the Heritage Minister (James Moore) famously claimed that opponents to a bill he was proposing in Parliament (C-32, relating to new copyright provisions) were 'radical extremists', seemingly including the 8,000 Canadians who had participated in the government's own consultation process. See commentary and analysis here: Michael Geist, 'Who are James

Moore's "Radical Extremists"', Michael Geist Blog, 22 June 2010, www.michaelgeist.ca/content/view/5137/125. Accessed 15 July 2010.

4. See H.G. Bown, *Telidon*, CRC Technical report ; no. 697-E₂ (Ottawa: Communications Research Centre, 1978).

5. See Government of Ontario, 'Ontario Computer Animation And Special Effects Tax Credit', 2009, www.omdc.on.ca/Page3402.aspx. Accessed 29 January 2010.

6. See Telefilm Canada, 'Canada New Media Fund – Product Assistance', 2009, www.telefilm. gc.ca/03/311.asp?lang=en&fond_id=3. Accessed 28 January 2010.

7. Forbearance was specifically inserted into the Telecommunications Act of 1993 as the government sought to increase market competition in telecommunication services. The first decision that took advantage of the new 'power to forbear' (i.e., to opt not to regulate in an area in which the regulator had a legal jurisdiction), was in 1994 in relation to 'non-dominant' (small, or new) cellular phone providers. Full text of the decision can be found on the CRTC website: www.crtc.gc.ca/eng/archive/1994/PT94-44.htm.

8. Internet forbearance came in July 1998 in Telecom Public Notice CRTC 98-17, 'Internet Forbearance'. The full text of the decision can be found on the CRTC website: www.crtc.gc.ca/eng/archive/1998/PT98-17.htm.

10. The principle was confirmed in a 8 July 2010 ruling from the Federal Court of Canada. Details available online at Michael Geist, 'Federal Court of Appeal Rules ISPs not Broadcasters', 7 July 2010, www.michaelgeist.ca/content/view/5176/125. Accessed 8 July 2010.

11. CRTC decisions are available from your library or at the CRTC website. Here is the link to decision 2009-677, 'Canadian Association of Internet Providers et al. and Vaxination Informatique– Application to review and vary certain determinations in Telecom Decision 2008-108 related to Bell Canada's Internet traffic management practices', Ottawa, 29 October 2009: www.crtc.gc.ca/eng/archive/2009/2009-677.htm.

12. See Telecom Decision 2008-108 (in which the case against Bell is considered, and dismissed) and Telecom Decision 2009-677 (in which the appeal is dismissed). Both decisions are available at the CRTC website: http://crtc.gc.ca.

13. Importantly for scholars, these fair dealing rights have been preserved in recent court cases such as 'CCH', in which a legal publisher sued a law library for sending copies of articles printed in its journals to researchers. The law library was deemed to be exercising a fair dealing right for the purposes of research. See CCH Canadian Ltd. v. Law Society of Upper Canada, 2004 SCC 13, [2004] 1 S.C.R. 339 available at http://csc.lexum.umontreal.ca/en/2004/2004scc13/2004scc13.html. Accessed 15 July 2010. See also the Department of Canadian Heritage's web page with advice on fair dealing in Canada, available here: www.canadianheritage.gc.ca/pc-ch/org/sectr/ac-ca/pda-cpb/publctn/cch-2007/102-eng.cfm.

14. Read the full posting here: Eric Hillman, 'Offline Book "Lending" Costs U.S. Publishers Nearly $1 Trillion', 15 January 2010, http://go-to-hellman.blogspot.com/2010/01/offline-book-lending-costs-us.html. Accessed 28 January 2010.

15. Michael Geist outlines the concerns, and provides a link to the Brazilian proposal, in this blog post: www.michaelgeist.ca/content/view/5180/125.

16. The term piracy is used six times in a briefing document created by the US Trade Representative, titled 'The Anti-Counterfeiting Trade Agreement – Summary of Key Elements Under Discussion'. It can be downloaded from the web, here: www.ustr.gov/sites/default/files/uploads/factsheets/2009/asset_upload_file917_15546.pdf.

17. See Ian Sparks, 'Internet access is a fundamental human right, rules French court', *Daily Mail*, 12 June 2009, www.dailymail.co.uk/news/worldnews/article-1192359/Internet-access-fundamental-human-right-rules-French-court.html#ixzz153SwOtiH). Accessed 12 November 2010.

18. See www.csmonitor.com/2003/0701/p07s01-woeu.html.

19. The Finnish law came into effect 1 July 2010. Press release from the Finnish Ministry of Transport

and Telecommunications, '1 Mbit Internet access a universal service in Finland from beginning of July', available online at www.lvm.fi/web/en/pressreleases/view/1169259.

20. See www.cebit.com.au/news/technology/spain-decrees-broadband-access-rights.

21. See http://news.bbc.co.uk/2/hi/uk_news/politics/8489870.stm.

22. See CRTC 1995, www.crtc.gc.ca/eng/HIGHWAY/HWY9505.htm.

23. The underlying principle of open software is not simply that it is freely available, but that the source code is made available to all users, who can modify it accordingly. The concept of 'free software' has been associated with Richard Stallman, who founded the Free Software Foundation.

Chapter 10

1. The actual percentage arriving in your email box or in your company's or university's main email service is variable day to day, month to month, and year to year as well as varying according to the activities of the members of that organization—have their email addresses been 'harvested' and sold to spammers, for example? Current data is maintained by a variety of agencies, including WebSense, a spam and virus prevention company, based in the US. Their 'Spam Percentage' page can be located here: http://securitylabs.websense.com/content/spamPercentage.aspx.

2. There is an emerging body of work that is re-marking on the importance of mobile social media in protests and resistance. Recent examples include the use of YouTube in the aftermath of the Iran election in 2009 or the use of Twitter during the G20. See, for example, Antonia Zerbisias, 'Coverage of the G20 proved Twitter's news edge', *Toronto Star*, 11 July 2010, www.thestar.com/news/insight/article/834367. Accessed 11 July 2010. See also the case study on the Citizen Lab in this chapter.

3. See also United States Court of Appeals, District of Columbia Circuit, USA v Mark Wayne Russell, No. 08-3120, 2 April 2010. Available at http://www.wired.com/images_blogs/threatlevel/2010/04/mark_wayne_russell.pdf.

4. The world of 'green broadband' is chronicled in detail by Canadian researcher—and former head of the CANARIE research network—Bill St. Arnaud. His blog, http://green-broadband.blogspot.com, is a gold mine of information on the topic and provides links to research papers, conference proceedings, and recent tests and trials.

5. See Richard Smith, 'University Data Centres and Climate Change', International Association for Management of Technology, Orlando, FL, March (2009).

6. David Eaves, a political commentator and blogger from Vancouver, provided an after the fact evaluation of the outcome of the interviews on his blog, here: http://eaves.ca/2010/03/17/youtube-interviews-strengths-and-weaknesses.

7. Check the answer for yourself, by visiting this page: www.flickr.com/cameras/apple/iphone_4.

8. These numbers were given by Jonathan Heiliger at a conference ('Structure 2010') in June 2010. The remarks were quoted in an article by Alex Williams, 'Twitter: Comparing its Velocity, not Downtime', *Readwrite Cloud*, 10 July 2010, www.readwriteweb.com/cloud/2010/07/twitter-how-its-down-time-comp.php. Accessed 10 July 2010.

9. See European Digital Rights, *Under Surveillance*, 2010, www.edri.org/campaigns/comic-book-under-surveillance. The site has this overview: 'The comic book *Under Surveillance* is an information and awareness tool for young adults created in the European project 'Sensitization and information of young European citizens on the protection of their personal data', where EDRi was one of the partners. The project is coordinated by the French League of Human Rights (LDH), in partnership with the European Association for the Defense of Human Rights (AEDH), European Digital Rights (EDRi), the Czech association Iuridicum Remedium (IuRe) and the Spanish association Comunicació per a la Cooperació (Pangea).' Accessed 15 July 2010.

10. See Noah Elkin, 'Looking Beyond the Staggering Mobile Stats in the BRIC countries', *eMarketer Daily*, 17 March 2010, www.emarketer.com/blog/index.php/staggering-mobile-stats-bric-countries. Accessed 20 March 2010.

11. That both of these online services were later sold to large American companies is both testimony to the success of them as business initiatives and an unfortunate commentary on this country's ability to sustain homegrown firms to the highest level of global competition.

12. Malware is an abbreviation of 'malicious software'. Malware is an omnibus term that includes many different types of software with the common feature of being designed to harass, annoy, or steal. It is generally introduced without the owner's knowledge or consent, often through downloaded programs, images, or web pages.

Bibliography

Aarseth, Espen. 2001. 'Computer Game Studies: Year One', *Game Studies: The International Journal of Computer Game Research* 1(1) www.gamestudies.org/0101. Accessed 25 April 2007.

Abramovitz, Moses, and Paul David. 2001. 'Two Centuries of American Macroeconomic Growth: From Exploitation of Resource Abundance to Knowledge-Driven Development', SIEPR Discussion Paper No. 01–05, Stanford Institute for Economic Policy Research, Stanford, CA: Stanford University.

Ahonen, Tomi. 2010. *Tomi Ahonen Almanac 2010: Mobile Telecoms Industry Review*. Tomiahonene Consulting. Hong Kong.

Akerlof, George. 1970. 'The Market for "Lemons": Quality Uncertainty and the Market Mechanism', *Quarterly Journal of Economics* 84(3): 488–500.

Aksoy, Asu, and Kevin Robins. 1992. 'Hollywood for the 21st Century: Global Competition for Critical Mass in Image Markets', *Cambridge Journal of Economics* 16(1): 1–22.

Aldridge, Stephen, David Halpern, and Sarah Fitzpatrick. 2002. 'Social Capital: A Discussion Paper', Performance and Innovation Unit, London, April.

Amabile, Teresa. 1996. *Creativity in Context*. Boulder, CO: Westview Press.

———. 2004. 'The Six Myths of Creativity', *Fast Company* 89, December, www.fastcompany.com/magazine/89/creativity.html. Accessed 22 April 2007.

Americans for the Arts. 2007. 'Research Services: Creative Industries', www.artsusa.org/information_resources/research_information/services/creative_industries/default.asp, updated 12 March. Accessed 3 May 2007.

Amin, Ash, and Nigel Thrift, (eds). 2004. *The Cultural Economy Reader*. Oxford: Blackwell.

Anderson, Chris. 2006. *The Long Tail: Why the Future of Business is Selling Less of More*. New York: Random House.

———. 2009. *Free: The Future of a Radical Price*. New York: Hyperion.

Anonymous. 2010. 'Mobile subscriptions hit 5 billion mark', *Ericsson press release*, 9 July 2010, www.ericsson.com/thecompany/press/releases/2010/07/1430616. Accessed 11 July 2010.

Anonymous. 2009. 'Network Effects', *The Economist*, 17 December 2009. Retrieved from www.economist.com/displayStory.cfm?STORY_ID=15108618, 30 December 2009.

Anthony, Ian. 2000. *Radio Wizard: Edward Samuel Rogers and the Revolution of Communication*. Toronto: Gage Publishing Company.

Arnison, Matthew. 2003. 'Open Publishing is the same as Free Software', www.purplebark.net/maffew/cat/openpub.html, first published March 2001. Accessed 28 April 2007.

Arthur, W. Brian. 1999. 'Competing Technologies and Economic Prediction', in D. MacKenzie and J. Wacjman (eds), *The Social Shaping of Technology*, 2nd edn, Buckingham: Open University Press.

Ashlee, Vance. 2006. 'Sun and Apple almost merged three times - Bill Joy', *The Register*, 12 January 2001, www.theregister.co.uk/2006/01/12/sun_apple_snapple. Accessed 11 November 2010.

Atton, Chris. 2001. 'Approaching Alternative Media: Theory and Methodology'. Paper presented to Our Media, Not Theirs, International Communications Association pre-conference, Washington DC, 24 May www.ourmedianet.org/papers/om2001/Atton.om2001.pdf. Accessed 1 May 2007.

———. 2002. *Alternative Media*. London: Sage.

———. 2004. *An Alternative Internet*. Edinburgh: Edinburgh University Press.

Australian, The. 2007. 'Ghosts of Blogging Haunt Net Celebrity', www.theaustralian.news.com.au/story/0,20867,21445581-2703,00.html, posted 26 March 2007. Accessed 26 March 2007.

Australian Broadcasting Corporation. 2001. 'This Time It's Different', broadcast on *Four Corners*, 30 April, www.abc.net.au/4corners/dotcom.

Australian Research Council Centre of Excellence for Creative Industries and Innovation 2005, CCI National Mapping Project: Conceptual Background https://wiki.cci.edu.au/display/NMP/

Conceptual+Background, created 11 November. Accessed 12 December 2006.

Baase, Sara. 1997. *A Gift of Fire: Social, Legal, and Ethical Issues in Computing*. Upper Saddle River, NJ: Prentice-Hall.

Bannermann, Sara. 2006. 'Copyright and the Common Good: An Examination of "the Public Interest" in International Copyright Regimes', in P.N. Thomas and J. Servaes (eds), *Intellectual Property Rights and Communications in Asia: Conflicting Traditions*. New Delhi: Sage, pp. 58–78.

Barber, Benjamin. 2000. 'Jihad versus McWorld', in F. Lechner and J. Boli (eds), *The Globalization Reader*. Oxford: Blackwell, pp. 21–6.

Bakardjieva, Maria. 2005. *Internet Society: the Internet in Everyday Life*. London: Sage.

Barabási, Albert-László. 2003. *Linked: How Everything Is Connected to Everything Else and What It Means*. London: Penguin.

Barbrook, Richard, and Andy Cameron. 1995. 'The Californian Ideology', *Muse* 3: 3–17.

Barlow, John Perry. 1995. 'Is There a There in Cyberspace?', *UTNE Reader*, March-April, pp. 31–6.

———. 1996a. 'A Declaration of the Independence of Cyberspace', www.eff.org/pub/Publications/John_Perry_Barlow. Accessed 22 January 2001.

———.1996b. 'Selling Wine Without Bottles: The Economy of Mind on the Global Net', in P. Ludlow (ed.), *High Noon on the Electronic Frontier*. Cambridge, MA: MIT Press, pp. 9–34.

Barnes, Brooks. 'Disney Acquires Web Site for Children', *The New York Times*, 2 August 2007. Accessed 30 June 2010 at www.nytimes.com/2007/08/02/business/02disney.html.

Barnes, Brooks. 'Club Penguin Misses Goals, Giving Disney a Half-Price Deal', *The New York Times*, 12 May 2010. Accessed 30 June 2010 at www.nytimes.com/2010/05/13/business/media/13penguin.html.

Barney, Darin. 2004. *The Network Society*. Cambridge: Polity Press.

Barr, Trevor. 2000. *newmedia.com.au: The Changing Face of Australia's Media and Communications*. Sydney: Allen & Unwin.

Bassett, Caroline. 2007. 'Cultural Studies and New Media', in G. Hall and C. Burchall (eds), *New Cultural Studies: Adventures In Theory*, Edinburgh: Edinburgh University Press, pp. 220–37.

Batterham, Robin. 2000. 'The Chance to Change: Discussion Paper by the Chief Scientist', August, www.isr.gov.au/science/review/ChanceToChange_17aug.pdf. Accessed 1 June 2002.

Baudrillard, Jean. 1988a. 'For a Critique of the Political Economy of the Sign', in M. Poster (ed.), *Jean Baudrillard: Selected Writings*. Cambridge: Polity Press, pp. 57–97.

———. 1988b. 'Simulacra and Simulations', in M. Poster (ed.), *Jean Baudrillard: Selected Writings*. Cambridge: Polity Press, pp. 166–84.

Baym, Nancy. 2005. 'Interpersonal Life Online', in L. Lievrouw and S. Livingstone (eds), *The Handbook of New Media: Social Shaping and Consequences of ICTs*, 2nd edn. London: Sage, pp. 35–54.

BBC (British Broadcasting Corporation). 2005. 'Building Public Value: Review of the BBC's Royal Charter', May www.bbc.co.uk/info/policies/bpv.shtml. Accessed 22 April 2007.

———. 2006. 'Blogosphere Sees Healthy Growth', http://news.bbc.co.uk/2/hi/technology/6129496.stm. Accessed 17 March 2007.

———. 2007. 'What is Digital Storytelling?', www.bbc.co.uk/wales/digitalstorytelling/about.shtml. Accessed 22 April 2007.

Bell, Daniel. 1974. *The Coming of Post-Industrial Society*. Harmondsworth: Penguin.

Bell, Steven, and Douglas Kellner. 1991. *Postmodern Theory: Critical Interrogations*. London: Macmillan.

Beniger, James. 1986. *The Control Revolution: Technological and Economic Origins of the Information Society*. Cambridge, MA: Harvard University Press.

Benkler, Yochai. 2001. 'The Battle for the Institutional Ecosystem in the Digital Environment', *Communications of the ACM* 44(2): 84–90.

———. 2006. *The Wealth of Networks: How Social Production Transforms Markets and Freedom*. New Haven, CN: Yale University Press.

Bennett, Tony. 1994. 'Research and Cultural Development', in M. Breen (ed.), *Enhancing Cultural Value: Narrowcasting, Community Media and Cultural Development*. Melbourne: Centre for

International Research on Communications and Information Technologies, pp. 17–23.

———. 1998. *Culture: A Reformer's Science*. Sydney: Allen & Unwin.

Berland, Jody. 1992. 'Angels Dancing: Cultural Technologies and the Production of Space', in L. Grossberg, C. Nelson, and P. Treichler (eds), *Cultural Studies*. New York: Routledge, pp. 38–55.

Berners-Lee, Tim. 2000. *Weaving the Web: The Past, Present and Future of the World Wide Web by its Inventor*. London: Texere.

Best, Kirsty. 2003. 'Beating Them at Their Own Game: The Cultural Politics of the Open Source Movement and the Gift Economy', *International Journal of Cultural Studies* 6(4): 449–70.

Bettig, Ronald. 1996. *Copyrighting Culture: The Political Economy of Intellectual Property*. Boulder, CO: Westview Press.

Bilton, Chris. 2007. *Management and Creativity: From Creative Industries to Creative Management*. Oxford: Blackwell.

———, and Ruth Leary. 2002. 'What Managers can do for Creativity: Brokering Creativity in the Creative Industries', *International Journal of Cultural Policy* 8(2): 49–64.

Blumler, Jay, and Stephen Coleman. 2001. *Realising Democracy Online: A Civic Commons in Cyberspace*. London: Institute for Public Policy Research.

Bocock, Robert. 1992. 'Consumption and Lifestyles', in R. Bocock and K. Thompson (eds), *Social and Cultural Forms of Modernity*. Cambridge: Open University Press, pp. 119–67.

Boden, Margaret. 1990. *The Creative Mind: Myths and Mechanisms*. London: Cardinal.

———. 1995. 'Creativity and Unpredictability', *Stanford Humanities Review* 4(2), www.stanford.edu/group/SHR/4-2/text/boden.html. Accessed 22 April 2007.

Bolter, Jay David, and Richard Grusin. 2000. *Remediation: Understanding New Media*. Cambridge, MA: MIT Press.

Boutell.com. 2004. 'WWW FAQs: How many Web sites are there?', www.boutell.com/newfaq/misc/sizeofweb.html. Accessed 19 December 2006.

Boutell.com. 2007. 'WWW FAQs: How many Web sites are there?', www.boutell.com/newfaq/misc/sizeofweb.html. Accessed 19 May 2007.

Bower, Joseph, and Clayton Christensen. 1999. 'Disruptive Technologies: Catching the Wave', in *Harvard Business Review on Managing Uncertainty*. Cambridge, MA: Harvard Business School Press, pp. 147–73.

Bowman, Shayne and Chris Willis. 2003. *WeMedia: How Audiences are Shaping the Future of News and Information*, www.hypergene.net/wemedia/weblog.php.

boyd, danah. 2008. *Taken Out of Context: American Teen Sociality in Networked Publics*. PhD Dissertation. University of California-Berkeley, School of Information.

Boyle, James. 1997. *Shamans, Software, and Spleens: Law and the Construction of the Information Society*. Cambridge, MA: Harvard University Press.

Braithwaite, John, and Peter Drahos. 2000. *Global Business Regulation*. Melbourne: Cambridge University Press.

Brand, Jeffrey. 2007. *Interactive Australia 2007: Facts About the Australian Computer and Video Game Industry*. Sydney: Interactive Entertainment Association of Australia.

Breen, Marcus. 2002. 'Convergence Policy: It's Not What You Dance, It's the Way You Dance It', in G. Elmer (ed.), *Critical Perspectives on the Internet*. Lanham, MD: Rowman & Littlefield, pp. 165–82.

Briscoe, Bob, Andrew Odlyzko, and Benjamin Tilly. 2006. 'Metcalfe's Law Is Wrong—*IEEE Spectrum.*' *IEEE Spectrum Online: Technology, Engineering, and Science News*. http://spectrum.ieee.org/computing/networks/metcalfes-law-is-wrong/0.

Brockman, John. 1996. *Digerati: Encounters with the Cyber Elite*. London: Orion Business Books.

Brook, James and Iian Boal, (eds). 1995. *Resisting the Virtual Life: The Culture and Politics of Information*. San Francisco: City Lights.

Brown, John Sealy, and Paul Duguid. 2000. *The Social Life of Information*. Boston, MA: Harvard Business School Press.

Bruns, Axel. 2005. *Gatewatching: Collaborative Online News Production*. New York: Peter Lang.

———. 2006. 'Wikinews: The Next Generation of Alternative Online News?', *SCAN: Journal of Media Arts Culture* 3(1) http://scan.net.au/scan/journal/display.php?journal_id=69. Accessed 28 April 2007.

———, and Joanne Jacobs. 2006. 'Introduction', in A. Bruns and J. Jacobs (eds), *Uses of Blogs*. New York: Peter Lang, pp. 1–7.

Bryce, Jo, and Jason Rutter. 2002. 'Killing Like a Girl: Gendered Gaming and Girl Gamers' Visibility', in F. Mayra (ed.), *Computer Games and Digital Cultures Conference Proceedings*. Tampere, Finland: Tampere University Press.

Buckingham, David. 2000. *After the Death of Childhood: Growing Up in the Age of Electronic Media*. Cambridge: Polity Press.

———. 2005. 'Children and New Media', in L. Lievrouw and S. Livingstone (eds), *Handbook of New Media*, 2nd edn. London: Sage, pp. 75–91.

Burgess, Jean. 2006. 'Hearing Ordinary Voices: Cultural Studies, Vernacular Creativity and Digital Storytelling', *Continuum: Journal of Media and Cultural Studies* 20(2): 201–14.

———, Marcus Foth, and Helen Klaebe. 2006. 'Everyday Creativity as Civic Engagement: A Cultural Citizenship View of New Media'. Paper presented to Communications Policy and Research Forum 2006, Sydney, Australia, 25–26 September, http://eprints.qut.edu.au/archive/00005056. Accessed 22 April 2007.

Burnet, Robert. 1996. *Canadian Railway and Telegraph History*. Etobicoke, ON: Telegraph Key & Sounder.

Burnett, Ron, and P. David Marshall. 2003. *Web Theory: An Introduction*. London: Routledge.

Bush, Vannevar.1996. 'Excerpt from "As we may think"', in M. Stefik (ed.), *Internet Dreams: Archetypes, Myths, and Metaphors*. Cambridge, MA: MIT Press, pp. 15–22.

BusinessWire. 'Club Penguin Waddles into Wii', *The New York Times*, 10 June 2010. Accessed 30 June 2010 at http://markets.on.nytimes.com/research/stocks/news/press_release.asp?docTag=201006100801BIZWIRE_USPRX____BW5430&feedID=600&press_symbol=89999

Butt, Danny and Axel Bruns. 2005. 'Digital Rights Management and Music in Australia', *Media and Arts Law Review* 10(4): 265–78.

Cahoone, Lawrence. 2003. *From Modernism to Postmodernism: An Anthology*. Malden, MA: Blackwell.

Cairncross, Frances. 1998. *The Death of Distance: How the Communications Revolution will Change our Lives*. London: Orion Business Books.

Calabrese, Andrew. 1999. 'The Information Age According to Manuel Castells', *Journal of Communication* 49(3): 172–86.

Callinicos, Alex. 2001. *Against the Third Way: An Anti-capitalist Critique*. Cambridge: Polity Press.

Campbell, Cole. 2000. 'Citizens Matter; And this is why Public Journalism Matters', *Journalism Studies* 1(4): 689–94.

Canada Media Fund. 2010. 'Recoupment Policy: Experimental Stream', www.cmf-fmc.ca/downloads/create/Recoupment_exp_en.pdf. Accessed 10 September 2010.

Carey, James. 1992. *Communication as Culture*. New York: Routledge.

———. 1995. 'The Press, Public Opinion, and Public Discourse', in T.L. Glasser and C.T. Salmon (eds), *Public Opinion and the Communication of Consent*. New York: Guilford Press, New York.

———, and John J. Quirk. 1992. 'The History of the Future', in J. Carey, *Communication as Culture*. New York: Routledge, pp. 173–200.

Carr, Diane, Andrew Burn, David Buckingham, Gareth Schott, and John Thompson, (eds). 2006. *Computer Games: Text, Narrative and Play*. Cambridge: Polity Press.

Carr, Nicholas. 2005. 'The Amorality of Web 2.0', http://roughtype.com/archives/2005/10/the_amorality_o.php. Accessed 17 March 2007.

Cassell, Justine, and Henry Jenkins. 1998. *From Barbie to Mortal Kombat. Gender and Computer Games*. Cambridge, MA: MIT Press.

Castells, Manuel. 1977. *The Urban Question: A Marxist Approach*, trans. A. Sheridan. London: Edward Arnold.

———. 1978. *City, Class, and Power*. London: Macmillan.

———. 1983. *The City and the Grassroots: A Cross-Cultural Theory of Urban Social Movements*. London: Edward Arnold.

———. 1989. *The Informational City: Information Technology, Economic Restructuring, and the Urban-Regional Process*. Oxford: Blackwell.

———. 1996. *The Rise of the Network Society*, vol. 1 of *The Information Age: Economy, Society and Culture*. Malden, MA: Blackwell.

———. 1998. *The Power of Identity*, vol. 2 of *The Information Age: Economy, Society and Culture*, Malden, MA: Blackwell.

———. 1999. 'Flows, Networks, and Identities: A Critical Theory of the Informational Society', in M. Castells, R. Flecha, P. Freire, H.A. Giroux, D. Macedo, and P. Willis, *Critical Education in the New Information Age*. Lanham, MD: Rowman & Littlefield.

———. 2000a. *End of Millennium*, vol. 3 of *The Information Age: Economy, Society and Culture*. Malden, MA: Blackwell.

———. 2000b. 'Materials for an Exploratory Theory of the Network Society', *British Journal of Sociology* 51(1): 5–24.

———. 2001. *The Internet Galaxy: Reflections on Economy, Society and Culture*. Oxford: Oxford University Press.

———. 2004. 'Afterword: Why Networks Matter', in H. McCarthy, P. Miller, and P. Skidmore (eds), *Network Logic: Who Governs in an Interconnected World?* London: DEMOS, pp. 221–24.

———, and Yuku Aoyama. 1994. 'Paths Towards the Informational Society: Employment Structure in G-7 Countries, 1920–90', *International Labour Review* 133(1): 5–33.

Castronova, Edward. 2005. *Synthetic Worlds: The Business and Culture of Online Games*. Chicago: University of Chicago Press.

Caves, Richard. 2000. *Creative Industries: Contracts Between Art and Commerce*. Cambridge, MA: Harvard University Press.

CBC. 2010. 'World of Warcraft Gamers can stay anonymous', www.cbc.ca/technology/story/2010/07/12/blizzard-world-of-warcraft-forums.html. Accessed 15 July 2010.

CCH Canadian Ltd. v. Law Society of Upper Canada, 2004 SCC 13, [2004] 1 S.C.R. 339

CCPR (Centre for Cultural Policy Research). 2003. *Baseline Study of Hong Kong's Creative Industries*, University of Hong Kong, September.

CDS (Centre for Digital Storytelling). 2007. 'What is Digital Storytelling?', www.storycenter.org/whatis.html. Accessed 22 April 2007.

CED (Committee for Economic Development). 2004. *Promoting Innovation and Economic Growth: The Special Problem of Digital Intellectual Property*, Report by the Digital Connections Council for the Committee for Economic Development, CED, Washington DC.

Centre for Citizen Media. 2007. 'About the Centre', www.citmedia.org/about. Accessed 28 April 2007.

Chakravartty, Paula, and Katharine Sarikakis. 2006. *Media Policy and Globalization*. Edinburgh: Edinburgh University Press.

Chandler, Alfred. 1977. *The Visible Hand: The Managerial Revolution in American Business*. Cambridge, MA: Harvard University Press.

Chee, Florence, Marcelo Vieta, and Richard Smith. 2006. 'Online Gaming and the Interactional Self: Identify Interplay in Situated Practice', in J.P. Williams, S.Q. Hendriks, and W.K. Winkler (eds), *Gaming as Culture: Essays on Reality, Identity and Experience in Fantasy Games*. Jefferson, NC: McFarland Publishing, pp. 154–74.

Cho, Kevin. 2006. 'Samsung, SK Telecom, Shinhan Sponsor South Korean Alien Killers', *Bloomberg News* www.bloomberg.com/apps/news?pid=email_us&refer=asia&sid=a2JvzciDnpB4, posted 15 January. Accessed 15 July 2007.

Christakis, Nicholas A., and James H. Fowler. 2009. *Connected: The Surprising Power of Our Social Networks and How They Shape Our Lives*. New York: Little Brown.

Christensen, Clayton. 2003. *The Innovator's Dilemma*. New York: HarperCollins.

Christopherson, Susan, and Michael Storper. 1986. 'The City as Studio, the World as Back Lot: The Impact of Vertical Disintegration on the Location of the Motion Picture Industry', *Environment and Planning D: Society and Space* 4: 305–20.

Citizen Lab. 2007. *Everyone's Guide to Bypassing Internet Censorship*. Citizen Lab

Clift, Stephen. 2000. 'The E-Democracy E-Book: Democracy is Online 2.0', www.publicus.net/ebook/edemebook.html. Accessed 7 April 2002.

Club Penguin Web Site, *Coins for Change 2009*. Accessed 30 June 2010 at www.clubpenguin.com/parents/coins-for-change-2009.htm

Coase, Ronald H. 1937. 'The Nature of the Firm', *Economica* 4 (16): 386–405.

Coleman, Stephen. 2006. 'New Mediation and Direct Representation: Reconceptualising Representation in the Digital Age', *New Media and Society* 7(2): 177–98.

———, and John Gøtze. 2001. *Bowling Together: Online Public Engagement in Policy Deliberation*. London: Hansard Society.

Collins, Jim. 1992. 'Postmodernism and Television', in R.C. Allen (ed.), *Channels of Discourse, Reassembled*. London: Routledge, pp. 327–53.

Community Broadcasting Foundation. 2007. 'What is Community Broadcasting?', www.cbf.com.au/Content/templates/sector.asp?articleid=30&zoneid=13. Accessed 1 May 2007.

Cooke, Philip, and Luciana Lazzeretti (eds). 2007. *Creative Cities, Cultural Clusters and Local Economic Development*. Cheltenham: Edward Elgar.

Coombe, Rosemary. 1998. *The Cultural Life of Intellectual Properties: Authorship, Appropriation, and the Law*. Durham, NC: Duke University Press.

Cortada, James. 2006. *How Computers Changed the Work of American Financial, Telecommunications, Media, and Entertainment Industries*, vol. 2 of *The Digital Hand*. Oxford: Oxford University Press.

Couldry, Nick. 2002. 'The Digital Divide', in D. Gauntlett and R. Horsley (eds), *Web Studies*. London: Arnold, pp. 185–94.

———. 2003. 'Beyond the Hall of Mirrors? Some Theoretical Reflections on the Global Contestation of Media Power', in N. Couldry and J. Curran (eds), *Contesting Media Power: Alternative Media in a Networked World*. Lanham, MD: Rowman & Littlefield, pp. 39–54.

Coupland, Douglas. 2009. *Extraordinary Canadians: Marshall McLuhan*. Toronto: Penguin.

Cowan, Ruth Schwartz. 1997. *A Social History of American Technology*. New York: Oxford University Press.

Cox, Melissa. 2000. 'The Development of Computer-Assisted Reporting'. Paper presented to the Association for Education in Journalism and Mass Communication, University of North Carolina, Chapel Hill, NJ.

Crandall, Robert, and J. Gregory Sidak. 2006. 'Video Games: Serious Business for the U.S. Economy', Entertainment Software Alliance, www.theesa.com/archives/files/2006%20WHITE%20PAPER%20FINAL.pdf. Accessed 30 April 2007.

Cranny-Francis, Anne. 2005. *Multimedia: Texts and Contexts*. London: Sage.

Crawford, Kate. 2003. 'Control-SHIFT: Censorship and the Internet', in C. Lumby and E. Probyn (eds), *Remote Control: New Media, New Ethics*. Cambridge: Cambridge University Press, pp. 173–88.

Creative City Network of Canada. 2005. *Making the Case for Culture*. Vancouver: Creative City Network of Canada.

Creative Commons. 2007. 'Creative Commons', Creative Commons, http://creativecommons.org. Accessed 24 April 2007.

Creeber, Glen, and Ben Hills. 2007. 'Editorial—TV III', *New Review of Film and Television Studies* 5(1): 1–4.

Critcher, Chas (ed.). 2006. *Critical Readings: Moral Panics and the Media*. Maidenhead: Open University Press.

Cross, Robert. 2004. *The Hidden Power of Social Networks: Understanding How Work Really Gets Done in Organizations*. Boston: Harvard Business School Press.

Csikszentmihalyi, Mihaly. 1996. *Creativity: Flow and the Psychology of Discovery and Invention*. New York: Harper Collins.

Cubitt, Sean. 2006. 'Tactical Media', in K. Sarikakis and D. Thussu (eds), *Ideologies of the Internet*. Cresskil, NJ: Hampton Press, pp. 35–46.

Cunningham, Stuart. 2002. 'From Cultural to Creative Industries: Theory, Industry and Policy Implications', *Media International Australia* 102, February: 54–65.

———. 2005. 'Creative Enterprises', in J. Hartley (ed.), *Creative Industries*. Oxford: Blackwell, pp. 282–98.

———. 2006. What Price a Creative Economy?, Platform Paper No. 9. Sydney: Currency Press.

———. 2007. 'Creative Industries Policy Discourse outside of the United Kingdom', *Global Media and Communication* 3(3).

———, and Jason Potts. 2007. *Four Models of the Creative Industries*. Unpublished paper.

———, Terry Cutler, Greg Hearn, Mark Ryan, and Michael Keane. 2004. 'An Innovation Agenda for the Creative Industries: Where is the R&D?', *Media International Australia* 112: 174–85.

Curran, James, and Myung-Jin Park, (eds). 2000. *Dewesternizing Media Studies*. London: Routledge.

Curtin, Michael. 2007. *Media Capitals: The Cultural Geography of Globalization*. Oxford: Blackwell.

Cutler & Company. 2002. *Producing Digital Content: A Report for the Department of Communications, Information Technology, and the Arts*, Melbourne, August.

David, Paul. 1985. 'Clio and the Economics of QWERTY', *American Economic Review* 75(2): 332–7.

———. 1999. 'Digital Technology and the Productivity Paradox: After Ten Years, What has been Learned?' Paper prepared for Understanding the Digital Economy: Data, Tools and Research, held at US Department of Commerce, Washington DC, 25–26 May.

David, Paul, and Dominique Foray. 2002. 'An Introduction to the Economy of the Knowledge Society', *International Social Science Journal* 171: 9–23.

Davies, William. 2003. *You Don't Know Me But … Social Capital and Social Software*. London: iSociety.

DCMS (Department of Culture, Media, and Sport). 1998. *Mapping the Creative Industries*, www.culture.gov.uk/creative/creative_industries.html. Accessed 5 May 2001.

de Bono, Edward. 1995. *Serious Creativity*. London: Harper Collins.

de Castell, Suzanne, and Mary Bryson. 1998. 'Retooling Play: Dystopia, Dysphoria, and Difference', in J. Cassell and H. Jenkins (eds), *From Barbie to Mortal Kombat: Gender and Computer Games*. Cambridge, MA: MIT Press, pp. 232–61.

de Castell, Suzanne, and Jennifer Jenson (eds). 2007. *Worlds in Play: International Perspectives on Digital Games Research*. New York: Peter Lang.

de Certeau, Michel. 1984. *The Practice of Everyday Life*. Berkeley: University of California Press.

Deibert, Ronald, and Rafal Rohozinski. 2010. 'Breaking up dark clouds in cyberspace', *The Globe and Mail*, 5 April, www.theglobeandmail.com/news/opinions/breaking-up-dark-clouds-in-cyberspace/article1524064/

de Kerckhove, Derrick. 1998. *Connected Intelligence: The Arrival of the Web Society*. London: Kogan Page.

Department of Communications and the Arts. 1994. *Creative Nation: Commonwealth Cultural Policy*. Canberra: AGPS.

Deuze, Mark. 2003. 'The Web and its Journalisms: Considering the Consequences of Different Types of News Media Online', *New Media and Society* 5(2): 203–30.

———. 2005. 'What is Journalism? Professional Identity and Ideology of Journalists Reconsidered', *Journalism* 6(4): 442–64.

———. 2006. 'Participation, Remediation, Bricolage: Considering Principal Components of a Digital Culture', *The Information Society* 22: 63–75.

Dewar, Kenneth C. 1982. 'The Origins of Public Broadcasting in Canada in Comparative Perspectives', *Canadian Journal of Communication*, 8(2).

DiMaggio, Paul, Eszter Hargittai, W. Russell Neuman, and John P. Robinson. 2001. 'Social Implications of the Internet', *Annual Review of Sociology* 27: 307–36.

Disappearing Computer. 2004. 'The Disappearing Computer Initiative', www.disappearing-computer.net/artefacts.html. Accessed 20 December 2006.

Dobb, Maurice. 1973. *Theories of Value and Distribution since Adam Smith: Ideology and Economic Theory*. Cambridge: Cambridge University Press.

Doctorow, Cory. 2006. 'Technorati State of the Blogosphere, Q3 2006', posting to BoingBoing: A Directory of Wonderful Things www.boingboing.net/2006/11/07/technorati_state_of_.html. Accessed 26 March 2007.

———. 2010. *For the Win*. New York: Tor Teen.

Dodgson, Mark, David Gann, and Ammon Salter. 2002. 'The Intensification of Innovation', *International Journal of Innovation Management* 6(1): 53–83.

Dodgson, Sean. 2003. 'The Internet of Things.' *The Guardian*, 9 October 2003, www.guardian.co.uk/technology/2003/oct/09/shopping.newmedia. Accessed 11 November 2010.

Donald, James. 2004. 'What's New: A Letter to Terry Flew', *Continuum: Journal of Media and Cultural Studies* 18(2): 235–46.

Doremus, Paul, William Keller, Lewis Pauly, and Simon Reich. 1998. *The Myth of the Global Corporation*. Princeton, NJ: Princeton University Press.

Dorfman, Ariel, and Armand Mattelart. 1984. *How to Read Donald Duck: Imperialist Ideology in the Disney Comic*. New York : International General.

Dorland, Michael. 1996. *Cultural Industries in Canada*. Toronto: James Lorimer & Company.

Dovey, Jon, and Helen Kennedy. 2006. *Game Cultures: Computer Games as New Media*. Maidenhead: Open University Press.

Drahos, Peter, and John Braithwaite. 2002. *Information Feudalism: Who Owns the Knowledge Economy?* London: Earthscan.

Du Gay, Paul, and Michael Pryke. 2002. 'Cultural Economy: An Introduction', in P. du Gay and M. Pryke (eds), *Cultural Economy: Cultural Analysis and Commercial Life*. London: Sage, pp. 1–19.

Duxbury, Nancy. 2008. *Under Construction: The State of Cultural Infrastructure in Canada*. Vancouver: Centre of Expertise on Culture and Communities.

Dyer-Witheford, Nick. 2002. 'E-Capital and the Many-Headed Hydra', in G. Elmer (ed.), *Critical Perspectives on the Internet*. Lanham, MD: Rowman & Littlefield, pp. 129–63.

———, and Greg de Peuter. 2006. 'EA Spouse" and the Crisis of Video Game Labour: Enjoyment, Exclusion, Exploitation, and Exodus', *Canadian Journal Of Communication*, 31(3).

———, and Zena Sharman. 2005. 'The Political Economy of Canada's Video and Computer Game Industry', *Canadian Journal Of Communication* 30(2).

Dyson, Esther. 1999. *Release 2.0: A Design for Living in the Digital Age*. New York: Broadway Books.

———, George Gilder, George Keyworth, and Alvin Toffler. 1994. 'Cyberspace and the American Dream: A Magna Carta for the Knowledge Age', www.pff.org/issues-pubs/futureinsights/fi1.2magnacarta.html. Accessed 3 February 2000.

Eco, Umberto. 1976. *A Theory of Semiotics*. Bloomington, IN: Indiana University Press.

Economist, The. 1999. 'The Net Imperative', Economist Survey: Business and the Internet, 26 June, pp. 3–5.

Electronic Frontier Foundation. (n.d.). 'Preserving Free Expression: Our Fundamental Rights of Freedom of Speech and Press', www.eff.org/freespeech.html. Accessed 20 July 2001.

Elmer, Greg (ed.). 2002. *Critical Perspectives on the Internet*. Lanham, MD: Rowman & Littlefield.

El-Nawawy, Mohammed, and Adel Iskandar. 2002. *Al Jazeera: How the Free Arab News Network Scooped the World and Changed the Middle East*. Cambridge, MA: Westview Press.

El Oifi, Mohammed. 2005. 'Influence without Power: Al Jazeera and the Arab Public Sphere', in M. Zayani (ed.), *The Al Jazeera Phenomenon: Critical Perspectives on New Arab Media*. London: Pluto Press, pp. 66–79.

Engelbart, Douglas. 1962. 'Augmenting Human Intellect: A Conceptual Framework', October www.bootstrap.org/augdocs/friedewald030402/aug-mentinghumanintellect/ahi62index.html, posted September 1997. Accessed 23 April 2007.

Ericson, Richard and Kevin Haggerty. 1997. *Policing the Risk Society*. Toronto: University of Toronto Press.

Ernst, Dieter, and Lin Su Kim. 2002. 'Global Production Networks, Knowledge Diffusion, and Local Capacity Formation', *Research Policy* 31: 1417–29.

ESA (Entertainment Software Alliance). 2006. 'Essential Facts about the Computer and Video Games Industry', www.theesa.com/archives/files/Essential% 20Facts%202006.pdf. Accessed 6 April 2007.

Farmer, James. 2006. 'Citizen Journalism Sucks', The Age, http://blogs.theage.com.au/media/archives/2006/10/citizen_journal.html, posted 5 October. Accessed 27 April 2007.

Feenberg, Andrew. 2003. 'Democratic Rationalization: Technology, Power, and Freedom', in R.C. Scharff and V. Dusek (eds), *Philosophy of Technology: The Technological Condition*. Malden, MA: Blackwell, pp. 652–65.

Feldman, Curt, and Tor Thorsen. 2004. 'Employees Readying Class-action Lawsuit against EA', Gamespot, 11 November, http://au.gamespot.com/news/2004/11/11/news_6112998.html. Accessed 7 April 2007.

Fiske, John. 1987. *Television Culture*. London: Routledge.

———. 1992. 'The Cultural Economy of Fandom', in L.A. Lewis (ed.), *The Adoring Audience: Fan Culture and Popular Media*. London: Routledge, pp. 30–54.

Fitzgerald, Brian. 2006. 'Creative Commons: Accessing, Negotiating and Remixing Online Content', in P. Thomas and J. Servaes (eds), *Intellectual Property Rights and Communications in Asia*. New Delhi: Sage, pp. 219–25.

Flanagin, Andrew J., Craig Flanagin, and Jon Flanagin. 2010. 'Technical code and the social construction of the internet', *New Media & Society*, Vol. 12, No. 2.

Flew, Terry. 2001. 'The "New Empirics" in Internet Studies and Comparative Internet Policy', in H. Brown, G. Lovink, H. Merrick, N. Rossiter, D. Teh, and M. Willson (eds), *Fibreculture Reader: Politics of a Digital Present*. Melbourne: Fibreculture Publications, pp. 105–13.

———. 2002. *New Media: An Introduction*, 1st edn. Melbourne: Oxford University Press.

———. 2004a. 'Creativity, the "New Humanism" and Cultural Studies', *Continuum: Journal of Media and Cultural Studies* 18(2): 161–78.

———. 2004b. 'Creativity, Cultural Studies and Services Industries', *Communication and Critical/Cultural Studies* 1(2): 176–93.

———. 2005a. *New Media: An Introduction*, 2nd edn. Melbourne: Oxford University Press.

———. 2005b. 'Creative Commons and the Creative Industries', *Media and Arts Law Review* 10(4): 257–64.

———. 2005c. 'Creative Economy', in J. Hartley (ed.), *The Creative Industries Reader*. London: Blackwell, pp. 344–60.

———. 2007. *Understanding Global Media*. Basingstoke: Palgrave Macmillan.

———, and Stephen McElhinney. 2005. 'Globalisation and the Structure of New Media Industries', in L.A. Lievrouw and S.M. Livingstone (eds), *The Handbook of New Media: Social Shaping and Consequences of ICTs*, 2nd edn. London: Sage, pp. 287–96.

———, and Jason Sternberg. 1999. 'Media Wars: Media Studies and Journalism Education', *Media International Australia* 90, February: 9–14.

———, Greg Hearn, and Susanna Leisten. 2006. 'Alternative Intellectual Property Regimes in the Global Creative Economy', in P.N. Thomas and J. Servaes (eds), *Intellectual Property Rights and Communications in Asia: Conflicting Traditions*. New Delhi: Sage, pp. 226–40.

———, Jason Sternberg, and Debra Adams. 2007. 'Revisiting the "Media Wars" Debate', *Australian Journal of Communication* 34(1).

Flichy, Patrice. 2005a. 'New Media History', in L.A. Lievrouw and S.M. Livingstone (eds), *The Handbook of New Media: Social Shaping and Consequences of ICTs*, 2nd edn. London: Sage, pp. 185–204.

———. 2005b. 'Internet: The Social Construction of a "Network Ideology"', in O. Couthard, R. Hanley, and R. Zimmerman (eds), *Sustaining Urban Networks: The Social Diffusion of Large Technical Systems*. London: Routledge, pp. 103–16.

———. 2007. *The Internet Imaginaire*. Cambridge, MA: MIT Press.

Florida, Richard. 2002. *The Rise of the Creative Class, and How it's Transforming Work, Leisure, Community and Everyday Life*. New York: Basic Books.

———. 2007. *The Flight of the Creative Class: The New Global Competition for Talent*. New York: HarperCollins.

Foucault, Michel. 1975. *Discipline and Punish: The Birth of the Prison*. New York: Random House.

Foundation Radiomuseum Luzern. n.d. History of the radio manufacturer Rogers-Majestic; Canada. Online resource. www.radiomuseum.org/dsp_hersteller_detail.cfm?company_id=8085. Accessed 31 March 2010.

Friedman, Thomas. 2005. *The World is Flat: A Brief History of the 21st Century*. New York: Farrar, Straus & Giroux.

Friel, Brian. 2002. 'Hierarchies and Networks', Openflows, www.openflows.org/article.pl?sid=0

2/08/02/2118227&mode=nocomment&tid=12, posted 2 August 2002. Accessed 21 January 2007.

Froomkin, Michael. 1997. 'The Internet as a Source of Regulatory Arbitrage', in B. Kahin and C. Neeson (eds), *Borders in Cyberspace*. Cambridge, MA: MIT Press, pp. 129–64.

———. 2003. 'International and National Regulation of the Internet', http://law.tm/docs/International-regulation.pdf, published 8 December. Accessed 21 May 2007.

Frow, John. 1994. *When was Postmodernism?* Sydeny: Local Consumption Publications.

———. 1995. *Cultural Studies and Cultural Value*. Oxford: Clarendon Press.

Galperin, Hernan. 2004. *New Television, Old Politics: The Transition to Digital TV in the United States and Britain*. Cambridge: Cambridge University Press.

Gandy, Oscar. 2002. 'The Real Digital Divide: Citizens versus Consumers', in L. Lievrouw and S. Livingstone (eds), *Handbook of New Media*. London: Sage, pp. 448–60.

García, Beatriz. 2004. 'Urban Regeneration, Arts Programming and Major Events: Glasgow, 1990, Sydney, 2000, Barcelona, 2004', *International Journal of Cultural Policy* 10(1): 103–18.

Garnham, Nicholas. 1987. 'Concepts of Culture: Public Policy and the Cultural Industries', *Cultural Studies* 1(1): 23–37.

———. 2004. 'Information Society Theory as Ideology', in F. Webster (ed.), *The Information Society Reader*. London: Routledge, pp. 166–83.

———. 2005. 'From Cultural to Creative Industries: An Analysis of the Implications of the "Creative Industries" Approach to Arts and Media Policy Making in the United Kingdom', *International Journal of Cultural Policy* 11(1): 15–29.

Gary, Loren. 1999. 'Beyond the Chicken Cheer: How to Improve Your Creativity', Harvard Management Update, July.

Gates, Bill. 1999. *Business @ the Speed of Thought: Succeeding in the Digital Economy*. London: Penguin.

Gauntlett, David. 2000. *Web.Studies: Rewiring Media Studies for the Digital Age*. London: Arnold.

———. 2004. 'Web Studies: What's New', in D. Gauntlett and R. Horsley (ed.), *Web Studies*, 2nd edn. London: Arnold, pp. 2–18.

———, and Ross Horsley (eds). 2002. *Web Studies*, 2nd edn. London: Arnold.

GBN (Global Business Network). 2002. 'Social Software and the Next Big Phase of the Internet, interview of Clay Shirky by Peter Leyden', www.gbn.com/, December 2002. Accessed 8 November 2005.

Geist, Michael (ed.). 2010. *From "Radical Extremism" to "Balanced Copyright": Canadian Copyright and the Digital Agenda*. Toronto: Irwin Law.

Geist, Michael. 2010. Who are James Moore's 'Radical Extremists,' Michael Geist Blog, 22 June 2010. Available at www.michaelgeist.ca/content/view/5137/125/, accessed 15 July 2010.

George, Cherian. 2006. *Contentious Journalism and the Internet: Towards Democratic Discourse in Malaysia and Singapore*. Singapore: Singapore University Press.

Giarini, Orio. 2002. 'The Globalisation of Services in Economic Theory and Economic Practice: Some Conceptual Issues', in J.R. Cuadrado-Roura, L. Rubalcaba-Bermejo, and J.R. Bryson (eds), *Trading Services in the Global Economy*. Cheltenham: Edward Elgar, pp. 58–77.

Gibson, William. 1984. *Neuromancer*. London: Gollancz.

Giddens, Anthony. 1990. *The Consequences of Modernity*. Cambridge: Polity Press.

———. 1998. *The Third Way*. Cambridge: Polity Press.

Gilder, George. 1994. *Life After Television*. New York: W.W. Norton & Co.

Gill, Rosalind. 2002. 'Cool, Creative and Egalitarian? Exploring Gender in Project-Based New Media Work in Europe', *Information, Communication, and Society* 5(1): 70–89.

———. 2006. 'Technobohemians or the New Cybertariat? New Media Work in Amsterdam a Decade after the Web'. Report prepared for the Institute of Network Cultures, Amsterdam.

Gillies, James, and Robert Cailliau. 2000. *How the Web was Born: The Story of the World Wide Web*. Oxford: Oxford University Press.

Gillmor, Dan. 2006. *We the Media: Grassroots Journalism by the People, for the People*. Sebastopol, CA: O'Reilly.

Gitelman, Lisa, and Geoffrey Pingree. 2003. *New Media 1740–1915.* Cambridge, MA: MIT Press.

Glass, Geoff. 2006. *Audience Labor: The Asymmetric Production of Culture,* A Whole Minute, 22 January 2006, www.geof.net/research/2006/audience-labor. Accessed 11 November 2010.

Glasser, Theodore. 2000. 'The Politics of Public Journalism', *Journalism Studies* 1(4): 683–96.

Gleick, James. 2000. *Faster: The Acceleration of Just About Everything.* New York: Vintage.

Godfrey, Donald G. 1982. 'Canadian Marconi: CFCF The Forgotten Case', *Canadian Journal of Communication,* Vol. 8, No. 4.

Godwin, Mike. 1998. *Cyber Rights: Defending Free Speech in the Digital Age.* New York: Times Books.

Golding, Peter, and Graham Murdock. 2000. 'Culture, Communications, and Political Economy', in J. Curran and M. Gurevitch (eds), *Mass Media and Society,* 3rd edn, London: Arnold, pp. 60–83.

Gore, Al. 1994. 'Remarks Prepared for Delivery by Vice-President Al Gore to the International Telecommunications Union', 21 March, www.goelzer.net/telecom/al-gore.html. Accessed 26 December 2006.

Gow, Gordon, and Richard Smith. 2006. *Mobile and Wireless Communications: An Introduction.* London: Open University Press.

Graham, Gordon. 1999. *The Internet: A Philosophical Inquiry.* London: Routledge.

Graham, Philip. 2000. 'Hypercapitalism: A Political Economy of Informational Idealism', *New Media and Society* 2(2): 131–56.

———. 2006. *Hypercapitalism: Language, New Media, and Social Perceptions of Value.* New York: Peter Lang.

Gramsci, Antonio. 1971. *Selections from the Prison Notebooks of Antonio Gramsci,* Q. Hoare and G. Nowell-Smith (eds). New York: International Publishers.

Granovetter, Mark. 1985. 'Economic Action and Social Structure', *American Journal of Sociology* 91: 481–510.

Gray, Carole. 2006. 'A Different Way of Knowing: Inquiry Through the Creative Arts', Proceedings of 1st International Symposium of Visual Studies,

Production as Research, Centro de las Artes, Monterrey, April, http://publicoutputs.rgu.ac.uk/CREDO/open/additionalpublication.php?id=3661. Accessed 22 April 2007.

Green, Lelia. 2002. *Technoculture.* Sydney: Allen & Unwin.

Grey, Michael. 2008. 'World of Warcraft hits 11 million subscribers', WoW.com, www.wow.com/2008/10/28/world-of-warcraft-hits-11-million-subscribers-worldwide. Accessed 15 July 2010.

Grimes, Sara M. 2008. 'The exploitation of children's affective labour in corporately owned virtual worlds'. Paper presented at the Joint Annual Meetings of Law and Society Association and Canadian Law and Society Association Montreal, Quebec

———. 2008. 'Saturday Morning Cartoons Go MMOG', *Media International Australia (126), Special Issue: Beyond Broadcasting: TV for the Twenty-first Century,* pp. 120–31.

Grossman, Lev. 2006. 'TIME's Person of the Year: You', *Time,* www.time.com/time/magazine/article/0,9171,1569514,00.html, published 13 December. Accessed 17 March 2007.

Habermas, Jürgen. 1995. 'Institutions of the Public Sphere', in O. Boyd-Barrett and C. Newbold (eds), *Approaches to Media: A Reader.* London: Hodder, pp. 235–44.

Hafner, Katie, and Matthew Lyon. 1996. *When Wizards Stay Up Late: The Origins of the Internet.* New York: Simon & Schuster.

Hague, Barry, and Brian Loader (eds). 1999. *Digital Democracy: Discourse and Decision Making in the Information Age.* London: Routledge.

Hague, Barry, and Brian Loader. 1999. 'Digital democracy: An introduction', in B.N. Hague and B.D. Loader (eds), *Digital Democracy: Discourse and Decision Making in the Information Age.* London: Routledge, pp. 3–22.

Hall, Peter. 2000. 'Creative Cities and Economic Development', *Urban Studies* 37(4): 639–49.

Hall, Stuart. 1982. 'The Rediscovery of "Ideology": Return of the Repressed in Media Studies', in M. Gurevitch, T. Bennett, J. Curran, and J. Woollacott (eds), *Culture, Society and the Media.* London: Methuen, pp. 56–90.

———. 1986. 'Cultural Studies: Two paradigms', in R. Collins, J. Curran, N. Garnham, P. Scannell, P. Schlesinger, and C. Sparks (eds), *Media, Culture and Society: A Critical Reader*. London: Sage, pp. 33–48.

Hallin, Daniel. 1994. *We Keep America on Top of the World: Television Journalism and the Public Sphere*. London: Routledge.

Haltiwanger, John, and Ron Jarmin. 2003, 'A Statistical Portrait of the New Economy', in D.C. Jones (ed.), *New Economy Handbook*. Amsterdam: Elsevier, pp. 3–24.

Halavais, Alex. 2008. *Search Engine Society*. Cambridge: Polity Press.

Hammond Museum of Radio. n.d., The Rogers Collection. Online resource. www.hammond-museumofradio.org/rogers.html. Accessed 31 March 2010.

Hardt, Michael, and Antonio Negri. 2000. *Empire*. Cambridge, MA: Harvard University Press.

———. 2005. *Multitude*. London: Penguin.

Hargreaves, Ian. 1999. 'The Ethical Boundaries of Reporting', in M. Ungersma (ed.), *Reporters and the Reported*. Cardiff: Centre for Journalism Studies, pp. 1–15.

Hartley, John. 1999a. *Uses of Television*. London Routledge.

———. 1999b. 'The Frequency of Public Writing: Time, Tomb and Tome as Technologies of the Public', presented to MIT Media-in-Transition Conference, 8 October, http://web.mit.edu/comm-forum/papers/hartley.html. Accessed 17 August 2001.

———. 2003. *A Short History of Cultural Studies*. London: Sage.

———. 2005. 'Creative Industries', in J. Hartley (ed.), *Creative Industries*. Oxford: Blackwell, pp. 1–39.

———. 2008. 'Journalism as a Human Right: The Cultural Approach to Journalism', in M. Löffelholz and D. Weaver (eds), *Global Journalism Research*. Oxford: Blackwell, pp. 39–51.

———, and Michael Keane. 2006. 'Creative Industries and Innovation in China', *International Journal of Cultural Studies* 9(3): 259–62.

Harvey, David. 1990. *The Condition of Postmodernity*. Oxford: Blackwell.

Haseman, Brad. 2006. 'A Manifesto for Performative Research', *Media International Australia* 118, February: 98–106.

Hassan, Robert. 2004. *Media, Politics and the Network Society*. Maidenhead: Open University Press.

Hauge, Atle, and Brian J. Hracs. 2010. 'See the Sound, Hear the Style: Collaborative Linkages between Indie Musicians and Fashion Designers in Local Scenes', *Industry and Innovation*, 17: 1, pp. 113–29.

Haussmann, Frank. 2002. 'Protecting Intellectual Property in the Digital Age', in A. Thierer and C.W. Crews (eds), *Copy Fights: The Future of Intellectual Property in the Information Age*. Washington, DC: Cato Institute, pp. 205–20.

Hawn, Carleen. 2004. 'If He's So Smart . . . Steve Jobs, Apple, and the Limits of Innovation', *Fast Company*, 78, January, www.fastcompany.com/magazine/78/jobs.html. Accessed 22 April 2007.

Healy, Kieran. 2002. 'What's New for Culture in the New Economy?', *Journal of Arts Management, Law, and Society* 32(2): 86–103.

Hearn, Greg, Abraham Ninan, Ian Rogers, Stuart Cunningham, and Susan Luckman. 2004. 'From the Margins to the Mainstream: Creating Value in Queensland's Music Industry', *Media International Australia* 112: 101–14.

Heilbroner, Robert. 2003 [1967]. 'Do Machines Make History?', in R.C. Scharff and V. Dusek (eds), *Philosophy of Technology: The Technological Condition*. Malden, MA: Blackwell, pp. 398–404.

Held, David, and Anthony McGrew (eds). 2002. *Governing Globalization: Power, Authority and Global Governance*. Cambridge: Polity Press.

——— (eds). 2003. *The Global Transformations Reader: An Introduction to the Globalization Debate*. Cambridge: Polity Press.

———, Anthony McGrew, David Goldblatt, and Jonathon Perraton. 1999. *Global Transformations: Politics, Economics, and Culture*. Cambridge: Polity Press.

Hermes, Joke. 2005. *Re-Reading Popular Culture*. Oxford: Blackwell.

Herring, Susan. 2004. 'Slouching Towards the Ordinary: Current Trends in Computer-Mediated

Communication', *New Media and Society*
6(1): 26–36.

Herz, J.C. 2002. 'The Bandwidth Capital of the World',
WIRED, no. 10.08, August, www.wired.com/wired/
archive/10.08/korea.html. Accessed 30 April 2007.

———. 2005. 'Harnessing the Hive', in J. Hartley (ed.),
Creative Industries. Oxford: Blackwell, pp. 327–41.

Hesmondhalgh, David. 2007. *The Cultural Industries*,
2nd edn. London: Sage.

———, and Andy Pratt. 2005. 'Cultural Industries and
Cultural Policy', *International Journal of Cultural
Policy* 11(1): 1–13.

Hill, David, and Krishna Sen. 2005. *The Internet in
Indonesia's New Democracy*. London: Routledge.

Hirst, Martin, and John Harrison. 2006. *Communication
and New Media: From Broadcast to Narrowcast*.
Melbourne: Oxford University Press.

Hirst, Paul, and Grahame Thompson. 1996.
Globalization in Question. Cambridge: Polity Press.

Hodgson, Geoffrey. 2000. 'Socio-Economic
Consequences of the Advance of Complexity and
Knowledge', in *Organization for Economic Cooperation and Development, The Creative Society of
the 21st Century*. Paris: OECD, pp. 89–112.

Hofstede, Geert. 1980. *Culture's Consequences:
International Differences in Work-Related Values*.
London: Sage.

Horst, Heather, and Daniel Miller. 2006. *The Cell Phone:
An Anthropology of Communication*. Oxford: Berg.

Howells, Jeremy. 2000. 'Knowledge, Innovation, and
Location', in J.R. Bryson, P. Daniels, N. Hentry,
and J. Pollard (eds), *Knowledge, Space, Economy*.
London: Routledge, pp. 50–62.

Howkins, John. 2001. *The Creative Economy: How People
Make Money From Ideas*. London: Allen Lane.

———. 2005. 'The Mayor's Commission on the
Creative Industries', in J. Hartley (ed.), *Creative
Industries*. Oxford: Blackwell, pp. 117–23.

Hudson, Heather. 2002. 'Universal Access to the New
Information Infrastructure', in L. Lievrouw and
S. Livingstone (eds), *Handbook of New Media*.
London: Sage, pp. 369–83.

Human Rights Watch. 2006. 'How Censorship Works
in China: A Brief Overview', www.hrw.org/
reports/2006/china0806/3.htm, August. Accessed
5 May 2007.

Humphreys, Sal. 2004. 'Productive Players: Online
Computer Games' Challenge to Conventional
Media Forms', *Communication and Critical/
Cultural Studies* 2(1): 37–51.

IEEE. n.d., The Alternating Current Tube. Online resource. www.ieee.ca/millennium/alternating_cur-
rent/ac_about.html. Accessed 31 March 2010.

IGDA (International Game Developers Association).
2004. *Quality of Life in the Game Industry:
Challenges and Best Practices*, www.igda.org/qol/
whitepaper.php. Accessed 26 April 2007.

Innis, Harold. 1951. *The Bias of Communication*.
Toronto: University of Toronto Press.

Internet Software Consortium (ISC). 2006. *Internet
Domain Name Survey* www.isc.org/index.pl?/ops/
ds. Accessed 3 December 2006.

Internet World Stats. 2006. 'Internet Usage Statistics—
The Big Picture, World Internet Users and
Population Stats', www.internetworldstats.com/
stats.htm. Accessed 3 December 2006.

Intven, Hank (ed.). 2000. *Telecommunications
Regulation Handbook*, prepared for World Bank,
Washington DC.

Ipsos Reid. 2010. 'Weekly Internet Usage Overtakes
Television Watching', *Ipsos News & Polls,* 22 March
2010, www.ipsos-na.com/news-polls/pressrelease.
aspx?id=4720. Accessed 11 November 2010.

ITU (International Telecommunications Union). 'Global
ICT Developments', www.itu.int/ITU-D/ict/statis-
tics/ict/index.html. Accessed 17 March 2010.

———. 2004. 'The Evolution to 3G Mobile-Status
Report', www.itu.int/itunews/issue/2003/06/thirdg-
eneration.html. Accessed 9 April 2004.

Jacobs, Jane. 1994 [1961]. *The Death and Life of
American Cities*. Harmondsworth: Penguin.

Jameson, Fredric. 1992. *Postmodernism, or, the Cultural
Logic of Late Capitalism*. London: Verso.

Jenkins, Henry. 1992. *Textual Poachers: Television Fans
and Participatory Culture*. New York: Routledge.

———. 2006a. *Convergence Culture: When Old
and New Media Collide*. New York: New York
University Press.

———. 2006b. *Fans, Bloggers and Gamers: Exploring Participatory Culture*. New York: New York University Press.

Jessop, Bob. 1998. 'The Rise of Governance and the Risks of Failure: The Case of Economic Development', *International Social Science Journal* 50(1): 29–45.

———. 2000. 'The State and the Contradictions of the Knowledge-Driven Economy', in J.R. Bryson, P.W. Daniels, N. Henry, and J. Pollard (eds), *Knowledge, Space, Economy*. London: Routledge, pp. 63–78.

Johnson, Steven. 2005. *Everything Bad is Good for You: How Today's Popular Culture is Actually Making Us Smarter*. New York: Riverhead Books.

Jones, Steven G. (ed.). 2003. *Encyclopedia of New Media*. Thousand Oaks, CA: Sage.

Juul, Jesper. 2003. 'The Game, the Player, the World: Looking for a Heart of Gameness', in M. Copier and J. Raessens (eds), *Level Up: Digital Games Research Conference Proceedings*. Utrecht: University of Utrecht, pp. 30–47.

Kahn, Robert, and Vinton Cerf. 1996. 'Excerpt from The Digital Library Project vol. 1: The World of Knowbots', in M. Stefik (ed.), *Internet Dreams: Archetypes, Myths, and Metaphors*. Cambridge, MA: MIT Press.

Kalathil, Shanthi, and Taylor Boas. 2003. *Open Networks, Closed Regimes: The Impact of the Internet on Authoritarian Rule*. Washington, DC: Carnegie Endowment for International Peace.

Keane, Michael. 2004. 'Brave New World: China's Creative Vision', *International Journal of Cultural Policy* 10(3): 265–79.

———. 2007. *Created in China: The New Great Leap Forward*. London: RoutledgeCurzon.

Kedrosky, Paul. 2007. 'Viacom v. YouTube: The Real Issue is a Consumer Rebellion, Not Intellectual Property', OpinionJournal, http://web.archive.org/web/20070317193609/http://www.opinionjournal.com/editorial/feature.html?id=110009788, published 15 February. Accessed 14 October 2010.

Keen, Andrew. 2007. *The Cult of the Amateur: How Today's Internet is Killing Our Culture*. New York: Doubleday.

Kelly, Kevin. 1997. 'New Rules for the New Economy', *WIRED*, no. 5.09, September, www.wired.com/wired/archive/5.09/newrules.html. Accessed 9 January 2001.

Kenney, Keith, Alexander Gorelik, and Sam Mwangi. 2000. 'Interactive Features of Online Newspapers', *First Monday* 5(1), http://firstmonday.org/issues/issue5_1/kenney/index.html. Accessed 27 December 2006.

Kerr, Aphra. 2006. *The Business and Culture of Digital Games: Gamework and Gameplay*. London: Sage.

Kingston, Margo. 2003. 'Diary of a Webdiarist: Ethics Goes Online', in C. Lumby and E. Probyn (eds), *Remote Control: New Media, New Ethics*. Cambridge: Cambridge University Press, pp. 159–72.

Kitchin, Rob. 1998. *Cyberspace: The World in the Wires*. Chichester: John Wiley & Sons.

Klein, Naomi. 2000. *No Logo*. London: Flamingo.

Kleinwächter, Wolfgang. 2002. 'Trilateralism, Co-regulation and Governance in the Global Information Society', in M. Raboy (ed.), *Global Media Policy in the New Millennium*. Luton: University of Luton Press, pp. 55–76.

Kline, Stephen, Nick Dyer-Witheford, and Greg de Peuter. 2003. *Digital Play: The Interaction of Technology, Culture and Marketing*. Montreal and Kingston: McGill-Queen's University Press.

Knights, David, Faith Noble, Theo Vurdubakis, and Hugh Willmott. 2002. 'Allegories of Creative Destruction: Technology and Organisation in Narratives of the e-Economy', in S. Woolgar (ed.), *Virtual Society? Technology, Cyberbole, Reality*. Oxford: Oxford University Press, pp. 99–114.

Kong, Lily, Chris Gibson, Louisa-May Khoo, and Anna-Marie Semple. 2006. 'Knowledges of the Creative Economy: Towards a Relational Geography of Diffusion and Adaptation in Asia', *Asia Pacific Viewpoints* 47(2): 173–94.

Koring, Paul. 2009. 'Canada placed on copyright black-list', *The Globe and Mail*, published 10 April 2009, retrieved 28 January 2010, www.theglobeandmail.com/news/technology/download-decade/article1127052.ece.

Kotkin, Joel. 2006. *The City: A Global History*. New York: Modern Library.

Kravets, David. 2010. 'U.S. Courts Split on Internet Ban', *WIRED* Magazine, 12 January 2010, www.wired.com/threatlevel/2010/01/courts-split-on-internet-bans.

Kress, Gunther. 1997. 'Visual and Verbal Modes of Representation in Electronically Mediated Communication: The Potentials of New Forms of Text', in I. Snyder (ed.), *From Page to Screen: Taking Literacy into the Electronic Era*. Sydney: Allen & Unwin, pp. 53–79.

Kumar, Krishan. 1995. *From Post-Industrial to Post-Modern Society: New Theories of the Contemporary World*. Oxford: Blackwell.

———. 2005. *From Post-Industrial to Post-Modern Society: New Theories of the Contemporary World*, 2nd edn. Oxford: Blackwell.

Kuo, David. 2001. *Dot.Bomb: My Days and Nights as an Internet Goliath*. New York: Brown & Co.

Ladly, Martha, and Philip Beesley. 2008. *Mobile Nation: Creating Methodologies for Mobile Platforms*. Toronto: Riverside Architectural Books.

Ladner, Sam. 2008. 'Laptops in the Living Room: Mobile Technologies and the Divide between Work and Private Time among Interactive Agency Workers', *Canadian Journal Of Communication*, 33 (3), pp. 465–98.

Lambert, Joe. 2002. *Digital Storytelling: Capturing Lives, Creating Community*. Berkeley, CA: Digital Diner Press.

Lamberton, Don. 1971. 'Introduction', in D. Lamberton (ed.), *Economics of Information and Knowledge*. London: Penguin, pp. 5–17.

———. 1999. 'Information: Pieces, Batches, or Flows?', in S.C. Dow and P.E. Earl (eds), *Economic Organization and Economic Knowledge: Essays in Honour of Brian J. Loasby, vol. 1*. Cheltenham: Edward Elgar, pp. 209–24.

Landry, Charles. 2000. *The Creative City*. London: Earthscan.

———. 2005. 'London as a Creative City', in J. Hartley (ed.), *Creative Industries*. Oxford: Blackwell, pp. 233–43.

Lapsley, Robert, and Michael Westlake. 2006. *Film Theory: An Introduction*, 2nd edn. Manchester: Manchester University Press.

Lash, Scott. 1994. *Economies of Signs and Space*. London: Sage.

———. 2002. *Critique of Information*. London: Sage.

———, and John Urry. 1989. *The End of Organized Capitalism*. Cambridge: Polity Press.

Lasn, Kalle. 2000. *Culture Jam*. New York: Quill.

Latour, Bruno. 2005. *Reassembling the Social: An Introduction to Actor-Network-Theory*. Oxford: Oxford University Press.

Lavery, David (ed.). 2002. *This Thing of Ours: Investigating the Sopranos*. New York: Columbia University Press.

Leadbeater, Charles. 2000. *Living on Thin Air: The New Economy*. London: Penguin.

———. 2007. *We-Think: The Power of Mass Creativity*, www.wethinkthebook.net/home.aspx. Accessed 18 April 2007.

———, and Paul Miller. 2004. *The Pro-Am Revolution: How Enthusiasts are Changing our Economy and Society*. London: DEMOS.

Lee, Terence. 2006. 'Going Online: Journalism and Civil Society in Singapore', in A. Romano and M. Bromley (eds), *Journalism and Democracy in Asia*. London: Routledge, pp. 15–27.

Legrain, Philippe. 2002. *Open World: The Truth About Globalisation*. London: Abacus.

Leiner, Barry, Vinton Cerf, David Clark, Robert Kahn, Leonard Kleinrock, Daniel Lynch, Jon Postel, Larry Roberts, and Stephen Wolff. 2003. 'A Brief History of the Internet', www.isoc.org/internet/history/brief.shtml, Version 3.32, last revised 10 October 2003. Accessed 3 December 2006.

Leiss, William. 1990. *Under Technology's Thumb*. Montreal: McGill-Queens University Press.

Lenhart, Amanda, and Susannah Fox. 2006. *Bloggers: A Portrait of the Internet's New Story Tellers*. Washington, DC: Pew Internet and American Life Project, www.pewinternet.org/Reports/2006/Bloggers.aspx, published 19 July. Accessed 14 October 2010.

Leo, Patrice, and Terence Lee. 2004. 'The "New" Singapore: Mediating Culture and Creativity',

Continuum: Journal of Media and Cultural Studies 18(2): 205–18.

Lessig, Lawrence. 2000. *Code and other Laws of Cyberspace.* New York: Basic Books.

———. 2001. *The Future of Ideas: The Fate of the Commons in a Connected World.* New York: Vintage Books.

———. 2004. *Free Culture: How Big Media Uses Technology and the Law to Lock Down Culture and Control Creativity.* New York: Penguin.

Levine, M.E., and Forrence, J.L. 1990. 'Regulatory Capture, Public Interest, and the Public Agenda. Toward a Synthesis', *Journal of Law Economics & Organization* 6, pp. 167–98.

Levinson, Paul. 1997. *The Soft Edge: A Natural History and Future of the Information Revolution.* New York: Routledge.

Levitt, Steven. 2008. 'Club Penguin Anonymous', *The New York Times*, 15 September 2008. Accessed 30 June 2010, http://freakonomics.blogs.nytimes.com/2008/09/15/club-penguin-anonymous/

Lévy, Pierre. 1997. *Collective Intelligence: Mankind's Emerging World in Cyberspace.* New York: Plenum Trade.

———. 1998. *Becoming Virtual: Reality in the Digital Age.* New York: Plenum Trade.

Lewis, Justin. 1990. *Art, Culture and Enterprise: The Politics of Art and the Cultural Industries.* London: Routledge.

Lewis, Michael. 2001. *The Future Just Happened.* London: Coronet Books.

Liestøl, Eve. 2003. 'Computer Games and the Ludic Structure of Interpretation', in G. Liestøl, A. Morrison, and T. Rasmussen (eds), *Digital Media Revisited.* Cambridge, MA: MIT Press, pp. 327–5

Lievrouw, Leah, and Sonia Livingstone. 2005. 'Introduction to the Updated Student Edition', in L. Lievrouw and S. Livingstone (eds), *The Handbook of New Media: Social Shaping and Consequences of ICTs*, 2nd edn. London: Sage, pp. 1–14.

Lipsey, Richard, Kenneth Carlaw, and Clifford Bekar. 2006. *Economic Transformations: General Purpose Technologies and Long-Term Economic Growth.* New York: Oxford University Press.

Lister, Martin, Jon Dovey, Seth Giddings, Iain Grant, and Kieran Kelly. 2003. *New Media: A Critical Introduction.* London: Routledge.

Litman, Jessica. 2001. *Digital Copyright.* Amherst, NY: Prometheus Books.

Livingstone, Sonia. 1998. *Making Sense of Television*, 2nd edn. London: Routledge.

———. 1999. 'New Media, New Audiences', *New Media and Society* 1(1): 59–68.

———. 2002. *Young People and New Media.* London: Sage.

———. 2005. 'Critical Debates in Internet Studies: Reflections on an Emergent Field', in J. Curran and M. Gurevitch (eds), *Mass Media and Society*, 4th edn. London: Hodder Arnold, pp. 9–28.

Lockard, Joseph. 1997. 'Progressive Politics, Electronic Individualism and the Myth of Virtual Community', in D. Porter (ed.), *Internet Culture.* New York: Routledge, pp. 219–32.

Lovink, Geert. 2002. *Dark Fiber: Tracking Critical Internet Culture.* Cambridge, MA: MIT Press.

Lovelock, Peter, and John Ure. 2002. 'The New Economy: Internet, Telecommunications and Electronic Commerce?', in L. Lievrouw and S. Livingstone (eds), *Handbook of New Media.* London: Sage, pp. 350–68.

Lyon, David. 1988. *The Information Society: Issues and Illusions.* Cambridge: Polity Press.

———. 2002. *Surveillance Society: Monitoring Everyday Life.* Buckingham: Open University Press.

McChesney, Robert W. 1999. *Rich Media, Poor Democracy: Communication Politics in Dubious Times.* New York: New Press.

———. 2000. 'So Much for the Magic of Technology and the Free Market: The World Wide Web and the Corprate Media System', in A. Herman and T. Swiss (eds), *The World Wide Web and Contemporary Cultural Theory.* New York: Routledge, pp. 5–35.

———. 2003. 'Corporate Media, Global Capitalism', in S. Cottle (ed.), *Media Organization and Production.* London: Sage, pp. 27–40.

———, and Dan Schiller. 2003. *The Political Economy of International Communciation: Foundations for the Emerging Global Debate about Media Ownership and Regulation*, United Nations

Research Institute for Social Development, Technology, Business and Society Programme Paper No. 11, October.

McKay, George. 1998,.'DIY Culture: Notes Towards an Intro', in G. McKay (ed.), *DIY Culture: Party and Protest in Nineties Britain*. London: Verso.

MacKenzie, Donald, and Judy Wacjman. 1999. 'Introductory Essay: The Social Shaping of Technology', in D. MacKenzie and J. Wacjman (eds), *The Social Shaping of Technology*, 2nd edn. Milton Keynes: Open University Press, pp. 3–27.

McLuhan, Eric, and Frank Zingrone (eds). 1997. *Essential McLuhan*. London: Routledge.

McLuhan, Marshall. 1964. *Understanding Media: The Extensions of Man*. New York: Mentor Books.

———, and Quentin Fiore. 1967. *The Medium is the Massage*. New York: Bantam.

McMillan, Sally. 2005. 'Exploring Models of Interactivity from Multiple Research Traditions; Users, Documents and Systems', in L. Lievrouw and S. Livingstone (eds), *Handbook of New Media*, 2nd edn. London: Sage, pp. 205–29.

McNair, Brian. 2003. 'From Control to Chaos: Toward a New Sociology of Journalism', *Media, Culture and Society* 25(6): 547–55.

———. 2006. *Cultural Chaos: Journalism, News and Power in a Globalized World*. New York: Routledge.

McNamara, Andrew. 2002. 'How "Creative Industries" Evokes the Legacy of Modernist Visual Art', *Media International Australia* 102, February: 66–76.

McPhail, Thomas, and Brenda McPhail. 1990. *Communication: The Canadian Experience*. Toronto: Coop Clark Pitman.

McQuail, Dennis. 2002. *Mass Communication Theory*, 3rd edn. London: Routledge.

———. 2005. *McQuail's Mass Communication Theory*, 5th edn. London: Sage.

McQuire, Scott. 2001. 'When is Art IT?', in H. Brown, G. Lovink, H. Merrick, N. Rossiter, D. Teh, and M. Willson (eds), *Fibreculture Reader: Politics of a Digital Present*. Melbourne: Fibreculture Publications, pp. 205–13.

McRobbie, Angela. 2005. 'Clubs to Companies', in J. Hartley (ed.), *Creative Industries*. Oxford: Blackwell, pp. 375–93.

Madden, Christopher. 2001. 'Using "Economic" Impact Studies in Arts and Cultural Advocacy: A Cautionary Note', *Media International Australia* 98, February: 161–78.

Malaysiakini. 2007. 'About Malaysiakini.com', www.malaysiakini.com/pages/general. Accessed 27 April 2007.

Malmstein, Ernst. 2001. *Boo Hoo: A Dotcom Story from Concept to Catastrophe*. New York: Random House.

Mander, Jerry, and Edward Goldsmith. 1996. *The Case Against the Global Economy: And for a Turn Toward the Local*. San Francisco: Sierra Club Books.

Manovich, Lev. 2001. *The Language of New Media*. Cambridge: MIT Press.

Marshall, David (ed.). 2006. *The Celebrity Culture Reader*. London: Routledge.

Marvin, Carolyn. 1988. *When Old Technologies Were New: Thinking about Electric Communication in the 19th Century*. New York: Oxford University Press.

Matlin, Julie. 'Digital Storytelling Workshops', NFB.ca Blog. Available online at http://blog.nfb.ca/2009/08/24/digital-storytelling-workshops. Accessed 5 September 2010.

Mattelart, Armand. 2003. *The Information Society: An Introduction*, trans. S.G. Taponier and J.A. Cohen. London: Sage.

Mayfield, Antony. 2007. 'What is Social Media?', Spannerworks e-Books, www.spannerworks.com/ebooks. Accessed 28 April 2007.

Mayfield, Ross. 2006. 'Power Law of Participation', Ross Mayfield's Weblog: Markets, Technology and Musings, http://ross.typepad.com/blog/2006/04/power_law_of_pa.html, published 27 April. Accessed 27 December 2006.

Meadows, Daniel. 2003. 'Digital Storytelling: Research-based Practice in New Media', *Visual Communication* 2(2): 189–93.

Melody, William. 1996. 'Towards a Framework for Designing Information Society Policies', *Telecommunications Policy* 20(4): 243–59.

Menser, Michael, and Stanley Aronowitz. 1996. 'On Cultural Studies, Science, and Technology', in S. Aronowitz, B. Martinsons, and M. Menser (eds), *Technoscience and Cyberculture*. New York: Routledge, pp. 7–36.

Mercer, Colin. 1994. 'Cultural Policy: Research and the Governmental Imperative', *Media Information Australia* 73, August, pp. 16–22.

Merrin, Chris. 2005. *Baudrillard and the Media: A Critical Introduction*. Cambridge: Polity.

Miège, Bernard. 2004. 'Capitalism and Communication: A New Era of Society or the Accentuation of Long-Term Tendencies?', in A. Calabrese and C. Sparks (eds), *Toward a Political Economy of Culture: Capitalism and Communication in the Twenty-First Century*. Lanham, MD: Rowman & Littlefield, pp. 83–94.

Milberry, Kate. 2009. *Geeks and Global Justice: Another (Cyber) World is Possible*. PhD Dissertation. Simon Fraser University. Burnaby, BC. Available online, here: http://geeksandglobaljustice.com/wp-content/Milberry-Dissertation-for-Library.pdf

Miles, Ian. 1997. 'Cyberspace as Product Space: Interactive Learning about Interactive Media', *Futures* 29(9): 769–89.

Miller, Daniel. 1998. 'Conclusion: A Theory of Virtualism', in J. Carrier and D. Miller (eds), *Virtualism: A New Political Economy*. Oxford: Berg, pp. 187–216.

———, and Don Slater. 2000. *The Internet: An Ethnographic Approach*. London: Routledge.

Miller, Paul. 2004. 'The Rise of Network Campaigning', in H. McCarthy, P. Miller, and P. Skidmore (eds), *Network Logic: Who Governs in an Interconnected World?*, London: DEMOS, pp. 207–17.

Miller, Toby. 2007. *Cultural Citizenship: Cosmopolitanism, Consumerism and Television in a Neoliberal Age*. Philadelphia: Temple University Press.

———, Nitin Govil, John McMurria, and Richard Maxwell. 2001. *Global Hollywood*. London: British Film Institute.

———, Nitin Govil, John McMurria, and Richard Maxwell. 2005. *Global Hollywood 2*. London: BFI Publishing.

Mills, C. Wright. 1956. *The Power Elite*. New York: Oxford University Press.

Milner, Andrew. 2006. 'Theorize This! Cultural Studies versus Utilitarianism', *Continuum: Journal of Media and Cultural Studies* 20(1): 111–25.

Milstein, Sarah. 2009. 'What would Jane Austen Have Twittered?', O'Reilly Radar, 30 November, http://radar.oreilly.com/2009/11/what-would-jane-austen-have-tw.html

Mitchell, William, Alan Inouye, and Marjory Blumenthal. 2003. *Beyond Productivity: Information Technology, Innovation, and Creativity*. Washington, DC: National Research Council of the National Academies, National Academies Press.

Mitrovica, Anthony. 2009. University of Toronto Magazine. Autumn.

MKW Wirtschaftsforschung GmbH. 2001. *Exploitation and Development of the Job Potential in the Cultural Sector in the Age of Digitization: Final Report*. Commissioned by European Commission DG Employment and Social Affairs, MKWCmbH, Berlin, June.

MobileTracker. 2005. 'Mobile Phone Users to hit 2 Billion this Year', 18 January www.mobiletracker.net/archives/2005/01/18/2-billion-mobile-phones. Accessed 10 December 2006.

Mommaas, Hans. 2004. 'Creative Clusters and the Post-Industrial City: Towards the Remapping of Urban Cultural Policy', *Urban Studies* 41(3): 507–32.

Montgomery, Lucy, and Michael Keane. 2006. 'Learning to Love the Market: Copyright, Culture and China', in P. Thomas and J. Servaes (eds), *Intellectual Property Rights and Communications in Asia*. New Delhi: Sage, pp. 130–48.

Moore, Christopher. 2005. 'Creative Choices: Changes to Australian Copyright Law and the Future of the Public Domain', *Media International Australia* 114, February: 71–82.

Mosco, Vincent. 1996. *The Political Economy of Communication*. Thousand Oaks, CA: Sage.

———. 1997. 'Citizenship and the Technopoles', *Javnost (The Public)* 4(4): 35–46.

———. 2000. 'Webs of Myth and Power; Connectivity and the New Computer Technopoles', in A. Herman and T. Swiss (eds), *The World Wide Web and Contemporary Cultural Theory*. New York: Routledge, pp. 37–60.

———. 2004. *The Digital Sublime: Myth, Power and Cyberspace*. Cambridge, MA: MIT Press.

MTI (Ministry of Trade and Industry). 2003. *Economic Contributions of Singapore's Creative Industries.* Singapore: Government of Singapore.

Murdock, Graham, and Peter Golding. 2004. 'Dismantling the Digital Divide: Rethinking the Dynamics of Participation and Excluson', in A. Calabrese and C. Sparks (eds), *Towards a Political Economy of Culture: Capitalism and Communication in the Twenty-first Century.* Lanham, MD: Rowman & Littlefield, pp. 244–60.

Murphy, Brian Martin. 2002. 'A Critical History of the Internet', in G. Elmer (ed.), *Critical Perspectives on the Internet.* Lanham, MD: Rowman & Littlefield, pp. 27–45.

Murray, Gil. 2003. *Nothing On but the Radio: A Look Back at Radio in Canada and How It Changed the World.* Toronto: Dundurn Press.

Murray, Janet H. 1997. *Hamlet on the Holodeck: The Future of Narrative in Cyberspace.* Cambridge, MA: MIT Press.

Musser, John, and Tim O'Reilly. 2007. *Web 2.0: Principles and Practices.* San Francisco: O'Reilly Radar.

Mussio, Laurence B. 2001. *Telecom Nation: Telecommunications, Computers, and Governments in Canada.* Monreal: McGill-Queen's University Press.

Nakamura, Lisa. 2000. '"Where Do You Want to Go to Today?" Cybernetic Tourism, the Internet, and Transnationality', in B. Kolko, L. Nakamura, and G.B. Rodman (eds), *Race in Cyberspace.* New York: Routledge, pp. 15–26.

National Endowment for the Arts. 2010. *Audience 2.0: How Technology Influences Arts Participation.* Washington: NEA.

Negroponte, Nicholas. 1995. *Being Digital.* Sydney: Hodder & Stoughton.

Negus, Keith, and Michael Pickering. 2004. *Creativity, Communication, and Cultural Value.* London: Sage.

Neilsen, Inc. 2010. 'Americans Using TV and Internet Together 35% More Than A Year Ago', *NeilsenWire.* 22 March 2010, http://blog.nielsen.com/nielsen-wire/online_mobile/three-screen-report-q409/, accessed 11 November 2010.

Newson, Emily. 2006. 'Celebrity Mags Embrace the Internet', Cardiff University Online Journalism, http://journalism.cf.ac.uk/2007/online/index.php?id=parse-195-0-0-251&article-551&author=Emily+Newson, posted 15 December. Accessed 6 May 2007.

Newman, James. 2002. 'The Myth of the Ergodic Videogame', *Games Studies* 2(1): 1–8.

Nie, Norman, and Lutz Erbring. 2000. *Internet and Society: A Preliminary Report.* Stanford, CA: Stanford Institute for the Quantitative Study of Society.

Nielsen, Jakob. 2000. *Designing Web Usability.* Indianapolis, IN: New Riders.

Nielsén, Tobias. 2004. *Understanding the Experience Economy: A Swedish Perspective on Creativity.* Stockholm: QNB Analys & Kommunikation AB.

Nip, Joyce. 2006. 'Changing Connections: The News Media, the Government and the People in China's SARS Epidemic', in A. Romano and M. Bromley (eds), *Journalism and Democracy in Asia.* London: Routledge, pp. 28–40.

Noam, Eli. 1991. *Television in Europe.* New York: Oxford University Press.

Nonnenmacher, Tomas. 'History of the U.S. Telegraph Industry'. EH.Net Encyclopedia, edited by Robert Whaples, 14 August 2001, http://eh.net/encyclopedia/article/nonnenmacher.industry.telegraphic.us

Nora, Simon, and Alain Minc. 1981. *The Computerization of Society.* Cambridge, MA: MIT Press.

Norman, Donald. 1998. *The Invisible Computer.* Cambridge, MA: MIT Press.

Norris, Pippa. 2001. *Digital Divide: Civic Engagement, Information Poverty, and the Internet Worldwide.* Cambridge: Cambridge University Press.

Northfield, Dianne. 1999. *The Information Policy Maze: Global Challenges—National Responses.* Melbourne: Centre for International Research into Communications and Information Technologies.

Nussbaum, Bruce. 2005. 'Get Creative! How to Build Innovative Companies', *Business Week*, 1 August, www.businessweek.com/magazine/content/05_31/b3945401.htm#. Accessed 29 December 2005.

Oakley, Kate. 2004. 'Not So Cool Britannia: The Role of the Creative Industries in Economic Development', *International Journal of Cultural Studies* 7(1): 67–77.

O'Brien, Damien. 2007. 'Viacom v. YouTube and Google: Copyright Challenges for User Generated Intermediaries'. Paper presented to ECUPL-QUT Legal and Policy Framework for the Digital Content Industry Conference, Shanghai, 28–29 May.

O'Connor, Justin. 1999. 'Popular Culture, Reflexivity and Urban Change', in J. Verwijnen and P. Lehtovuori (eds), *Creative Cities*. Helsinki: University of Art and Design Publishing Unit.

———, and Xin Gu. 2006. 'A New Modernity? The Arrival of "Creative Industries" in China', *International Journal of Cultural Studies* 9(3): 271–83.

OECD (Organisation for Economic Co-operation and Development). 1996. *The Knowledge-Based Economy*. Paris: OECD.

———. 1999. *The Economic and Social Impacts of Electronic Commerce: Preliminary Findings and Research Agenda*. Paris: OECD.

———. 2003. *The e-Government Imperative*. Paris: OECD.

O'Neil, Mathieu. 2006. 'Rebels for the System? Virus Writers, General Intellect, Cyberpunk and Criminal Capitalism', *Continuum: Journal of Media and Cultural Studies* 20(2): 225–41.

O'Regan, Tom. 2002. 'Too Much Culture, Too Little Culture: Trends and Issues for Cultural Policy-Making', *Media International Australia* 102, February: 9–24.

O'Reilly, Tim. 2005. 'What is Web 2.0: Design Patterns and Business Models for the Next Generation of Software', www.oreillynet.com/pub/a/oreilly/tim/news/2005/09/30/what-is-web-20.html, published 30 September. Accessed 17 March 2007.

———. 2006. 'Web 2.0 Compact Definition: Trying Again', O'Reilly Radar, http://radar.oreilly.com/archives/2006/12/web_20_compact.html, posted 12 October. Accessed 17 March 2007.

Orlowski, Andrew. 2005. 'On Creativity, Computers, and Copyright', *The Register*, www.theregister.co.uk/2005/07/21/creativity/, published 21 July. Accessed 22 May 2007.

Ó Siochrú, Seán. 2004. 'Civil Society Participation in the WSIS Process: Promises and Reality', *Continuum:*

Journal of Media and Cultural Studies 18(3): 330–44.

———, and Bruce Girard, with Amy Mahan. 2003. *Global Media Governance: A Beginner's Guide*. Lanham, MD: Rowman & Littlefield.

Osborne, Thomas. 2003. 'Against "Creativity": A Philistine Rant', *Economy and Society* 32(4): 507–25.

Outing, Steve. 2005. 'The 11 Layers of Citizen Journalism', www.poynter.org/content/content_print.asp?id=83126&custom=, posted 11 June. Accessed 28 April 2007.

Papacharissi, Zizi. 2002. 'The Virtual Sphere: The Internet as a Public Sphere', *New Media and Society* 4(1): 9–27.

Paré, Daniel. 2003. *Internet Governance in Transition: Who is the Master of this Domain?* Lanham, MD: Rowman & Littlefield.

Park, Myung-Jin, Chang-Mai Kim, and Byung-Woo Sohn. 2000. 'Modernization, Globalization and the Powerful State: The Korean Media', in J. Curran and M.-J. Park (eds), *Dewesternizing Media Studies*. London: Routledge, pp. 111–23.

Peck, Jamie. 2005. 'Struggling with the Creative Class', *International Journal of Urban and Regional Research* 29(4): 740–70.

Penfold, Carolyn. 2003. 'Global Technology meets Local Environment: State Attempts to Control Internet Content', in K.C. Ho, R. Kluver, and K.C.C. Yang (eds), *Asia.com: Asian Encounters the Internet*. London: RoutledgeCurzon, pp. 83–96.

Penley, Constance, and Andrew Ross. 1991. *Technoculture*. Minneapolis, MN: University of Minnesota Press.

Perelman, Michael. 2002. *Steal This Idea: Intellectual Property Rights and the Corporate Confiscation of Creativity*. New York: Palgrave.

Phillips, Walter P. 1879 [1975]. *The Phillips Code, Telephone and Telegraph Age*. New York. Available at www.radions.net/philcode.htm, retrieved 29 December 2009.

PMSEIC (Prime Minister's Science, Engineering, and Innovation Council). 2005. *Imagine Australia: The Role of Creativity in the Innovation Economy*, published 2 December.

Podolny, Joel, and Karen Page. 1998. 'Network Forms

of Organization', *Annual Review of Sociology* 24: 57–76.

Poletti, Teresa. 'Can Research In Motion climb out of its slump?' *Marketwatch*. 1 July 2010. Available online at: www.marketwatch.com/story/research-in-motion-caught-in-a-perfect-storm-2010-07-01

Pool, Ithiel de Sola. 1983. *Technologies of Freedom*. Cambridge, MA: Belknap Press.

Porter, Michael. 1998. 'Clusters and the New Economics of Competition', *Harvard Business Review* 76(6): 77–91.

Poster, Mark. 1990. *The Mode of Information: Poststructuralism and Social Context*. Cambridge: Polity Press.

———. 1995. *The Second Media Age*. Cambridge: Polity Press.

———. 2001. *What's the Matter with the Internet?* Minneapolis, MN: University of Minnesota Press.

———. 2005. 'Culture and New Media', in L. Lievrouw and S. Livingstone (eds), *Handbook of New Media*, 2nd edn. London: Sage, pp. 134–40.

———. 2006. *Information Please: Culture and Politics in the Age of Digital Machines*. Durham, NC: Duke University Press.

Postman, Neil. 1993. *Technopoly: The Surrender of Culture to Technology*. New York: Vintage.

Potts, Jason. 2003. 'The Prometheus School of Information Economics', *Prometheus* 21(4): 477–86.

Pratt, Andy. 1998. 'A "Third Way" for the Creative Industries?', *International Journal of Communications Law and Policy* 4(1), www.digital-law.net/IJCLP/1_1998/ijclp_webdoc_4_1_1998.html. Accessed 29 May 2007.

Prensky, Marc. 2001. 'Digital Natives, Digital Immigrants', www.marcprensky.com/writing/Prensky%20-%20Digital%20Natives,%20Digital%20Immigrants%20-%20Part1.pdf. Accessed 2 December 2006.

Putnam, Robert. 1995. 'Tuning In, Tuning Out: The Strange Disappearance of Social Capital in America', *Political Science and Politics* 28(4): 664–88.

———. 2000. *Bowling Alone: The Collapse and Revival of American Community*. New York: Simon & Schuster.

Quah, Danny. 2003. 'Digital Goods and the New Economy', in D.C. Jones (ed.), *New Economy Handbook*. Amsterdam: Elsevier, pp. 289–321.

Rainie, Lee, and Peter Bell. 2004. 'The Numbers That Count', *New Media and Society* 6(1): 44–54

Ramsay, Randolph. 2007. 'GDC '07: Chris Taylor says "No more overtime"', Gamespot AU, 8 March, http://au.gamespot.com/news/6167123.html?msg_sort=1. Accessed 7 April 2007.

Ravensbergen, David. 2008. 'Be Nice to the 'Creative Class!', The Tyee, http://thetyee.ca/Views/2008/08/05/CreativeClass/

Raymond, Eric. 1998. 'The Cathedral and the Bazaar', *First Monday* 3(3), www.firstmonday.dk/issues/issue3_3/raymond. Accessed 28 December 2003.

Redden, Guy. 2003. 'Read the Whole Thing: Journalism, Weblogs and the Re Mediation of the War in Iraq', *Media International Australia*, 109: 153–65.

Redhead, Steve. 2004. *Paul Virilio: Theorist for an Accelerated Culture*. Edinburgh: Edinburgh University Press.

Reeves, Byron, and Clifford Nass. 2002. *The Media Equation: How People Treat Computers, Televisions, and New Media Like Real People and Places*. Cambridge: Cambridge University Press.

Rennie, Elinor. 2003. '"Trespassers are Welcome": Access and Community Television Policy', *Javnost (The Public)* 10(1): 49–62.

———. 2006. *Community Media: A Global Introduction*. Lanham, MD: Rowman & Littlefield.

Rheingold, Howard. 1994. *The Virtual Community: Finding Connection in a Computerized World*. London: Secker & Warburg.

Rheingold, Howard. 2002. *Smart Mobs: The Next Social Revolution*. Cambridge: Perseus.

Rice, Ronald. 1999. 'Artifacts and Paradoxes in New Media', *New Media and Society* 1(1): 24–32.

———. 2002. 'Primary Issues in Internet Use: Access, Civic and Community Involvement, and Social Interaction and Expression', in L. Lievrouw and S. Livingstone (eds), *Handbook of New Media*. London: Sage, pp. 105–29.

———, and Carolyn Haythornthwaite. 2005. 'Perspectives on Internet Use: Access, Involvement and Interaction', in L. Lievrouw and S. Livingstone (eds), *Handbook of New Media*, 2nd edn. London: Sage, pp. 92–113.

Ricks, Christopher. 1968. 'McLuhanism', in R. Rosenthal (ed.), *McLuhan: Pro & Con*. Baltimore, MD: Penguin.

Rifkin, Jeremy. 2000. *The Age of Access: How the Shift from Ownership to Access is Transforming Modern Life*. London: Penguin.

Rimmer, Matthew. 2003a. 'Virtual Countries: Internet Domain Names and Geographical Terms', *Media International Australia* 106, February: 124–36.

———. 2003b. 'The Dead Poets Society; The Copyright Term and the Public Domain', *First Monday* 8(6), www.firstmonday.org/issues/issue8_6/rimmer/index.html accessed 25 August 2003.

Robins, Kevin, and Frank Webster. 1999. *Times of the Technoculture: From the Information Society to the Virtual Life*. London: Routledge.

Robinson, Evan. 2005. 'Why Crunch Mode Doesn't Work: 6 Lessons', International Game Developers Association—Articles, www.igda.org/articles/erobinson_crunch.php. Accessed 7 April 2007.

Robinson, Ken. 2001. *Out of Our Minds: Learning to be Creative*. Oxford: Capstone.

Rogers, Everett. 2003. *Diffusion of Innovations*, 5th edn. New York: Free Press.

Rogers, Mark, Michael Epstein, and Jimmie Reeves. 2002. 'The Sopranos as HBO Band Equity: The Art of Commerce in the Age of Digital Reproduction', in D. Lavery (ed.), *This Thing of Ours: Investigating the Sopranos*. New York: Columbia University Press, pp. 42–57.

Romano, Angela. 2003. *Politics and the Press in Indonesia: Understanding an Evolving Political Culture*. London: RoutledgeCurzon.

Romer, Paul. 1994. 'The Origins of Endogenous Growth', *Journal of Economic Perspectives* 8(1): 3–22.

———. 1995. 'Interview with Peter Robinson', *Forbes* 155(12): 66–70.

———. 2007. 'Economic Growth', in D. Henderson (ed.), *The Concise Encyclopedia of Economics*, www.econlib.org/library/enc/EconomicGrowth.html. Accessed 14 February 2007.

Rosen, Jay. 2000. 'Questions and Answers about Public Journalism', *Journalism Studies* 1(4): 679–83.

———. 2007. 'PressThink: Ghost of Democracy in the Media Machine', http://journalism.nyu.edu/pubzone/weblogs/pressthink. Accessed 28 April 2007.

Rossignol, Jim. 2006. 'Sex, Fame and PC Baangs: How the Orient plays host to PC gaming's strangest culture', *PC Gamer UK*, http://rossignol.cream.org/?p=284, posted 4 January. Accessed 15 July 2007.

Rossiter, Ned. 2006. *Organized Networks: Media Theory, Creative Labour, New Institutions*. Amsterdam: NAi Publishers, Institute of Network Cultures.

Rowland, Wade. 2006. *Spirit of the Web: The Age of Information from Telegraph to Internet*. Toronto: Thomas Allen & Son.

Rushkoff, Douglas. 1996. *Playing the Future: How Kids' Culture Can Teach Us to Thrive in an Age of Chaos*. New York: HarperCollins.

Rutter, Jason, and Jo Bryce, (eds). 2006. *Understanding Digital Games*. Thousand Oaks, CA: Sage.

Sale, Kirkpatrick. 1995. *Rebels Against the Future: The Luddites and the War on the Industrial Revolution—Lessons for the Computer Age*. Reading, MA: Addison-Wesley.

Sassen, Saskia. 1991. *The Global City: New York, London, Tokyo*. Princeton: Princeton University Press.

———. 1999. 'The State and the New Geography of Power', in A. Calabrese and J.-C. Burgelman (eds), *Communication, Citizenship, and Social Policy: Rethinking the Limits of the Welfare State*. Lanham, MD: Rowman & Littlefield, pp. 17–31.

———. 2001. *The Global City: New York, London, Tokyo*. Princeton: Princeton University Press.

Sawyer, Ben. 2002. 'The Next Ages of Games Development', The Adrenalin Vault, Developer's Corner, www.avault.com/developer/, posted 30 September. Accessed 28 October 2002.

Schaffer, Jan. 2007. *Citizen Media: Fad or the Future of News? The Rise and Prospects of Hyper-Local Journalism*, www.kcnn.org/research/citizen_media_report. Accessed 6 May 2007.

Schiller, Dan. 2000. *Digital Capitalism: Networking the Global Market System*. Cambridge, MA: MIT Press.

———. 2006. 'Digital Capitalism: A Status Report on

the Corporate Commonwealth of Information', in A.N. Valdivia (ed.), *A Companion to Media Studies*. Malden, MA: Blackwell, pp. 137–56.

Schiller, Herbert. 1995. 'The Global Information Highway: Project for an Ungovernable World', in J. Brook and I.A. Boal (eds), *Resisting the Virtual Life: The Culture and Politics of Information*. San Francisco: City Lights, pp. 17–33.

Schuler, Douglas. 1996. *New Community Networks: Wired for Change*. Reading, MA: Addison-Wesley.

Sclove, Richard. 1995. *Technology and Democracy*. New York: Guilford Press.

Scott, Allen. 2004. 'Cultural-Products Industries and Urban Economic Development: Prospects for Growth and Market Contestation in Global Context', *Urban Affairs Review* 39(4): 461–90.

Scott, Ben. 2005. 'A Contemporary History of Digital Journalism', *Television and New Media* 6(1): 89–126.

Scott, John. 1986. *Capitalist Property and Financial Power: A Comparative Study of Britain, the United States, and Japan*. Brighton: Harvester Wheatsheaf Press.

———. 1991. *Social Network Analysis: A Handbook*. London: Sage.

Seaman, Bruce. 2000. 'Arts Impact Studies: A Fashionable Excess', in G. Bradford, M. Gary, and G. Wallach (eds), *The Politics of Culture: Policy Perspectives for Individuals, Institutions and Communities*. New York: New Press, pp. 266–85.

Sell, Susan. 2002. 'Intellectual Property Rights', in D. Held and A. McGrew (eds), *Governing Globalization: Power, Authority, and Global Governance*. Cambridge: Polity Press, pp. 171–88.

Seltzer, K., and T. Bentley. 2000. *The Creative Age: Knowledge and Skills for the New Economy*. London: DEMOS.

Shanker, Daya. 2006. 'Copyright, Competition Policy and Prevention of Monopolistic Abuses in the TRIPS Agreement', in P.N. Thomas and J. Servaes (eds), *Intellectual Property Rights and Communications in Asia: Conflicting Traditions*. New Delhi: Sage, pp. 79–102.

Shapiro, Carl, and Hal Varian. 1999. *Information Rules: A Strategic Guide to the Network Economy*. Boston, MA: Harvard Business School Press.

Shaw, Russell. 2005. 'Web 2.0? It Doesn't Exist', http://blogs.zdnet.com/ip-telephony/?p=805, posted 17 December. Accessed 17 March 2007.

Shearmur, Richard. 2010. 'Space, Place and Innovation: A Distance-based Approach', *The Canadian Geographer/Le Géographe canadien*, 54, no. 1, pp. 46–67.

Shenton, Karla, and Todd McNeeley. 1997. *The Virtual Communities Companion*. Albany, NY: Coriolis Group Books.

Shirky, Clay. 2003. 'Social Software and the Politics of Groups', http://shirky.com/writings/group_politics.html, posted 9 March 2003. Accessed 8 November 2005.

———. 2009. *Here Comes Everybody: The Power of Organizing Without Organizations*. New York: Penguin.

———. 2010. *Cognitive Surplus: Creativity and Generosity in a Connected Age*. New York: Penguin.

Sholle, David. 2002. 'Disorganizing the "New Technology"', in G. Elmer (ed.), *Critical Perspectives on the Internet*. Lanham, MD: Rowman & Littlefield, pp. 3–26.

Silver, David. 2000. 'Looking Backwards, Looking Forward: Cyberculture Studies 1990–2000', in D. Gauntlett (ed.), *Web.studies: Rewiring Media Studies for the Digital Age*. London: Arnold, pp. 19–30.

Siwek, Stephen. 2002. *Copyright Industries in the U.S. Economy: The 2002 Report*. International Intellectual Property Alliance, Washington DC.

———. 2004. Copyright Industries in the U.S. Economy, prepared for the International Intellectual Property Alliance, Washington DC.

Slater, Don. 2002. 'Social Relationships and Identity Online and Offline', in L. Lievrouw and S. Livingstone (eds), *The Handbook of New Media*. London: Sage, pp. 533–46.

Smith, Anthony. 1991. 'Towards a Global Culture?', in M. Featherstone (ed.), *Global Culture, Nationalism, Globalization and Modernity*. London: Sage, pp. 171–92.

Smith, Richard. 2006. 'New media industry in Vancouver', Proceedings of the Colloque De L'Association d'Économie Politique (AÉP): La Compétitivité Urbaine À L'ère De La

Nouvelle Économie: Enjeux Et Défis, Montreal, 5 November 2005.

———. 2004. 'A Model for the Study of Clustering: A Case Study from New Media Firms in Vancouver', in L. Morel-Guimaraes (ed.), *Key Success Factors for Innovation and Sustainable Development*. Oxford: Elsevier.

Smith, Richard and Ellen Godfrey. 2009. 'Foundation for the Future: Establishing baseline measures for assessing the impact of broadband in BC communities'. Vancouver, CPROST Report 2009–06.

Smythe, Dallas. 2001. 'On the Audience Commodity and its Work', in M.G. Durham and D.M. Kellner, (eds), *Media and Cultural Studies: KeyWorks*. US: Blackwell Publishing, pp. 253–79.

Sood, Ashish, and Gerard Tellis. 2005. 'Technological Evolution and Radical Innovation', *Journal of Marketing* 69, July: 152–65.

Stadler, Felix. 2006. *Manuel Castells and the Theory of the Network Society*. Cambridge: Polity Press.

Standage, Thomas. 2007. *The Victorian Internet: The Remarkable Story of the Telegraph and the Nineteenth Century's On-line Pioneers*. New York: Walker & Company.

Stein, Joel. 2007. 'Have Something to Say? I Don't Care', LATimes.com, www.latimes.com/news/print-edition/opinion/la-oe-stein2jan02,1,918996.colu mn?track=rss&ctrack=1&cset=true, published 2 January. Accessed 28 April 2007.

Stein, Laura, and Nikhil Sinha. 2002. 'New Media and Communication Policy: The Role of the State in the Twenty-First Century', in L. Lievrouw and S. Livingstone (eds), *Handbook of New Media*. London: Sage, pp. 410–31.

Sterling, Bruce. 2005. *Shaping Things*. Cambridge, MA: MIT Press.

Sternberg, Robert (ed.). 1999. *Handbook of Creativity*. Cambridge: Cambridge University Press.

Stevenson, Deborah. 2004. '"Civic Gold Rush": Cultural Planning and the Third Way', *International Journal of Cultural Policy* 10(1): 119–31.

Stevenson, Nick. 1995. *Understanding Media Culture: Social Theory and Mass Communication*. London: Sage.

Stillman, W.J. 1891. 'Journalism and Literature', *The Atlantic Monthly*, (Vol 68, No. 409, November). pp. 687-698.

Stokman, Franz, Rold Ziegler, and John Scott. 1985. *Networks of Corporate Power: A Comparative Analysis of Ten Countries*. Cambridge: Polity Press.

Stoll, Clifford. 1995. *Silicon Snake Oil: Second Thoughts on the Information Highway*. London: Macmillan.

Storper, Michael. 1997. *The Regional World*. New York: Guilford.

Streeter, Thomas. 1987. 'The Cable Fable Revisited: Discourse, Policy, and the Making of Cable Television', *Critical Studies in Mass Communication* 4: 71–97.

———. 2004. 'Romanticism in Business Culture: The Internet, the 1990s, and the Origins of Irrational Exuberance', in A. Calabrese and C. Sparks (eds), *Towards a Political Economy of Culture: Capitalism and Communication in the Twenty-First Century*. Lanham, MD: Rowman & Littlefield, pp. 286–306.

Streitz, Norbert, and Paddy Nixon. 2005. 'The Disappearing Computer', *Communications of the ACM* 48(3): 33–5.

Stueck, Wendy. 'Club Penguin Founders Strike it Rich', *The Globe and Mail*, 2 August 2007. Accessed 30 June 2010 at www.theglobeandmail.com/news/technology/article774336.ece

Suh, Bongwon, Gregorio Convertino, Ed H. Chi, and Peter Pirolli. 2009. *The Singularity is Not Near: Slowing Growth of Wikipedia*, WikiSym'09, October 25–7, Orlando, Florida.

Sunstein, Cass. 2002. 'The Law of Group Polarization', *Journal of Political Philosophy* 10(2): 175–95.

Supreme Court of Canada. 2002. Théberge v Galerie d'Art due Petit Champlain Inc, 2 SCR 336.

Sweeny, Alistair. 2009. *BlackBerry Planet: The Story of Research in Motion and the Little Device that Took the World by Storm*. Mississauga: Wiley.

Tapscott, Don. 1998. *Growing Up Digital: The Rise of the Net Generation*. New York: McGraw Hill.

Taylor, Peter, D.R.F. Walker, and Jonathon Beaverstock. 2002. 'Firms and their Global Service Networks', in S. Sassen (ed.), *Global Networks, Linked Cities*.

New York: Routledge, pp. 93–115.

Tellis, Gerard J., and Peter G. Golder. 1996. 'First to Market, First to Fail? Real Causes of Enduring Market Leadership', *Sloan Management Review* 37(2): 65–75.

Terranova, Tiziana. 2004. *Network Culture: Politics for the Information Age*. London: Pluto Press.

Thompson, Grahame. 2003. *Between Hierarchies and Markets: The Logic and Limits of Network Forms of Organization*. Oxford: Oxford University Press.

Thompson, Graham. 1990. 'Sandford Fleming and the Pacific Cable: The Institutional Politics of Nineteenth-Century Imperial Communications'. *Canadian Journal Of Communication*, 15(2).

Thompson, John. 1991. *Ideology and Modern Culture*. Cambridge: Polity Press.

———. 1995. *The Media and Modernity: A Social Theory of the Media*. Cambridge: Polity Press.

Thoreau, Henry David. 2000 [1882]. *Walden*. Vol. 1. Boston: Houghten Mifflin.

Throsby, David. 2001. *Economics and Culture*. Cambridge: Cambridge University Press.

Thussu, Daya Kishan. 2006. *International Communication: Continuity and Change*. London: Arnold.

Toffler, Alvin. 1970. *Future Shock*. New York: Random House.

———. 1980. *The Third Wave*. New York: Bantam Books.

Tofts, Darren. 2005. *Interzone: Media Arts in Australia*. Melbourne: Craftsman House.

Townsend, David A. 2004. *Report On the National Antenna Tower Policy Review*. Ottawa: Industry Canada, www.ic.gc.ca/eic/site/smt-gst.nsf/eng/sf02037.html.

Tsagarousianou, Roza, Damian Tambini, and Cathy Bryan, (eds). 1998. *Cyberdemocracy: Technology, Cities and Civic Networks*. London: Routledge.

Turban, Efraim, Jae Lee, David Kung, and Michael Chung. 2000. *Electronic Commerce: A Managerial Perspective*. Upper Saddle River, NJ: Prentice Hall.

Turkle, Sherry. 1997. *Life on the Screen: Identity in the Age of the Internet*. New York: Touchstone.

Turner, Graeme. 1990. *British Cultural Studies: An Introduction*. Boston, MA: Unwin Hyman.

———. 1999. 'Tabloidisation, Journalism and the Possibility of Critique', *International Journal of Cultural Studies* 2(1): 59–76.

———. 2004. *Understanding Celebrity*. London: Sage.

———. 2005. *Ending the Affair: The Decline of Television Current Affairs in Australia*. Sydney: UNSW Press.

UNCTAD. 2004. 'Creative Industries and Development', www.unctad.org/en/docs/tdxibpd13_en.pdf. Accessed 10 May 2007.

———. 2005. World Investment Report 2005: Transnational Corporations and the Internationalization of R & D, United Nations, New York and Geneva.

UNESCO. 2003. Culture, Trade and Globalization: Questions and Answers, www.unesco.org/culture/industries/trade/html_eng. Accessed 4 June 2003.

United Nations. 1948. Universal Declaration of Human Rights, adopted by the General Assembly of the United Nations, 10 December, www.un.org/Overview/rights.html. Accessed 5 May 2007.

Vaidhyanathan, Siva. 2001. *Copyrights and Copywrongs: The Rise of Intellectual Property and How it Threatens Creativity*. New York: New York University Press.

———. 2004. *The Anarchist in the Library: How the Clash between Freedom and Control is Hacking the Real World*. New York: Basic Books.

van Dijk, Jan. 1999. *The Network Society*. London: Sage.

Vastag, Brian. 2004. 'Does Video Game Violence Sow Aggression?', *Journal of the American Medical Association* 291(15): 1822–4.

Venturelli, Shalini. 2005. 'Culture and the Creative Economy in the Information Age', in J. Hartley (ed.), *Creative Industries*. Oxford: Blackwell, pp. 391–98.

von Hippel, Eric. 2005. *Democratizing Innovation*. Cambridge, MA: MIT Press.

———. 1988. *The Sources of Innovation*. New York: Oxford University Press.

Wagstaff, Jeremy. 2004. 'Korea's News Crusaders', *Far Eastern Economic Review*, 7 October, pp. 34–7.

Wang, Jing. 2004. 'The Global Reach of a New Discourse: How Far Can "Creative Industries" Travel', *International Journal of Cultural Studies* 7(1): 9–19.

Ward, Ian. 2003. 'An Australian PR State?', *Australian Journal of Communication* 30(1): 25–42.

Wardrip-Fruin, Noah, and Nick Montfort. 2003. *New Media Reader.* Cambridge, MA: MIT Press.

Warren, Christina. 2010. 'Facebook Teams Up with British Government to Curb Deficit', *Mashable!*, 9 July 2010, http://mashable.com/2010/07/09/uk-government-facebook-deficit. Accessed 9 July 2010.

Wasserman, Stanley, and Katharine Faust. 1994. *Social Network Analysis: Methods and Applications.* Cambridge: Cambridge University Press.

Webster, Frank, and Basil Dimitriou. 2003. *Manuel Castells*, 3 vols, *Sage Modern Masters in Social Thought Series.* London: Sage.

Weinberger, David. 2008. *Everything Is Miscellaneous: The Power of the New Digital Disorder.* Calgary: The Times Press.

Weiss, Glenn. 2007. 'Glenn Weiss: Architecture, Design and Public Art', www.glennweiss.com. Accessed 5 May 2007.

Wellman, Barry. 2001. 'Physical Place and Cyberspace: The Rise of Personalized Networking', *International Journal of Urban and Regional Research* 25(2): 227–52.

———. 2004. 'The Three Ages of Internet Studies: Ten, Five and Zero Years Ago', *New Media and Society* 6(1): 123–29.

———, and Milena Guila. 1998. 'Virtual Communities as Communities: Net Surfers Don't Ride Alone', in M.A. Smith and P. Kollock (eds), *Communities in Cyberspace.* London: Routledge, pp. 167–94.

———, and Carolyn Haythornthwaite. 2002. 'Moving the Internet out of Cyberspace: The Internet in Everyday Life—An Introduction', in B. Wellman and C. Haythornthwaite (eds), *The Internet in Everyday Life.* Malden, MA: Blackwell, pp. 3–41.

———, Anabel Haase, James Witte, and Keith Hampton. 2001. 'Does the Internet Increase, Decrease, or Supplement Social Capital? Social Networks, Participation, and Community Commitment', *American Behavioral Scientist* 45(3): 436–55.

Westerway, Peter. 1990. *Electronic Highways: An Introduction to Telecommunications in the 1990s.* Sydney: George Allen & Unwin.

Whitton, Nicola. 2010. *Learning with Digital Games A Practical Guide to Engaging Students in Higher Education.* New York: Routledge.

Wikipedia Contributors. 2007. 'Mod (computer gaming)', Wikipedia, The Free Encyclopedia, http://en.wikipedia.org/wiki/Mod_%28computer_gaming%29, modified 6 April. Accessed 7 April 2007.

Williams, Raymond. 1965. *The Long Revolution.* London: Chatto & Windus.

———. 1974. *Television: Technology and Cultural Form.* London: Routledge.

———. 1976. *Keywords: A Vocabulary of Culture and Society.* London: Fontana.

Williams, Robin, and David Edge. 1996. 'The Social Shaping of Technology', *Research Policy* 25(4): 865–99.

Williamson, Oliver E. 1975. *Markets and Hierarchies.* New York: Free Press.

———1985. *The Economic Institutions of Capitalism.* New York: Free Press.

Windschuttle, Keith. 2000. 'The Poverty of Cultural Studies', *Journalism Studies* 1(1): 145–59.

Winner, Langdon. 1986a. 'Technologies as Forms of Life', in L. Winner, *The Whale and the Reactor: A Search for Limits in an Age of High Technology.* Chicago: University of Chicago Press, pp. 3–18.

———. 1986b. 'Do Artifacts Have Politics?', in L. Winner, *The Whale and the Reactor: A Search for Limits in an Age of High Technology.* Chicago: University of Chicago Press, pp. 19–37.

Winseck, Dwayne. 2002. 'Wired Cities and Transnational Communications: New Forms of Governance for Telecommunicatons and the New Media', in L. Lievrouw and S. Livingstone (eds), *Handbook of New Media.* London: Sage, pp. 393–409.

Winston, Brian. 1998. *Media Technology and Society—A History: From the Telegraph to the Internet.* London: Routledge.

WIPO (World Intellectual Property Organization). 2006. *WIPO Patent Report 2006: Statistics on Worldwide Patent Activities*, www.wipo.int/ipstats/en/statistics/patents/pdf/patent_report_2006.pdf. Accessed 27 May 2007.

Witt, Leonard. 2004. 'Is Public Journalism Morphing into the Public's Journalism?', *National Civic Review* Fall: 49–57.

Wolf, Gary. 1996. 'The Wisdom of Saint Marshall, the Holy Fool', *WIRED* 4(1), www.wired.com/wired/archive/4.01/saint.marshal.html. Accessed 29 May 2007.

Wolfe, David. 2009. *21st Century Cities in Canada: The Geography of Innovation*. Ottawa: Conference Board of Canada.

Woods, Tim. 1999. *Beginning Postmodernism*. Manchester: Manchester University Press.

Woolcock, Michael. 2001. 'The Place of Social Capital in Understanding Social and Economic Outcomes', *ISUMA: Canadian Journal of Policy Research* 2(1): 11–17.

Woolgar, Steve. 2002. 'Five Rules of Virtuality', in S. Woolgar (ed.), *Virtual Society? Technology, Cyberbole, Reality*. Oxford: Oxford University Press, pp. 1–22.

World Bank, The. 2003. 'Social Capital for Development', www.worldbank.org/poverty/scapital. Accessed 10 January 2004.

World Bank, The. 2010. 'Indicators', http://data.worldbank.org/indicator. Accessed 10 September 2010.

WSIS Civil Society Plenary. 2003. 'Shaping Information Societies for Human Needs: Civil Society Declaration to the World Summit on the Information Society', Geneva, 8 December.

Yeon-Ho, Oh. 2004. 'The Revolt of 727 News Guerillas', http://cnglish.ohmynews.com/articleview/article_view.asp?no=153109&rel_no=1, published 19 February. Accessed 5 May 2007.

———. 2007. '10 Preconditions for the Value of User-Generated Content', OhMyNews CEO Oh Yeon-ho's address on the 7th anniversary of OhMyNews, http://english.ohmynews.com/articleview/article_view.asp?article_class=8&no=347268&rel_no=1, published 26 February. Accessed 28 April 2007.

Yoo, Christopher S. 2009. 'The Convergence of Broadcasting and Telephony: Legal and Regulatory Implications', *Communications & Convergence Review*. Vol. 1, p. 44. December.

Yoo, Christopher S. 2008. 'Network Neutrality, Consumers, and Innovation.' *University of Chicago Legal Forum*, Vol. 25, pg. 179.

Young, Sally. 2006. 'Not Biting the Hand that Feeds? Media Reporting of Government Advertising in Australia', *Journalism Studies* 7(4): 554–74.

Yúdice, George. 2003. *The Expediency of Culture: Uses of Culture in the Global Era*. Durham, NC: Duke University Press.

Zetie, Carl. 2004. 'Convergence or Divergence: What's Next for Mobile Devices?', *InformationWeek*, 15 May, www.informationweek.com/story/showArticle.jhtml?articleID=18311545. Accessed 12 December 2006.

Zelizer, Barbie. 2004. *Taking Journalism Seriously: News and the Academy*. Thousand Oaks, CA: Sage.

———. 2005. 'The Culture of Journalism', in J. Curran and M. Gurevitch (eds), *Mass Media and Society*, 4th edn. London: Arnold.

Zhang, Xiaoming. 2006. 'From Institution to Industry: Reforms in Cultural Institutions in China', *International Journal of Cultural Studies* 9(3): 297–306.

Zhang, Yonghua. 2006. 'China's Efforts for International Cooperation in Copyright Protection', in P. Thomas and J. Servaes (eds), *Intellectual Property Rights and Communications in Asia*. New Delhi: Sage, pp. 149–63.

Index